REMOTE

a story of St Helena

REMOTE

a story of St Helena

LINDSAY GRATTAN COOPER

PORCUPINE PRESS

Johannesburg, South Africa

ISBN-13: 978-1512087512 | ISBN-10: 1512087513

Published by Porcupine Press
PO Box 2756
Pinegowrie, 2123
South Africa
Tel: 27 (0)117914561
Fax: 27 (0)117912399
info@porcupinepress.co.za
www.porcupinepress.co.za

Distributed by Porcupine Press
Set in 11 point on 14 point Minion Pro
Layout and typesetting by wim@wimrheeder.co.za
Printed by CreateSpace

For Stedson, our friend

"It is impossible to approach and see this singular island, for the first time, without wondering how the deuce it got there. A vast mass of rock, rising abruptly from nearly the centre of the great Atlantic ocean, jagged and irregular, cut and slashed as it were into pieces by the great hatchet of nature – too large to be passed without examination, and too small, and unfruitful, and badly situated, to be of much use..."

– Lieutenant James Prior, 1813

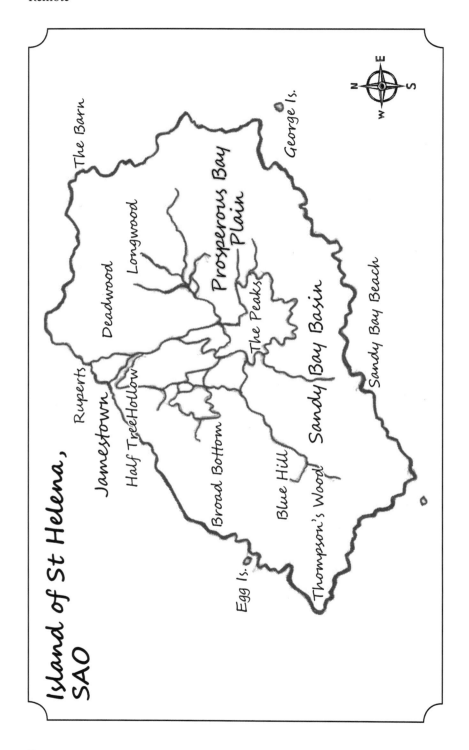

Island of St Helena, SAO

Prologue

Late June 1999

The Honorary French Consul is opposite me, slouched in a club chair, legs outstretched, arms folded, an uncharacteristic picture of glumness amidst the relaxed jollity of a first day at sea. Everyone else in the chatter-filled Sun Lounge seems to be smiling.

"What's the matter, Michel?" I inquire.

He manipulates a huge Gallic shrug. "This is *such* a long bus ride," he sighs, blowing frustration through the corner of his mouth in an exasperated *phfff*, "and it's only our first day!"

I gape. This is no impersonal cruise liner, after all, packed with jaded strangers. Rather, a voyage on this unique little cargo-passenger vessel, barely 7 000 tons, is one of the world's best-kept secrets; and who would sanely pass up, for more touristy options, five days of gentle pampering by St Helenian crew, the company of interesting co-passengers, and the promise of St Helena at the end of it – the ten by seven miles of rock sitting pretty in the middle of the South Atlantic Ocean, towards which we are all now headed? When I find my voice it is a squeak of incredulity. "*This* ship – a long bus ride? It's a *wonderful* ship!"

"When you've done this trip a few more times you'll see what I mean," Michel advises with the wisdom of experience. And though my current purchasing of a second home on that island means that this will soon become my family's annual commute from first-base in Cape Town, I already have a few trips on the RMS *St Helena* under my belt, and so meet his opinion with open disdain.

"Well, *you're* obviously not eager for an airport!" challenges South African JJ from the other chair, bestowing a grievously pitying look on my living-in-the-past attitude. "I can't wait! The sooner we get air service the better!" Clearly also bored already, he rises to head into the noonday sunshine on deck, followed by Michel. An Airport is an issue already, I realise: For or Against.

I am not alone for long before a stranger plops into Michel's vacated chair, introduces himself as Duncan Hill, orders me a gin and tonic, and starts chatting knowledgeably about the island even though, he confesses, he has never seen it before. The extent of his homework is hugely impressive until it dawns on me that this is the incoming new Governor, a man now travelling to St Helena to take up a three-year contract as the island's Commander-in-Chief and Envoy of Her Majesty the Queen in that tiny British Overseas Territory – one of the few surviving 'pink bits' on a seriously depleted map of the once-great British Empire. He is the man who knows what's really happening there. "All this talk of an Airport…?" I prompt with interest.

His whole face lights up. "That is the British government's primary project at the moment. And I can tell you now, within just *five years* an Airport – named after me – will be up and running in St Helena. I promise you." I can almost see the runway lights.

"I'm not especially in favour of an airport there," I venture carefully.

He regards me tolerantly over his glass, a man of outwardly benign demeanour. "An Airport is the only thing that will save St Helena from extinction. The British government wants the island to become self-sufficient, and air tourism will make her viable." Strong words, I think. This island is clearly a millstone around Britain's neck.

I glance around at our co-passengers. Some are from DfID (the British government's Department for International Development). There is nearly always a bunch of their experts on board, some bowed diligently over laptops, most revelling in the joy of a free five-day sea cruise. But the bulk of other non-St Helenian travellers are tourists of varying age who, conversation has proved, have already been everywhere else in the world and now are interested only in remote places. "St Helena is a niche market. People who travel there do their homework and know what to expect. Tourists who fly in will not be the same species," I courageously suggest.

"We'll still have an Airport."

My thoughts streak to that adored little island I have been in love with all my adult life, and I try to picture its brave new world of fly-in tourism. But all I can imagine are hordes of disgruntled package-holiday Brits huddled on the windy seafront, whingeing about its lack of beaches, nightclubs and nice resort-wear on this tropical island, and dying to go home.

"It won't be easy to build."

"Five years," insists the Governor-Designate happily. "It *will* be there."

Along on the voyage are a fifty-something Airport Surveyor and two barely pubescent female assistants, also dispatched by DfID. All three have been slightly irritating in their free-cruise liveliness on board, rowdy in their beer-swilling and loudly hectic in holiday mode. Not one has produced a laptop nor displayed the slightest knowledge of or interest in St Helena, yet they will earn a rewarding remuneration from the British government for this exercise. And when I sound out the surveyor about his expectations on the island, he is alarmingly gung-ho.

I hide my smile, and on the morning we sail up to the island I take up a position beside him at the bridge-wing railings, just to watch his face – especially since the ship's Master is drawing purposefully close to the shoreline to afford these experts a fair view of the allotted Airport site.

It is early dawn, and at first all that is discernible is a shadowy hulk looming out of the darkness, an oblong patch of solid blackness laid across the star-glittered backdrop of the north-westerly horizon. This island stands solitary in an immense ocean, a thousand miles from Africa, more from Brazil, and seven hundred miles from her nearest neighbour, the even smaller Ascension Island. At this hour, her peaks and gorges are still undefined, but the surveyor's eyes are eagerly pinned on the blurred outline.

Then the light comes up and details flare into focus. I know what we are looking at on this southern side. A little to port of the bow is the huge rugged amphitheatre of Sandy Bay, which we lose when we turn eastwards and start hugging tall perimeter cliffs gashed by gullies, crevices, and tiny bays outlined by crashing white foam, all great walls of brown rock rising perpendicular out of the ocean. Save for a lone guano-white rock enjoying the illustrious name of George Island, the scene from the bows is still murky brown or black in a gunmetal sea until, as the skies brighten further, the sun suddenly shows us verdant flashes of the inland heights: the green meadows of Woody Ridge, the shimmering 2 700 foot peaks behind, Diana and Actæon, even the tall Norfolk Island pine piercing the sky beside Napoleon Bonaparte's last home, at Longwood House. And then, high above the unexpectedly grassy sea cove of Prosperous Bay with the knotted Turk's Cap beside it – both overshadowed by the great ugly massif of The Barn – the barren and knobbly plateau of Prosperous Bay Plain is pointed out by our Captain. That is where the airport will be built.

I turn my attention to the surveyor. He is ashen. Lines furrow his cheeks, horror glazes the eyes. "So what do you think now?"

"Bloddy 'ell!" he exclaims. "I never imagined anything like *this*!"

"You still think building a runway up there will be easy?"

He covers his face with his hands, shaking his head. That's all the answer I require. I smile my sardonic Airport smile to myself; the one that says: *By the time your government has paid all you experts to look at this difficult site, to measure it, assess it and work out how on earth to get the requisite machinery to it, they could have built Jamestown a breakwater and got a faster ship.*

But the Airport isn't directly my affair at all and I won't lose sleep over it. Governor-Designate Hill has assured me it will happen, and all that really concerns me and my family is access – by either sea or air – to the new secondary lives we are building in St Helena. And because we are so nearly there now, gliding inexorably closer under slowed and quieter engines and a gently lapping sea, my heart is beating crazily with excitement.

The area around the huge grey Barn and Flag Staff Hill, on our port side, was where everything started 14 million years ago, the first of three huge volcanic sheet eruptions that gave birth to St Helena and, like so many other shoreline features, today is completely devoid of vegetation. I find The Barn's looming black presence strangely disconcerting, forbidding almost, and the scene brightens only when the ship has slipped past it and the towering and sheer coastal wall of Flag Staff beyond, where, from under its lee, today a small boatful of fishermen wave as we pass. One of our crew recognises the boat, and across the water a cheerful greeting is called to the fishing friends, and a little joshing returned, almost unintelligible to foreign ears as the islanders spontaneously lapse into their own sing-song English patois.

Our quiet group of early risers on the bridge-wings is a chattering camera-clicking throng by the time we pass Flag Staff, and now all that is left is to round the island's northeast corner. And there they are! The familiar moored fishing boats bobbing in James Bay, punctuated by one or two late-visiting yachts, confirming the presence of the town just ahead of them, the morning sun painting them brightly as they sway on a grey morning sea. We slide slowly past Rupert's Valley, the so-called industrial quarter of the island with its fish factories, fuel farm and power plant; slowly past the old ruined 17th Century military batteries on Munden's Hill above, past the cliff-hanging now-derelict house where three Bahraini dissidents were imprisoned under house arrest during the 1950s. And the next bay is Jamestown's.

The dark blue St Helena flag with its yellow crest has already been run up our mast and, catching a brisk breeze, is standing out importantly, acknowledging the Union flag that has just been hoist high on Ladder Hill to advertise our august arrival. And now, with engines quite silent, the RMS has turned again, artfully nosing towards the moored fishing craft in James Bay, to face the long thin capital straggling up its narrow gorge ahead. Rows of cars are already parked all along the seawall at the mouth of the valley to welcome us, and knots of people can be made out patiently waiting near the Customs house for the rattling blue Wharf-transport to offload us in an hour or so. At the Landing Steps, the small ferry sways impatiently as it waits to bring the Immigration officials across the quarter mile of water to the ship as soon as we have dropped anchor.

And, a moment or two later, down the anchor goes, squealing and groaning through a reverberant clanging of its heavy chains. There is an instant's pregnant pause, and then the ship's whistle echoes over the bay and all the way up the steep valleys, across the bluffs and up to the very peaks themselves, sending its clear message of greeting as far as it can. A mellow, familiar roar in one sustained heart-melting hallo to family and old friends. The RMS is home.

Remote

1.

A Country House in Town

July 1999 to April 2000

The new pontoon at the bottom of the gangway makes all the difference to my innate clumsiness. But even so I am glad of the strong, rough fishermen hands that grab my arms to swing me off the surging metal staircase beneath my feet, across the swaying platform, and over the gunwales of the small ferry before I fully realise that I am executing a giant leap. And now that I am seated alongside a group of returning islanders on the ferry bench, more or less enveloped by an obligatory Mae West issued for this short journey to shore, I gaze back up the walls of the ship that brought us here, wave a final goodbye to officers lounging at the railings, at crewmen working the cargo already swinging from the ship's derrick for transfer to lighters waiting below, and at co-passengers and new friends who wave back as though they'll never see me again even though they themselves will be on the next boat to shore. Then, as a paroxysm of engine splutters finally suggests that the ferry has her complement of passengers for now, I find that we are suddenly cutting past the bows of the RMS *St Helena,* past moored yachts and a hundred small fishing boats at rest in the bay, and our ship is receding behind us. Rapidly growing in stature ahead, the island looms like some haughty Victorian duchess, nestled within her dark taffeta ruffled skirts, ready to receive us, while in my stomach butterflies are frenetic with excitement.

Donny is one of the familiar islanders helping out at the Landing Steps, immaculate in ship's whites and as dashing as ever, even though he left the RMS some years ago. But his broad grin of recognition gleams as he leans down and hoists me from the ferry gunwales where I have now been obliged to pirouette momentarily until the sea gets its rhythm right and allows me to ascend to dry ground. "Hey, good to see you back!" he exclaims. "Stayin' long?"

"Just a week this time."

"That no way long enough!"

"I'll stay longer next time – we're buying a house here!"

"*Buyin'*? Wow!" Though the expert flick of his wrist catapults me up the Landing Steps, quickly away from the wash of sea behind me, I still register his surprise; for the sale of a house to a South African national on this fiercely British island is a rare thing indeed.

When I've shed the life jacket at the top of the steps, dropping it into a tea chest of sorts, I am free to find a cramped seat on the aged and rattling blue bus that plays St Helena's ambassador for a teeth-jangling run past a few containers, an obsolete crane and various late 18th Century buildings hacked into the high brown cliffs, that have, over time, served their uses for almost everything from dwellings for lascars to Her Majesty's Customs. And it is outside the barrel-roofed latter that we all are disgorged to claim and explain our luggage that has miraculously arrived ahead of us, and then face the welcoming mass of strange faces excitedly crowding the barricade a little further on.

My heart is beating fast now, emotion making it hard to breathe. And even before I forge forward towards the crowd, my eyes are involuntarily drawn to the great familiar cliffs that dominate Jamestown, the solid grey church nestling at the foot of the soaring Jacob's Ladder, the white walls of the Castle and brown walls of the empty moat outside it, the tarred Wharf lining the curve of James Bay…

Then I see him and just know that he's the man. Tall, rangy, head and shoulders above the crowd, his faded hair the colour of the cigarette smoke that shrouds him, a silky brown and white Springer spaniel at his side, wagging its stumpy tail ingenuously. Although I have forborne to pin a flower in my hair for recognition, he somehow knows me too and steps forward with a wide smile, his voice emitting the soft rolling accents of a Dorset man – tones familiar to me after many months of anguished negotiation across transatlantic phone lines, but whose face I do not know. "Well, I'm glad we finally sorted it all out!" he chuckles, slinging my suitcase into the boot of his car and then settling himself behind the wheel. "You do know the house, don't you?"

My stomach suffers a lurch of nervousness. "I know where it is and what it looks like from the outside – but I've never been through the gate," I admit. Years back, when I first introduced my husband, Christopher, and our then-young children to this island that so completely obsesses me, we holidayed for two months directly behind this new purchase, so I know its position perfectly – its convenient proximity to town and yet soothing distance from it; its tall white walls and long double verandas visible from the road, and the length of its garden.

"Never been inside!" he exclaims in horror. "I didn't realise that! I hope to goodness you like it."

I hope so, too, most fervently. An odd configuration of rooms wouldn't bother me, nor would aesthetic anomalies; and we've already been assured by a friend that electrics are safe and the house structurally sound. Nevertheless, the very last words I had uttered to my dear husband before I sailed away to set our seal on this extraordinary transaction, were: "What do I do if the *atmosphere* is awful?"

The answer was simple really: nothing. For after the incredible rigmarole of forms and faxes that we were required to submit, recommendations from bankers, medics, police and pillars of Cape Town society, after scrutiny of all these by Island Councils, after postings of intent advertised to the general public and then another month-long wait for a final decision of acceptance to issue forth from the Governor-in-Council to buy this particular house, it was unlikely that we would find the stamina to do it all again for a different property. Assuming another such perfect place ever again so miraculously presented itself. It is this house or none at all – with or without an oppressive atmosphere. "I *will* like it," I assure the Dorset man, hardly able to voice my silly apprehensions at this late stage. "This whole thing is a dream come true, and my husband and I can't thank you enough for pulling out every stop you could!"

He smiles wryly, both of us knowing that he had wanted a guaranteed cash sale as desperately as we wanted the house. "I never really wanted to sell," he says wistfully as he whisks me over the moat, through the Town Arch and across the Grand Parade, past the lined-up Georgian edifices of Main Street, executes a turn at the tiny roundabout outside the Canister that is Jamestown's great divide, past the old Victorian Market building and up the long incline of Market Street. "But though my wife was born in St Helena, she's lived all her adult life in the UK and she finds this island too small for her now. She's already gone back and left me to pack up here."

He does a quick right and a left that causes the spaniel to slide off his seat, and we are then on a quieter, narrower road, still climbing a little, until the car slows down alongside a long white wall with a big black gate at the end of it, and he silences the engine. "I hope you will be happy here," he smiles. "Think of this as your house now – I'm really just caretaking it until I join my wife."

He opens the gate and lets me in, and the first thing I notice are the vivid blooms of hibiscus and bougainvillea tumbling alongside the yellow brick path to the door, and over the boundary walls. There is colour everywhere even though it is midwinter, and pinks, scarlets, oranges and mauves shriek their hues against the bright white of my new home which is positioned sideways on to the road, grandly dominating the garden at its feet. The house stands at the very top of Jamestown, just where the valley makes a gentle dogleg and then narrows quite spectacularly into a jungle of mango trees and palms until it eventually is lost in the folds of the green inland hills. On either side, the raw brown cliffs of James Valley rise up almost sheer, proffering cacti and spiky agaves as a gesture of vegetation above the long string of close-packed Georgian houses that comprise the island's capital. From the seaside to the house the town measures exactly one mile.

"I love this house and am really sorry I can't stay on," he says, opening the front door for me. And when I cross the threshold, I know why he waxes so lyrical. Though I haul a deep breath, almost waiting for some dreaded intimation that all might not be quite well within these thick Regency walls, there is no threat at all. The house's perfumed melange of polish and old smoke, of spices, dust, cigarettes, dog, dampness, rich wood and well-used furnishings at once envelops me with warm, welcoming arms. This is a house that has been lived in, for better or worse, for two hundred years. It's a house with history and real soul. I feel the Dorset man's hopeful eyes fixed on me. "This is gorgeous!" I exclaim as I thankfully let out my breath. "You have absolutely nothing to worry about!"

The floor of the lower veranda, accessed by five stone steps and bounded by thigh-high walls, is painted green – an ages-old colonial stalwart, I note wryly, and he grins: "Green paint or red here, no other choice. You'll need to bring stuff with you when you move in."

And by *stuff* it is clear that he means more than exterior cement paint. For there are indeed some changes to be made inside, I decide as I begin my explorations. The house – *our* house now, our wonderful, marvellous hard-won prize – still retains numerous old furnishings which the Dorset man himself has not changed in the short time he has lived here, but some will not bide long with me. Heading the list will be the red-and-gold carpet that climbs the main staircase, an off-cut, surely, from some derelict Eastbourne boarding house, along with other wall-to-wall carpets that obscure original teak foot-wide floorboards throughout the house. Seventies sun-filter curtains will come down, their rods with them. And the sets of narrow glass-panelled double-doors downstairs that lead into the sitting room and dining room – elegant in theory but in reality ornamented by panes of spotted translucent bathroom glass – bother me just as much as the upstairs hollow-board interior doors with their modern chrome handles...

"Are you *sure* you're happy?" insists the Dorset man, trying to read my face for chinks of doubt. In truth, people don't often buy houses they have never visited.

"I'm ecstatic! Really!" Where are words good enough for the euphoria of a lifelong dream coming true? Something longed for in all your waking hours for years and years, and talked of in your sleep; something that turns out to be so much more than your wildest dreams. "Two years ago when we were last on the island," I tell him, "Christopher and I decided that the time was at last right to look for a cottage here. All I really wanted was to own some of this island's earth. 'A flowerpot of soil will do' was what I actually said. And look at what we have now! A beautiful old house on half an acre of garden in the part of Jamestown that I love best!"

"A Country house in Town is what the islanders call Villa Le

Breton," says the Dorset man with a flush of pride, and adds: "But a flowerpot would have been cheaper!"

In the unseasonal heat of the late June afternoon, for it is winter in this southern hemisphere, I walk downhill past the old low cottages of Market Street, returning the spontaneous hallos and waves I am served by every passer-by. This famous friendliness keeps a happy smile on my face and a sense of tremendous privilege to be back among such a truly welcoming people, world-renowned for their courtesy and unrestrained greetings. Some faces are familiar, some are not, and I am hailed by one wizened old woman who inquires in her sing-song tone, when I pause to gaze at the traffic winding down Ladder Hill Road high above us: "Who you is, dearie? You come on de ship?"

I realise that she is not supposing that I might have flown to this airportless island or magically arrived by train, but that she means, quite pertinently, *today's* ship, the one still holding court in James Bay. "Yes, I arrived this morning."

"How long you stay?"

"Just a week."

"You work wit' de Gowmen'?"

"No. I've come here to buy a house."

There is a brief pause before she remarks somewhat enigmatically, "Oh, my," and then lays a bony hand reassuringly on my arm, "Well now, God bless you, lovey." Feeling heavily imbued with God's blessings already, I somehow doubt that I will need to take up any more of His valuable time with regard to our marvellous new acquisition, but I smile gratefully before we continue on our separate ways, she trudging uphill with her little shopping bag, me quickening my pace so as not to be late for the new Governor's inauguration.

Gathered in front of the Market building, I notice knotted groups of uniformed bands watching the slow-moving hands of the silver Victorian clock near the White Horse bar, drums at their feet and brass gleaming. Then I negotiate the dog-leg behind the white Canister building and eventually I am in the broad Main Street, heading down to the Grand Parade where a larger crowd is gathered.

I find shade with an assembly of local onlookers under a scarlet flame tree, gathered to watch the proceedings from the library end of the long, low cannon-guarded Courthouse building to one side of the large public square. The inauguration of a new Governor is a novelty to me, never having coincided with such a colonial ceremony on the island before, and I take in all the details of the scene with the starry eyes of a teenager completely in love. Studiously eschewing any distinctive national trait – no colourful national costume, no indigenous music or dance, no local art or surviving craft, no definably St Helenian cuisine – reserved St Helena devotedly adheres instead to a so-called *culture* that bares all the marks of post-war 1950s England. Only its famous friendliness and its language are its great distinctions, and – like that of so many British islands across the globe – the latter is faintly rhythmic, sometimes throwing up smidgens of Old English which delight new ears; but even that, in this modern age of telecommunication, is swiftly and sadly giving way to slang and Americanisation. So, colonial trappings are not out of place here. Indeed, I think as I wait for something to begin, this island – perhaps more than any other place I know – is still all about colonialism: about depending on others to make decisions, about depending on others to take the blame for them, especially about depending on others to keep the coffers filled. In this context, and in support of St Helena's marvellous history, such a delightfully outmoded formal ceremony finds its mark in this far-flung forgotten world.

The Grand Parade is the hub of Jamestown in a slightly dislocated fashion. A full street's length from the shops, pubs and hotel that draw the masses, this large space marks the official entrance to the island, gained through an historic Arch in the old military curtain walls built when the English East India Company introduced a settlement here in 1659. To the east of the Arch, accessed by the first opening on the left, stands the white-painted Castle – seat of government and something of a misnomer for this unthreatening 18th Century edifice – and through its own archway, brilliantly bougainvillea-swathed and also guarded by two small cannon, a cobbled courtyard and a handsome raised portico are visible.

The west of the parade square is rimmed by various warehouses, themselves historic stone buildings, and in the far corner huddles

Her Majesty's Prison, disarmingly flaunting its drying laundry on the blue-painted wooden upper balcony. All of these are backed by the awesome 699 steps of a near-vertical Jacob's Ladder shimmying up the cliff face to another set of domineering battlements on top of the hill.

It is, however, the tall grey St James' Church that commands the square, the oldest surviving Anglican Church in the southern hemisphere. *Newly-built* and much admired by Captain James Cook in 1775, it has at various times enjoyed two towers and two consecutive steeples. Presently limited to only one tower and no steeple, it still exerts a motherly presence over the town; and though it is not the island's cathedral – that privilege having been awarded to the rural heart of the countryside because the populace of Jamestown were considered too reprobate at the time – there is a profound sense of history within its walls.

As a reminder of its authority, while we patiently stand waiting, the tower clock strikes the quarter hour, several minutes out of time as always yet somehow befitting this island's inbuilt disregard for punctuality. And its strident clang triggers a sudden bugle squeal from the upper reaches of Main Street; a first hesitant note, and then the full-lunged drum-beaten marches that bring into view the proud Salvation Army and the various other musicians I had seen gathered at the Market.

Bringing up the rear are the police, blue-black and stiff-shouldered, snow-white gloves swinging in perfect synchrony, British chequerboard insignia dizzyingly bright and ready for review by the new Commander-in-Chief of St Helena once the inauguration has taken place. Polished brass along the length of the procession reflects the blazing afternoon sun as it relentlessly flogs the Parade, the heat worsened by humidity that is now rendering the air so stifling we can barely breathe. Even so, our necks immediately crane to watch the marchers, and the bored young Scouts and Girls Guides all lined up in our corner of the square and grown restless and fidgety through the long wait, now straighten their backs at the fervour of the music. Even the small Brownie who, to the consternation of her leader, had determinedly seated herself cross-legged on the ground against the heat, staggers to her feet.

Right on cue, by our time, the new Governor and his wife

arrive. We have watched the gleaming Rover turn from the dog-leg near the Market into the top of Main Street, and then cruise slowly down towards us, the Governor's pennant hanging dismally limp in the dearth of a breeze. A chauffeur/aide-de-camp in braided uniform leaps out to open doors and both the Hills are disgorged outside the Courthouse to mount a few shallow steps to the podium, taking their places beside the purple-cassocked Lord Bishop and the Lady Sheriff. Behind them are ranged besuited dignitaries of Legislative and Executive Councils – those same officials, I note wryly, who recently delved with such depth into our humble application to buy property here. Everyone looks hot, not least His Excellency who, fond of shorts and T-shirts on those lazy shipboard days, is now swaddled up to the neck in a starched white uniform with a high embroidered collar and cuffs. He wears thick white gloves, a heavy sword at his side, and a tall chin-strapped white helmet topped by layered white and scarlet plumes. Swan's feathers, we are told, though London's Foreign & Commonwealth Office irreverently calls them 'dead chicken'. His cheeks are already pinked by the heat.

Mrs Hill, of formidably decisive personality I discerned during our five days at sea, is no less uncomfortable. She, somewhat inappropriately, is wearing a smart but thick wool suit in this intense heat, having been warned by her predecessor that temperatures can be perishing on the island in June, yet without forewarning that the climate in Jamestown bears no relation whatsoever to that of the inland heights where they are lodged in their huge damp residence, Plantation House. I feel for her in the focus of scrutiny; yet, while the rest of us, sodden by humidity, fall back into the shade of our flame tree to lean on any support we can find, she steadfastly holds her own without a glimmer of capitulation, while Bishop, Sheriff and new Governor intone their various formulae. His Excellency's speech is all about flying of course, about airports, air-services, far-flung destinations and great intentions; but with the Union flag dead on its Ladder Hill mast this afternoon and no swan's feather stirring on the hat, it is almost impossible to imagine anything flying around this island. Unsurprisingly a Brownie faints, just a few rows from me, soon mimicked by a young policeman who keels over like a tin soldier, both causing scuffling and disruption among nurses and bystanders who stretcher them away.

When, eventually, the bugles are raised again, an excruciatingly inexact rendition of *God Save the Queen* yowls cat-like across the valley-mouth, and I instinctively glance again towards Latin-American Gloria Hill who is involuntarily wincing, shoulders unconsciously hunched against the noise. She is too new here to have yet experienced the idiosyncrasies of St Helena that make us all smile, but she will discover them in time, just as my family and I still have much to learn about actually living here. After all, a whole new era is beginning: A new Governor with big dreams, a new part-time life for me and mine, and a whole new flying future for this dear little place.

The review is over now and as the crowd disperses, I deem it time to return to my new white house up the hill, taking the road slowly and happily as I head for home, deciding that, whatever the time when I get there, that will be the right moment to open the half bottle of champagne Christopher sneaked into my suitcase for quiet celebration. The tail-wagging spaniel and I – and the Dorset man if he's around – will take it to the dappled shade of the old jacaranda tree just inside the gate, so artistically gnarled and bent by wind, that offers a view of the house, all the garden, and the afternoon sun on the towering brown cliff opposite, and there we will toast new ownership of this Country House in Town.

The Dorset man has set up a succession of meetings for me through my seven days on the island, among them a signing-over session at Legal & Lands which will finally seal the purchase. There are also insurances to sort out at Solomon & Company which more or less rules the commercial island, a transfer of telephone names for phone book update at Cable & Wireless, and an appointment with the Chief Secretary at the Castle concerning a work permit for letting out Villa Le Breton's small attached self-catering 'cottage' in which I am presently living, if we so wish.

But in between meetings, with manic dedication, I wield a lengthy tape measure around the house, aware that before we freight over furnishings for this new endeavour, make curtains, or buy floor rugs or furniture, we should be sure they'll fit. Nothing in this house is truly symmetrical, I discover, and this procedure entails more hands-and-knees work, more stretching and reaching, more drawing, and more muttering of imprecations than I could ever have foreseen. My lists are endless. Sheets of paper flutter across the floor, notebooks pile up, my hand gets writer's cramp. The large dining room is dispensed with first, and I am mightily thankful that the huge oval table and chairs we so impulsively bought for this room before confirmation of the sale ever came through, will fit perfectly, even alongside the hefty, ugly (but capacious) resident sideboard that I have not the strength to dispose of.

The kitchen keeps me captive for hours with its nooks and crannies, and eventually I am released to make my way up a second staircase, this of green-painted stone, perilously steep and uneven, that leads from the kitchen to a small back landing where our newly-adolescent son's room will overlook the lush mango orchards of Cambrian House behind us. The main house's only bathroom sits alongside, and for a moment I am mesmerised by its yellow plastic *art deco*-styled bath-panel, the blue-flowered shower-curtain, the orange-trimmed net on the window, the patchy and ancient carpet that curls at the corners – and most especially the redolence of the damp that lies with it. I lift the carpet warily, in the dim hope of discovering fine teak beneath, and am not surprised to see that these boards are beyond hope of revival. The tape-measure goes to work again: new shower cubicle and taps, new floor covering and panelling for the bath, new basin, and a Roman blind.

I cross the awkward angles and turns of the half landing on the main hideously red-and-gold carpeted staircase – the mathematics of these variant steps will be tackled another day – and arrive on a sunny landing at the upstairs front of house, the space flanked by a large bedroom on either side. Double-doors open from the landing on to the upstairs veranda and I am magnetically pulled to view my estate from these lofty heights. "The garden's a bit much for me to care for, all on my own," the Dorset man had apologised as he initially showed me around the grounds, but since it sports avenues of mango trees, forests of hibiscus, guava trees, banana palms, a reasonable lawn, and a whole world of birds, I do not feel it's anything to be ashamed of. From here

I can see the world pass by, cars chugging up the high, climbing Side Path pass on one side, and others winding away from us up Ladder Hill Road ahead on the opposite side of our valley. The *sea view* offered by my seller in the official advertisement for this house was, I discover, an exaggeration since the triangle of wide ocean offered from the extreme western end of the veranda measures little more than two inches of horizon; but as Christopher and I personally prefer a view of mountains to one of empty ocean, this is not troubling.

In the right-hand room I nearly chop off my fingertips. The sash windows of this house bear a quirk about which I've received no warning. And when I release the lock on one of them, it crashes southwards with such unexpected violence that the force cracks one of the small Georgian panes across one corner – an unfortunate accident but not embarrassing since the house is now ours. But it does dawn on me that, without my swift reflexes, I might easily have been found still affixed to the window by bleeding fingers when the Dorset man eventually returned from his afternoon's outing, and the wielding of my trusty tape measure would necessarily cease. Perhaps yet more troubling, I decide, is the realisation that if I hadn't so timeously escaped, my temporary incarceration would have been in a room that sports – to my utter incredulity – no fewer than *eleven* different floral designs in pink, none co-ordinating.

In the bedroom across the landing, I refrain from meddling with the temperamental sashes but, while measuring up the numerous discrepancies of their antique specifications, discover a small scratching on one of the panes. *HJT.* I dive at once into my new large envelope of ancient documents pertaining to this house, but on the face of it HJT did not exist among the various actual owners or lessees that have inhabited the house since the turn of the 19th Century. It was a bored child, I decide fondly – or perhaps a lovesick daughter mooning over an absent suitor – who left that little remembrance.

Once floors and walls are measured and sketches of all the irregular doors and windows are drawn, I start on the specifications of the furniture we will keep. And it is while examining a dainty Regency table that a pile of leaflets flutters to the floor. *Fly or Die*, they warn as I gather them up, propelling me right back into the Airport argument. "Where do these come from?" I ask the Dorset man.

He grins. "I printed them. I've been running a campaign here, trying to explain to people that this island stands no chance of survival without air access."

I quirk a doubtful eyebrow at him.

"Some enlightened people see the advantages," he quickly argues. "For one thing, we'll be able to fly medevacs out without forcing sick people into days on the ship, and tourists will fly in. But the old people are too afraid of change. If we don't change, the island will shrivel away – just as the brochure says."

"Then you'll be pleased to know that the new Governor says we'll have an Airport within five years." I give him the gist of the Governor's speech and our conversations at sea.

"Within five years!" he repeats. "He told you that?"

"Perhaps he means it," I offer naïvely.

His smile is now enigmatic. "Remember this: the key to surviving on this island is to believe very little of what you hear. Though Lord knows, this place needs that airport."

I smile back in a way that offers to change the subject, and he suddenly leaps from his chair. "Speaking of keys," he says, "this is yours. Take it home to show your husband. I'll use the other lock until I leave." And he places on my palm a huge piece of heavy moulded iron.

I look down at it overlapping the span of my hand. It is black and worn shiny in the place where two hundred years of fingers have turned it in the lock of the huge front door. My front door now, I correct myself. Mine and my family's. I look around at the tired curtains, the bilious stair carpet, the myriad other cosmetic changes that I will make when we finally move in. But for all that, one thing is clear. I am already in love with this house as deeply as I am in love with this island. I close my fingers tightly around the key and warm it against my heart.

If the RMS *St Helena* hadn't broken down quite so spectacularly in the dying weeks of the year, we would have celebrated the last Christmas of the decade in our new second home. As it was, something dramatic happened in her engine room just off the coast of Brest in France as she set sail from England for southern waters in late November that year, and we did not see her in Cape Town again until the following March. Our crates of meticulously-measured newly-acquired furnishings – sofas, armchairs, three dining tables and seating, veranda chairs, beds, tallboys, pictures, bedding, custom-made blinds and curtaining for nineteen irregular windows, kitchen utensils, waste-paper baskets, ornaments, cutlery, books, CD players and music, floor rugs, wine, garden irrigation hose, a car, extra car-parts, and ten custom-made Victorian interior doors... Well, all of these things, and much more, sat in two Cape Town garages we had commandeered until normality was restored to St Helena.

On the island this catastrophe caused havoc. The enforced cancellation of a few hundred holiday plans was insignificant in the light of possible starvation. And within hours of the news breaking, island shops were stripped bare of cigarettes, beer, cooking oil, margarine, flour, lavatory paper and sugar, pretty much in that order. No Christmas fare arrived, no turkeys, no toys, no mail, no long-planned millennium fireworks or frivolous party favours. Medicines threatened to run short and the hospital went into overdrive until the Castle leapt to action; and so, from somewhere remote, was eventually scrounged a bouncy Greek ship that offered to carry St Helena's medevacs to Cape Town. However, visitors marooned on the island were not all lucky enough to talk themselves into passage on this ship, and some did not get off the island in time to save their employment at home after their unlikely excuses fell on the deaf ears of bosses who commanded: "I'm *ordering* you to get the next plane out of there or you're fired!" In today's world of easy communications, it remains difficult for outsiders to even vaguely comprehend the remoteness of a place served solely by one fairly sporadic ship.

Apart from that, the island quietly pottered on about its business. Constant shortages of one kind or another have bred a phlegmatic race blessed with the philosophical assumption that at some time or another before death doth them assail, whatever they are short of will eventually arrive. And it generally does. Just as the RMS did. Eventually.

With engines restored to working order, it finally skimmed south, dumped its long-overdue British cargo on a relieved St Helena, then continued to Cape Town where we determinedly prised our teenage children from their respective halls of learning, settling ourselves and our extensive freight on board for a move already delayed by nearly four months.

But the tall white house with its double verandas, Georgian windows and bird-filled garden still looks the same when we finally get there, only it is now bare of the Dorset man's personal furniture, his silky dog, and his kindly presence. The rooms stand clean and empty, barring the various pieces of furniture we are adopting, while the tired pink curtains still hang at the sitting room windows and the red-and-gold carpet sullies the stairs. But there is a quiet grace about the house, which Christopher acknowledges immediately. "This *feels* like home," he announces, pausing on the stairs to take in our new domain as I excitedly lead my family from room to room. "We've done the right thing."

And now we set to work. Within hours the wall-to-wall carpets are gone, exposing broad teak floorboards throughout, which bring our darling daughter, Virginia, to her knees, scrubbing and rubbing them with nourishment and all the exertion of an enslaved 17-year-old. Pushing trails of blond hair from her eyes, she pauses occasionally to suggest with light rancour: "Tell me again why I'm doing this?"

"To bond with this new part of our lives."

"I hope Richard's also bonding," she ventures suspiciously, hinting that her younger brother might not be as diligent. But he too is enslaved and is ripping old curtains from their rods with all the reckless verve of a 13-year-old who, while relishing the distance from his Cape Town school, would also prefer to be liberated from these chores. "How long will this all take?" he repeatedly demands. But to this we have no reply. Chris and I are too busy shifting adopted furniture about and rearranging rooms before our own new household eventually starts arriving from the Wharf on the back of a growling open truck.

With the veranda littered with opened boxes, cupboards are packed, pictures hung, the kitchen organised to my liking. But by the second week we are running out of steam. Not a family of adept do-it-yourselfers we have already begun to flounder. And then our friend

Greta the Sheriff, a St Helenian businesswoman of many connections, miraculously steps in. "A handyman came looking for work this morning," she says on the phone. "I wondered if you could use him?"

We fairly kiss him when he arrives at our door, a strapping young man with strong arms and a drill in his hand. "Clyde," he introduces himself. "An' my wife Bonnie happy doin' cleanin' if y'all want. The whole two us lookin' for wark."

Bonnie and Clyde work like Trojans. Bonnie runs as she vacuums and polishes, and sings as she irons, while Clyde and Chris become best buddies. Together they lay down the miles of irrigation hose that our broad half-acre deserves, and set the sprinklers going. Together they cart our new custom-made interior doors to be planed to size at a carpenter's shop and afterwards hung by Clyde. Chris holds the screws as Clyde fixes new Victorian brass door-knobs in place, and steadies the ladder while Clyde screws in new iron curtain-rails, hangs the ceiling-to-floor curtains, and fits a custom-made Roman blind into each of eight completely irregular windows. Under their care the house becomes home, and we rejoice in our wonderful team. "What a fabulous find!" I tell Greta when I phone to thank her for them, and she sighs with relief: "I don't know the couple at all, you know – they've been working in the Falklands for some time. But he certainly looked strong and capable. I'm glad they've turned out so well."

"They're pleasant and friendly and very hard-working," I repeat. "Everything's taking shape here so fast!"

By the end of a hectic month, the house bears our own stamp, and Clyde sets to work laying a concrete hardstanding under the jacaranda tree where grass refuses to grow. It will be a soothing place to sit, especially when the setting sun lights up the cannon and brownstone fortifications of Sampson's Battery on the high eastern cliff-top above us, and the pair of gleaming white fairy terns that roost on the wind-bowed branches over our heads settle down for the night. Chris and I plan, over the years ahead when life is more leisurely here, to enjoy many a bottle of fine Cape wine in this spot.

The hardstanding is not yet complete by the time we have to return our children to school in Cape Town, but Clyde is happy to continue building it in our absence. He will care for the garden too, watering the lawns and plants regularly, trimming the hibiscus hedges and bougainvilleas, and nurturing the fruiting mangos and young banana palms. A couple of times a week he will rev up our car – a strong SUV-type nine-seater – to ensure the battery doesn't go flat, and he'll finish off some sanding, painting and several other odd jobs inside the house, generally acting as maintenance man while Bonnie makes a noise around the place to keep white ants (termites) at bay and scare away Jamestown's importunate cockroaches. Greta will pay the staff and the utilities bills in our absence, and keep an eye on the property until October when I will come back alone, as vanguard, to oversee some renovation of the kitchen before Christopher and the children – and his mother on her first visit to St Helena – arrive for the Christmas school holidays. There is still much to do here, and we don't want to leave, but our primary lives in Cape Town need to be resumed.

The afternoon light is painting Jamestown golden as we take up places against the deck-railings of the departing RMS. Below us some young people are knee-boarding from a speedboat that is enjoying a rare opportunity for mild exhibition. It surges back and forth across the bay, sometimes weaving between anchored boats, sometimes taking a wide turn behind our ship, and another group of teenagers watching from the Wharf let out a teasing cheer whenever a knee-boarder falls off. There are still crowds on the Wharf, lingering in happy conversation long after the ferry has brought all the RMS passengers to the ship, and some will remain until she slowly swings westwards, emitting three long soulful blasts (and a half) of farewell, and then glides out of sight beyond the cliffs of Ladder Hill to round the island at the western end. There are rituals to island life, and the movements of this vessel, we already know, govern them all.

A sudden clanking stirs me from the reverie I have fallen into as I watch the scene around us. The noisy anchor is rising. The gentle swell beneath us becomes real movement and with that realisation, an ache clutches my heart with the talons of farewell. It is always the same – every time I leave this place. Frantically I lean towards the island as the ship inches away, eyes seeping in every last adored detail from the emerald sweep of the inland peaks to the town packed into its cramped and arid-flanked gorge, imprinting the scene on my mind, drawing it into my soul all over again, afraid of ever losing it. And then as Rod Stewart's immortal *Sailing* blares through the ship's tannoy – a stirring anthem not only synonymous with this ship but also her brave predecessor's voluntary service in the long-ago Falklands War – my tears flow unrestrainedly. Even though I will be back within the year, I never want to leave.

2.

As it was in the Beginning

October to December 2000

"I hope you won't be too disappointed," Greta offers nervously as she stops her car outside my gorgeous house. It is October at last, and after six months' absence I am back, itching to start cheering-up work on the kitchen and establish myself in the way of St Helena life. "He bolted the gate from inside, you see, so I couldn't get in until I sent Larry 'Nails' over the wall."

Disappointed? She opens my front gate and ushers me into the Vale of Desolation. "Larry was a bit – eh – *surprised* at what he found..."

I am ravaged. My heart soars to my throat and then lurches out of me altogether. And I see at once why Larry was *surprised*. My face pales almost to swooning but there is nothing to clutch for support, for Greta, ready to run, still stands by the gate. Where, six months ago, Chris and I left our half-acre of tropical dream in the arms of that tender caretaker and his sweet wife, here lies a desert. No blade of grass shows its brave little ears, knotted banana palms lie in brown tangles, the pawpaw trees clearly will spawn no more. I see twelve ancient mango trees shrivelling before my eyes, and twenty-two fully-grown hibiscus bushes drawing their final gasp. Ten appear already dead. The usually rampant plumbago hedge and four massive bloomless bougainvilleas are drooping sickly under the death-rattle of parched leaves.

Only along the border of the garden path does a stiff row of valiant marigolds lift bright faces to greet me, plants that were not growing there when we left in April. Flowers of deception, these; for while the huge front gate was uncooperatively bolted, this meagre offering – in the only flowerbed visible through the slats of the sturdy entrance – was cunningly designed to fool Greta into assumption that all was well elsewhere in the grounds. I turn my stricken face to her now, mouth rounded, mute with shock.

"You'd better come and look inside the house," she suggests grimly, summoning the courage to slide past me. I follow, knowing this won't be good.

In the sitting room a large sheet of corrugated roofing is propped against my pristine new yellow sofa, taking up most of the room itself, impossible to ignore. And in the rest of the house the same theme of casual disregard is carried through in half-sanded doors, half-painted walls and stairs, and ugly bleach splash-stains on our newly-nourished teak floors. In the guest cottage the bed is rumpled and scattered with cigarette butts and ash for added effect, while in the ironing room lies a tiny pile of un-ironed clothing, abandoned by Bonnie who clearly declined to do even that small kindness for us in our absence – a fact disproportionately irking to me in the scheme of things.

"We saw them in Cape Town!" I exclaim to Greta whose cheerful features have taken on an expression of rare gravity. "We met them off the RMS, showed them the whole Peninsula, bought them lunch, delivered them to their London flight in the evening… And they told us everything was 'good' here!"

"So you knew they'd left the island?"

"We knew they'd found work in England, and we understood their need to earn more money overseas. Greta, we *hugged* them when they left!"

Greta giggles, from hysteria I expect. "I bet you don't want to hug them now!"

"I might seize them by the throat if we ever meet again," I venture boldly to the Sheriff, but she looks as though she might assist me. She recommended them, she remembers.

When Greta leaves me I walk the garden, tears pouring down my face. All Chris's lovingly-laid irrigation has been ripped up, and now only a small ring of hose encircles the traces of Clyde's own dead potato plants. All the rest is wasteland. Shrivelled foliage hangs everywhere, rustling tiredly in the breeze. Even the grassless earth is grey, no more than dust when I take it in my hand, and the barren whole is littered with rubble.

Rubble? Clyde clearly used stones for the foundations of the hardstanding under the jacaranda tree, which, miracle of miracles, was actually completed and now is the sole aspect of the garden to offer any solace. But why spread the surplus all over the grounds? And why should he have such surplus, anyway? Because, I learn later when Greta returns with my utilities bills, at some point he hired a mighty electric stone-grinding machine, running it here for days on end to make gravel from lorry loads of stone, which he sold. My electricity bill bears this out. No doubt he also transported his loads in our car which, it turns out, was spotted in parts of the island *"where even 4x4s don't go"*, I am informed. Although a tough vehicle, our car is not a four-wheel drive. According to further reports, we had barely passed Southwest Point on our southward voyage last April, when he sold his own car, put Bonnie behind the wheel of ours and started teaching her to drive. The exercise was not without mishap, I note, for there are bruises and abrasions to our formerly gleaming car that are new, and when I first climb inside I find the air con broken and the speakers ripped out. The final touches to that picture are painted when, one evening, a stranger arrives at my gate and asks for the car keys. In blank amazement I question his reasons. "Well," he explains with a hint of impatience, "Clyde say I can use dat bus anytime I want. Dat machine his'n anyway."

Our anger is so large that Chris and I agree across the miles that a telephone call of upbraiding to England might release some of our ire. And with a stroke of luck I actually remember the name of the establishment where Bonnie and Clyde had secured employment. But when I get through to the manager there, his fury with them is greater even than ours. "They worked here for three days," he splutters down the line to me, "and I never want to hear their names again! I can't talk about them I am so angry!"

"Join the club," I say, but I never find out exactly what they have or haven't done there.

And then Christopher rings me again from Cape Town. "You'll never believe what I've just received!" he announces jubilantly. "A fax from Clyde in England – with a contact number! He's asking for job references for himself and Bonnie!"

"And so you'll fax him back a glowing testimonial of their good conduct?"

"I'll be brutally honest," says Chris. "Now I have a chance to tell them *exactly* what we think of them."

It's a good idea, I agree. Though I very much doubt that that was what Clyde had in mind, or that it will gain him further employment.

Swinging London, on the cusp of the 1970s, was still in full pendular motion when those of my generation in Cape Town spread their wings and, almost without exception, flew to England to grab the action. But, by and large, people of my youthfulness did not wilfully elect to explore remote islands at that stage of their lives. "Why then," is the inevitable question in slightly incredulous tones, "did you choose *St Helena*? What on earth took you *there*?" The fact is, I had already travelled England twice, and had also explored Europe quite extensively. After that I had a job to do and a living to earn, so when I suddenly developed a yen for a sea cruise that slotted into the brief leave my employment allotted me, I put a pin in a map.

Waving the point rather arbitrarily around the southern hemisphere *(Mauritius, maybe? Reunion? Even exotic Madagascar?)*, it came to earth on the other side of Africa. *St Helena Island* it said, necessitating a cross-eyed squint to see the minuscule dot that it pierced. And while I failed to dredge up so much as a glimmer of knowledge about the place other than Napoleon Bonaparte's exile and death there, I might have suffered the smallest tremor of doubt about this mission. Nevertheless I went to visit Thomas Cook, where the woman at the desk gave me a pitying look. "No one goes there," she said. "In fact, you can't get there!" And so I knew at once that that was where I was going.

At the Union Castle Building I was better received. In fact *two* ships served the island in those far-off days, trim 12-passenger cargo carriers that skimmed between South Africa and England at a brisk twenty-six knots, offering the rare tourist a choice of either one week or a full month's stay on St Helena, and taking a mere two and a half days to get there from Cape Town. I booked for a week, still clueless as to what I would find, the local libraries also having no enlightenment on offer at that time. And the moment I stepped ashore, I realised my terrible mistake: I should have booked for a month.

Some places are like that: you simply *know*. And over a generation later that same passion, consolidated by later visits and three decades of close communication with St Helena, has never diminished, even though the path of true love was, along the way, beset by long absences brought about by the normal hurdles of real life: fiscal trials, limited leave, family commitments. A distracting shift of focus into marriage not unnaturally took up a clump of years and the welcome onslaught of tiny children another busy clump. Yet through it all St Helena was there, just over the horizon, frequently on the lips – always, always in the heart.

A late '80s Christmas saw our first family visit, my poor husband trailing along in self-defence, I suspect, having long been married by proxy to this island he had never seen, and resigned from the outset to an inevitable voyage of discovery at some stage of his life. He is the quintessential Englishman whose home is his castle, and he does not care for the glories of travel with the same passion I bestow upon them. The toting of our siege-rations, too, came as a massive revelation to him – thirteen cabin-trunks and crates various for a two-month island-stay – though he is over that shock now and currently is an unsurpassed carrier of wide-world comforts for life at Villa Le Breton. The children came too, of course: Virginia, grudgingly released from pre-school by a nun who did not deem travel to much benefit anyone; and a toddling Richard accompanied by 523 disposable nappies and a dog lead attached to his baby-reins. The dog lead was donated by a friend who, taking one horrified look at our aged transportation, clutched his own daughters to the safety of his bosom and held them there. By then the speedy Union Castle ships had given way to an infinitely slower erstwhile paper-carrier from the coast of British Columbia that was now St Helena's very own 72-passenger cargo-ship. "I would *never* risk *my* children on that!" he admonished us, as though we did not sufficiently care for our offspring, and swiftly bore his progeny back to suburbia. But the dog lead was a useful thing, for Richard spent the greater part of the five-day voyage tied to a central post on the sun deck, enabling him to run about without risk of inadvertently leaping overboard through various gaps on deck where the railings did not always meet.

Those two months passed as a watershed holiday at Cambrian House – an early 19th Century private house in its garden acre in the upper reaches of Jamestown, where mynah birds squawked and peach-flavoured mangos fell from the trees in their hundreds. Set in its idyllic area, quiet as the countryside yet close to town, the lovely old house wove wondrous spells, sowing strong seeds of attachment to the island into the hearts of Chris and our children almost as securely as St Helena had long ago taken root in my own. A happy coincidence indeed, for when, a full twelve years later, the house immediately below it miraculously appeared on the market, we knew exactly what we wanted.

And so here I am now. Owner of a property somewhat larger than the *flowerpot* I had originally set my sights on. Owner, in fact, of a 200-year-old Grade II Listed house in serious want of cosmetic attention, and a desert with which I am barely coping at the present moment.

Painfully feeling the absence of my family and any shoulder to cry on, my Season of Desolation drags itself into weeks. Day after miserably lonely day I wake at 4am with the insomniac rooster next-door, rise with the mynahs at five, and for four hours in the cool of morning valiantly battle the uncountable metres of wrecked irrigation system. I barely know how it works, but I forge on relentlessly. Then, when the heat of the day brings me indoors, I labour with unfamiliar paints and cleaning fluids, trying to eradicate the new stains on the floor and complete the painting of the main staircase (now thankfully devoid of its virulent boarding house runner), mulling over my lack of practical experience in these matters while I struggle.

By late afternoon I am back outside, stumbling about the garden, again attempting to mend tens of blocked minuscule sprinkler spouts, some horribly damaged, most just suffocated by dust. It is a seriously exhausting pastime, monotonous and frustrating, requiring endless trudges up the sloping garden to turn the tap on, down again to check the spout that I've tweaked too little, and another trudge up again to turn off the tap. Up and down, up and down, praying for water, praying for help, exhorting my poor dying garden to hold on because, though slow in getting there, my dedicated attention is at hand. At the end of the evening, dripping wet from spouts I've tweaked too much and too exhausted to think of food, I pour a whisky, weep into it, fearfully dispatch a couple of hideous cockroaches in the kitchen and small scorpions on the stairs, that take an unconscionable goose-fleshing time to die, and fall asleep by eight. Then Zander saves my life.

The first day that Zander appears, he says nothing. I show him the well-stocked tool shed, mercifully still intact, and he hauls out a rake and spade which he bears off to the loneliest reaches of my wilderness. And there he stands all day, leaning on the spade, the rake unused, bleakly gazing around him. I won't urge him to action, for I sympathise with the untenable weight of his apprehension as he views the work ahead. Deciding where to begin probably looms like Everest, and he is not yet even at Base Camp, for the most daunting labour before him lies not in the creative design of garden beds or the generating of an essential vegetable patch, but in the initial removal of Clyde's legacy of rubble. He requires time to acclimatize.

And at last his miracle work begins; the digging and clearing, sowing and growing, cutting and planning. At a steady, unflappable pace, with steady, unflappable determination to get the garden cleared and at least a little resuscitated by the time Chris arrives to show off our new house to his mother, Zander's work gradually begins to show progress. At last, with a pillar to lean on, strong, upright, steady, solid, I begin to feel less abandoned.

Then the telephone rings. "If you're looking for a cleaning woman," says JJ who found me Zander, "I can recommend Annette. I've just interviewed her for myself and she's good, but I've employed Zander's wife instead. I think you'll like Annette." I am weak with gratitude now, and as Annette bustles in, all smiles and motherly bosom and takes over the house with cheery confidence, I dissolve like a ball of candy-floss in her hands. With the silent rooms now ringing with gossipy chatter and busy footsteps, I can at last begin to think straight. I lift up the phone to announce to our patient kitchen-fixer-in-waiting: "Pat, I'm ready for you now!"

Pat, Gibby and Growler, the 'decorators' – a magical trio of happiness – work impressive and diligent hours. They arrive at seven forty-five, enjoy breakfast under the jacaranda, and have their sleeves rolled up by eight. They bring their own radio, and above the strident Country-&-Western selections of Radio St Helena, their chatter and laughter lifts each day out of the realms of the domestic into a sphere of merriment. There is hammering going on as they fix and fit, mending leaking taps and troublesome lavatories. The doors abandoned by Clyde are painted and rehung; they second-coat the now-white main staircase to finished professionalism. Whole rooms are refreshed by lighter walls and old window frames are remoulded. In the kitchen the greatest transformation takes place as a shabby single basin is ripped out and replaced with a smart double sink and modern taps, surrounded by a handsome timber counter of wood brought from South Africa. This makes all the difference. New doors are hung on every kitchen cupboard too, tongue-and-grooved and painted creamy *Calico* to brighten up the south-facing kitchen, and now furnished with a large Cape yellowwood table and its six purposely mismatched second-hand chairs from Cape Town; it is as homely and inviting as any farm kitchen. My trio hang blue and cream Roman blinds on the big windows to compliment the Provençal hint of blue and yellow I have introduced, clean the panes to shining brightness, and we are well-pleased with the job.

They even make their contributions to the garden. With innocent visions of lush foliage and colour abounding upon my return, I had brought with me a garden urn and pedestal in two parts which now require cementing together. With the island temporarily out of cement, the trio have just enough left of their own to do the job, and after trooping off together to plant and secure this elegant piece of garden ornamentation near the bottom of our Gobi where it would draw the eye down the length of the eventual garden, stand looking around them and shaking their heads. The next day I am presented with a plum tree. "It ain't strong," apologises Pat, their leader, "but maybe it will like this place." Also in his bucket are a white-bloomed endemic St Helena ebony bush and a small cabbage bush of maroon-coloured foliage which, he explains, should grow *"quite big"*. As *quite* is not usually a term of mediocrity in St Helena – a "quite nice party" usually describing some fabulous affair – we designate plenty of space for its growth.

The following day Annette brings me exotic amaryllis bulbs and, with word evidently spreading about my calamity, soon everyone who enters my gate is carrying a plant of sorts – neighbours, friends, carpenters, electricians, painters, plumbers, the postman, passing acquaintances or total strangers, shocked by my garden's condition and the treachery of their compatriots. Zander contributes more than labour, scrounging and searching for seedlings with the fervour of a new father, though some of his greatest and most worthwhile contributions materialise as welcome sacks of *soil* (in local terminology), defined for my benefit as *mannew* and gleaned from the donkeys of Deadwood Plain.

In these hectic days of resuscitation, too hard-driven towards reviving the vital garden-water supply and saving our gasping property, Zander and I have no opportunity to relandscape the garden. So these generous offerings are simply stuck in the ground where the area has so far been cleansed of rubble, a bed on one side of the lower garden already dubbed The Shrubbery. The gifts are overwhelming, and all the more precious since no garden nursery exists on the island, where I might wander leisurely among assorted plants picking out what I would like. It is an eclectic diversity of offerings; everything from brilliant hibiscus, dramatic bromeliads, two young purple jacarandas, two young African thorn trees promising flame-red blooms someday, white and blue agapanthuses, orange daylilies, a spidery red *Crucifixion* plant, sunflowers and orange daisies, to vast clumps of pink bizzie lizzie which St Helena romantically calls *Venus Rose*. My friend Gay even arrives with nine naked branches off her frangipani tree which, if I plant while the moon is waxing as she advises me, will soon grow into a beautiful pink-blooming heavy-scented arbour.

Meanwhile, with Zander in charge, sods and seeds slowly begin to spread into the making of an actual lawn, and – once the island is eventually replenished with cement after the current shortage – with the help of his friend, Stickman, he will build two gracious sets of shallow concrete steps leading the eye from the shade of the gnarled jacaranda tree beside the gate, down the gentle grassed terraces and a short path to focus on the new garden pedestal. Down there he maps out a semi-circular bed which he fills with large daisy bushes, cannas, geraniums and a guava tree, while behind these the ten dead hibiscuses, miraculously reviving under his healing hands, are slowly developing into part of a thick screen against the ugly General Hospital that lies at the foot of our garden, into whose unshielded windows I uninterruptedly gazed through the worst of this season of sweat and tears.

The past two months have been pretty awful, really – lonely and exhausting. But with Annette and Zander on my side, I am on top of things at last. And now that I am no longer counting weeks, but days, until the family arrives back on the island, I feel I can afford to relax at last. We have done everything in our power to restore the property to rights. The house is clean and organised, and I wander happily from room to room, admiring the changes we have made. The solid Victorian doors have worked wonders in pulling the place together, and teak floors gleam where they are smooth, while still showing the wear of two centuries in other patches that I refuse to obliterate with a sander. These are character marks, the scratches and irregularities, legacies from earlier families who also have called this house home, and which have a right to be here.

I run my hand along the silky surface of our huge yew dining-table which so perfectly suits its place, and which, although we will probably live in the cool outdoors of our fresh-air veranda most of the time, cries out for dinner parties, for candles glowing off its warm yellow wood bringing to life the elegant green, red and gold colourings of curtains and upholstered dining chairs. Pictures already hang on the walls, a small serving table is packed with silver, the monstrous old inherited Victorian sideboard full of wine glasses. All we need is to summon guests. In the sitting room golden-yellow has been introduced to brighten what might have been a too-sombre space, shielded as it is from direct light by the roof of the veranda, and it works well. With so much dark inherited furniture in this house, Chris and I have been at pains to brighten our shaded rooms, and the black steel four-poster bed in our bedroom is now offset with wafting white voile curtains at the windows, white bed linen, and bright lamps.

Ours is my favourite room, cool, quiet, inviting. With its bruised black iron trunk at the foot of the bed (a well-worn relic of my father-in-law's naval career), its old-fashioned ceiling fan and screeching mynah birds outside, the room echoes some old colonial home of bygone ages and a time of elegant, unrushed living. Which perhaps it still is, I reflect as I sit on the trunk, gazing through the wavy glass of old window panes at the white fairy terns performing a ballet of breathtaking beauty above the garden, and I can't help but think it fitting that we furnished this room this way. I am content, happy in this house, so thankful that things here are on the mend.

And so it is that at dawn on the Sunday that my beloved Chris, Virginia, Richard, and Fee, my mother-in-law, will board the northbound ship in Cape Town, I awake early in a jubilant mood. Five days and they will all be here! Happiness springs me from my high wide bed and, picking up the glass of fruit juice I left on the chest of drawers overnight, I take it out to enjoy in tranquil splendour on the upper veranda. Below me my new world is slowly waking, brought to consciousness by the raucous yells of the cocky mynahs who dominate James Valley with their shrieks and strutting importance. Between them the soft tweeting of Madeiran canaries and grey-velvet Java sparrows sweeten the morning as they rustle the leaves of the neighbours' banana palms; and on the path, unfazed by anything, gentle peaceful doves from distant New South Wales are tamely going about the business of breakfast. Above the house, the beautiful bright-white fairy terns flutter and dance according to their whim, the newly-risen sun gleaming through their graceful wings as they play. Undoubtedly, all the world is blessed. Until I rise from the chair.

The tear in my back is audible. A ligament rip that crackles in my brain and plunges white-hot irons through the very depths of my being. Every nerve in my body screams, though no sound issues from my constricted throat because my voice is dissolved by pain. Instead, with the reactions of a headless fowl, I miraculously continue elevation from the chair and, apparently floating on some unknown levitation, make it to my bed. There I lie prostrated, shivering with shock and agony, contemplating the fact that suddenly, severely disabled, I might die of either agony or thirst before I am discovered here. From my bed I can see the upstairs telephone on the landing, but in that place it is of absolutely no use to me. I will simply have to wait for Annette to find me next Tuesday.

I lie there for hours, groaning softly. But eventually, with Nature far beyond calling now and positively screeching, I somehow sidle off the high bed on to my feet and agonisingly feed myself along various bed-posts and banisters till I reach the bathroom. This is no less than an assault course, executed at a graceless forty-five degrees. The journey involves five steps down, a gap across an angled landing, two steps up and a passage. I am whimpering pitifully. When I retrace this awkward route back to my bed, I am clutching a box of painkillers under my chin as I slide myself along, while a glass of water in one shaking hand slops its precious commodity at every step. I pass the phone and contemplate it. But the only person in the world I want to call is Chris, and I cannot do this to him at the very moment he is leaving. He's all eagerness in Cape Town today.

Should I phone a doctor? What would he do but offer painkillers which I already have? Rest is best, I decide. I do not want to be carted off to hospital and pummelled by a physiotherapist, if such a species exists on this island. Rather, I will lie here quietly and be a martyr until comforting Annette eventually happens upon me.

Annette clucks around me soothingly when she finds me on Tuesday, and by Friday I have spent enough time on my back to be able, at last, to stand shakily. Hobbling with a walking stick, I direct my feet to the car which I gently cajole to the Wharf to greet my happy family. It is the crack of dawn, and I have not yet heard the ship's warm greeting echoing up the valley, but I am so eager to see them that I go early anyway.

Down Main Street, across the Parade, driving extra-carefully with my insubordinate legs, through the Arch. And then my mouth falls open. The sea is a roaring, crashing, maelstrom of viciousness, and monstrous rollers are towering above us, exploding as they hit the shore, smashing across the Wharf in great surges of froth. This is an annual event, dubbed either December or February Rollers according to their timing, but never before have I seen them so terrifying. More daunting still is the notion that either my precious family will leap from ferry to Landing Steps in this ocean fury – or they won't. I am not sure which thought is worse. I park the car near the public swimming pool, as far from deluge as I can, and when I spot a seasoned fisherman I know further down the Wharf, I limp over to him. He, too, is watching the waves with an expression of wonderment. "The passengers on the ship won't be able to get off today, will they?" I venture in trepidation.

"You got family on board?" he asks somewhat irrelevantly. When I nod bleakly, his voice takes on a reassuring tone. "You got nothing to worry about now. The local people knows this sea – they knows every move it make. It could take a while in these rollers, but they'll get everybody off today, you'll see."

But the rollers continue to crash and bellow. In a momentary break between them I observe that the RMS still is not yet in the bay, and so I break out the rations brought with me and share them with friends now filtering down to the seaside to meet their own relatives, or simply to watch the spectacle. Freshly-brewed coffee in a flask, homemade ginger biscuits baked with love and immeasurable difficulty yesterday.

The arrival of the RMS, with or without rollers, is an event that draws the crowds. Mostly it is sheer curiosity that brings us to the railings near the Customs area as the rickety blue bus trundles from the Steps with its new arrivals. For strangers are to be scrutinised, and returning islanders are to be recognised so that word of their homecoming might spread more quickly. It is also a social time, an occasion for catching up with news and gossip. Certainly, for the five days this week that I have spent flat on my back, I have missed all the chat not delivered by Annette; but today everyone is in awe of the rollers, the subject of our conversations. Those who know I am also expecting an elderly mother-in-law are encouragingly absolute in their conviction that she will be safe coming ashore in the Air Taxi – a rather grand name bestowed upon a bench-lined container suspended by a hook and swung by crane from deck to barge and barge to Wharf, sparing elderly and infirm the leap from ferry to Steps. But I know my mother-in-law. However great the perils of the rollers, Fee will not submit to the Air Taxi, and I only hope she makes the leap in one piece.

The ship finally arriving, blasts her siren jubilantly, looking so serene sitting out there in the calmness of the bay it is hard to believe that aquatic hell still froths at the shoreline. The crashes are deafening, tarmac is sodden, and spray bejewels all the parked cars along the Wharf, spectators huddled near them, trying to shelter. Then, after an aeon of impatience, someone points out the ferry stoically butting out towards the anchored vessel, reassuring us that at least the Immigration officials were able to board the *Gannet Three* safely from the thunderous Steps. This is comforting: if the boatmen could get their own off the island in the ferry, they would get mine on it. Settled in the boot of our car now, its hatchback roof up and offering some respite from spray while I hold court with gathered friends, I sit up and take notice. And eventually, after another age, the ferry starts back once more. But we soon lose sight of it again behind the waves and the turn of the bay. My hunches tell me Chris and company are in this launch, as anxious to get ashore as I am frantic to see them, and I crane my neck to no avail.

The sun is fairly high in the sky by now. It is growing uncomfortably warm. I am dying for a late morning coffee or, very soon, a midday glass of wine. And I am still waiting for passengers – especially my passengers – to come ashore. And suddenly, a cheer in the crowd announces the arrival of the rickety blue bus. It stops on the other side of the railings at the Customs shed and disgorges… oh look! There they are! One, two, three, FOUR of them! "What did I say!" I exclaim to Gay who is watching beside me. "I told you Fee wouldn't come on the Air Taxi!"

They are flushed with excitement when they have passed through the Customs' formalities and rush to hug me: "The ferry made SEVENTEEN passes at the Steps before we could land!" they each inform me. "And just before the boatmen gave up there was a short break in the waves!" I notice there is not a drop of water anywhere on my elegant mother-in-law; as my fisherman friend promised they have got her ashore completely unscathed. *The local people knows this sea, they knows every move it make.* This is a fact of life here. Why should I ever have doubted it?

3.

The Road Less Travelled

December 2000 to January 2001

Christmas has passed with a large happy gathering of friends and family arranged around our yellow yew table for a feast, just as I had imagined our first Christmas at Villa Le Breton to be; the whole season's lead-up spiced with all the bands and parades and carol-singing events close to island hearts. There is a short hiatus now before Christopher's brother and his wife arrive to view our new acquisition, and we need to draw breath.

"Now that the rain has stopped at last," I tell Virginia who is at home washing her hair, "we're taking Granny for a drive. I don't know where we're going or when we'll be back. We'll simply follow the sun. We're taking midday drinks with us."

"That's okay," says Virginia, half listening. "You'll be back for lunch?"

"Probably."

It's weeks since I wrenched my back, but I'm still in huge pain. "Be very careful," advised one of the doctors during dinner with friends next door at Blundens. "Tear another millimetre and you'll spend the rest of your life in a wheel-chair." I take that warning to heart and am really trying to be careful; but while I am obliged to entertain my visiting mother-in-law, rest is almost impossible. Now Chris helps hoist me into the high front seat of our car and packs pillows around me for steadiness, adjusts the special girdle Gay has lent me, and straps me in tightly. Fee, in the back seat, is nursing 'flu, a frightful cold and a frozen shoulder. We two women, at least, should be luxuriating in bed, but the weather has been foul for five full days and now, with patches of blue between clouds at last, we're itching to get out of the house.

And so we follow the sun. It leads us out of town up the winding Ladder Hill pass, between the historic military installations dominating the top of that cliff, up and up through the lamentably unplanned settlement of Half Tree Hollow so haphazardly splattered across a barren cactus-ornamented plateau, and past the omniscient High Knoll Fort straddling its strategic hilltop above. Then, just around a bend, we're into stunning countryside of green meadows, deep valleys and shimmering flax-covered peaks. The roads begin to narrow as we head further inland, blue skies leading us westwards past signposts to Broad Bottom and Blue Hill, a drive of quite stupendous beauty as the sun alternately filters through tall forest foliage or blazes down on emerald pastures.

There is a viewpoint some way along this road that shows a rolling landscape of green mountains and velvet farmlands on one side, and the breathtaking natural amphitheatre of Sandy Bay on the other, all shades of pinks and greys as naked rock plunges downhill to meet the rugged little cove at Sandy Bay Beach.

For decades, until I happened upon a geological study of St Helena by Ian Baker who knows the island well, I had laboured under the romantic misapprehension that Sandy Bay was the crater of a magnificent volcano, and never for one moment did I doubt that the round little bay at the bottom was the core of that turmoil. To the novice all the signs of dramatic subterranean activity are there, with its shifting colours and tall fingers of rock punctuating the apparent lava ridges, and for years I have erroneously informed listeners – just as I was originally informed myself – that the other half of this beautiful crater has, over time, sunk into the sea. In fact, I even learned that the peaks and ridges of the hidden half are, like some wondrous and exciting Atlantis, sometimes spotted by fishermen. But now I discover that the beginnings were not quite so picturesque after all, rather that sheet eruptions of landmass simply rose from the ocean's deep through submarine volcanism, and that over time all this present-day splendour has been caused by boring old erosion. That's according to the scientific view, and while I know that Ian Baker is yet another passionate devotee of this island and his findings are declared with qualification and no malice, I rather regret that this knowledge has (for me, at any rate) stripped a little romance from the quite spectacular beauty of Sandy Bay. Wind and waves wrought this. And more wind, wearing away, over nine million years or so, the softer blanket of earth that we no longer can see.

Fee has already admired this magnificent view a few times so, without stopping now, we carry on to the very end of the ridge where large graffiti on a lonely garage building has long advised rather disarmingly: *Sex is bad for one but good for two*. This is our usual turning place, but instead of retracing our path home to Jamestown, today we continue past the garage and head down a steep, forested hill towards the broad, barren mountain pasture of Thompson's Wood (this is St Helena, after all, where Longwood has no trees either, and Levelwood perches perilously on a vertiginous hillside). On the way, we draw into the roadside shade and break out our drinks. It's half an hour after noon already and high time for refreshment. After this we'll turn for home.

The beer goes down well. The three of us chat about the countryside in this distant corner of the island, listen to birds twittering above us and cows lowing at Thompson's Wood, and comment yet again on the amazing variety of scenery that St Helena can offer in the space of its scant forty-seven square miles. "It's like a cake," says Christopher. "You enjoy it best by taking a slice at a time, rather than all at once." And today our slice has been the unpeopled west.

It's tricky to turn the car on this steep switchback, Chris decides when we have packed away our empties, and so he drives down to Thompson's Wood to turn at the gate there. But then I notice a narrow country road dead ahead that is unfamiliar, and ask, rhetorically really: "I wonder where that goes?"

The rough road curves round the hillside southwards, we soon discover, and affords us a glorious view down a plunging valley with part of razor-sharp Speery Island sitting in blue waters far below – a narrow landmark peninsula of dangerous pinnacled rocks at the south-western corner of the island. "This is nice. We'll turn at the top of this road," suggests Chris who is enjoying the climbing track in this strong and able car (the one that isn't actually a 4x4).

At the top it is worth the painful effort for both Fee and me to clamber out of our seats and gasp at the view laid before us. The Gates of Chaos are below us, topped by great jagged rock formations that menace the sky. Here is Earth at its wild best. Angry ravines tumble over themselves in their rush for the sea, hills between them fumble and fall and rise again in triumph. And the colours of their barrenness are startlingly vivid – glaring orange, earthy browns, purples and reds, golden angles of light yellow sunshine glittering across them in contrast. Azure sea miles below. And above, along the faraway skyline, the dark green trees and shimmering flax fields of the Peaks on the rim of this amazing basin.

We're finally turning the car for home when we spy the noticeboard. Here, sitting at the very teeth of hell it points tantalisingly down a continuation of our track to *Fairyland*. And this is a place we know – an area of grassy meadows and small woods set against an enchanting blue and green backdrop fronted by Sandy Bay's huge stone pillar of Lot. We have visited it along another road before. "Fee would love Fairyland!" I suggest, and Chris, scrutinising the terrain concedes: "The road actually looks alright along there, and we have high ground clearance. If we're all up to it…?"

We are. The sun is still gleaming between scattered clouds, casting splendid shadow patches on this amazing countryside, and we are in no hurry for lunch. We head on down the track that soon levels out, we discover, to run parallel with the long ridge road above us which had led to the garage graffiti, though we are now halfway down the mountainside. We round a bend and pass a delightful stone ruin where a lone man is digging a vegetable patch. Back in the late 1600s, soon after the English East India Company moved into St Helena, John Luffkin built this house a day's horse ride from Jamestown and no doubt grew his own crops here, but today's man waves with no less surprise as our car trundles past. This is not a regular road at all, though I do know that occasional Land Rover tours used to be run along here for interested tourists, and having once upon a time walked some of the route I recall how beautiful it is.

Fee, despite her 'flu and sore shoulder, is enjoying the drive immensely and, acknowledging that I am somewhat immobilised by my straps and pillows, is the one who gamely dismounts from the car to open five successive gates along the road for Chris to drive through. This is an adventure for all of us, and the splendour of our surroundings in this loneliest slice of the island is reward for her labours. As we progress, huge volcanic boulders looming from the roadside eventually give way to woodlands, and then to a forest of tall endemic St Helena gumwood trees, their grandeur dwarfing the five thousand sapling gumwoods we know only from new plantings in a brilliant save-the-environment project called the Millennium Forest in the distant north-east of the island. Full grown, the gumwood is a handsome tree with gnarled boughs and shiny umbrella foliage, though rarely seen in maturity these days. History tells us that before the island was first discovered, thick forests of these gumwoods, growing in a swathe at between four and six hundred metres altitude across the island, would have been home to not only the now-extinct but much yearned after endemic giant earwig, but also a flightless rail that would have joyfully foraged on the thickly-carpeted forest floor for the plethora of insects at its disposal. However, reputedly cleansed by early English settlers seeking fuel and building materials, the old forests are gone now, creating in their stead such great plains as Longwood (formally known as the Great Wood), and the sadly descriptive Deadwood.

When we pass through a garden I am terribly excited, craning my neck for any signs of a ruined house in the forest to the right of us. There is trace of a mossy gate-post, I think, but no dwelling that I can see, though either side of our track is now thick with fuchsias, hibiscus, agapanthus, and various domestic trees. It is a riot of growth, and though tangled and undisciplined by years of abandonment, speaks of a once-loved family home these many miles from civilisation. I have no idea who lived here.

Past the garden the track becomes overgrown with long grass, and starts declining steeply towards a bend in the road. Our car is doing well with its generous ground clearance, and sitting high in its seats we are enjoying magnificent views of our surroundings and loving this exploration. Up and up, round the bend. And here's a surprise! A blue-painted habitable country cottage suddenly appears, set back just a little way from the road – lonely, indeed, without sturdy transport. There are lace curtains in the windows which are closed, I notice as we drive past, but goats are roaming nearby, munching up the garden. The house is in good repair, obviously lived in. The map tells us this is Peakdale Cottage.

The thick forest falls away just past the cottage, and suddenly my breath is expunged by the vista that unexpectedly opens up below us. "Look at that!" I exclaim in excitement – and Chris looks, for one instant taking his eye off the road…

The mud that promptly swallows our wheels is feet deep. It reaches to the very gunwales of the car which stops dead with a jolt and refuses to budge. Some rare words of irritation escape Chris's lips as he climbs out and investigates. "We'll have to push," he announces grimly.

We? Push this car? There is a momentary female resistance to the idea, but as neither Fee nor I are natural whingers, out we get. I unstrap my straps, unbunch my pillows and lay them to one side, readjust Gay's girdle around my midriff, grip my country walking stick and lever myself into the mud. I lean limply against the back of the car, which is about as much as I can manage in this condition. Fee is resolutely positioning her only good shoulder to the thrust. Nothing happens, not surprisingly, and eventually Fee gets behind the wheel and Chris pushes. Still the car does nothing but scream in protest. The exercise, I notice is merely digging the wheels deeper into the mire.

I turn round and scrutinise the little blue cottage behind us. The goats are very much at home, but clearly no one else is. Perhaps at the end of the workday someone will appear and we can phone for help. Assuming, in this island's lack of mobile phones, that there is a landline phone here, of course. I voice this optimism aloud, but Fee says darkly: "It will be quite late by then, and we're due for dinner with the Governor at seven. We should lay a base of stones under the wheels."

My octogenarian mother-in-law sets to work searching for stones. Chris searches for stones. I appoint myself stone-spotter-in-chief, unable as I am to bend and lift. But even in this helpful act I fail. We are in grassland. There are no stones. Instead there is a trickling stream passing between our fore and rear wheels, steadily compounding, by its determined flow, the result of five days' worth of heavy rain already wreaking havoc on this muddy track.

"Cedar branches," I suggest. So we all gather cedar branches from the trees a few yards below the road, those we can break with our bare hands, at least. We have no useful saw in the tool box, no cutters, no knife. We do have rope, but no friendly vehicle to tie it to. Our puny cedar branches are thickly tucked under the wheels to provide some purchase, but this too fails. The mud creates slime on the oily foliage, and nothing in our status changes. Then lo! We spy a sheet of corrugated iron halfway up the hillside, and off Chris goes to fetch it. As he climbs back in behind the wheel, Fee lays it in position and I encouragingly nudge it in with my toe. She and I are both covered in mud and pain; but this is definitely going to work. The engine starts with a roar, gear engages – and the tyres shriek again but do not budge.

Fee and I climb tiredly back into our seats, and placid Chris dredges up a few more words of irritation. "Gloria said she wants the Plantation House staff to leave by eight so we mustn't be late," Fee reminds us helpfully. The once-high sun is dropping and the air already has a decided chill. By four-thirty we will lose the direct sun behind the tall Ridges above us, and it is not far from that now. We have been here four hours. We drank our beer at Thompson's Wood and have brought nothing to eat in the car. We have no blanket to keep us warm through the night, no access to a telephone, no strength to walk away from here. And at home my children are in a flat spin of anxiety since we did not come home for lunch. They don't even know which side of the island we are on.

"I'm going to leave you two alone here," announces Christopher at last. "I'm going for help." That seems an eminently good idea since we have tried everything else, but help is probably a night away, I reckon. A passing car perhaps, once he's made it to the tarred ridge road some daunting distance above us; then a drive to a telephone; then the assembling of Jamestown's fire-department from various corners of the island, and a truck that can pull us out; and finally the realisation that the Fire & Rescue Service can do nothing in the dark down here... Fee and I watch Chris walk away as though he is leaving for the arid wastes of the Arctic. A tired lonely figure, he marches off around the bend in the track and we lose sight of him until, an aeon later, he reappears as a tiny movement ascending the next hill. His path has climbed quite considerably by now, and he's still climbing. Then the road turns again and he is gone for good. Fee settles down for a light nap in the back seat, but I am too sore, too anxious, and too jolly cold to sleep. I am also finding this place a bit creepy.

Five o'clock comes and goes and no owner returns to the little blue cottage – I have barely taken my eye off it through the wing mirror – but I do notice the goats ambling off to pastures greener. So we are completely alone now, Fee and I, and I wonder how many ghosts wander this part of the island. Since they're evidently fairly prolific everywhere else in St Helena, they probably move in droves around here...

And suddenly I hear voices. *Oh, God, are these humans or...?* They're humans. Several of them on foot. They are approaching around the nearest bend in the track ahead and, joy of joys, Chris is with them! "I found a cottage," he hisses through the window. "They are going to get us out of here." There are some boys and an older man, and none of them is familiar to me. "They're country people," he adds, as though I might be in doubt, and only later do I learn what he found as he sought help for his precious women. The cottage was situated in the middle of nowhere. He had walked for miles before he spotted a dwelling way down in a valley and had made his way there, watched from a great distance by a girl who, scantily clad and chewing on a long stem of grass, lounged in the cottage doorway and at no time displayed the slightest flicker of animation at his approach. On the narrow veranda sat a boy plucking a guitar. This was a scene eerily reminiscent of a Jon Voigt film he had seen back in the '70s – one set in the lonely backwoods of West Virginia or somewhere similar – and the memory of it caused Chris a vague flutter of misgiving. But as soon as an adult appeared and our predicament was explained, the man scooped both Chris and the plucking boy into a truck and at speed drove up and over the dales to another distant cottage. Here more youths were assembled before the truck plunged deep into some further valley, piled further muscle power into the back, and finally set off for the little blue cottage and our marooned car.

I prostrate myself with apologies as he draws near, for having dragged this stranger from his distant home. "We had hoped someone might return to the cottage here, and help us," I gabble.

He chuckles. "You woulda be wait a long time," he says. "It a ole lady done live there – and she dead last mont?" The man takes charge with efficiency and determination, evacuates Fee and me from our seats and climbs behind the wheel. He is shouting instructions to the boys who are light years from enthusiasm for this job but apply their shoulders to the car nonetheless. "Are they going to push us all the way?" I inquire, unaware that their truck is parked around the bend on the far side of an even worse mud-patch. There is a lot of pushing going on but our car has not moved an inch.

"You gotta lif'!" the man instructs, and as a body, the boys turn their baseball hats back-to-front and bend to the task again. The rear comes up with reticence under their unified heaving, slowly, clinging to the mud which eventually makes a gutturally squelching sound just as the engine roars. It's in gear. It moves forward on its front wheels, just a few inches but enough for acceleration. This man knows how to drive. His timing is exact. The power is gauged just right. And out of the bog flies our exhausted chariot.

Now, he tells us, we all have to sit in the boot to weigh down the back of the car as he negotiates the rest of this sticky area to get the car around the bend. So Fee and Chris and I (heartily mindful of that last protected millimetre of ligament I am not supposed to tear) duly climb in with the boys, and the car sails forward. But the mud pond around the corner still beckons – and naturally it claims us. Down we go again, the slime almost over the bumpers. But help is still at hand. The boys are cajoled into activity once more, the car is heaved through, and it bursts in triumph on to dry land on the far side, nose to nose with the man's own truck. "She be good now," the man assures us, unwitting that our car is definitely a male, "but I see you through Fairyland anyway, just to make sure you safe." And so his great truck, laden with youthful power, leads the way up the winding mountainside, down through valleys and around narrow bends, until he hoots cheerily and waves us on our way. "You be a'right now, not far to the tar!" Fairyland has never looked better. Country people have never been kinder.

From the top of the ridge, when we finally get there, we see the sun is sinking even on that side of the mountain. There is a distinct evening glow upon the world, turning shadows to deep green, the sea to gold, and setting High Knoll alight as we speed past it, back through Half Tree Hollow, down the steep and weaving and now shadowed Ladder Hill Road. It is six-thirty as we bustle through the door – we must be at Plantation House in half an hour, by order of the Governor's wife. Virginia and Richard are watching television. "Oh, hi," they say, barely shifting eyes from the screen.

"Weren't you panicking about us?" I ask.

"No, not really. You said you were going for a drive. You could have gone anywhere."

I haven't time to remonstrate, or to recount our ordeal. In fifteen minutes flat I have showered the mud off my limbs, washed and dried my hair, slapped make-up on, changed my clothes, and am stumbling back to the car with the haste and dignity of a knockabout clown. Chris and Fee, racing to break records, are ahead of me. "We thought we were going to be late..." Fee gasps to the Governor and his wife as we pass through their little portico at precisely seven o'clock.

Gloria is looking unusually relaxed. "That wouldn't have mattered," she smiles. "It ees vehrry casual, only us five for supper tonight, and the staff can wait until we feenish. There was no rush."

It's the tent that has scandalised the nation. First impressions count, and ever since a rock recently fell through the drum roof of the historic Old Customs Shed on the Wharf, the first thing to greet tourists in St Helena is a large marquee, open on all sides, serving as that venerable port of entry. In the stiff breezes of our present summer it flaps and sways over the baggage and arrivals accumulated there, and we have no doubt that in time – which moves slowly in this place – it will develop dramatic rents and tears and perish marks and still, stoically, continue to present itself as Her Majesty's Customs Shed. It sits there night and day, through all weathers, whether the RMS is in the bay or not. Until, quite suddenly, it vanishes.

This is a mystery. Especially since the bay is currently chock-a-block with yachts enjoying this final destination of the biennial Governor's Cup Yacht Race from Cape Town, and yachties are moving along the Wharf all day and night. Even the mother ship RMS, hovering over them as they sailed here, is anchored out there. But no Customs Officer is in sight. Added to this conundrum is a disconcerting mountain of containers marooned on the Wharf as shopkeepers are advised that due to the absence of HM Customs Shed from its usual locale, our festive season goods cannot be released to the public between Friday and Tuesday. So where has the tent gone?

To the hills, it turns out. The reverberations reach us, spilling down the deep island *guts* from the central highlands where the scandal has occurred. A cocktail party has been held at Plantation House to welcome the yacht race participants; and with the title of Governor's Cup Yacht Race, nothing less would be expected, especially since His Excellency and Mrs Hill themselves travelled all the way to Cape Town just to fire the starting gun.

But Gloria, it turns out, is no fan of yachtsmen. "I weell not allow them inside my house," she pronounces. "Yachties are unwashed and slovenly – look at the way they dress in Jamestown. There is no alternative but to set up a marquee and entertain them in the grounds." So the Customs Shed has been requisitioned, carted up to Plantation and erected, under her stringent instructions, on the hard tarmac of the car park. The front door of the house is to be kept closed throughout the party, and the new unisex cloakroom she has recently installed in the house accessed only by a side door.

And so the upper-crust of Cape Town's yachting fraternity and their private-school crews, rightly anticipating a party within the shelter of the large Regency residency, are somewhat chagrined to find themselves welcomed by His Excellency under cover of flapping canvas in the freezing, breezy temperatures of a central island evening. The men are dressed in long shirtsleeves, or at best are wearing light jackets, but the women, in summertime evening spaghetti straps, are blue with cold.

So now the streets are ringing with criticism. Islanders are outraged by such inhospitable behaviour, and the yachtsmen angrier still at the slur. "Tent" is on everyone's lips.

But Gloria remains adamant. "I have spent many hours restoring furniture in thees house," she insists, "and the last theeng I want is dirty hands on my possessions." Though Gloria and I get on well, I am too new on the island – or too cautious – to point out that the house and its furniture are not hers, exactly. All of it, in fact, is property of the Island of St Helena.

Through my personal miasma of painkillers, our Christmas holiday has passed happily. It is, after all, the season to be jolly and I have tried my very best. We've enjoyed home-cooked meals on the repainted green veranda where we have spent our happiest hours, attended the concerts and parties and parades that are part of an island Christmas season, taken drives to show Fee the splendours of St Helena, hosted Christmas lunch for sixteen people, and later found ourselves back on the Wharf to greet Chris's brother and his wife coming from England, through Cape Town, to visit for a week. It's all been fun and time has sped along while sister-in-law Diana has painted superb watercolour landscapes around the island, and brother-in-law Anthony, currently involved with the Royal Navy's hydrography department, has honed up on surrounding seabed structure. Fee has even played a few rounds of golf at the famed nine-hole golf course at Longwood – a somewhat rough-turf wind-blown course on an inland plateau where a tethered donkey marks one of the holes, and a tree blocks another.

Virginia and Richard meanwhile, old hands at St Helena, have developed their own island lives, and we've seen little of them. Crime is so rare here that they are free to walk anywhere in safety, even late at night. And for teenagers reared in a South African city, this security is the greatest gift we could give them. They have good friends, are happy, and both revel in this tiny world.

But now it's time for us all to go. With sagging hearts we lock the great heavy front door once again, gaze lovingly upon our reviving garden, and leave for the Wharf. Annette and Zander are in charge now, with our absolute trust, and I will next see them when I return as family vanguard once more in October, after I have resumed my primary life in Cape Town for the next nine months. Chris and the children will follow in December again for the Christmas holidays. They wave us off from the front gate like family – Chris and me, Virginia and Richard, Fee, Anthony and Diana, all leaving together.

The sea is not kind on the homeward voyage. I am green all the time and seasick for most of it, and I spend nearly all of it on my bunk, flat on my back, sleeping. But the others have a ball. And when it comes to Fancy Dress Night, they arrive to pick my brains. "What shall we go as?" they ask. I have done this costume thing so many times before that I am now running out of ideas. I have dressed Chris as a macaroni penguin from Tristan da Cunha (a sister island), Virginia as a Rising Sun, Richard as a coffee mug (*What a mug I am!*), and as a goldfish (*Small fry*) when he was little.

And once, when travelling on my own, I was ambitious enough to go as Diana's Peak – the highest point on St Helena. This involved cladding myself to my knees in a cardboard cone of green crepe paper - arms pinned to my sides, of course – and a cardboard Norfolk Island pine attached precariously to my head. The costume took me a day to make, closeted alone in my cabin with sticky tape and scissors borrowed from the Bureau, and a sheet of cardboard scrounged from the galley, but the result was satisfactory. I went down to dinner that night in my pre-prandial Captain's cocktail party clothes, and then repaired to my cabin to don the great surprise. The joke, however, was on me. What I had not calculated was the height of my structure, and while it fitted well and looked exceedingly splendid in the cabin mirror, it was much taller than the doors through which I must pass to reach the festivities. Besides, the first obstacle was merely opening the cabin door with arms incapacitated. So I called a friend. But while he stood outside it offering suggestions, he was actually powerless to help me bend low enough to exit. Instead he howled with mirth while I executed a perilous angle and finally burst from my cabin to collide with the opposite wall. Getting through the main lounge door was only marginally easier. Since then I have not really gone in much for fancy dress.

And now the whole family is here, gathered in our cabin, pleading for inspiration. There are a lot of them to accommodate. Fee is just as eager as Anthony and Di to join the fun, and Virginia and Richard wouldn't miss it. Chris and I will feel very unsporting if we don't join in as well, but time is marching steadily towards zero-hour and I am feeble and seasick. There is no way I could rise off my bunk and make costumes today. "Go as The Tent," I offer weakly. That requires little work and will deal with all of them in one go.

The Tent? The whole lot of them stare as though I have hurled my senses into the Atlantic. His Excellency and the Governor's wife are, after all, on board with us, *en route* to making their annual official visit to Tristan da Cunha from Cape Town. And so are a substantial number of those very same yachties who were so rudely snubbed at Plantation House. But I can think of absolutely nothing else, especially as a St Helena theme is generally more fun. "Hang an *HM Customs* sign on the front," I suggest. "Everyone's been through it."

"But the Hills…"

"All we need is a sheet and a sign. It's easy," says Chris, evidently coming round to the idea, and the party is dispatched to practice tenting. Yet by evening, strangely enough, I am really ill, and Chris has sympathy seasickness. We lurk in our cabin while only five of our family join the Fancy Dress. But as the great white sheet wavers through the parade, it draws a roar of laughter from the yachties, we later hear. And even Gloria was seen to smile ruefully.

4.

Into the Vortex

October to December 2001

Zander has parked my car at the Wharf, shining and familiar after my nine months' absence from the island, with keys ready in the ignition to drive myself home; and, rather than waste time waiting for my disembarkation, has scurried back to Villa Le Breton to titivate the garden's thriving vegetables for my homecoming inspection. After eventually passing through formalities in the monstrously ugly chipboard shed that now replaces the wind-ripped Customs tent (barely an improvement), negotiating the ship-day traffic in town, and at last entering my big front gate, I see his gentle face crinkled with proud smiles. And before being allowed to enter Annette's gleaming interior, I am hijacked to admire the transformation from last year's desert. The sky-blue plumbago hedge, shielding the vegetable patch from summer winds with its pale galaxies, is in full flower this year, and such activity has taken place beyond it that scarlet-fruited chilli bushes have sprung up in flashes of brilliance. Among the sprightly bean rows and eager carrot tops making a confident showing, a row of infant lettuces are turning faces to the thin October sun. Even spindly papaya trees are already craning long necks to show off the young green fruits that will ripen just in time for Chris to knock them down for breakfast when he arrives in December.

Across the path in The Shrubbery – that physical evidence of the kindness of strangers – the area is a riot of luminous colour, newly-dominated by a Persian lilac tree which has sowed itself dead-centre of the bed and sprung up of its own volition, promising palest purple-pink fronds someday soon. Gay's nine waxy, heavy-scented frangipani slips, diligently planted when the moon was on the wax as she commanded, are already showing first signs of heady summer flowering. The lawns are in good shape too, demarcated into two distinct terraces, joined – with cement at last back on the island – by two elegant sets of shallow steps that Zander and his friend, Stickman, have built. In due time gravel will follow this route, sweeping past the once-lonely ornamental pedestal rooted there by Pat and his team a full year ago, the completely-revived hibiscus hedge behind it, past a replanted stand of whispering Sandy Bay banana palms, and all the way back to the house through the deep shade of the ancient mango trees that once formed an avenue alongside our eastern boundary wall of island red-stone. On either side of us, the high brown cliffs frame this narrow neck of the valley, while birds dart and dance between them. I am so thrilled with everything I want to dance too.

"There's things we need from down-the-street," Annette informs me between bosomy hugs and months' worth of chattering gossip. "But they can be easily wait till Thursday." That's good, because this afternoon I must collect my luggage and twenty-eight boxes of *stuff* from the Wharf, which Zander will heft for me, and tomorrow, Wednesday, it must all be unpacked. Thursday, anyway, is prime shopping day. It is then that fresh vegetables come in from the smallholdings, and beef or pork delivered from the killing fields. It is also when even country people come to town, resplendent – if they are over seventy – in sedate hats and best cardigans. Only forty years ago country-folk still made this weekly expedition by donkey, necessitating a pre-dawn start and often a dusk return, but now they arrive by car to make their way through town, steady-footed and straight-shouldered, heads held high against a world that has evolved beyond their credibility. Several will have known the rise, and the sudden demise in the 1960s, of St Helena's vital and lucrative flax industry. Many have weathered meagreness and hardship most of their lives, some even sending their brothers to fight a World War that barely touched the island itself. And while a few who still can't read or write now dwell in a world dominated by emails in this distant place, others can remember the importation of the very first motorised vehicle to the island in 1929, an Austin 7 – the germ, in fact, that spawned an epidemic of car buying on an island that today supports almost more cars than people.

The population of that time was deeply divided on the prospect of motorcars, I was amused to learn, many stating with innate St Helenian reluctance to change that, as they had got on very well with horses and donkeys in the past, motorisation was not necessary. But the car came anyway, as I suspect the Airport will eventually descend upon the island, and though admittedly a useful transport against the mountainous hairpins of this island, cars are now ubiquitous, noticeably noisy and polluting in their present excessive numbers.

On Thursday I seek out Annette's list, but by midmorning the only available parking left in Jamestown is way down on the Wharf. Our little ship, readying herself for departure to Ascension this afternoon, is still in the bay, lighters busily ferrying last containers of baggage from the Steps, the large Wharf crane going flat-out. Apart from occasional tuna exports to Spain, little of monetary value will depart in those containers as neither St Helena's excellent coffee is produced in enough quantity for extensive export, nor will bananas survive the sea voyage. All along the seafront runs the special quiver that accompanies her motherly presence in the bay, for at embarkation time for northbound passengers later today, this long narrow area will be crowded with cars and people again, just as it was when I arrived the day before yesterday. Two hours later, however, after she has roared her familiar three and a half blasts of farewell and turned towards our sister island, Ascension, seven hundred miles northwest of us, everyone will quickly disperse and St Helena will once again settle back on its heels, getting on with its own solitary life.

Crossing the moat and passing through the Town Arch I scrutinise all familiar landmarks for slight changes in the months that I have been away, but nothing has been altered, of course. The Grand Parade looks exactly the same – the bougainvillea-swamped Castle entrance, the cannon-guarded jacaranda-shaded Courthouse, austere St James' Church, the blue balconied gaol, the old stone warehouses, even Cyril's Fast Food kiosk, are all just as we left them last January. But energetic hammering from behind the Public Works' warehouse indicates that the Old Powerhouse at the foot of the Ladder is well on its way to metamorphosing into the long-planned, much talked-of New Museum. One of the things I really want to do, now that I shall be established in St Helena over the next nine months, is join the Heritage Society, overseers-in-chief of this grand museum project, and a group of what I presume are like-minded history lovers. The Heritage Society and the animal-protection RSPCA are high priorities for which, now that last year's Season of Desolation is over, I will have lots of time to spare in my new, more settled, life here – a stark truth having descended on Chris and me over this past period in Cape Town, that we have actually not bought a lock-up-and-go which we would visit for three months a year as originally intended, but an establishment that, it turns out, requires full-time nurturing. Long absences from my family now lie ahead, previously unforeseen, if we are to make this far-flung dream work to our advantage, while I hold the fort in this island house, and Christopher keeps Cape Town's home fires burning. Wide-world friends are shocked at the very notion, but history shows that marriages have for centuries survived enforced separations, and we see no chink of doubt that ours can do the same. Besides, in this remote place, separation is all around us.

Fat feral pigeons are everywhere, uncouth mynah birds strutting about, gentle peaceful doves daintily scavenging for crumbs between the cars packed together in designated *parks* on the Parade. Above the resonant traffic, their pretty *cu-cu-cu-cu-curoos* and the strident mynah yells are archetypal sounds of Jamestown; those, and the slightly inaccurate church clock chiming. Like so many cameos in St Helena's history, this clock, naturally, has its own quaint story of misdirection and confusion. Though specially imported from England for St James' Church in 1787 it was, upon arrival, inexplicably installed not in the church-tower but in the Courthouse across the way, where it resided for some fifty-eight years, bemusedly ticking away the decades before it eventually, rightfully, found its way to St James'. Extensive alterations to the church at the time perhaps had something to do with its delay, but it was barely installed there before another rash of renovation was instigated in 1869 after termites were found to have chomped up nearly all the building's woodwork. And today, we are advised, St James' is in need of yet more renovation, so I am soon warned of many, many fundraising games of Scrabble ahead to scrounge money for this project.

Unblemished by coyness, and never camped up to be cute, Georgian Jamestown remains a treasury of matter-of-fact history with inhabited houses and business-filled shops, where little architecture has changed since the capital thrived as a busy retail-stop for sailing vessels from the East during the 18th and mid-19th Centuries. Only the cobbles of those years have gone, and the former spacious divide in the middle of Main Street is now a crowded car park, dubbed the Stand. Gas lamps eventually gave way to electricity, and though an elaborate Victorian fountain that once tinkled at the head of the street has vanished without trace, two old peepul trees still cast welcome shade across public benches placed outside the imposing bay-windowed Canister building nearby. Notorious trees, these, for here it was that the sale of slaves was conducted – unwilling captives from South East Asia, Madagascar, Africa and India whose blood, blended with that of British militiamen garrisoned here through the centuries, make up St Helena's evolved coffee-skinned population. Yet it is these simple details that fire imaginings of those frightened people clustered beneath these trees, wealthy gentlemen sizing up sale-wares while their English women in bonnets giggle among themselves from a distance; farmers clip-clopping in from the country on horseback or with mules bearing heavy baskets of produce; soldiers and servants going about their daily duties; sailors diving in and out of 'The First and Last' ale-house, now Harris Guesthouse but once a popular seafarers' pub reputed to be the first upon entering Jamestown, the last upon leaving.

It is a cheery, if ponderously slow, passage for me up Main Street in this land of shouted hallos as, in no obvious hurry, I am regularly halted by friends to discuss their health, my health, and the weather, before moving on. But in the doorway of the new Spar Supermarket, Muriel grabs my arm: "Welcome home! Can I put your name down for Scrabble in aid of St James'?" Then Liz bounces up: "Glad I've seen you! The League of Friends has bagged *Bridget Jones' Diary* for a cinema evening at Donny's Place in December! Could you make fudge for it?" Cathy catches up with me as I ponder the distressingly empty vegetable bins: "We're short of lesson readers at St James' on Sunday mornings, I'll put your name down – thank you!" Then, as I delve into the freezer, searching for treasures – learning as I go that the island is currently short of both local beef and its world-class local tuna – Patsy greets me with a cry of good cheer: "We've a Corona Society charity coffee morning next week, would you like to come?" I am a creature feeble at saying no, and so log a mental note of all these dates while

I continue with my shopping. It is my duty to involve myself in this small place, I understand, simply because I am a New Face.

Passing by the secretive recesses of Eva Benjamin's shop, I spot a be-hatted country woman inside, waiting while assistants obligingly climb ladders to reach for tins of sweetened condensed milk for her tea, and the rice, measured in brown paper bags in this old-style grocer, that forms the basis of so much St Helenian cooking. The high dark wooden counter here still holds, like old children's book illustrations, huge scales and glass jars of rainbow-coloured gob-stopping sweets. The country woman is engrossed in chatting with ancient Eva herself who famously watches hawk-eyed over her till, but the English conversation is in such strong colloquial accents that it is barely intelligible to an outsider like me. At ease in this familiar place, the country woman undoubtedly prefers it to the air-conditioned neon brilliance of the nearby Spar that draws modern crowds, but whose greater choices cause her more decision-making than she is used to.

At the tiny Growers' Market kiosk, I am shown the best of the mean fresh vegetables on offer, for clearly nothing has come from the country today after all. One huge white cabbage and emaciated sweet-potatoes are all that are on offer today, though I want onions, regular potatoes, lettuces, tomatoes, eggs. At Thorpe's Grocery, American Country-&-Western music from the ubiquitous Radio St Helena, inviting us to *Lay a Bli-anket on the Gri-ound*, jollies up the shoppers – a definitive reminder of where one is in the world. But there're no eggs here either, or cake flour, so I stock my basket instead with a bottle of whisky, one of gin, and a hunk of rubbery mild cheddar (the island being out of mature), and hand over a fist of sterling-allied St Helena ten pound notes for these expensive indulgences.

Shopping is a dedicated trudge, alternately extended by social chitchat and dashed hopes. At 'Horse's' – properly called the Queen Mary Stores – a huge truck of goods from the ship is parked across the store entrance, and cartons are being loaded into a crate on a rope just inside, serving as a loading lift to the warehouse above. I squeeze past the truck but, for my own safety, am detained from proceeding while the loaded box gingerly swings upwards, guided by the truck driver and the helpful arms of shop assistants. Then I am allowed to enter the long dark store that stretches back and back. Within the frustrating retail limitations of this island, one can buy almost anything at Horse's except clothes. I come here for my favoured washing powder and chocolate, but also find the offer of freezers, cornices, paints, wood, and window panes. There are radios and microwave ovens, buckets of lurid plastic flowers, ornaments, saucepans, candles, pet food, plumbing fixtures and whole shower units, piled high in the deep shadows of this wonderful place. Today, above the cooler-counter where I happily find some feta cheese (long past it's sell-by date, actually, but a happy find nonetheless), a chalk board is advertising misspelled spices in enchantingly bold capital letters:

CIMMANO STICKS
TIMMERECK...

But they cannot, either, offer me eggs, flour or potatoes, tomatoes, lettuce, plain yoghurt, fruit, long-life cream or custard (no fresh milk ever sullies this island!), or any other cheese. It's probably time to give up the search and simply wait to see what gets unpacked from the RMS in the next few days. "Cargo late today," they tell me. Already, I'm back in the swing of things.

Saturdays are Open House at Hallams, and though this generous hospitality extends only to a smallish group, the so-called *openness* implies an expectation that certain of us will show up promptly at noon every week, willy-nilly, and for these chosen few nothing less than a watertight excuse is accepted for not making that midday drive into the country. The host is John Beadon, my oldest friend on the island in every sense of the word, who holds court from a wingback chair by the fire of his inland home while his Man dispenses small bowls of crisps and large tankards of Castle Lager, even to the women present. That John himself drinks a superior quality beer on these occasions – lugged up from the RMS in person by the ship's senior Captain, Martin Smith – is a perk of his great age, I suppose, or evidence of our particular fondness for him, because somehow he cleanly gets away with this antisocial quirk. From his corner he says little, but listens hard, thinks deeply, reminisces on his colonial-era bank career in Malaya and Ceylon with great humour, and anonymously draws on deep wells of generosity when necessary.

Beside his post, a capacious armchair is left vacant for the Lord Bishop, but even before His Lordship arrives, it is made clear that we usurp it at our peril. So, very early on, I adopted a small yellow club chair that lives against the wall and, since it is never readied for my august arrival week after faithful week, I regularly haul it forward myself to a spot where I can hear every conversation and observe the assembled company with the same watchful eyes that John hides under crinkled lids. This is where I learn what's really happening on the island.

I've met both the new bishop and his predecessor at Hallams, and neither of these princes of the church quite fitted my stereotypical image of men of such rich cloth. But then I should have remembered earlier the story my parents told of an official party they once threw for judges of the Circuit Court in the city where my father was then solicitor-general. As the invitations went out, so each recipient speedily rang up and asked if they might bring along their bishop houseguest while the Anglican Synod took place at the same time. Though horrified at the thought of a sombre and possibly tee-total event, they naturally agreed; but the first bishop to arrive set the pattern by running up the garden path and demanding a double whisky. The party was a riot, and by the end of the night my father's generous cellar was pretty much stripped. I should have learned from that. Why start with one tot when you can have two? Give a bishop an inch, I have learned, and he'll take a yard…

Bishop Peter, the predecessor, was a tall, thin, ascetic man with a shock of dark hair, who spouted Latin and Classical Greek like mother tongues but otherwise spoke little. Then, sailing with him on the RMS as I made my way home from the house signings in '99, I received my first surprise when the Captain invited him to say grace at dinner. Prepared for a solemn head-bowed prayer, I dutifully clasped my hands. But Bishop Peter had already leapt from his chair beside me and, gathering his cassock around him like a milkmaid's skirts, proceeded to skip with skinny-legged strides around our large table, singing a jolly little prayer-song from Walt Disney's *Johnny Appleseed:*

The Lord is good to me
And so I thank the Lord
For giving me the things I need
The sun and rain and an apple seed
The Lord is good to me!

The next morning, soon after breakfast, I was reading in the ship's Sun Lounge when the Bishop ascended from his distant accommodation, weighed down with books and files. He selected a small low coffee table across the room, dumped the books on it, fluffed his papers about, retrieved a fallen pen, and then leaned forward to write. A moment later he was standing up to contort himself sideways into the chair and awkwardly skew around to reach the table, not unlike some knotted snake. The compellingness of my thriller began to waver. When I next looked up he was on the floor, his legs arranged like a spider, one drawn in, the other at an ungracious angle, while his neck was stretched just above table-height while he tried again to write.

"You don't look very comfortable, Bishop," I commented conversationally.

"I'm not!" he exclaimed. "There's no desk in my C-Deck cabin and I have much work to do!"

So up spake innocence. "There's a desk in my cabin," said I. "You could use that for an hour or two while I'm up here."

In a trice he had gathered all his paraphernalia and leapt to his feet. "Show me where it is!"

I led him down one flight of stairs and ushered him through my cabin door. "So kind, so kind," he muttered, immediately flinging his work across both the desk and my bunk. "I'll let you know when I've finished!"

At five-to-six in the evening, some eight hours later, the Bishop was still hunched over my desk while I danced from foot to foot in the corridor outside my cabin. My make-up, hairbrush and other bedside clutter had, I noticed, been stowed somewhere invisible, but the dress hanging from a peg on the wall was mercifully still there. Within the next five minutes I must arrange myself in that dress for the Captain's Cocktail Party, do my hair, my face, and complete various other details of *toilette* in order to shake the illustrious hand in greeting at precisely six o'clock as ship protocol demanded – the same Captain with whom I had dined last night, of course, but that's just one of shipboard's rituals. I cleared my throat.

"Uh – umm – Bishop? I'm afraid I must change for Captain's Cocktails…"

"Nearly finished," he called without looking up. And at six-fifteen he rose from the chair, smiling as he finally permitted me, once again, to cross the threshold of my own cabin. "Most kind," he mumbled, "most kind." *Give a bishop an inch…*

So, soon after we met the new Bishop John at Hallams last Christmas – as portly and bald as Bishop Peter was thin and blessed with hair, and earthier than Peter's wildest imaginings – I was not surprised when he'd speculatively eyed up Chris and me. "When will you next be off-island?" he had asked without preamble. I mentioned the dates. "Good. That house of yours will suit me very well as a townhouse while the Vicar of St James' is on leave. When I have late or early services in town, I'll sleep at your place and it will save me the country drive." And so he had, making himself thoroughly at home at Villa Le Breton during several weeks of our latest absence, reported Annette.

Therefore, when he phoned as soon as I returned this October, inviting me to drinks with a group of friends at Donny's on the Wharf on Friday evening, I should first have asked what he wanted of me. But I didn't. And now that I am captive in his car on the way to the seafront, he admits that we first have a small meeting to attend.

A very small meeting, as it turns out. A Chairman, a Secretary, a Treasurer – and me. Up until now I had felt I could cope with fundraising Scrabble now and then, with obligatory bingo for the aged at occasional Corona Society coffee mornings, with attending rare barbecues and movie evenings for the League of Friends who help the hospital, and even the unnerving business of sometimes reading lessons in church. But this seems to be a turning point into major involvement. I am not sure I like the idea. The Heritage Society is still my prime interest should I actually *join* a Society, and the RSPCA its close second.

"But the St Andrew's Society is important!" advises Deirdre,

Treasurer-cum-Social Secretary, impatiently knotting her long hair into a decisive bun. "Every year in late November we hold a Ball to mark St Andrew's Day; and at the end of January we do a Burns' Night Supper. It's mid-October already and we need to get started with both of these. You can see there aren't many of us."

That much I can definitely see. The Secretary/Chieftain – the slightly acerbic, white-bearded Editor of the *St Helena News* – does not look to me like a Ball kind of guy, even though he holds the distinction of being a true Scot, while the proudly English veins of the Society's Chief – our Bishop himself – are sullied by no dastardly drop of Scottish blood. Neither of them will be eager to hang St Andrew's flags, I'm sure. On my left sits Deirdre, a St Helenian whose exact Scottish lineage is, for all I know, like mine, a good five generations removed from the bonnie banks of Loch Lomond. My heart is not palpitating with eagerness for this endeavour.

But across the table, the Bishop, whose usually twinkling brown eyes now appear serrated with menace, is clearly determined that I have no reason to eschew doing something practical for the cause as I am, after all, a lady-of-leisure-without-ready-excuses. I shuffle my feet beneath the table, hem and haw, play for time while three pairs of eyes bore into me painfully. But in the end, because I am still the new girl on the block and bowed by pressure, I warily agree to help with the upcoming Ball.

And that's the nod that fires the starting-gun – eliciting with it a blinding flash of presentiment that henceforward the weeks, months, and eventually years that follow this feeble acquiescence will no longer be my own. I dimly suppose there might be some hours freed for doing things I actually prefer, but leisure, I know, will fly off on the wings of the wind. And my presentiment is not without foundation, for Deirdre turns out to be a natural-born organiser, terrifyingly efficient, and within five minutes has embroiled me not only in the numerous challenges of the St Andrew's Night Ball, but also the even greater challenges of a Burn's Night Supper – an event I have, all my life, studiously and successfully sidestepped among Scotland's far-reaching tentacles. But for some unexplained reason, Deirdre claps her hands and I am obediently there.

So, now sucked into the vortex, I roll up my sleeves and Deirdre and I get to work. November's prestigious black-tie St Andrew's Night Ball, first on the list, comes about not without some difficulty. A last-minute let-down by a promised disc jockey has obliged us – in the inconvenient off-island absence of 'King George', a recognised local keyboard maestro – to resort to an unknown quantity manning CDs for the dancing, an eleventh-hour panic imperturbably handled by Deirdre. Without a clue of whom to call, and a complete novice at St Andrew's Night protocol anyway, I stand about wringing my hands while Deidre makes calls, marshals troops, and copes, turning the event into a grand affair. At least, by island standards.

I have thrown many parties in my time and am not bad at them when I put my back into it. I threw a 1940s theme party for Chris once that people talked about for twelve years; and notwithstanding the demands of clamouring small children, another time single-handedly cooked him an eight-course restaurant-calibre dinner for a decorative, elegant, fun-strewn New Year's Eve birthday party for twelve. I once catered every morsel, arranged every bloom, made the cake and all but the bride's dress, for a friend's wedding in our small garden that, at the last moment, was shifted inside because of an unanticipated storm, and a sophisticated elderly guest proclaimed it the best wedding she had ever attended. I could efficiently handle a St Andrew's Night Ball quite alone, if things here weren't so utterly foreign from anything I've known before.

The Consulate Hotel Ballroom is crowded, and full of chatter backed by a Scottish music CD Deirdre has proffered to the disc jockey. Men are smart in black dinner jackets tonight, women in long dresses. This is one of the Events of the Year, Deirdre assures me, and I see that guests comprise all the upper echelon of island society. Long hotel-owned red-clothed tables flanked by their resident multi-coloured plastic chairs are set down the length of the room, stopping short of the alcove that is the dance floor.

One of my delegated missions was to buy all the blue candles I could muster in Jamestown (no easy task at all), which now burn brightly on each table, representing the royal blue of St Andrew's white-crossed flag; and I tentatively trust their significance is noted because, frankly, little else lends a Scottish atmosphere to the room. Notwithstanding our supposedly blue-and-white night, the swathes of orange tinsel that permanently hang from the ceilings of this islander-run hotel ballroom still twinkle in place, and on support pillars in the big room, large red cardboard cut-out stars add another quaint embellishment. There are not enough of these to emulate a real galaxy, of course, so fluorescent red, yellow, and orange sale stickers fill the gaps – the circular kind with a hundred jagged edges to catch the eye, which they do. Orange crepe paper streamers still back the small performing platform at one end, and between our hard-won royal blue candles and the royal blue paper napkins I have also trudged for, the hotel's small vases of red plastic flowers dominate the tables. This clashing backdrop, being part of permanent in-house decoration, may not be dismantled under any circumstances, even for this event, I learn.

After the buffet dinner table has been cleared of the gammon, non-assertive St Helena curry and jelly-and-custard trifle that constitute traditional island fare at such gatherings, the dancing gets going. And now I can pick out the few genuine Scots among the hundred-plus guests – five, to be exact – who, in Highland dress and excited by the CD bagpipes, are energetically flinging themselves through the Gay Gordons, kilts and sporrans flying. Even the tartan-sashed St Helenian amateur Scottish dancers from Longwood, waiting in the wings to demonstrate a reel, can barely contain their eagerness to join in. It's all jolly and hectic, and guests, I note, are thoroughly enjoying themselves. It spells huge relief for me, still feeling a little like *Alice Through the Looking Glass* as dancers laugh and yodel with delight under the handful of blue-and-white flags pinned on the back wall in our puny efforts to advertise the theme, in what is to me a very slightly bizarre event. I try not to notice that the flags, of course, are completely dominated by a mammoth poster covering one wall of New York at night, haplessly focussing on the brightly-lit, very recently late (only two months back) twin towers of the World Trade Centre. I swish my skirts a bit and cheerfully kick out my feet now and then, in a manner of enjoyment, but my heart tells me I yet have a lot of adjusting to do in Island Life.

St Andrew's Night has finally brought us to the tail end of November and again I am excitedly on countdown to the arrival of Chris, our children, and Fee. My happy trio of decorators – Pat,

Growler and Gibby – is back in harness at the Villa, Radio St Helena in full spate and laughter ringing over the garden as they balance on long ladders, repainting the gleaming white exterior of this tall house, their work almost done. Pre-Christmas social life is slowly gaining momentum and early in December, just days before my family is due to arrive, I am invited to Sunday lunch at Irene Harris's guesthouse in Lower Jamestown, the hostess a delightful English visitor with whom I became friendly on the northbound voyage in October. I park my car on the Stand in the middle of Main Street, just opposite the guesthouse, and am welcomed inside.

There are ten of us together, all friends, seated around a steaming Sunday meal of roast island pork and trimmings just laid before us, when a loud hammering shakes the front door. Irene investigates, only to reappear a moment later looking perplexed. She leans over me. "It's the police," she hisses. "They want a word with you."

In all my history, no policeman has ever initiated an official conversation with me. I rise and go to the door, not a little mystified. An immensely tall young figure stands there, towering over both me and his smartly uniformed colleague. "Dat your car dere?" he gestures over his shoulder. I crane my neck to see behind him, and there behold my poor maroon wagon impaled on the drainpipe of an empty house on the far side of the street. It looks helpless, one front wing slightly crumpled by contact with a wall, a light broken, its hindquarters ungraciously protruding onto the path of upcoming traffic – should any cars pass on this somnolent Sunday noon. "Us escort you now to Headquarters, ma'am, and us talk about dam'ge to public property an' obstruttin' traffic," I am informed. And before I can turn to excuse myself from the lunch party, I am frogmarched down the street, an officer of the law gripping my arms on either side. In what is perceived to be an almost totally crime-free island this sight must prove an amusing distraction to onlookers from behind their lace curtains, I muse as my legs barrel along with them.

In a small office at the back of the Courthouse building, I am sat down and grilled. *Have I been drinking?* No. In fact, since the hostess of the lunch-party is of the B'hai faith we are, willy-nilly, drinking apple juice. *Do I often park my car like that?* No. *What reason do I offer for parking in that way?* I rack my brains. I had parked quite normally, pulling up the handbrake, of that I was certain – though perhaps I had left the gear in neutral? In any event my friends, Tommy and Gay, had arrived a good fifteen minutes after me at Harris Guesthouse and my car was still in its proper place when they parked their own nearby. "I really don't know how it happened," I offer in despair, without benefit of any reassuring smile from the two officers.

"Us now gi'e you a breat'alyser tasst," the tall one announces, placing before me an unfamiliar black box. "You see it say '000' before you begin? Us see what it say after." I huff into the hose, and some glimmer of consternation passes over the young officer's face when he sees the three little zeroes untainted by alcohol fumes.

"I've been drinking apple juice," I remind him reproachfully, thinking of cold pork and congealed gravy on my party plate.

"Yes, ma'am, I see dat now. You free to go after I read you a warnin' for drivin' wit'out due care 'n 'ttention." And before I can retort that the whole point was that I was far removed from my car at the time of its journey into the drainpipe, he reads me a formal warning. When I finally emerge from the small back office, promising that my car will never take off without me again, I find Tommy Dunne waiting outside, puce with fury – a colour unusual for one of the gentlest Irishmen I have known. "Let's get you out of here!" he directs into the general hearing of the police, and seizes my arm with the same grip of purposefulness with which they had propelled me down this street twenty minutes earlier. "They're lunatics! They have no right at all to treat you like this! And don't you worry about that drainpipe – I'll fix it myself as soon as the shops open tomorrow!"

Amused in retrospect, I phone the Bishop to share a laugh over my story when I return home from the interrupted party. He guffaws in appreciation: "But you heard about the expat Nurse Tutor, didn't you? About a week ago her car was neatly parked in the Stand when a local chap drove down Main Street and crashed into it. So the police came along, hauled the Nurse Tutor out of the post office where she was buying stamps, and breathalysed *her*! The other chap went off home."

I am still bemused by official logic here, but somehow these two incidents tell me that this is the real start of Island Life.

5.

Goodnight, Sorry for Sinking You

December 2001 to January 2002

Among this summer's visitors is a Royal Fleet Auxiliary vessel, come to pay respects to its late sister, the RFA *Darkdale*, who languishes at the bottom of James Bay. It's a signal event, for just over sixty years ago the 8 145 ton *Darkdale* had lain peacefully at anchor in this off-the-beaten-track anchorage, when a German submarine, *U-68*, commanded by *Korvettenkapitän* Karl-Friedrich Merten, sneaked up behind it and, with four salvos of torpedoes, blew the whole ship to pieces. Its effect is still recalled by some of the island's elderly, woken by the explosion that rocked the town shortly after midnight on an October night in 1941 and caused a fire on board that raged for three hours before the broken remains of the ship finally sank to the seafloor. On board were forty-six crewmen who perished in the attack; the only survivors, two men knocked off the ship by the force of the explosion, and seven others who were ashore when it happened – her Captain Thomas Card among them, the Chief Engineer, the Chief Steward, one seaman, and three others in hospital at the time.

A special, if belated, ceremony of remembrance is to be held at the Cenotaph today, conducted by the Lord Bishop; and the visiting RFA ship has journeyed here with a wreath expressly designed for the occasion, which they will lay with all solemnity in memory of this disaster. Christopher, a child of the Royal Navy, his mother, and I join the modest crowd gathered on the Wharf this morning, taking up places against the seaside railings with our new friends Liz and Martin Drury. Martin, a former head of the National Trust in England, is presently on the island to kick-start a National Trust of our own, due to open next May, on St Helena's Day.

By due time, all is ready on the seafront. The white Cenotaph, which already bears a new bronze plaque describing the names of the dead we are to honour, waits in mute dignity while clergy amass within its shade, surplices gently teased by the morning breeze. Nearby, neatly-aligned RFA participants are patiently poised in anticipation of the ceremony as the appointed hour approaches. Eventually St James' clock strikes and, give or take a few minutes, the appointed hour passes. This is no great surprise in this inherently unpunctual place, of course, but as time plods on even the local dignitaries grow restive.

Chris and I meet eyes, registering simultaneously that while the RFA crew are here, their special wreath is not. And then we remember the culmination of fierce warnings posted along the seafront: *Your Last Chance to Discard Vegetable Matter!* For strictly no foreign fruit must sully this island's good earth without extensive phytosanitary tickets, no vegetable, no seedling, and no flower. And certainly no lovely wreath of fresh blooms caringly transported across half an ocean, even if the cooler that protected it *en route* most likely killed off all its ugly threats days ago. Our group of friends exchange raised eyebrows, judging, from our wide-world wisdom, that this adherence to the letter might be a little pedantic in this instance. The chilled wreath would, after all, never travel further inland than the stone steps of the Cenotaph perching on the outside of the sturdy city walls; so surely a simple cellophane covering could suffice to contain any surviving horrors that still lurk within the buds? Nonetheless, the A&NRD – in short, the Agriculture department – is adamant: no phyto ticket, no wreath. But, they magnanimously inform the RFA, they will be pleased to deliver a substitute wreath of local flowers to the Wharf when it is ready. "Marigolds!" I mutter to Chris in trepidation of the stiff, evil-smelling favourites for local church posies. *When it is ready...*

So, while someone saunters among the hills in search of sparse island flowers, we wait. And wait and wait. Caught under the glaring noon sun, our small party begins to wilt but, absolutely determined to see this through to its end, we stay. Twenty more minutes drag by, thirty, forty. And then, with a sudden flurry among the clergy, the Bishop breaks loose from his throng and, in a flounce of surplices, leaves the Wharf at unprecedented speed, heading over the moat, through the Town Arch and out of sight. I tentatively suggest that, now out of patience, he is heading for the hills himself, perhaps to do murder up there, and our group shares slightly hysterical giggles at the turn this solemn ceremony is taking. What if he doesn't return?

But, as suddenly as he departed, he soon returns, racing back over the moat, this time transporting a large circle of red plastic Remembrance Day poppies. "Can't delay any longer," he growls as he speeds past us. "I swiped it from the storeroom in St James'. It'll have to do!"

With a flourish he presents it to the RFA's designated wreath layer, begins the service, and has just reached that poignant moment for which we have all long suffered the day's heat, when our attention is diverted by the screeching arrival of a large vehicle in our midst – nothing less than the A&NRD's new mobile veterinary clinic. And from its wide-flung double doors emerges a wreath. Not, of course, the selected one that had travelled the oceans deep to adorn St Helena's Cenotaph but, instead, a cobbled-together garland of assorted blooms designed to suffice – including in its circle many, many marigolds. It is to the great credit of the RFA visitors that they are laughing at the incident, in public, at least; most particularly as they now are laying two wreaths for the dead of the *Darkdale* – the Bishop's plastic poppies, and this tardy donation from the Agriculture department.

Perhaps, someone suggests hopefully, the original offering might be allowed to ride the oily waters above the wreck itself, floating in isolated glory where foreign ills will not taint the island. But I have already been here long enough to suspect that it will more likely travel far inland, through dangerously vulnerable territory, merely to be incinerated. As for the rest of us, we're ready for home now, for a rollicking post-mortem over ice-cold gin and tonic.

Far from lying alone in James Bay, the *Darkdale* is probably kept company by more wrecks than we can imagine, given the sheer numbers of wooden sailing vessels that history has seen off the island's coast. While many of those who might have come to grief are probably buried under silt and detritus from the bounding cliffs, unknown and unremembered, certainly the SS *Papanui* is still partially visible just a stone's throw from Donny's sundowner deck. But the *Papanui*, a New Zealand ship carrying 364 emigrants from Southampton, England, to Freemantle, Australia, does not share the *Darkdale's* tale of bloody tragedy. Certainly her passengers and the crew of 108 must have been nearly scared to death by the fire consuming their ship as they limped into James Bay's safe haven in September 1911, exploding soon afterwards. But happily, all survived to be later transhipped to the SS *Opawa* to continue their journey.

The proximity of the 17th Century Dutch East Indiaman *Witte Leeuw* is, however, vastly more romantic. Heading home from the East Indies in 1613 with a full cargo of spices and a reputed stash of 1 311 diamonds, this mighty sailing ship, in company with three other Dutch East Indiamen, rounded the headland of Munden's and came, with some surprise, upon two Portuguese carracks peacefully at anchor off Chapel Valley (the old name for James Bay). This was a bit of luck! Two tiny armed merchantmen stood little chance against the power of the Dutch, and the latter bore down on the enemy with fearsome drum rolls and the blaring trumpets of battle. The Portuguese, unable to manoeuvre, could do little but fight for their lives – which they did with stunning effect, for two of the stout Dutchmen fled and a battered third quickly followed, unable to continue the battle. The *Witte Leeuw*, biggest of them all, receiving brave bombardment from the carracks, exploded and soon sank beneath the waters right before the Portuguese eyes.

Over the years various parties have dived for the treasures listed on her manifest, identifying her position by several dated cannon found lying above her sandy burial ground, with a prodigious mass of peppercorns around them. She had reputedly carried thirty guns along her one hundred foot hull, and 15 171 bags of pepper which, unlike other spices, had survived centuries of seawater. The diamonds, probably scattered by the stern blast, have never been found, but an enormous quantity of valuable late Ming porcelain was brought to the surface, much of it completely intact and now residing in the Ryksmuseum in Amsterdam.

The island's connection with the SS *City of Cairo* has closer parallels with the *Darkdale* than any other local sea adventure. Unescorted, though carrying one hundred passengers and 196 crew through the hazardous seas of World War II, the ship left Bombay on 1 October 1942, called at Cape Town, and then set out for Pernambuco

(Recife), Brazil. She was on this lonely leg of ocean when, on the night of 6 November, disaster struck – in the form of two torpedoes from the very same *U-68* that had sunk the *Darkdale* at St Helena just a year earlier, with the same Karl-Friedrich Merten in charge. As the *City of Cairo* rapidly started to sink at the stern, the order was given to abandon ship, whereupon the U-boat promptly surfaced. Their position was approximately two thousand miles east of Brazil, Captain Merten courteously advised the *Cairo's* frightened passengers, one thousand miles west of Africa, and five hundred miles from St Helena Island, in which case the latter landfall was recommended. Then he uttered the famous words that have immortalised this efficient German submariner: "Goodnight, sorry for sinking you."

Eighteen people died in the blast, and the radio officer, refusing to leave his post, went down with the ship. But with two lifeboats damaged, the 275 survivors were crammed into six remaining open boats put out by the *Cairo's* Captain Rogerson who, supplied with only one sextant and one chronometer among them and striving to keep all the boats together, valiantly set out towards St Helena. Thirteen days later, with three boats separated, the remaining three were finally rescued by the *Clan Alpine* within sight of the island, highlighting Captain Rogerson's extraordinary navigational skills. One hundred and forty-eight living passengers and crew were put ashore at St Helena by the *Clan Alpine*, and for the next three months they enjoyed the generous hospitality of the islanders until eventually two ships of the Royal Navy picked them up. But, of those put ashore, two Indian lascars died on the island (two others had died on the lifeboat), and two Europeans.

I met the daughter of one of these dead, making the pilgrimage not only to visit her father's grave in St Helena but also to meet the people who had made her parents so welcome. Her mother had survived a nightmare journey during those arduous days in the lifeboat, nourished for two weeks solely by Horlicks tablets while a baby girl grew in her belly, then, at the end of the journey suffering the death of her husband on shore. But the baby daughter, unwittingly along for the adventure and now recounting the story, had suffered only one after-effect of her mother's traumas: a life-long repulsion for Horlicks; that most nourishing of winter drinks.

Apart from one boatload of fifty-four survivors rescued in mid-ocean and taken to Cape Town, tales from the other two strayed lifeboats are not as happy. One had helplessly drifted towards the coast of Brazil for fifty-one days before rescue arrived, but by then only three passengers were still alive, one of those dying on the German ship that picked them up. The last boat, slowest of the six, had – to everyone's horror – inexplicably set the longer course for South America after separating from its small St Helena-bound fleet. It boasted only two survivors of its own fifty-four passengers at the end of its voyage.

Though Christopher, young Richard and my mother-in-law all returned to the Cape after the Christmas holidays, I still have Virginia with me. Lately completing her final school year, she now intends spending six months of a gap year on the island, helping out at Prince Andrew Secondary School, and I am thrilled, even though with so much on my plate I barely have time to see her. The dreaded Burns' Night is upon us, but with the Bishop breathing hard down my neck, I dare not renege on my word. Deirdre, anyway, is an old hand at it, so I once more trot obediently in her wake, doing as directed. This time it's a black-tie dinner in the Wellington Guesthouse dining room. With speeches, I learn. Scottish speeches, and quite a lot of Robert Burns.

It's a somewhat quirky ritual for a remote subtropical island, I feel as the evening slowly unfolds. For in a room of nearly forty St Helenians, there are still only five true Scots, presided over by the defiantly English Chief who continues to vehemently deny the smallest drop of Scottish blood. Also, on a sweltering midsummer's night in the humid heart of Jamestown, the thick wool kilts and velvet jackets of Burns devotees seem, if not a heavy cross to bear, at least quite a distance out of place.

The heat in the dining room is relentless, despite the huge Regency sash-windows flung wide behind us. But soon we discover that these present an open invitation to January's flying cockroaches to participate in our gathering. They zoom in with the whirr of helicopters, huge and grotesque, refusing to leave until our hostess, Ivy 'Wellington', has marshalled an army to deal with them; and drawing flimsy curtains against such fly-pasts is no deterrent. Eventually we close the windows and turn on the ceiling fans. But their draught promptly extinguishes the multiple candles ornamenting the tables, splattering blue wax far and wide, and so, by public demand, the fans are switched off and the candles relit. It therefore is not long before the dignity of dinner jackets is entirely abandoned, ties loosened, and perspiration flows freely down female décolletages.

The meal, which is abysmal, is indeed punctuated by the numerous speeches and antics demanded of a traditional Burns' Night Supper, and even I, with forewarning, am challenged to perform – a thrown-down gauntlet which I stoutly pick up regardless of my ineptness at public-speaking. *A Toast to the Laddies* is my lot, following a varied recitation of toasts to the Haggis, the Lassies, Burns himself (poor Rabbie, for sure, is spinning in his grave!), and innumerable others – and to suit the occasion I offer a desperate dawn-worked skit on Burns' *A Man's a Man for a' that*. It goes alright, I suppose, notwithstanding my fake Scots accent, but by now a great deal of neat whisky has been consumed in a party turned heady in the suffocating heat, and I am way beyond caring. The potato and leek soup, brewed with best intentions by our Chieftain, somehow curdled during the day and certain members of the party turn green quite early on, while others persistently whine about this unfortunate accident all evening. Followed by boiled mince untainted by seasoning, mashed potato, and boiled pumpkin in place of buttered Swedes (*neeps & tatties* is a Burns' Supper requisite, evidently), and a best-forgotten pudding, I note immediately that there is infinite scope for gastronomic improvement should I unfortunately be involved in next year's dinner. *But will I be?* Not if I can summon courage enough to say *No* to Deirdre.

The Christmas lights in Main Street are finally down now that January has almost passed, and all the Santa Clauses that frame the Market area over the Festive Season have been put away for a year. But a palpable frisson of activity is running through the island. 'Q5' cometh and much is afoot.

Q5, St Helena's Quincentenary, celebrates five hundred years of recorded history since the island's accepted discovery. And what a history it's been! This event is something I am keenly interested in. But though I am brimming with ideas for the great celebration, planning was completed by a committee months ago, while I was still off-island, and preparation is already well underway. All I can do now is help in small ways.

And so, in the first of my celebration duties, I find myself installed at the newly-opened Q5 Information and Exhibition Centre in Lower Main Street, appointed to "chat and be friendly" to tourists venturing in from the rash of passing cruise ships the island expects to entertain this summer season. This is an easy and enjoyable task for me, and I chat to my heart's content, deftly selling T-shirts and knick-knacks as I go. But the star of exhibits in this ground floor showroom is, in fact, a collection of some 5 000 spectacular photographs in a computer-generated slide show, covering every angle of St Helena from its breathtaking scenery and the varied faces of its mixed population to the island's earliest sepia prints of built heritage and local landmarks. However, in sneaked moments of enjoying the show myself, I soon detect a problem: when the morning sun of this southern summer beams so cheerfully into the east-facing windows, the scenes vanish from the computer screen – even when the sun-filter curtains are drawn. So, mortified by this terrible waste of a brilliant presentation, I start rummaging at home in high cupboards and finally manage to unearth two pairs of thick lined curtains which I bear downtown in triumph.

I seek out young Jason, who gives me a look of some resignation when I coerce his able body from a back room at the Centre. But he obligingly searches out a tall ladder and such objects as he may need for the hanging of heavy curtains, and ascends towards the high ceilings, my copious cloth bunched under his arm. My curtains had once over-generously extended from ceiling to floor at Villa Le Breton, even with a metre or so to spare. But now, as Jason dramatically unfurls the first drop to its full length, I see it blocks out barely two-thirds of the light, still allowing the full force of summer to stream onto the computer screen through these majestic 18th Century townhouse windows. Jason shrugs and descends, dumping the curtains at my feet and carting the ladder away while my help-mate at the T-shirt desk utters "Never mind" on a slightly indifferent sigh. And I learn (with some residual difficulty) a stout lesson in St Helenian pragmatism: one attempt is enough; and *perseverance* is not a St Helenian word. The slide exhibition had, after all, initially been set up when sun was not shining and the screen was visible. But the fact that we cannot not see the pictures now is nothing less than the fault of the sun – a matter utterly beyond our control. I have a great deal still to learn here.

Much as I revel in the obligatory chatting, our actual role at the Q5 Centre is something of a puzzlement; for surely the purpose of celebrating five hundred years since discovery is to remember the island's past? Yet, strategically stuck on the wall, is the chosen slogan for May's up-coming festivities: *Looking up, looking forward.* This emanates from a Q5 motto competition offered to students at Prince Andrew Secondary School, I learn, and not only did this curious phrase win the contest, but many of their posters now ornamenting these walls show aeroplanes. Huge Boeings, sometimes two at a time, landing and taking off from this very island. Even a T-shirt bearing that ubiquitous emblem is for sale, causing tourists to recoil with distaste: "An airport will ruin St Helena!" They know, of course, that the sea voyage provides the essence of adventure, the notion of expedition, and half the memorable experience of visiting this remote place – because they have done it themselves.

But the Airport is already a local obsession, vigorously fuelled by a Governor keen to name it for himself, and his docile Council of followers. Giving more credibility to its prospects, however, is SHELCO, an interested overseas venture capital investment consortium with a recently-established permanent representative on the island. SHELCO's impressive prospectus, in fact, leaves no stone unturned, clearly detailing not only the planning and construction of an airport, but also the running of an actual airline. In addition, their 'three-legged stool' – the newly-coined phrase-about-town – proposes the construction of a low-volume high-income eco-friendly hotel in the countryside (with full-sized golf course), promising to neither blemish the landscape nor draw on St Helena's meagre utilities resources. Nor will it benefit the islanders much, I feel, unless the locals merely aspire to the menial tasks they perform for worthwhile salaries in the Falklands and prefer not to exercise at home. But if anyone is equipped to handle this gargantuan project, SHELCO – with financially stable, internationally respected backers – would get my vote, even though I still doggedly question the wisdom of attracting fly-in tourism to the middle of nowhere for a tropical destination with a capricious climate and no beaches.

The building in which we sell plane-emblazoned T-shirts is oddly relevant to our Portuguese past; though this gem of interest is not widely advertised to either populace or visitors. But it so happened that the three terrace houses known as 'One Two Three Main Street', one of which the Q5 Centre now occupies, rest firmly on the site of a chapel built by the early Portuguese visitors. Interestingly, though there is ample written proof that the Portuguese navigator, João da Nova Castello, discovered Ascension Island in the previous year, 1501, no absolute proof has ever confirmed his discovery of *this* island a year later. Nonetheless it's generally accepted by historians that he was our man, and he gives us an intriguing hook on which to hang an old Portuguese hat.

And so, the story goes, it was on 21 May 1502 that da Nova happily spotted this uncharted rock rearing from a stormy horizon, and immediately named it *Ilha da Sancta Elena* for the blessed Saint (Helena, mother of the first Christian Emperor Constantine) who had brought them safely hither on her name-day. His was one of three small ships weighed down with pepper, ginger, cinnamon and cloths from Cochin in the East, destined for Portugal. What they saw was an apparently uninhabited island, devoid of four-footed beasts and fruit trees, but thickly verdant with forests of endemics. In the surrounding waters, fish leapt to the hook, and seals, sea lions, and even turtles were plentiful. A lively stream of sweet water bubbled down the valley, emptying into the bay where da Nova anchored, and the strategic usefulness of this island was at once noted.

The story also goes that, touchingly grateful for their survival through the storm that had tossed them here, they immediately gave credence to the old adage that the first building erected by the early Portuguese discoverers was always a church (by the Dutch a fort, and by the English a pub!), and broke up a carrack that was not faring so well at sea, using its beams and ironwork to raise a small wooden chapel ashore. Inevitably, however, this charming tale is refuted in an exhaustively researched work on our early Portuguese visitors in which we learn, with some slight disappointment again, that there seems to have been no carrack to break up (because all three ships originally setting sail from the East returned to Portugal together and intact) and it would appear that they possibly did not build a chapel on the island for many decades.

For reasons best known to the Portuguese sailors, the discovery of St Helena was not widely publicised in Europe in those earliest days; and for several years the island was visited solely by their own ships homeward-bound from the East. Here they collected vital fresh water from the streams for their continuing journeys and sometimes sent sick sailors ashore to live or die, depending on their condition.

It was also they who introduced the first animals and fruit trees into this pristine environment, not least to offer succour to a shy, grossly mutilated Portuguese soldier, Fernão Lopes, who had jumped ship *en route* from India to Portugal in 1515. Lopes, a Portuguese nobleman and Christian renegade stationed in Goa, had deserted from the army of the remorseless naval general, Aphonso d'Albuquerque, only to be surrendered back to him as a prize, with others, by his fearful opponent, Rasul Khan of Goa, in 1512. So, niftily circumventing promises to spare their lives, Albuquerque then inflicted three days of grisly torture on his traitors, severing right hands and the thumbs of their left, cutting off noses and ears, and pulling out beards and hair. More than half the captives died in the process, but Lopes survived for three years as a miserable beggar in Goa, derided by his own countrymen and shunned by his former Muslim friends. In 1515, however, he saw the chance to stow away on a homebound ship, and it was during this voyage that he debated the wisdom of returning to similar humiliation in Portugal, and so crept ashore on the uninhabited St Helena to hide in the woods until the ship set sail. At least the sailors, futilely searching for him until it was time to leave, showed compassion, and left for him *"a barrel of biscuit and some pieces of hung beef, and dried fish, and salt, and a fire, and some old clothes, which each one contributed"*. And so, leaving supplies each time they called, Portuguese ships respected his solitude. And apart from one eventual voyage north to pay homage to the King and Queen of Portugal, and beg Absolution of the Pope for having forsworn Catholicism to embrace the Moslem faith while serving in India, he spent a span of thirty years living quite alone (except for a pet cockerel) in a small cave in what is now called James Valley. Though we know that he died here around 1545, neither his bones nor his cave have ever been identified.

Nonetheless, Records show that by 1530 at least, St Helena was visited by other nations as well – in that particular year certainly by two troubled French ships that managed to drop anchor in the bay and provision themselves with fowls and pigs *"and other things"* (many goats, by further accounts) with which the Portuguese had furnished the island from time to time. Then, by 1571, the Portuguese clearly believed it time to build a chapel, and this they did.

"Tiled, and whitened on the outside very fair" according to the notorious English privateer, Thomas Cavendish, who offered his impressions in 1588 – the little church was built with a porch. Also, on a stone causeway at the nearby stream was, he tells us, *"a frame erected whereon hang two bells wherewith they ring to Mass, and hard unto it is a Cross set up....very artificially of free-stone"*. On this, the date *"1571"* was carved. Inside the church, he informs us, was set an altar and pictures of Christ upon the Cross, *"and the image of Our Lady praying, with divers other histories painted curiously on the same. The sides of the church were hung around with stained cloths having many devices drawn on them"*. This is a welcome description and a useful aid to picturing this proud little House of God presiding over its rushing stream and the gardens of pumpkins and melons, of herbs, juicy figs, oranges, lemons and pomegranates that now flourished beside leafy walks through Chapel Valley. But what Cavendish did not admit was that he himself had mysteriously seen fit to destroy both that altar and the Cross while he was there. This fact came to light only the following year when the Dutchman, Jan Huygen van Linschoten, a pilot for the Portuguese fleet, gleaned the gossip from some recuperating sailors dropped off at St Helena from a previous Portuguese ship. The English, he was told, had left behind only a sword and a kettle.

Today there is no trace at all of the Portuguese chapel. No stone, nor bell, nor any shred of *"drawn devices"* remain, other than the accepted fact that the site of the Portuguese chapel lies directly under the foundations of the late 18th Century One Two Three Main Street – and the Quincentenary Centre.

✳

Thanks to the upcoming celebrations, the tiny dot of St Helena Island is temporarily enlarged on the world's map, and for the moment we are graced by one cruise liner after another. From the modest to the very grand they drop anchor in James Bay, and the populace rushes to greet them. Taxis, mostly freelance, line up along the Wharf offering personalised tours, while buses old and new claim those who prefer travelling in groups. The famous charabanc is there too, of course, smelling nostalgically of oil and old leather - a bottle-green open-topped fourteen-seat Chevrolet bus, vintage 1929, with a revitalised engine once donated from an American visitor's back yard. The charabanc is a local institution, and from Villa Le Breton the sound of its droning motor is distinctive as it labours up the steep gradients of Side Path above our house, the staccato voices of its tourists ringing out in exclamation.

But things do not go smoothly with all the liners. Especially with the *Aurora*, a brand new ship of momentous proportions and awesome grandeur, that almost fills the bay with its towering presence. On television, we've lately been treated to documentaries about the construction and furnishing of this luxury P&O liner, and the island has looked forward to its arrival with excited anticipation – not least because it carries 1 699 passengers who, if they all come ashore, will benefit our meagre coffers by nearly £20 000 in landing fees. This ship, like others, is equipped with its own smart tenders, and I am among a watching crowd on the Wharf as they cut a dash from ship to shore. Weather-wise, the gods are with us on this day – blue sky, windless air, millpond sea – and 405 passengers make it ashore before arrogance gets the better of the *Aurora's* tender-crew. As the local boatmen know, there's an art to broaching the Landing Steps, which relies on heading *past* them to approach from east to west, which the tenders are stringently advised to do. However, the *Aurora's* Staff Captain evidently knows better; and, rigidly refusing to take advice from simple island people, approaches from west to east, promptly bumping the pier-head and damaging the brand new tender. So, with a petulant swish of petticoats, all shore-trips from the mother ship are forthwith cancelled. Passengers already ashore enjoy their day tremendously, while the others fume. But their wrath is nothing compared to the rage of the Governor and the Bishop who both happen to be on the Steps at the time of the incident. "Take your bloody ship away!" they command the *Aurora's* know-all Staff Captain angrily, "and don't come back!" All along the Wharf are thwarted taxi drivers who have proffered an ill-afforded £10 each for this day's licence to carry passengers about, money now irrevocably lost to them.

When the *Crown Odyssey* visits, their Captain – perhaps overly-fearful of lawsuits should anyone stumble on the Landing Steps – baulks at permitting any tourists at all to travel ashore, even in his own tenders. Yet he has no compunction in inviting His Excellency the Governor of St Helena, the Lord Bishop, and the Honourable Attorney General to make the apparently hazardous journey from shore to ship in a diminutive ferry, in order that he might enjoy lunch with these dignitaries. There are other hitches too: the *Coronia*, the elderly *Monterey* and the *Saga Rose*, unsuspecting of St Helena's occasional oddities, make the grave mistake of visiting on early-closing Wednesday afternoons or Sundays, only to find Jamestown sealed and barred to tourism – a curious myopia from which the Chamber of Commerce suffers, notwithstanding their vociferous support of future air-tourism. But others stop long enough to cast ashore such luminaries as Sir Jimmy Saville who, for reasons that somehow evade me, causes massive excitement in the streets of Jamestown. More worthy, I feel, is my personal hero, the hugely impressive Terry Waite, with whom I am invited by the Bishop to share a fish-and-chips lunch at Donny's – a man whose strength of character brought him through deprivations we can barely imagine. Taken hostage in Lebanon in February 1987 and held captive in solitary confinement for nearly five years, chained by wrist and ankle to the wall of a dark cell, his meals served through a hatch lest he glimpse the face of his captives, a lesser soul would have lost his mind. But this man, though of a towering height compounding his discomfort in a cramped space, now appears relaxed, humorous and clear-minded, and unstintingly continues his humanitarian work.

The elegant blonde Ben Fogle of BBC fame, visiting a little later, causes tumult, and because I actually have no clue who he is, am deprived of the fluttering and faintness that assails other expatriate women as he wanders up the street. He's here to research a book, I learn, but he is only one of many interesting people attracted to St

Helena. In a single week once, Chris and I entertained film actors, a television producer and a multiple award-winning environmental journalist at Villa Le Breton, all of whom he had casually befriended on the RMS. At other times artists, writers and one or two scientists have also enjoyed wine on our veranda, and it is worth a moment's consideration to accept that none of these interesting associations would ever occur on an aeroplane.

Over time St Helena has hosted many figures known through history, the early years bringing such privateers as Francis Drake, and the swash-buckling Cavendish already mentioned, with Lancaster hot on their heels. The dashing Prince Rupert of the Rhine (third son of Frederick V of Bohemia and Elizabeth, the sister of Charles I of England), was another figure of romance who turned to piracy to assuage boredom after an outstanding career during England's Civil War. We have it on the good authority of Jan van Riebeeck, the Dutch Commander then *en route* to colonise the Cape of Good Hope in 1652, that Prince Rupert was expected to be lurking somewhere around St Helena at the time. Notwithstanding the pursuit of Admiral Blake just behind him, it was Rupert's intention, van Riebeeck believed, to lie in wait and nab an old East Indiaman or two returning home with treasures. *"As he doubtless knows that the Hon. Company has resumed the war against the State of Portugal in their Indian possessions,"* writes van Riebeeck, pulling no punches, *"he would probably make little distinction between English and Dutch East India ships, seeking to disguise his action under a cloak of righteousness, on the pretext of having a Portuguese commission."* Legend tells us that the unscrupulous Rupert lurked in what was then known as Seine Valley Mouth, the bay just east of Chapel Valley, and his presence in those waters is now remembered instead as Rupert's Valley.

More prosaically have followed scientists and naturalists: Edmund Halley (Halley's Comet) in 1677 to map out the stars of the southern hemisphere; William Dampier, famous English explorer, naturalist (and also buccaneer) in 1691; and Captain James Cook on board the *Resolution, en route* to Ascension Island in 1775, who stayed six days on St Helena and loved the place. Captain Bligh, formerly of the *Bounty*, called in 1792 on return from his second voyage to the South Seas, and *en route* with his cargo bound for Jamaica left plants and seeds of breadfruit and sago in St Helena as an inexpensive food option for the island. Though the breadfruit was received quite well, the sago proved a bit of a mystery to the locals, so Bligh's Otaheitan (Tahitian) travelling companions were called upon to cook it for them as a means of demonstration, but, inevitably, those plants soon died from lack of attention and neither breadfruit nor sago is evident in St Helena now. Governor Janisch of St Helena makes a passing reference to Bligh's visit, including mention of the introduction of mangoes to the island, but rather sadly I can't substantiate this report, though I like to think fondly of him for the probability of this delicious contribution.

Charles Darwin honoured us with a visit, arriving in the *Beagle* on 8 July 1836, and spent nearly a week examining flora and geology – recording an amazing 746 species of plant in that time, fifty-two of which he found to be indigenous. He made a grave error in the avian department, however, claiming quite erroneously that the St Helena's single surviving endemic bird, the wirebird *(charadrius sanctaehelenae)*, was imported.

The 19th Century seemed to bring with it royalty of many nations. Prince William Henry Frederick of Holland in 1838; Prince Alfred, second son of Queen Victoria and a serving officer on HMS *Euryalus* in 1860; in 1880 the grieving Empress Eugenie, widow of Napoleon III, on a pilgrimage to the grave of her 23-year-old son, the Prince Imperial, who had died in an ambush in Zululand the previous year; and Prince Albert William Heinrich of Prussia, grandson of Queen Victoria, on a German frigate *Prinz Adalbert* just one month after her. The Duke and Duchess of Connaught and their daughter Patricia started the flow for the next century, *en route* to South Africa on HMS *Balmoral Castle* in 1910; and in 1925 the Prince of Wales (the future King Edward VIII) arrived on the HMS *Repulse*, the largest ship ever to have visited St Helena up to that time, which brought crowds to the seafront to view the spectacle. Another grandchild of Queen Victoria, this time the Princess Marie-Louise of Schleswig-Holstein, passed through in 1938; and in 1947, when HMS *Vanguard* dropped anchor in James Bay, the island enjoyed the first-ever visit of a reigning monarch to St Helena – King George VI of England with his wife, the Queen Elizabeth and their daughters, the princesses Elizabeth and Margaret. They were followed ten years later, on HM Yacht *Britannia*, by Prince Philip, Duke of Edinburgh, by then the husband of the newly-crowned Queen Elizabeth II, the former Princess, and in 1984 by their second son, HRH Prince Andrew the Duke of York, after whom the Secondary School is named.

Then there were prisoners. From Seyyid Khalid, former Sultan of Zanzibar and then pretender to that throne, who was detained in St Helena at His Majesty's pleasure for four years (with his harem) before transfer to the Seychelles in 1921, to three political dissidents from Bahrain kept under house arrest on the perilous edge of Munden's cliff from 1957 to 1961, the island has long presented itself as a natural detention centre.

Of course, it was Napoleon Bonaparte's exile on St Helena that firmly fixed the island into the annals of history. But just fifty years after his body was removed from its quiet tomb near Hutt's Gate for repatriation to France in 1840, King Dinizulu, taken during the Anglo-Zulu Wars, found himself secluded by ocean for seven years, along with some of his wives and two angry uncles. He had no sooner been returned to the land of his fathers in 1898, than St Helena was swamped by 6 000 South African Boer prisoners taken during the Anglo-Boer War at the turn of the century – nearly all of them housed in tents across the great plains of Deadwood and Longwood, with an overflow of crusty independent Free Staters placed at Broad Bottom, some miles away from friction. However, back in Natal, the land of the Zulus, rebellions had continued to wreak havoc after the return home of Dinizulu; and in mid-1906, following a bloody but unequal battle between colonial troops and 5 000 ceremonially-sprinkled warriors in the Bambatho Uprising, 4 700 Zulu prisoners were taken. Of these, the twenty-five ringleaders were tried and sentenced to *"long terms of imprisonment"* on St Helena where they arrived a year later with two Natal warders, to be housed in the Ladder Hill Barracks. Though strong by reputation, many of these powerful Zulus turned out to be medically unfit for work, and despite the *"very liberal diet"*, tobacco allowance, social care, short working day, and excellent medical care reportedly administered to them, seven died of tuberculosis or heart disease before the remaining eighteen were pardoned by the Governor-General at the Opening of the first South African Union Parliament in 1910, and allowed to return home.

The island, flanked by one thousand miles of open ocean to the east and 1 300 miles to the west does not present itself for easy escape. And though one or two less high-profile prisoners have got away in their time, undoubtedly with collusion from a passing ship, the sheer cliffs are a prison wall. Perhaps these factors, more than any other, form the real story of St Helena.

6.

Unsure and Uncertain Hopes

February to March 2002

The Airport crunch time comes when it is eventually decided to hold a referendum. And here we are, finally faced with a decision that the people must make for themselves – ostensibly, at least. With too many centuries of slavery leaving an unwarranted legacy of dependency on the lords in London, autonomous thinking does not come readily to many St Helenians. But now the ball is in this court, and pens are poised.

"*I would like to have an airport on St Helena, with alternative arrangements being made for shipping*" reads the ballot paper. "*Or: I would not like to have an airport but would like to have a replacement RMS St Helena*"

To some, the questions appear artfully disguised in obfuscation, presenting the voter with no significant choice in the matter. And it's especially the *alternative arrangements being made for shipping* that confuses. With the lifespan of the RMS already on the wane, the island *must* have a new ship; not only for cargo, but also for certain medical patients unable to fly – significantly those stretcher-borne, or with heart problems, hypertension, advanced pregnancy, or fear of flying – and even for tourists who simply prefer sea travel. But this subject is sheathed in vague mumblings about the probability of non-passenger-carrying cargo calls from intermediate ships, and nothing is spelled out by DfID who are pushing the airport project for all it is worth. No questions are answered about where a shipping service will come from, or who will run it or pay for it. And while I suspect that the great majority of St Helenians actually wish for both an airport *and* a new RMS - because life on the island would never be the same without our own ship in the bay – that choice simply isn't there.

"The people of St Helena are asked to forego a replacement RMS (our lifeline) together with an operating subsidy, a total...which will be used to construct a 2 000 metre strip of concrete on Prosperous Bay Plain, in the unsure and uncertain hope that an airline will land an aeroplane on it..." writes our St Helenian friend, Stedson, to the local newspaper. *"The people of St Helena must be told the full story. They should be told what the risks are, and what the benefits could be. Public participation in the decision making should be encouraged, but the pros and cons must first be articulated. Then, and only then, a referendum should be held."* Another learned, but agitated, St Helenian writes: *"I can't believe [we] have been asked to vote for either a replacement ship or an air service. Who made [this offer] and agreed to this? Who tossed the coin and put us in a Catch 22 situation...? Voting for one means voting against the other. If the vote comes down in favour of an airport it will be a vote against sea access or the other way around."* So now that weekly newspapers are swamped not only with pie-in-the-sky rallies *for* the airport, but also sober arguments *against*, I recognise with relief that I am not the only Cassandra out there.

What we do learn just before the referendum, however, is a lot about costs. For one thing, in less than two years the Airport's price has soared from £27 million to £50 million, and it is doubtful that the ascendency will cease there. Also, ignoring the fact that our present RMS (after shortcuts) cost £30 million to build thirteen years ago, DfID has indicated willingness to fund our whole access project up to £26.3 million – their estimated cost of a replacement RMS. This seems to present a shortfall of some £23.7 million which, they blandly suggest, could be made up from 'private funding'. *From here?* we ask, appalled. Well, they offer magnanimously, maybe a loan will cover the shortfall; in which case DfID will reap the rewards of our successful tourism upturns when air access brings in the hordes.

London's other suspect move is the inclusion of the Falklands and Ascension Island in the referendum's voting line-up. While the votes of RMS crew are acceptable, since most are islanders based in St Helena, St Helenians earning substantial salaries in Ascension Island, and especially so in the Falklands, would unarguably be biased. Letters from such overseas workers describing jubilation at the prospect of air travel often appear in the local paper, and from their unambiguous wording it is clear that an airport solely means speedy homebound travel for holidays. No further thought is exercised over the physical impact of an airport on the island, or the environmental impact on the families they are coming to see – and least of all do they pause to consider the enormous expense of airfares which will certainly prohibit frequent returns. It is euphoria again, rife with contagion the closer we come to the referendum – and those most diseased are the islanders furthest from home.

I do not vote. I would like to, but that privilege is not accorded to me despite having owned property on St Helena for twenty-seven months already, or that I'm showing all signs of permanent residency here. Neither does it count that I was born in the British Commonwealth, nor that I am married to an Englishman who still holds British citizenship and is co-owner of our property. Yet Sue, an English consultant whose two-year term on the island is very nearly expired and who, by her own admission, will never again take the trouble to return to St Helena, *is* allowed to vote. The paradox is something that irks both of us, and it was she who suggested: "I couldn't give a toss whether this place gets an airport or not, so the result doesn't matter to me. Tell me what *you* would vote, and I'll mark whatever you decide." And so, thanks to Sue, I have my clandestine say after all.

With the results due this afternoon, the Bishop arrives on my veranda calling for coffee, and for an hour and a half we sit glued to Radio St Helena which is announcing results throughout that time. The count is taking place at the Consulate Hotel in Main Street, about as central as could be, and for the interest of the general public many chairs have been set up to watch the process. And yet, when the Bishop looked in there on the way to my house, not a soul was watching. The town itself is silent, he says, with thick apathy clogging the air despite the potentially momentous occasion. Even Side Path above us, as we enjoy the afternoon cool on the veranda, is empty of cars usually droning up its steep incline.

The RMS *St Helena* figures are the first to come in, and I find myself gaping over my cup in astonishment. The crew on our *ship* – those deckhands, stewards and stewardesses, the Bureau staff and the

St Helenians who are Officers, the galley staff and the engine-room boys, all people in highly lucrative employment on the high seas – have made their decision. They want an airport.

For a few stunned moments we stare at one another in disbelief. Then Bish clears his throat. "Well," he pronounces in a voice resonant with doom, "the RMS is the weather-vane. The whole vote will go with the Airport now. It was the phrasing of the questions that did it."

And so the Airport wins the day. After a provocative rendition of *The Final Countdown* offered at deafening volume on the radio, the total results are announced. The St Helena home vote, added to those treacherous votes from Ascension, the Falklands and the RMS, amount to 71 percent in favour of the Airport against a trivial 28.4 percent in favour of a new ship. What is not so loudly advertised is that St Helena itself barely came to the polls at all – accounting for just 1 500 votes in a thriving community of nearly 5 500 people.

Next day on the street, no one talks about it much. Age-old apathy still clings to this island nation. What will be, will be. "It won't happen," says Stedson, "not in my lifetime." "Nor mine," says much younger Donny. The first airport surveys took place way back in the 1940s; and we could have had an airport in the '60s, I learn, when the South African government offered to build one at their own expense as a refuelling stop for long-haul flights; but either the island or the British government (no one can quite remember) declined the offer, so they built in the Cape Verde Islands instead. In the '80s, talk about an airport raised its head yet again, but nothing materialised then either. Why should this time be different? Soon there's much less talk of airports. Far more important are the rituals of ordinary island life: the all-important arrivals of the RMS with goods, between them the endless treasure-hunt of shopping, and simply dealing with the sultry heat of February that shrouds us like a soaked velvet blanket between the stifling walls of Jamestown.

Today the town is humming. It's not only Shrove Tuesday in this Anglican community, but Careers Fair Day. The dilapidated old Customs tent has been hauled out of storage where it has reposed since the hideous new shed took its place, and its remains tugged westwards towards Donny's on the Wharf where it is now filled with kiosks and displays. The fair has even overflowed into the hitherto ignored Leisure Centre across the moat, a recent development dubbed 'the White Elephant' for its ugly bus shelter look-alikes dotting a cramped area of strip lawns, and a tennis court whose tight boundaries forestall any ball service from one end. And though this is the first time the park has ever been used, it's buzzing.

The shirt-sleeved Governor Hill is wandering about engaging the stallholders in chatter, and media are swarming all over the place – cameras clicking, microphones at the ready – feasting on the activity. I scoot around the offerings for a while, admiring nursing displays, dental mouldings, primary school essays, and the wondrous attractions of working for the government. And when I have seeped in all that is on offer – though I am not at all in search of career ideas – I wander off to keep Deirdre company at the New Museum for a few hours. The building's finally completed metamorphosis is on public show today to anyone who might be interested, and even though we are not anticipating a stampede, the building is beautiful enough to be admired. With mere details left to complete before the fifty museum showcases the Heritage Society cannot yet afford are shipped out from Cardiff (I am by now a member of that august society), the shell of the old Powerhouse is no longer filled with dust and planks as it was just a few months ago. Instead, it rises as a splendid and gracious space in which to accommodate objects of St Helena's exceptional history, with all the dignified aura of age and maturity behind the extraordinary job that Tommy Dunne has pulled off. Also, not only is a corner of the ground floor already partitioned off with large-paned windows to designate what will eventually be the Curator's office and a museum shop, but from one side of the main hall an exquisite double staircase in varnished wood rises gracefully to the second-storey gallery. Superb museum space though it might turn out to be, it is, to my eyes, a God-given auditorium, with the added gift of fantastic acoustics which cry out to be heard.

An embryonic idea regarding an interim use for this gorgeous place has just begun sprouting in my mind as I sit there chatting to Deirdre, when a stranger wanders through the front door. Noting an unfamiliar face, Deirdre's curiosity is immediately aroused, and in the time-honoured way of St Helena, she promptly extracts answers to the three questions spontaneously demanded of new visitors: *Who are you? What are you doing here? How long are you staying?* These are not unfriendly queries, merely a need to place the new arrival into a pigeon-hole where he might be recognised for his role on the island; and this newcomer is happy to explain that he has been sent to us by DfID, as The Airport Planner.

I regard this information with contained wryness for at least a second, speedily calculating the recent movements of the RMS before succumbing to utter compulsion: "The Airport Planner! So please tell me, what exactly would you have planned had we by chance voted *against* an airport while you were already steaming here on the ship from Cape Town?"

He has the grace to look abashed at London's perspicacity. "Well, I am a general planner, not just for airports," he offers lamely. "I would have found something else to plan." Yeah, right. Yet he knows enough about airports to be certain we will have ours within the next six years. *2008?* From where we sit now, that is already four years later than our Governor's confident 2004 expectations on that inauguration voyage he and I shared two and a half years ago.

In the notable absence of locals interested in the new museum, the next visitor is also a stranger, one who prowls quietly around the empty building, inspecting details with close concentration, paying scant attention to either Deirdre or me as we share takeaway French fries from Cyril's Fast Food. Only on his way out does he open his mouth for the first time – and I immediately see fit to leap into it. His American accent is the giveaway. "I know who you are!" I exclaim without preliminaries. "You're the Anguilla Man! The person who is bringing £34 million a year to St Helena every year for ten years!"

Beside me Deirdre sways slightly with the shock of my pronouncement. His scheme has not yet hit the local headlines, though I've heard all about it from Chris in Cape Town who met him at a party there; and the implications of such enormous wealth for St Helena are astounding.

I sit him down and offer him the remains of our lunch on which he happily munches while I tremble in anticipation of details from the horse's mouth. Barely able to contain myself from asking the vital question that has plagued me since Chris's first hints of this windfall, I listen to his lengthy explanations of how the scheme will work. Illuminated with get-rich-quick slickness, it involves large shipments of cars *en route* from Japan or Korea to Europe, which, about once a month for the next ten years, will pause offshore while passing St Helena – and thereby we will make our fortune. Apparently all it requires is a local agent to meet with the passing ship, receive revenue for the cargo on behalf of the St Helena government – duty that would otherwise be paid in some other EU port – and enormous wealth will be our reward. It barely makes sense.

"Why *us*?" croaks Deirdre, still in shock.

"Why not you?" he drawls. He is a thin and pallid man, studiously self-effacing. "Three years ago the EU wrote into its constitution that St Helena and other such dependencies are entitled to the same living conditions as enjoyed by its mother country. You could use the money here. Your Governor is keen on this scheme, by the way, and the Foreign & Commonwealth Office approves, and the EU is also happy with it. Also, your Attorney General has known about this scheme for the past three years." *But does our true-blue Attorney General approve?* I wonder. Notoriously wary of any easy money-making scheme, I feel confidence and approvals trip too lightly off this man's tongue, while the worm of doubt wriggling in my stomach grows ever larger as he speaks.

"I don't see how it can be legal," I announce at last, inevitably the party pooper. I assume, privately: *these people will be smuggling drugs...*

"It's completely legal," he promises. "And I'll tell you something else: transhipment is almost in the bag. The whole thing could be up and running in two months' time, as soon as April this year." Nothing gets going that fast in St Helena, I remind myself.

"How do you fit into the picture? What company do you work for?" Deirdre asks.

He drops his eyes, smiling enigmatically. "Me? You know, I'm not really a businessman. I was invited only to set this thing up. I live in Anguilla in the Caribbean, and my real interests are history and the environment – that's why I came in here this morning to look around your lovely new museum building. And I collect postcards as a hobby. History, environment and postcards, that's me." He hastily looks at his watch, "Well, ladies, I have a meeting to attend. Good talking t'ya."

The Anguilla Man is just about to leave the island when I next bump into him, nearly a month later. "So, have you enjoyed your stay?" I inquire. "Have you seen much of the island?"

"Y'know what," he drawls, "I've just been in Jamestown the whole time. Aw, I did get into the country for meetings on two occasions but it was dark both times." So – the lover of history and the environment has made no effort in four weeks to savour the wealth of ages, the stunning beauty of this diverse island, or any of its environmental interests. I wonder if he has collected many postcards here.

What he really collects – I have already heard along the ubiquitous grapevine – is aliases. Oh, and also child brides from Asia. Tales of his two Caribbean-based henchmen, co-directors of the transhipment company that was, in truth, set up as recently as mid-February while the Anguilla Man was already here, sound just as shady, and are run through with drugs, death, intrigue and many people in high places. (But then, we should not, I remind myself, believe everything we hear in St Helena.) Nonetheless, to our stupefaction, the deal here seems to be steaming ahead. The *St Helena Herald*, once the story breaks, takes a commendably cynical viewpoint, notwithstanding that newspaper's ties to the local government, while people in the street call the scheme "that pirating thing". Yet our own Governor – surely learning at least some of that which I have heard, but who is perhaps befuddled by dollar signs – has lately been busy recommending the proposal to the FCO (whom the Anguilla Man, back in February, claimed had already approved it). By August his new company's St Helenian agents are appointed and feted in Anguilla. By October the whole thing has *"gone through, all bar dotting the i's"*. And then comes silence. No more is said about transhipment. The Anguilla Man is strangely forgotten, and no car-carrying vessels from Korea or Japan bob around our ocean. If it was all so above board, it's a pity we never signed the deal...

After the Anguilla Man hastens off to his meeting from that casual browse around the museum building on Careers Day, and before I rush off to coax Virginia into frying fabulous pancakes for Shrove Tuesday afternoon festivities in Main Street, I broach my new idea to Deirdre. "This building is crying out to be heard," I suggest. "What if we raise some more money for it by organising a Music & Poetry Evening here before the display-cases arrive? I see a sort of semi-circular theatre, a soiree-type event, to give an easy but elegant atmosphere to proceedings. The ideal spot for performers would be against the wall opposite the staircase, so that latecomers can sit on the steps if they like, or watch from the upper gallery."

"And?"

"We'd serve sparkling wine at interval and really delicious cocktail snacks. And the programme would be a mix of songs and instrumental music, all kinds of poetry, something for everyone. It would at least attract people into this building who would never otherwise bother to come here. Then, when they've seen it, maybe they'll be keen enough to support it."

"Good idea," said Deirdre getting to work on the instant. "I'll make a list of musicians and guests, you handle poetry readers and organise invitations, and we'll do this before Alison Forbes leaves on the RMS." Alison, a talented pianist and vital to proceedings, is due for expat leave in five weeks' time, which allows us just four weeks to production. "In the meantime, go and find the dentist and ask for his input."

I find the dentist, our lead violinist, still in the Careers tent, explaining his dental mouldings to an interviewer from Radio St Helena. When I get my turn to speak with him he is full of enthusiasm for the concert, and reels off a list of suggestions and dates for musicians' practices. I rush back to Deirdre with the good news, pick up my car keys and, running proposed invitation wording through my head as I drive, dash up to the country to fetch Virginia from the Secondary School where she's currently a voluntary classroom assistant. At home the frying pan awaits her.

Miss O'Connor's Pancake Recipe is one of the finest gems that Virginia extracted from twelve years of expensive schooling. Not to say that the rest of her education was inadequate, but merely that her Grade 3 teacher's personal recipe for pancakes is the best in the world, which now, on Shrove Tuesday, proves to be an extremely useful bit of tutelage. Virginia learned the art well. Shoving eggs and flour at her to keep up impetus, and with one eye on the clock – since these offerings are to be delivered to Father Fred's Vicarage in Jamestown within the hour – I flounder about trying to help as best I can, though pancake-making is out of my orbit. Meanwhile, her artistry grows into mountains of sweet-scented, butter-yellow discs of enticing delicacy, with Virginia, whose omniscient vision is legendary, periodically exclaiming: "No, Mum, you're not allowed to steal!" even though her back is fully turned to me.

Everyone is in town when we get there, and as I wander past the Pancake Race organisers, a yellow flag is thrust at me. "You're Number 5 Marshal," Ann Sim commands. "You go down near the bottom of the Stand, where the runners turn to come back up the next side of the street, and you don' let nobody pass who drop their pancake, see!" I obey Ann, as one does, and take up position as the last marshal on the downward run, giggling at the antics of the racers as I stand in the cool early evening shadow of tall Association Hall. Jamestown at this time of evening is at its finest, the old buildings kissed with a delicate blush, high cliffs behind them painted orange in the lowering sun. Mynah birds roosting in the trees of Castle Gardens alongside the Courthouse are already home for the night, their screaming raucousness drowning out all other city sound, even the cheers and laughter of the Main Street spectators. Beyond the Parade, through the Arch, the sea glitters prettily while the sky shows every promise of a spectacular sunset.

With the first-ever Careers Fair such a success in the Leisure Park, a party feel still lingers in the town; so there is no shortage of participants for races. The youngest children run first, in shortened bursts, with small pans, faces creased in concentration. Then come the agile, competitive to the death, tossing madly as they go. But the truly side-splitting company is the over-sixties, all friends of mine including the Bishop in purple shirt and dog collar, pectoral cross flying out as he gallops, and lithe Tommy Dunne with sexy legs stretched fully in khaki shorts, who hurtle past tossing extra-thick hunks of half-cooked dough, clumsily colliding with one another on the way. The public is screeching with laughter, while tourists gathered on the steps of the Consulate Hotel and the Wellington Guesthouse and joining the hilarity, will write home about this comedy. All of which gives birth to a thirst that can only be assuaged at Donny's afterwards, in a rowdy celebration that sees us through the rest of the evening. The party finally breaks up when the Bishop suddenly remembers that he has mislaid the Ashes for tomorrow's Ash Wednesday services, and must immediately start a search.

That night I dream of car-carriers queuing up in James Bay to buy pancakes. But each one is paid for with a song or a poem, and just before I awake I distinctly see our Customs Chief walking up Main Street with a massive wad of money in his arms and a happy smile on his face.

"It will be alright on the night," Father Joe assures me. Father Joe is St Helena's sole Roman Catholic priest, a wise and erudite man with a sharp eye, analytical mind, true heart, and an Irish sense of humour. We sit together drinking tea in the cosy vicarage of the Church of the Sacred Heart in Upper Market Street, that boasts just about the same dimensions as his meagre local flock. Predominantly an Anglican island with eleven Anglican churches under the Lord Bishop's care, but also giving ground to Seventh Day Adventists, New Apostolics, Jehovah's Witnesses and B'hai, the Roman Catholics are mostly expatriate, and thin on the ground at that. "They always say that the worse the rehearsal, the better the performance."

I gaze back at him bleakly. The Music & Poetry evening is mere days away, and after weeks of tactful cajoling I have barely managed to eke from key performers any idea of what poetry they're willing to read. From the Assistant Attorney General, a talented actor on whom much emphasis relies, I have just received eighteen faxed pages of Edward Lear which seem to head his inclination list. Cathy Hopkins, whose soprano voice is special, has offered to sing Glenn Miller's *Little Brown Jug*. Deirdre – in answer to my casual jest that if Cowper's *Diverting History of John Gilpin* were *much* shorter it might have made an amusing reading – had crisply informed me that "that sort of poem is far too deep for this crowd". God help us. What sort of moronic crowd, exactly, are we expecting? We have His Excellency and Mrs Hill and all the Executive Council on the invitation list, all the Legislative Councillors, heads of department, education principals, and an entire complement of contracted expatriate executives. Hardly any hoi-polloi – that is, those unfortunates not meriting St Helena's curious habit of attendance-by-invitation-only – will sully our hall. In any other society, occasions such as this might be advertised in the local press so that anyone may attend, contingent upon their willingness to pay the requested entrance fee. But here, to nearly every event, invitations are issued – entrée to upper echelon society, I suppose, and I am flattered to be included in many of these – yet I would have thought it better that Mrs Joe Soap (who hasn't made The List but *really* would like to attend) could book herself a place and bring three friends for company if she wanted to.

Nonetheless, to this end I have obediently drawn up and printed attractive invitations to the 130 guests Deirdre and I felt we could accommodate in the museum building. Then, with some help, the envelopes were addressed and each one delivered by hand, purposefully bypassing the perfectly efficient local postal service in lieu of paying for stamps. This is the local way, and all mail but bills arrives like this.

"I'll happily read Yeats for you, especially as it's the night before St Patrick's Day," says Father Joe with a twinkle in his eye, "and I'll pick a couple of poems that strike a fair balance between Lear and absolute ridicule." I laugh, releasing a moderate cascade of pre-performance nerves. "And Susan O'Bey will, I know, also read something intelligent. Your Robert Frost suggestion will probably appeal to both her and the audience. Go and see her."

And so I do, with some welcome meeting of minds on the subject. It is not that I had planned an evening of dry academia. On the contrary, in my hopeful mind was a melange of great variety, a thoroughly mixed bag. And I already know that within our substantial audience, there are guests who would enjoy a little Mozart just as much as a jig on a fiddle. It is striking that happy medium that is taxing.

The evening before the event it is all-systems-go. When I arrive at the museum, Tommy is already rushing about, fussing over details for the official launch of his beautiful baby. The remodelled building still smells invitingly of new wood and varnish, exuding an air of dignified anticipation, its welcoming atmosphere reaching out to a whole new crowd of potential visitors. Already there is music too, as the dentist, in a far corner, is offering up his violin to the amazing new acoustics. Gay – herself a proficient musician – is trying out the worn old piano that has been hauled in.

But the piano is in the wrong place, stationed somewhat unsociably at the furthest end of the auditorium. I approach Deirdre gingerly, who, with an expatriate Helper, is already setting up chairs in stiff narrow rows facing the fire escape. "I think the piano's meant to be opposite the staircase," I remind Deirdre. "And the seating is supposed to form a semi-circle around the musicians."

"It's not done that way in St Helena," Deirdre snaps tartly. She is wearing her hair in a knot again. "It's against our culture."

I carefully engineer a voice of reason. "This is a different sort of event from the usual. The whole atmosphere depends on being a little bit soirée-like, relaxed but elegant. And in a semi-circle over here, people from all corners of the room can have an equal view. I suggested that right from the start when I dreamed up this whole thing." I boldly seize up a group of three or four stacking chairs and demonstrate what I originally planned. "You see, it's more informal like this."

"The people won't like that!" snaps the Helper, in a distinctly you're-still-a-newcomer voice as she snatches away my chairs and faces them once more to the distant limits of the hall.

"We're going to do this the proper way," Deirdre adds. "Performers are at the far end, people sitting in straight rows."

I swallow, choosing words carefully. "Another query: if the readers' lectern is under the gallery, won't they need light to see by?"

"I'll bring a lamp tomorrow," retorts the Helper. "Everything is under control. I don't think there's anything more for you to do here."

I don't think so either. So, being a Friday evening, I go in search of my good friends at Donny's. "You look as though you need a strong drink," remarks Stedson's wife, Joyce, as I sit down.

"Probably a double whisky," suggests the Bishop.

"Mostly likely quite a few," I say. I am irked by Helper's dismissive attitude when she had nothing to do with original plans and is not even a member of the Heritage Society. Also, I am disappointed that what I visualised in this spectacular auditorium has been completely turned on its head.

Nonetheless, the next evening I am back at the museum for the performance. My stomach is clenched with nerves, and I am no longer sure what to expect of the evening. Even the sparkling wine I ordered for Interval – the driest of a nauseatingly sweet selection carried in the grocer shops – has been criticised by Deirdre, so there might well be no solace for the poor audience even then.

Father Joe, at least, is brimming with optimism. "Just feel the buzz," he says conspiratorially, pushing through the arriving crowd with Yeats tucked under his arm. "This is going to go well. People are excited, and they're thrilled to see this beautiful building renovated and put to fine use. I told you it would be alright on the night!"

And it is. Punctuated by a happy Interval of sparkling wine contentedly imbibed by all, and savouries served by Virginia and two pretty friends (one of whom later applauds the evening in an enchanting review for the *St Helena Herald*), the performers do us proud. Everything from Mozart to popular music is wrought by an ensemble consisting of piano, five violins and two recorders. There are piano duets, violin duets, and floor-stomping St Helenian jigs played on the fiddle by an islander who cannot read a note of music. Cathy, thankfully spurning the *Little Brown Jug*, has gone fishing instead, treating us to Schubert's *The Trout* in dulcet tones, while a bit of Michael Flanders gets the audience loudly participating in the chorus of his *Hippopotamus Song*. In between, Robert Frost gets an airing, as does Edward Lear, Father Joe does great justice to Yeats, and Nurse Tutor Vivienne reads some extraordinary and moving poems written by her own mother. Hilarious anecdotes of island life in the old days are unwrapped from cotton-wool by Greta the Sheriff, but the roof nearly caves in under laughter when, in the strongest of St Helenian country accents, an old island ballad is sung. All tastes have been served after all.

It is just a pity, I think when it's all over – amazed that Deirdre and I have pulled this off in less than a month – that the people at the back of the auditorium saw nothing from their regimented rows, while even the front seats faced a large green notice on the fire escape, backdrop to the musicians, exhorting them to LIFT BAR TO OPEN THE DOOR. And the readers read by a faint glow from the most hideous lamp on earth, duly furnished by the Helper-who-knows-how-things-are-done-here.

7.

This is the way, walk ye in it

February to May 2002

The outstanding success of the *Music & Poetry Evening* is still reverberating around the island, when I am gripped with regrets over my involvement with the Heritage Society. I voice them to Bish (so nicknamed now, within the family, to differentiate him from the four other Johns in the Saturday Hallams circle), and he smiles with cruel smugness: "Didn't I tell you so?"

I concede that he did. In fact he repeatedly warned me against joining that group in the first place, and I should have listened. For one thing, I have quickly learned how little history is discussed among them (except, to my horror, to suggest that the Napoleonic legacy here is superfluous), for the society is obsessed with the Museum Project – a current concern given the imminence of Q5 Day, of course – but one might have hoped for a passing mention, perhaps, of preservation of built heritage or historic things related. Also, around that long Courtroom table where their meetings are held, sit bounteous Chiefs and few Indians. Power games rule the day and I'm bothered by this, even though I've been a zealous Indian myself, feverishly writing – at the Chairman's own request – begging letters to worldwide charities when the museum suddenly ran out of enough money to pay for the museum's fifty custom-built showcases already awaiting export from Cardiff docks. That was my first mistake. "Resign," advises Bish.

"I can't. Not yet."

"Why on earth are you still involved with the museum when you're so unhappy with the Heritage Society?"

"Because before all their incredible viciousness started, and before members crossed the street to avoid me as I walked through town, I promised to help set up their museum shop in time for Q5," I shrug. "And Chris and I are too damned proud to break our word. I'm not going to make a scene; my dignity is all I've got left."

"They'll come back to bite you," he warns gloomily, "even though these people call themselves Saints."

Saints: a moniker to be used sparingly by strangers, but preferably only among friends. Thankfully I've not yet been brazen enough to cross this line before I bump into Greta the Sheriff in Jamestown. She's a whirling dervish of indignation, spitting metaphorical tacks as she exits a meeting conducted by a visiting DfID Expert. "He *really* irritated me!" she exclaims. "He's never visited before, and hasn't been on the island five minutes before he's calling us *Saints* – and in a public meeting too, never once referring to us as *St Helenians. Saints* is our own local nickname, not meant to be bandied about by outsiders!"

In fact, the beginnings of *Saint*hood are blurry, since early visitors to St Helena were infrequent, given the long months at sea to and from the East Indies. As a general rule, outward-bound sailing vessels from Europe preferred the trade winds that carried them almost to Brazil, before turning eastward towards the Cape of Good Hope and then to the Indies; but, on the homeward leg, ships would exploit the Cape's southeast trades and the strong Benguela Current that brought them to St Helena. Because of such time-lapses, reliable reports on this newfound island were spasmodic and, with vast gaps to fill, St Helena's early days are punctuated by intriguing question marks and contradictions.

It is the fogs surrounding first human habitation here that swirl thickest. And with the exception of the legendary hermit Fernão Lopes's thirty lonely years on St Helena, and a Portuguese Franciscan friar who remained for fourteen years and was buried here when a ship timeously arrived to dispose of his corpse, it is reasonably certain that few other early Portuguese, French, Dutch or English actually chose to live here. However, in the Records we are served an annoyingly cryptic message that *"before 1557"* two black men from Mozambique, a Javanese man, and two women slaves swam ashore from a ship and hid themselves in the woods until their vessel had sailed. *"They soon multiplied to twenty"* apparently, and this is truly intriguing because, just two decades later, in 1578 when the island should have abounded with Mozambican and Javanese teenagers, Philippo Pigafetta mentions only that near the chapel was one small cottage *"wherein, for the most part, some Portuguese do remain, sometimes three, sometimes two, yea, and sometimes but one alone..."* He makes no mention of other residents anywhere on the island. And in fact we are told by William Barret, who made notes for the famous chronicler Richard Hakluyt on a visit around 1580, that by Order of the King of Portugal no more than two people, namely *"Cremites"*, were permitted to inhabit the island – the better to conserve fruit and vegetables for victualing ships, as well as to help sick sailors to recovery. *Cremites?* Friars, perhaps? I fail dismally to trace further references to these Samaritans.

So there we are, 1580 and still in square one. No population to speak of except for the two unexplained Cremites, and absolutely no hint of that supposed new generation of teens. Various sailors still called, Francis Drake purportedly among them in 1580, on the homeward leg of his circumnavigation of the world, followed by three illustrious Japanese Ambassadors on their way to visit the Pope, and the destructive pirate Cavendish who smashed up the Portuguese chapel in 1588. A year later, the wonderful chronicler, Jan Huygen van Linschoten, drew what are possibly the earliest sketches of the island; and then we learn that his fleet, departing St Helena in May 1589, left behind fifteen sick men *"and some slaves who, escaping from the ship, had swum ashore"*. Given the obfuscation of so many historical Records, we never ever find out what became of these swimmers. Did they escape on a friendlier ship? Or did they, like their mysterious forerunners, stay and multiply? Perhaps, possibly, they *were* the mysterious Mozambican-Javanese party, simply arriving later?

From 1659, Records take a considerable turn for the better after Captain John Dutton of the English East India Company (EEIC) arrived with a small garrison and forty chosen settlers to take possession of St Helena and build a fort and settlement here. With the Cape of Good Hope newly settled by Jan van Riebeeck under the Dutch East India Company flag in 1652, the English saw their chances of a prosperous way station slipping past. And at that point, with Portugal's diminished interest in St Helena and Holland's focus on the Cape, this little island developed enormous strategic value for England.

John Dutton and his wife, a Dutchwoman from Batavia (today's

Djakarta) in the East Indies, set sail with their fleet early in February that year – accompanied by a man-o'-war with thirty-six guns and 150 men under orders to *"convey home"* any returning ships that might be found at St Helena. This order essentially staked England's claim to this island, even though English ships had already been under orders to supply roots and trees to St Helena for some time past, in preparation of settlement. Then in June that year, the ship *Truro* was commissioned to touch at St Iago in the Cape Verde Islands, *en route* to Madras, to collect further provisions for St Helena. These turned out to be plantain roots, large yams, potatoes, *"cassandra sticks, bonavist, pease, gravances, and beanes of all sorts"*, as well as oranges and lemons which, according to early visitors, were already thriving as *"wild woods"* in St Helena. But added to the list of those luscious provisions from St Iago, are: *"Five or six blacks or negroes, able men and women, we desire you to buy them, provided they may be had at or under 40 dollars per poll…"*

Whether those *negroes* were actually bought on that voyage is not precisely known. But within six years the marvellous resident Henry Gargen offers a detailed census of inhabitants, complete with English wives and children – though the times being what they were, the Blacks were not graced with names in the list. Nonetheless, thanks to his efforts we know that resident on St Helena around 1665 were thirty men and two boys, thirteen women and ten children, making a grand total of fifty-three English men, women, and children – among whom Young and Greentree are surnames that still survive on the island today. *"Of ye Blackes"*, he tells us, there were seventeen men and four women, numbering twenty-one altogether. Gargen also informs us that approximately six people had died between 1661 and 1665, and that about five "ran away" – quite a feat in this desolate ocean. In 1664 *"two women gone home and I hope they home"*, he announces, lending an impression that either he feared for their safety or was decidedly relieved to be rid of them. In 1667, a year after the Great Fire of London, the *Charles* was sent out with around thirty new settlers made homeless by the blaze. Yet, instead of swelling the numbers, they merely replaced twenty-five former settlers who, as Gargen informs us, had returned to England, or moved on to Bantam in Java with Captain Dutton four years previously – Gargen's own wife and child among them, evidently caring little for the rusticity and remoteness of life in the South Atlantic.

But it was the increasing importation of slaves that eventually changed the demographics of the island, as new blood arrived from the East Indies, India, Madagascar and the Maldives, and, during the Abolition of Slavery, indirectly from West Africa. In the early 1800s indentured Chinese labourers were imported for quarry work, but though accorded only a number instead of a name, these hard-working people were not officially slaves. Nevertheless, neither they nor the multinational slaves, nor the English soldiers garrisoned in St Helena until 1906, seem to have resisted spawning children of mixed heritage during their tenure, and features of those ancestries are still recognisable in many St Helenians to this day – the Chinese descent most easily discernible in the Sandy Bay region.

With such an eclectic history – some of it troubled by unspeakable cruelty – it is surprising that the mixed race now known as St Helenians have become world-famous for charm and friendliness. And on any day that I might now feel apprehensive of broaching the public, my mood is soon cheered by a friendly wave as I drive downtown, then another, so that by the time I have parked my car I am calm and smiling. Not all are so blessed with charm, obviously, for I have recently experienced the worst of the Heritage Society's shocking and inexplicable vengefulness after registering some success in my fundraising efforts, and those wounds are raw and stinging. But friendly greetings go a long way to soothe hurt and anger.

The museum shop, with its Dickensian window divider and wooden shelves straddling the door into the Curator's office, holds every promise of charm in the museum. But it needs stock to sell – and I have excellent contacts. Enlisting, as our runner, a super-efficient friend in Cape Town, I some time ago (before the society's appalling unpleasantness) designed T-shirts for which she's already supplied sepia-print St Helena postcard pictures and scouted the Cape for quality T-shirt-makers. In addition she's organised a logo for golf shirts, and the printing of tablemats and mugs. On the island, meanwhile, I had designed certain knick-knacks for the shop and a variety of labels for jam jars ultimately to be filled with mango jam and other local delights. And ultimately it falls to Christopher himself to settle the South African bills on behalf of the museum, to assemble the hundreds of T-shirts, jars, labels, mugs and tablemats from all over Cape Town and pack them, and then to tote them freight-free to the island under his own name to save the museum further expenses. With him now back on the island for the approaching festivities, the stock has already been priced during boisterous family sessions at our huge yellow dining room table; and though Richard has had to return to Cape Town after short school holidays, Virginia is still here, and we've all had our sleeves rolled up. T-shirts have been grouped in size and design, stacked in slippery piles of plastic sleeves which cascade across the floor when we pass. Dozens of printed tablemats are prettily tied with raffia and adorn the piano. Sticky labels are fixed to rows of jars of homemade mango jam from Villa Le Breton's own trees, and china mugs have been checked for chips and cracks, and carefully repacked. Then all this is hefted to the museum by Chris.

And now Deirdre and I must go in search of furniture for the shop.

Shelves are all in place, completed to Tommy Dunne's perfection, and a high rack over the door into the Curator's office already flaunts an effective row of antique bottles dug up around the island through the years. But what the room still needs is a large table for displays. An antique table, and possibly a sideboard, we decide. Deirdre knows where to look.

Behind and below the handsome Georgian facades of Jamestown lie mazes of unseen buildings, courtyards, and basement warrens. And it is into one of the latter that we now descend from rough street steps, ducking under a low doorway. A key manifests itself and we let ourselves into a dank, cobwebby room with minimal light from the pavement above. *Did slaves live here,* I wonder? The air is thick with damp and dust and the evocative smell of forgotten furniture.

When my eyes grow used to the dimness, I see a treasure trove of old picture frames, spinning wheels, mottled mirrors, broken chairs and tables, stacked against walls and in piles on the floor – *who used these?* And almost immediately we spot a large carved sideboard and a good-sized drum table, perfect for the museum. Protected by inches of dust and cobwebs, they require only a good cleaning to shine them up, and all that is needed now is transport to haul them over to the shop. Deirdre and I go in search of Tommy's truck. We will, of course, find him at the museum.

We cross the Parade together, towards the foot of the Ladder, and walk down the short alley to the open museum door. I enter the building just a few steps behind Deirdre and, somehow anticipating gentle Tommy's reply, I spontaneously call out *hallo*. And indeed I am answered by an instant rasping of chairs on the upstairs floor, a rush of feet across wooden boards, and a row of intimidating faces promptly materialises over the gallery railing. Clearly, I realise too late, half the Heritage Society is busy here. I recognise the voice that sharply demands: "What are *you* doing here, Lindsay? What do you want?"

And before I can catch my breath, up speaks Deirdre: "It's okay. She's with me."

In the milliseconds that follow, a thousand emotions fast-frame through my head, coloured by the notion that in St Helena one is supposed to keep a sense of humour at all costs. But the entertainment value of the Heritage Society has finally outrun its scant worth. I cease smiling and, in one swift movement, turn on my heel and go home. The cleaning of the beautiful carved sideboard, the shining of the table, the setting out of all those goods still tied up in Christopher's organised parcels and stacked in the corner, will happen without me.

"Please tell me," I ask Bish, whom I find enjoying midday wine with Chris on the veranda, "*why* are they like this?"

"Well, dear," he pronounces sombrely, "you're not only an expat, but a willing Indian who speedily raised £30 000 for them when they urgently needed money to pay for their showcases. Now you are bitterly resented. Resentment of anyone's success, I'm afraid, is a sad St Helenian trait. I warned you a long time ago not to join the Heritage Society."

A mynah bird suddenly screams in irritation from the roof, a long drawn-out shriek resonant with frustration and epithets. I want to do the same and let out my rage at this small-minded group of power-hungry individuals. But Bish is right, of course, and to him I have no response. He did warn me.

The Quincentenary celebrations begin at midnight with a Eucharist at St James', and at twelve o'clock its church bell joyously heralds arrival of the great event, heard even above the lusty singing of a packed congregation. We are, of course, singing not only in celebration of the discovery of this island five hundred years ago, and in praise of the Christian saint after whom it was named, but also in thanks for the end of an arduous campaign to have British citizenship restored to St Helenians. Back in the early 1980s, with the end of Hong Kong's British sovereignty looming and the British government of the time taking fright at the spectre of an England swamped by Chinese refugees, one way to avert this catastrophe was the removal of British citizenship from nearly all Britain's fourteen Crown Colonies. To the outrage of tiny St Helena, this naturally included its own paltry 5 500 people who, in their entirety, would barely fill an average English village cricket stand. And while Britain's action spurred many other colonies to seek independence, impecunious St Helena – promptly renamed a British Dependent Territory – began its long campaign to have right-of-abode in Britain restored to them. And finally the harassing has paid off. The British government's 500th birthday present to St Helena, by now proclaimed a British Overseas Territory in an apparent orgy of status-changing over the past twenty years, is restored British citizenship. A gift of true celebration.

Across the Parade, a podium of wooden planks has been erected directly in front of the Courthouse, from which ceremonies will be conducted in the morning. And even at this hour, as we drift from the church, the capable JJ and a few straggling helpers are putting final touches to massive foliage festoons that adorn its unvarnished timber. Apart from their shadowy forms and the exiting congregation, it seems the rest of the island has gone to bed, and I am longing for mine; but both the Bishop and his overnight guest at Bishopsholme – a chaplain off the visiting RFA *Grey Wolf* – are clearly still wide awake. *Whisky* is written all over them. "Coming up to the house for a nightcap?" Chris asks, visually pressed for the invitation.

At 3am they finally rise to go home. Virginia has long since retired to bed upstairs, and Christopher has periodically dozed in his chair, as is his habit beyond a certain hour, notwithstanding the garrulous humour of the two churchmen ensconced on our veranda. But now seriously tired, my mind's eye is inflexibly lodged with cellophane-wrapped raffia-tied boxes of fudge moving sluggishly along a mental conveyor belt, and it's all I can see. Fudge is the very last of our promises-to-be-kept for the galling museum shop, and as our kitchen is already stacked with expensive ingredients bought weeks ago, this last obligation is one that Virginia dutifully elects to keep – her fudge as famous as her pancakes. "I have a favour to ask," I request Bish as the pair eventually heads for the gate. "You have a designated parking place at the Parade tomorrow morning, but the rest of us aren't allowed to take cars to town. Could you pick up the three of us and a ton of fudge on your way down?"

Bish *hurrumphs*, as is his way with favours asked. "I suppose so," he responds without discernible enthusiasm. But at nine-thirty tomorrow he and the chaplain will, I am reasonably certain, crunch to a halt on our gravel drive anyway.

And so it happens that on St Helena's Day – this long-awaited hard-planned Quincentenary celebration – Chris and I awaken at dawn to the sickly scent of cooking fudge pervading the furthest recesses of the house, and a daughter already mopping sweat from her brow. Down in the kitchen, vanilla-sweet blocks slide off her racks, pile after pile in their hundreds, as Chris and I pack and label and tie the bright little boxes with raffia. "I'll never make fudge again," grumbles Virginia. "I'll be ill if I smell this anymore!" But she finishes at last and at nine-thirty we load everything into the Bishop's car.

And this time the museum people are pleased to let us through the door, weighed down as we are with cartons of confectionary for their selling. But we do not stay to offer further assistance. We merely dump everything and leave other busy people to set them on the shelves. "Done!" I say to Chris with a sigh of relief as I finally turn my back on the whole Heritage Society and its unpleasant Museum Project, and head back towards the Grand Parade. "I've kept my word on everything all the way through this ghastly saga, but I am done with them now – chapter closed!"

"We're all done with them," Chris reminds me dryly, "because I definitely won't be ordering, or fetching, paying for, or shipping, so much as a label for them after this."

"And just remember, I'm never making fudge again," repeats Virginia. "For anyone!"

*

Under streamers of red-white-and-blue bunting strung throughout Jamestown, shining brass, and gleaming boots, familiarly resonant marches announce the stirring start of ceremonies at ten o'clock as the local uniformed bands advance down Main Street. Today they are also leading visiting contingents from the small RFA *Grey Wolf* anchored in the bay, smartly disciplined visiting French sailors capped with their quirky little pompoms, and even a small division of RAF Underwater Divers – *surely a contradiction in terms?* – who have spent some weeks diving the 1613 Dutch wreck *Witte Leeuw* and have brought up, among other artefacts, a perfect Ming meat platter which they will donate to the museum today.

By the time the festivities are launched with an ecumenical church service, chairs under the podium's shady bower are comfortably occupied by the suits and garden party hats of dignitaries; while before them the greater masses, offered neither seating nor shade on the open Parade, stand unsheltered in the tropical heat of this late May morning. Even the fulsome awning of the library's flame tree has been claimed by the uniformed bands, and there is no succour left for the public. But this is St Helena's finest hour, and so we show fortitude as the Bishop, be-cuffed in Elizabethan frills today, and garrulous in his moment, joyfully belabours the successes of restored citizenship for which his predecessors have long wielded the sword of battle.

The temperature rises, melting sun cream and sending rivulets of perspiration down our backs. Within the bower of the podium, even the hats slowly begin to wilt, and under her funereal black creation, light years removed from celebration, the Governor's lady looks weary and down-at-the-mouth. She would vastly prefer to be at home with her four thousand beloved books, her expression tells us. Then His Excellency takes his turn, cheery in his whites today though the hat's plumes barely flutter. From him we hear the news that a Royal visit is arranged for November, as part of this year of celebration. Unfortunately HRH the Princess Royal will be limited to a very short stay, he explains, but she is nonetheless delighted to be coming. And with that a ripple of restrained applause rattles across the square from a nation that, though obsessively British, is not overtly monarchist. On the podium, however, a frisson of greater excitement rustles the expatriate dignitaries, the people most likely to benefit from a royal visit.

The hands of the church clock progress upon their designated route, showing steady advancement towards eleven, long past eleven, closing on twelve noon when the museum – today's undoubted focus – will be officially opened. And eventually the podium speeches are over. As a body the crowd turns towards the museum alley, ready to move on – but no! In St Helena's inimitable fashion, awards must be presented at the least convenient time. Again we are constrained to watch the platform, and a hundred ribbons pinned for this or that, a hundred hands shaken, and a hundred lethargic ovations are wrung from jaded onlookers now beginning to steam under a fine drizzle. It is long past noon by the time we eventually move down the alley to the finally-completed New Museum for the next round of speeches. We have already been on our feet, in the sun, for nearly three hours.

Master of ceremonies here is the Heritage Chairman. Normally an articulate man, capable of eloquent English, this is not his shining hour. Today he is strangely committed to an expatiated history of fundraising for the New Museum – a sore point about which I'd personally prefer to hear as little as possible. Nonetheless, the entire gathering is treated to a penny by penny account of monies gained and lost along this rocky path, and how the Heritage Society tried to get more but were denied it, but then gained some after all… It seems, in the extreme heat of midday, that every stone of the building is about to be re-laid, every floorboard hammered into place all over again. His Excellency, trussed like a fowl in his too-tight ice cream suit, pushes the handsome feathers to the back of his head like a fireman's helmet, exposing a neon-red face, his lady in black emulating a death's head beside him. Somewhere 'twixt podium and this stifling alley into which nearly a quarter of the population is now compressed, the Bishop has shed his ruffles and is in a black suit over a purple short-sleeved shirt, but his bald head bears the overhead sun without mercy. He rolls his eyes our way as discomfort levels soar, and still the speech goes on. Contributors to this great edifice are now being thanked: Tommy for his building work; the young Canadian curator for setting up the museum displays so expertly; Deirdre for the amazing feat of singlehandedly organising all the stock for the Museum Shop which is now ready for business… And last but not least, thanks to those whose unstinting dedication to fundraising has provided the money needed to bring the whole project to fruition: the government – and the wonderful Friends of St Helena Association in England. The Friends, five hundred of them, have raised a massive £90 000 over a period of just two years, we are told. What a feat! With grovelling thanks to their visiting Chairman we all applaud our appreciation loudly, but over our clapping hands Chris and Bish and I exchange knowing glances. In just three months I, completely unaided, had raised an extra £30 000 – a full third equivalent of the Friends' contribution. I listen, without flinching, for the mention that is not uttered, expecting nothing more than I hear. And that, in itself, is a sad indictment of those chiefs who have all so needlessly spilt blood.

After interminable ages, Heritage Chairman's monologue eventually gives way to a drawn-out peroration from the visiting Friends' Chairman, during which the Governor, perusing his own notes, frantically begins to edit his script by discarding whole pages of it. Gloria's smart black hat dips down to hide set features beneath it, and the Bishop, pink-faced in the heat, shifts restlessly from foot to foot. Dying of heat and boredom, Chris and I long to go, having heard more than enough already, but are trapped by the crowd behind and speakers ahead. At last Friends' Chairman lays aside his tedious readings for a solicitor from Bristol to follow with his own oration, but who this man is or why he is here at all no one in the crowd has the slightest idea. After all of that, a speech by the RAF Divers is a blessed relief. They at least have something interesting to offer – the blue-and-white Ming meat-platter, proudly shown off with some succinct descriptions of their underwater explorations around the *Witte Leeuw*. The Governor, by now swaying dangerously from the heat - discarded pages in one hand, relevant notes in the other – finally gets his chance, and we are obliged to hear him too. But by this time the Bishop is practically on points. "I promise this next will be the shortest part of the whole proceedings," he announces, and massive relief resonates through the crowd as he swiftly executes a blessing on the renovated building. The ceremonial ribbon is snipped, and a thousand people surge across the threshold into the coolness of the beautiful museum, faint and fanning themselves. It is already well after one o'clock and the newborn National Trust awaits us.

In the mid-afternoon Chris, Virginia and I trudge home on foot. Bish, on a cranky fuse by the time he'd discharged his multiple duties, expediently escaped in his car an hour ago, evaporating all hopes of a lift home for us while I was a captive judge at the Little Miss May Queen competition – a somewhat bizarre pageant of seven-year-olds dressed in make-up, heels, and evening gowns. This hasn't been the most festive of days after all, we agree as we limp up the shady footpath alongside the tiredly dribbling Run. It was the protracted speeches that drowned frivolity at birth. That, and the alarming scarcity of food and drink to be found. "But this is a holiday for *everyone*," we are curtly reminded when we ask why refreshments are so hard to come by – a response that also explains why promised shuttle buses aren't operating when we need them. We're exhausted, dehydrated, ravenous, foot-sore, and in pretty ill-humour. Virginia has gone suspiciously silent. Chris is threatening his death or some equivalent fairly soon. And the ankle I severely sprained yesterday in a tumble on Main Street, and on which I have relentlessly stood all day, is now polychromatic and screaming righteous indignation. Perhaps this evening will be more fun.

"I'm not going to town tonight," Christopher advises us defiantly as he collapses into a wicker chair on our veranda. "You can go on your own." But we want him to share the continuing magic of this special day; so we bring him water to cheer him up, about thirty gallons of it, and revival eventually sets in. By six o'clock, we are all in better humour, and even Chris is ready to watch the float procession after all. "But this time," he announces, "come hell or high water, we are taking our car into town." With time to spare before the procession starts, we can still get ahead of it to find convenient parking.

Virginia has already disappeared with friends, so Chris and I leave alone. But just metres from the house, as we reach the China Lane link between Ladder Hill Road and Market Street, we hit a dead stop. Traffic from the country is tightly backed up in single file all along the steeply curving descent of Ladder Hill pass, we notice; while below us, on the only artery to town, floats are already lumbering down Market Street. With a sinking heart, I watch the procession gathering momentum. "There's no point in us both missing the floats," I bleat to Chris who's behind the wheel. "If you stay with the car, I'll take the video camera and walk down with them." And before he can reply I abandon him.

Immediately in front of us the Governor's Rover is also stuck in the queue, and Gloria, alone in the rear seat, hails me as I pass. "What a *day*!" she exclaims. "I have just learned that the floats started half an hour earlier than announced, and they did not even tell the Governor! I see you're doeeng the same as Duncan – he is also walkeeng with the floats. But me, I am stayeeng right here, like Chrees!" Without a chauffeur, Chris does not have her options, but as I disappear around the corner I give him an encouraging wave and, with ankle screeching in protest, take off down the rough-paved mile through Jamestown. Past the tall post-war flats on the corner of China Lane, and the lovely walled garden and verandas of Palm Villa opposite. Past the low single-storey dwellings that stagger along Upper Market Street, many built in the 1700s when this road was known as the Southwark Side, and the buildings were townhouses for country gentlemen who opened stores when wealthy travellers called on their way home from India. With bountiful ships in the bay, those were days of booming commerce in Jamestown.

This night the street is lined with its residents seated on front steps for a ringside view, or leaning from windows, some leaping up to dance beside the floats as they slowly roll past. Given an historical theme, better suited to the Quincentenary than *Looking Up, Looking Forward,* I reflect, each district has chosen an event in the island's past and put their hearts into their work. With caravels, and slaves with jingling chains – and an inevitable aeroplane ridiculously in their midst! – the most captivating float of all is handsome pink Alarm House, star of the little Mutiny of 1783, now swarming with redcoats as it makes its stately way down Market Street. Even if details are dimmed by enshrouding dusk, the festive lights on floats are enough to brighten the proceedings. Music blares from every truck, their decibels squeezed upwards by the narrow street to echo back and forth against the cliffs, and the whole valley is filled with the sound of fiesta. Alongside the floats, participants in fancy dress jig and dance and sing, exhibiting an emancipation of spirit rare among St Helenians. This is carnival! This is actual *fun*!

I arrive at the Grand Parade in thickest darkness. But now I have perked up. The air has cooled down. My poor ankle, sorely tried today, is numb. The floats are fabulous, and this is one big party. Virginia is somewhere here with her friends – but now Chris is missing. With no mobile phone connections on the island, I have no idea if he even made it to town by car or whether, faced with nowhere to park, he's given up and gone home again. The whole population is at the seafront tonight – five and a half thousand people milling around the parked floats or taking up position on the Wharf for a good view of the RAF Diving team's next great contribution to our celebrations – fireworks! The night is pitch black, heavy as velvet, and the lights of the floats illuminate only their immediate space while I blindly search the pressing crowd for my husband without success. Even the coloured lights jauntily strung along the seafront do not cast enough radiance to make out facial features.

I wander about rather aimlessly, prowling around the stationary floats on the Parade, searching the Wharf again and again for his dark hair among a whole nation of dark heads; and suddenly I feel his familiar hand on my shoulder. "Ha! It's lucky we've been married such a long time," he offers ambiguously, "or I'd never have found you in this crowd…"

I am glad he made it in time. I would have hated him to miss the spectacular show. The RAF are doing the island proud tonight, culminating their friendly visit with twenty minutes of stunning continuous illuminations. Ignited not far from the Landing Steps at the far end of the Wharf, their reflections splinter across the bay as they zoom skywards against the black shadow of Munden's cliffs behind them. The noise is unspeakable, of course, like cannon crashing, thunder claps, the detonation of bombs above the roar of earthquakes. "I hope that tomorrow," I sombrely suggest to Chris, "the pitiful corpses of all the cliff-roosting fairy terns aren't strewn along the Wharf, dead from shock. That, or rockfalls."

But tomorrow there aren't. Luckily no small white corpses are anywhere to be seen. And, by special good fortune, considering our unstable cliffs, no rocks either. Tomorrow, instead, we have post-mortems; the most graphic from Bish who apparently opted to follow the procession from his comfortable armchair at home and was happy to relay the radio version to us. Radio St Helena had been working that night from their smart new mobile studio, with boss Tony Leo inside, and Ralph Peters and Paul George on its roof, all offering a running commentary of events:

Ralph: "And here comes a very nice float!"

Paul: "What is it?"

Ralph: "I don't know, but it has nice bright lights."

Tony (inside the windowless van): "I can't quite make out what it is."

Paul, with joyful exclamation: "Oh! I'll tell you what it is. It's a car turning on its headlights!"

And so goes the commentary, each float minutely discussed in this vein until the sobbing of a small child unexpectedly interrupts the professional proceedings. "This is Paul's child, a little upset," announces Ralph equably, and the two radio men then embark on a lengthy session of *koochee-koochees* that intersperse the commentary until the yelling stops. The infant, it turns out, is also on the roof of the Radio St Helena van.

Finally the procession winds down, and at last comes the *piece de resistance*: "My goodness!" one of them exclaims. "Look at *this* float! What a *superb* job they've done here!"

"Yes," agrees the other, "this must have taken *hours*! What *is* it?"

"Well, I think it's meant to be a fire engine. What does it look like to you?"

"It certainly *looks* like a fire engine."

A pause, as it passes by and sweeps towards the end of the Wharf where the fireworks are about to begin.

"Well, actually," they finally agree, "it *is* a fire engine."

Radio St Helena had clearly had a long – but perhaps not-so-thirsty – day.

8.

Worse than Kosovo

June 2002

Gloria Hill has never liked St Helena. It is not her fault really, just a bitter disappointment that her husband, for whom she had intended the post of British Ambassador to Rome, was awarded Governorship of St Helena instead. And she is not one to be trifled with.

She singled me out early on, marking me down as a friend, discovering in me someone with a passing knowledge of Western history which is not only her passion, but her late-in-life university degree. And I happily hike along with her across the safe ground of this subject whenever possible – listening mostly, because her expertise is miles beyond my league. But my greatest asset is neutrality. Unlike so many expatriate women in her domain, as a South African settler I am a safely independent entity without any of the political attachments to government that other wives carry. And, quite honestly despite her general unpopularity, I enjoy her company. A woman of spirit and of great intelligence, she hosts a pedigree whose particular blood has anointed her with patrician and sometimes intriguingly outmoded opinions that go right to the bones of any matter. However, her single greatest failing is that she does not vent them quietly. Gloria is certainly a character, effervescent and never boring, fulfilling her duties to the best of her temperament – sometimes with grace and marked aptitude, sometimes with roughshod boots. The thing is, St Helena is simply too small for her. London, Paris and Rome are her favoured territories, and the confines of such a tiny island are both constricting and humiliating. However, she busies herself with the four thousand books she brought for company, energetically dedicates herself to cleaning and cataloguing the old library and antiques at Plantation

House, and also, by appointment, gives informed historical tours of the residency. In between, she tirelessly battles the FCO for large bronze statues to be sent out for her hall: "Like the British Embassy has in Rome," she insists.

Her other failing she cannot help. She is not British. And I can relate to this deficiency at first hand, having 'made the grade' myself – as far as many British are concerned – only by marrying an Englishman. Gloria has done the same, but her history is worse. While I am at least a child of the Commonwealth (albeit usually forgotten), her background is utterly foreign, her accent marked, her temperament vibrant, and her inborn conservatism part and parcel of her own Latin-American heritage where, until lately, there was never a middle-class – only fair-skinned 'upper-crust' or dark-skinned 'peasants'. And this is all too strange for St Helena to swallow.

The mutual antipathy began early, at her first official Plantation House cocktail party. When someone stumbled and accidentally broke a small antique table, she made it clear around the island that St Helenians were not welcome at her abode again. However, soon learning that she could not execute her husband's official duties without entertaining certain of them – Councillors and heads of department, for instance – she now proceeds with a set jaw, a careful eye on liquor consumption, and ugly plastic mats on the antique tables that destroy the elegance of the occasion. "Because," she tells me, "the locals won't know how to use coasters." I mutter that I think they do, but this is water off a duck's back.

She likes her own way, with the merest tendency to sweep aside suggestions from anyone else – which is why she and I occasionally run head to head. And the most flamboyant of our collisions occurs on a full ship, island-bound, when she and I are both travelling without our spouses. Things start well, while the RMS is still tied up at Cape Town docks, with a small group of us in the Sun Lounge waiting to get going. The Bishop is there, also a young Hugh Grant look-alike on his second or third business trip to St Helena, the expatriate Chief of Police, Royce Hipgrave with his wife Denise, Gloria, and I. "I want *every*one to understand one theeng on thees sheep," the affable Gloria suddenly announces to our assembled party. "Seence I am travelling without Duncan, I weesh to be treated just like *every*one else. Theenk of me only as a tour guide on holiday." That's easy enough, since this particular assortment of friends is not prone to kowtowing. She rises to her feet, a good-looking woman with today's sparkling eyes and cheerful smile, shoulder-length hair swinging youthfully at her middle-aged shoulders, and pads over to the bar to order a round of drinks. But across the lounge her voice rings out like a clarion bell as she accosts the barman: "*I am the Governor's wife…*"

She returns to her chair with another pronouncement. "You, Leendsay, and you, Hhugh, will be on *my* quiz team."

A fleeting trapped-bunny glance passes between Hugh and me, but we do the maths simultaneously. Most of us in this little party will be seated at the Captain's table for the voyage, and traditionally that table forms its own team when required. Which means that Gloria, Bish, Hugh and I will all be together on the Captain's team anyway – *should* there be a quiz on this voyage. We smile benignly and let the remark pass, deeming it superfluous to commit ourselves at this early stage.

This voyage's Captain's table proves the most unusual I've yet experienced, ranking only in the vague orbit of a voyage during which all my dinner companions – including the Captain himself, a Conservative British MP, a North Carolina Republican businessman, an English Chief Justice, and their spouses – gave a spontaneous musical rendition of *Jerusalem* over the pudding. And this one starts rather unexpectedly with the opinions of a bad-tempered old man and his cowed wife who are already seated at the table when, on our first night out, the Bishop and I arrive simultaneously to find ourselves placed on either side of them. The Bishop introduces himself as he sits down, and is greeted by a grunt. "Huh, I wouldn't have thought St Helena merited a Bishop," is the rude response from the crusty old man.

The Bishop, straightening his shoulders with pique, resettles his large pectoral cross. I detect fire in his eyes. But these warnings are lost on Mr Bad-Tempered who then goes on to dispute everything our Lord Bishop says. The crunch comes when, inevitably, the subject of British Citizenship for St Helenians is broached, together with Margaret Thatcher's part in that history, and Charles II's Charter for the island – a campaign long waged by the Anglican

Church in St Helena, with involvement in it a prerequisite for her several successive bishops since the '80s. But Mr Bad-Tempered throws himself back in his seat with another snort. "Enough of that!" he commands His Lordship. "You don't know *what* you're talking about!" It is not beyond the realm of possibility, I think, watching the changing colours of Bish's face, that our senior cleric might suffer an apoplexy right now. But instead, we both sink into a stunned silence broken only by Cowed, his sweet wife, who whispers to Bish: "He's the *most* difficult man I have *ever* had to live with!"

The others join the table, unsuspecting of the trials Bish and I suffer in our given seats, and begin their own cheery chatter. But I am stuck with Mr Bad-Tempered on my left and for a while I rehearse a few safe subjects before I dare open my mouth to him. And then – following on his recent holiday tour of Simon's Town in the Cape – I venture an item about the African penguins that breed there. "You don't know what you're talking about!" he snaps, though I have watched that penguin colony grow since inception. And so, by degrees, we move on to Australia from where my younger child and I have just returned from holiday, and the mid-Outback underground opal-mining town of White Cliffs in particular. "It must be the ugliest town on earth," I offer casually, desperate to levitate the atmosphere a bit. "Bah!" he explodes. "You don't know *what* you're talking about!"

The soup arrives. We have a long way to go. And in the interests of civility (and also because we are stuck on the opposite side of a large table from our laughing Captain, the amiable Hugh, and the far more interesting Gloria), I make a last-ditch attempt at conversation. Speaking with supreme authority on matters marine, Mr Bad-Tempered frequently refers to himself as a Naval Man, and so I tentatively explore that territory given the fact that my husband's father was a Royal Fleet Air Arm admiral and Chris's brother a naval commander. It is hardly worth the effort, for Mr Bad-Tempered's relationship with the sea is, it transpires, solely limited to the RNVR from 1942-46, during which time his greatest achievement appears to have been the acquisition of some very large tattoos that I discover on his forearms.

I give up then. The Bishop has long ago lapsed into a dangerous silence, completely ignoring the grumpy old man and the poor cowed wife and speaking to no one. I am thoroughly beaten too. Indigestion is definitely on the cards tonight.

The following evening it is Gloria's chance to perform. After twenty-four hours at sea she is already bored and crotchety, and the *tour guide on holiday* role is clearly wearing thin. Her voice is loud and her criticisms louder as she finds vociferous fault with the limited shipboard world in which she now dwells. "*My God!* You can't eat *that*! They are tryeeng to POISON us!" she cries at the ship's excellent food. "Is this some dead animal from the *street* – MY GOD!"

But the real battle commences on Sunday night, when Captain Martin Smith sits down for dinner with a happy beam on his face. "Well, we have the Quiz tonight – and I'm looking at my team," he announces genially.

And up springs Gloria, ram-rod straight. "No-no, you are not! Leendsay and Hhugh are on *my* team and I have collected *my* people!"

The Captain looks perplexed, and the Bishop, evidently on special dispensation to boost an all-Saints team rather than ours, leaps into the fray. "The Captain's table is traditionally a team of its own, Gloria."

"But Leendsay and Hhugh are with *me*!"

Hugh, travelling on business, sinks deeply into his collar, fearfully hissing at me, "What do I do? My job depends on her husband!"

Across the table, the Captain fixes me with a questioning eye. A glance around the gathering shows that without the Bishop, or Gloria, Hugh and me, the Captain's team will consist solely of Mr Bad-Tempered and his wife. That would be unfortunate indeed for the poor Captain. So, requiring no favours from the Governor myself, and with Martin a family friend of many years, I rise to the skirmish. "The Bishop's right, Gloria. The Captain's team is a tradition…"

Before I finish, optic daggers whirr across the table. "Very well," she announces. Her voice is not soft. "You decide, Leendsay, but *ree*-memberr thees – I WILL *NEHVERR* ASK YOU AGAIN!" *To what? To Plantation House? To join her quiz team on the next voyage we might share?*

I draw a deep breath, my decision made. I am, after all, a guest at Martin's table – and she *just a tour guide on holiday*. Besides, she herself is expected to be part of this team. "I'll stay with the Captain's team."

Now there is an exultant chinking of glasses and cutlery as she furiously leaps to her feet, betrayed by perceived revoking of our support. And in mid-course she is gone, striding about the crowded dining saloon to canvass other diners, exhorting them to fall in with her. We are left watching open-mouthed as passengers cringe at her approach. When she eventually returns to her place, having co-opted twelve players in place of the requisite six to eight, her fire has not yet died. With effect, she lays her palms upon the festive board and leans as far across it as she can, fixing me with antagonism: "It would be well, Leendsay," she advises me, succinctly enough for every other table and all the pole-axed dining stewards to hear, "if you would *ree*-memberr that the Captain is a married man, for I am going to tell Chrees that the two of you are carry-ingg on!"

Martin nearly chokes. "Oh!" he exclaims in justifiable astonishment, for we share the most unthreatening of associations. "Now *that's* a novel idea – perhaps we should give it a try, Lindsay!" The Bishop guffaws loudly. Hugh's raised wineglass shivers with pent-up laughter. Mr Bad-Tempered and Cowed, already agog, descend into a state of total shock.

Unsettled by the theatrics, all the other diners are in distinct disarray by the time they eventually ascend from the dining saloon to the A-Deck lounge for coffee and liqueurs. Instead of settling into relaxed groups, passengers are now wearing the look of hunted deer as they shift uneasily from group to group, unsure where it is safe to sit. There is no sign of Gloria. But terrified of finding themselves captive by her, they scramble for the furthest corners of the room. Even the Police Chief and his wife, usually joined at the hip, wrench themselves apart in their anxiety, and Denise ends up with us, Royce at a far-flung table across the lounge. The twelve co-opted teamsters are mercifully separated by the Purser into two workable teams of six, but neither group knows where the eagle will land – until, just as the Purser rings his starting bell, the double doors fly open. "Where ees *my* team? *Where* ees my team?"

She pauses for a moment to assess the layout, and finding no massive team of twelve awaiting her formidable general knowledge, immediately homes in on the nearest table. There she attaches herself, determined towards victory. But a doctor on the team – from shock, perhaps – gets all the medical questions wrong, and to Gloria's fury, they lose the contest, soundly beaten by the Captain and his friends.

She *has* invited me again, to whatever it was that she swore not to. There are dinners and functions at Plantation House that I attend, and she and Duncan come to dinner with us. We share a very occasional coffee together or social telephone gossip, and her company is lively and stimulating. But I am sometimes aghast at her unconcealed rudeness to islanders. She is clearly unhappy here, and on a bad day she is loud and omnipresent, wreaking havoc even on unsuspecting tourists, explicitly dramatizing her hatred for St Helena, its people, its ship, its walks, roads, food, climate, her predecessors at Plantation House, and numberless other obsessions. And when a well-known BBC war correspondent, offered a free holiday to "anywhere in the world", chooses St Helena, even he becomes a victim. On his last night he reels from a reception at Plantation House, commenting that though he has covered wars all over the globe he has never felt so shell-shocked in his life. "That woman," he exclaims, "is worse than Kosovo!"

This invitation is different: a cocktail party on board the SAS *Drakensberg*, a South African Navy ship visiting St Helena as part of the island's Quincentenary celebration year. Dubbed *South African Connection Week*, the visitors will entertain St Helena with Zulu dancing exhibited by some crewmen from that nation, pay homage at the graves of two babies of King Dinizulu, who are buried in the cathedral graveyard, and visit the South African Boer Cemetery.

It was mostly typhoid that carried off the one hundred or so Afrikaner prisoners of the Anglo-Boer War who now lie peacefully at rest on the green slopes of Knollcombes, St Helena. Surrounded by deep-grassed fields and bird-filled woodland, gazing on green mountain peaks ahead, the graves' neat white markers climb their hill in stepped formation, watched over by two guardian memorials on which the victims' names are inscribed. This verdant place is a far cry from the harsh South African hinterland from which so many of them hailed, with its familiar scrubby bushes, hard dry earth and endless horizon broken only by a few dumpy *kopjes* here and there. But though distant from the small family graveyard they may have anticipated on the farm back home, they have secured a gentle peace in this pretty valley.

With the islanders instructed by the British Governor Sterndale to *"treat the prisoners with that courtesy and consideration which should be extended to all men who have fought bravely for what they considered the cause of their country"*, the first shipment of 514 Boer prisoners arrived on the troopship *Milwaukee* in April 1900. Soon to be followed by 4 500 more, they were immediately taken to Deadwood Plain where a tented camp was set up, and a community of sorts was established. Nine months later a smaller additional camp was established at Broad Bottom in the west of the island to separate the fiercely independent Free Staters from other Boers; but most of the prisoners were housed at Deadwood for the duration of their internment.

The Boers were not an idle people, and they soon started both a camp school for their accompanying children and a newspaper known as *Die Krijgsgevangene*. Around the island their contributions were manifold, erecting a new crane on the Wharf, extending the seafront road to West Rocks, and building a desalination plant at Rupert's Bay which, though unused, still stands today. The sturdy proportions of New Ground House bear their practical stamp, yet the artistry of their delicate carvings was legend. In 1902, when the popular Governor Sterndale agreed that Boer handiwork was also to be shown at an island-wide exhibition of industrial arts, the prisoners brought forward so many contributions that an entire room was given over to these alone. Working only with improvised saws fashioned from of old table knives, and hammers made from stones, they turned out tobacco pipes, walking sticks, miniature furniture, and model carts carved from wood or bones. So expert were these talents that, somewhat ironically, the Loyal Address illuminated by the Governor and joyously dispatched to England on the coronation of King Edward VII in 1901, was accommodated in a casket of endemic St Helena ebony wood – exquisitely carved by a South African Boer prisoner.

The Boer General Cronje and his wife, also arriving on the *Milwaukee* with the first batch, were not subjected to a tent at Deadwood. Instead they were accorded the comfort of Kent Cottage, a modest double-storey house in the shadow of High Knoll Fort, some six miles from the camp. Somewhat aggrieved that he was not shown the proper respect of a mounted guard to watch over him, the General immediately demanded one – throwing the government into instant consternation since there was no mounted guard at all on the island. Nonetheless the obliging Governor Sterndale promptly gave orders that some men of the St Helena Volunteers be supplied with horses and given a crash course in riding – a sport to which these men did not readily adapt. However, as soon as they could sit a horse without falling off, the troop was dispatched to Kent Cottage to mount guard over General Cronje, and to accompany him whenever he went riding.

So delighted was the General, that no sooner did they arrive at his house than he decided to pay a cross-country visit to Deadwood to inspect his men at the prisoners' camp, and immediately leapt to his horse. Practically born in the saddle, he set off at a hard gallop, leading the way up hill and down dale with his insecure guard lolloping on behind, until eventually they arrived at the Camp. There the exhausted guard dismounted, and while the General talked to his compatriots, they drew breath, girded their loins for the homeward leg, and waited for signs of Cronje's readiness to return to Kent Cottage. When the moment came, the General leapt on to his horse again and immediately turned it for home – but not one of the unpractised guards, each holding a rifle in one hand, managed to remount. This was an awkward situation indeed, not a little humiliating for the Volunteers who were now watched with hilarity by a huge audience of Boers, every one of whom was an accomplished horseman. But at last the day was saved by the General himself who instructed one man to hold the rifles while each guard ungainly clambered on board his horse, and eventually they set off westwards for Kent Cottage – the prisoner once again riding confidently ahead while the unhappy guard trailed behind.

The amusing thing about this special invitation from the South African Navy is a quaint phrase tacked to the bottom of the card, by way of instruction: *Guests to meet at the Landing Steps at 5.30pm, where they will be uplifted to the SAS Drakensberg. Uplifted?* Why not just say *accompanied, transported, ferried,* since I assume we'll be riding the crest of the wave as is the way here? So, on the due date, I make my way to the Wharf, heading for the Steps. But plans have changed in the interim. Realising that the *Drakensberg's* boarding platform is too small for civilians and its rope-ladder hazardous to public safety, the navy has, at the last minute, sent its helicopter to fetch us – a true *upliftment*, it seems – and there it stands in all its military glory in a broad area cleared of traffic between the public swimming pool and the sea. This is fun, and enough of a novelty for half the island to turn up at the seafront to watch our transportation; only rarely do helicopters cut the air of St Helena, and those mostly as convenience for some visiting dignitary between a naval ship and Plantation House.

Everyone is there, including the police who have thrown up a cordon to hold back the spectators and, at the far end of the Wharf, an impressive phalanx of fire engines with spinning lights and men at attention to watch over our safety. Alongside the police, navy personnel are assiduously checking names on a list and once ticked off, guests are permitted to vault over the ribbon. On the other side, we are issued with "flotation harnesses and ear-defenders", and in groups of fifteen are loaded without great elegance into the cramped seating of the helicopter. Though I once enjoyed a glass-bubble chopper tour of Reunion Island, this is my first experience of military flying and it reminds me a bit of Vietnam war movies, though the journey is fortunately too short for much further resemblance. With the door slammed shut for our preservation, and the small windows allowing only the briefest of rare aerial glimpses of our cliffs already shining copper in the sunset glow, the flight is dark and noisome, but such an adventure.

We are disgorged on the gently swaying grey bows of the *Drakensberg*, thanks to cocktails being served aft on the helipad where we should have landed; and an impressively long red carpet leads the way past oily fixtures and secret doors as we head for the stern of the ship. The decks are narrow and, watching my step carefully, all I notice at first of the tall receiving officer are his spotless white shoes marking the open space of the helipad where earlier arrivals are already enjoying wine and canapés. "Welcome aboard," he offers in a distinctive voice that I know, and my head jerks up with surprised recognition. "*Mac?*"

"*Lindsay?* What in the world are you doing *here?*"

What, indeed, in the desolate wastes of the South Atlantic Ocean. "I'm living here!"

"No!" he exclaims in the only viable response to such madness. When he has completed his task of greeting party guests, he comes over to chat. One of the last times I saw Mac Bisset was during my distant teenage when, on holiday in the semi-desert plains of Kimberley, South Africa, we spent a day together searching for bully-beef tins and military buttons on the Boer War battlefield of Magersfontein. I already know that he's now a respected military historian back in South Africa, but this was the last place I expected to see him. "I've been awarded the honorary naval rank of Commander for this voyage," he explains. "And I'm actually rather enjoying it. Mainly, though, it's offered me a wonderful chance to visit these Boer sites, and I'm very excited about getting ashore tomorrow."

I am looking forward to having him to dinner, to showing him my lovely house and to catching up with him; but it seems the navy will be kept so busy with things historical while in St Helena that I'll barely see him again. However the unexpected encounter, though brief, was a delightful surprise.

The *Drakensberg's* visit is hailed as one of the highlights of all the Quincentenary celebrations, the entire island captivated by the South Africans' smartness, friendliness, and hospitality; and most particularly by their genuine interest in St Helena. I am *hugely* proud of them. But after an incident with Gloria that once again leaves us open-mouthed, I am fairly bursting with patriotism. The South African visit, happening in June, coincides with the Queen's Birthday – an event roughly contiguous with Trooping the Colour in London to celebrate Her Majesty's Official birthday. In the colonies it evokes (in essence only) the summer garden party annually hosted by the Queen at Buckingham Palace. In St Helena, this is an occasion when protocol is paramount, a dreg of surviving colonialism left over from a long-forgotten Empire. Punctuality is key (arrive late at your peril), and stopping short of requiring tails to be worn these days, medals are still mentioned on the invitation. It is, of course, accepted that women of substance will wear hats and smart attire, but in the heart of a St Helena winter, held inland in the soggy climes of Plantation House, the event does not lend itself to a garden party atmosphere. It usually rains. So a protective marquee (a new one, at last) is rigged up, and once again guests are deterred from entering the house. "If guests want the loo," we learn from Gloria in advance, "they must go there round the side of the house. I weell not have them tracking mud across my floors!"

Most of the dastardly mud actually stems from her odd arrangement of holding the party on the tarmac area in front of the house; so, because of this, cars are forced to park on the squelchy field below and a mucky negotiation follows to gain the sheltering marquee. In high heels it's no fun, and while the dutiful couple post themselves under protective cover just inside its entrance, shaking hands and directing guests to sign the Visitors' Book on a table immediately in front of them – an arduously delaying process – other guests in their smart suits and fragile hats are impelled to wait their turn for admittance in the fine rain outside.

This year's party is not the best of occasions. The Governor, a man short in stature, exudes an embellished self-importance echoed by his somewhat inept speech. Clad once again in the straining white suit with plumed hat comically tilted, he insists on delivering it from the shallow steps of his porch, but as the frills of the marquee hang low, those under cover see only his chubby lower half while his words are carried away on the breeze. There appears to be no band present on this occasion either, which is odd, for the red-jacketed Gettogethers are a Queen's Birthday tradition, offering pleasant background music throughout the party and a stirring brass rendition of the British national anthem when the appropriate moment arises. Yet, we discover very much later, they are there after all; Gloria has situated them around a corner, out of sight, in the rain, and no one hears their valiant *God Save the Queen* at all.

With the South Africans present this year, five officers from the ship are graced with invitations which they have been pleased to accept. But Gloria – having upset the island's protocol department to the point of total confusion with constant rearrangements of guest lists to include her own preferences – comes upon a frightful error when she discovers that the helicopter pilot on the list is... a black African! This is an appalling situation for her. "Blacks don't know how to behave!" she explains without a twinge of humility, and promptly issues instructions to the Castle for the pilot to be disinvited. However, quite unbeknownst to her, this cancellation has provided a fortuitous opening for the Castle to rectify another glaring error of protocol regarding the guest list. For the one person inadvertently omitted from the list altogether, was the most senior of them all: Rear Admiral Magalefu!

Admiral Magalefu duly arrives, in full Dress uniform with rows of gold braid and medals as required, a charming and dignified Tswana man of entertaining conversation. But his chocolate skin colour is not lost upon Gloria. As soon as the reception line can be abandoned she bears down on him, jaw set, stride purposeful. A path is spontaneously carved for her progress. Somehow we can tell she is not about to welcome this honoured guest. "Did you receive an invitation to come here?" she demands, and those of us in her hearing almost faint away. She might as well have asked straight out for the admiral to leave.

All eyes are on him now, but there is no flinching, no spark of antagonism in his manner. He remains as cool as a cucumber. "I certainly did, and am delighted to be here," he replies, graciously inclining into a gentlemanly bow. It is done with such ease, such effortless aplomb that Gloria is stumped, the air whisked from her wings. "Well, I don't recall inviting you," she retorts, and moves away. The admiral smiles and turns back to our interrupted conversation: "Excuse me, you were saying…?"

A few nights later, at another party on his ship, he sustains his good manners in a speech in which, without audible rancour, he mentions "His Excellency's beautiful wife". Only the few who were in earshot at Plantation House that day – and those whom the story has already reached along the island's ubiquitous grapevine – can imagine his true feelings for this rude white woman. But he will not display them publicly. I am so proud of South Africa and my gracious countrymen I weep as I watch the *Drakensberg* finally sail away.

"I cannot wait for my Staff Officer!" Gloria announces to me one day, "He is comingg on the next sheep." The luxury of a batman is allowed to all British Governors, but up to now no Commander-in-Chief of tiny St Helena has deemed one necessary. Except Gloria. "I told Duncan that we cannot continue without one, for I will find him *vehrry* useful to me. *Twenty-five percent* of his job, you know, is to help *me* get what I want." *Large bronze statues for Plantation's hall?* The FCO no doubt has advised her to stop nagging them, so rearguard action is the next move.

When he arrives it becomes clear just what state the FCO is in, for a more unsuited couple for St Helena could not have been devised in fiction. A man in mid-fifties with hair of regenerated blackness including goatee, impenetrable sunglasses and a penchant for formal black three-piece suits and dark tie on a tropical business day (while His Excellency is familiar with short-sleeved shirts), he soon acquires the nickname of Machiavelli for reasons that are slightly foggy. That it remotely alludes to that Florentine's diplomatic career is unlikely, and connotations with his famous *Prince* are also vague; but if nothing else, the new Machiavelli quite frequently resembles a member of the Italian underworld in that sombre attire – or at the very least a resident of the shady side of Anguilla. He is, however, a native of England's industrial midlands, a fact borne out by his indubitable accents, and so he lacks the natural *esuberanza* of the average Italian. However, he evidently does not lack all romantic spirit for it soon transpires that the voluptuous and loquacious mid-twenties girl he has brought with him, soon dubbed Cleavage by sharp-eyed Father Joe, was, four years ago, rescued from the ravages of a troubled Eastern European state by the warrior himself.

Cleavage had long since grown used to metropolitan life – New York's in particular – by the time she found herself cast away in mid-ocean, and scanty leather miniskirts, stiletto-heeled knee-high boots and jaunty fashion hats bear testimony to this. However, she carries them off well, given her youth and her natural aplomb, even if they are notably out of place in the remote tropics. But Gloria is in seventh heaven. With the bronze statues no longer a lost hope, and a real cosmopolitan with whom to give vent to her permanent cabin-fever, the new couple is feted at every turn. Dinners, luncheons and more dinners launch them into St Helena society. Gloria's eyes sparkle, her face transformed with happiness, allowing the island a rare glimpse of the *femme fatale* that once captivated Duncan Hill. All is well for the moment.

The first dinner of welcome is at the long table in Plantation's elegant Regency-style dining room, set for once with the crested china and glass usually deemed too grand for 'locals'; but as tonight's party of twelve is a solely expatriate affair it receives a rare airing. My initial introduction to the celebrated couple is made over drinks in the drawing room beforehand. But on this occasion, while Machiavelli circulates diplomatically, talking at me for some prescribed minutes before we permanently run out of conversation, Cleavage is completely silent. Perhaps her décolletage has stunned the others, for her quietness seems to have exerted a domino effect on the rest of the guests by the time we move into dinner, and it turns into the dullest gathering I have attended anywhere. Only Gloria shows animation, from her end of the table loudly upbraiding the staff in front of the guests, as is her embarrassing habit, while the Governor at the other end – desperately working on the dampness of the gathering – becomes more inane as the meal wears on.

The meal itself is a matter of intrigue to me tonight, since there has been much ado about the theft from Plantation House of the Governor's permanent cook by the Chief Secretary's household. Gloria is not in a forgiving mood over this affair and it goes on rankling. But by the time Machiavelli and Cleavage arrive, a new cook – better known for his keyboard talents – has already been instated at the residency, and this is his grand debut. I can't help but look on the dinner fare with trepidation, and am not surprised. A first course of chewy calamari is followed by turkey 'with trimmings' – in reality a marble of stuffing and a fractured Vienna sausage enrobed in bacon. Fresh green beans and carrots pass the test, but the potato wedges are commercially pre-frozen. The cream caramels later served with mercifully real caramelised apple wedges, bear the indisputably plastic taste of a packet-pudding. And we learn that the new 'chef', anyway, is proving his greater skills at a dance tonight.

A few weeks later Gloria rings me. "I would like to know the truth, Leendsay. What was the real reason you did not come to Cleavage's birthday lunch? I am askingg you *vehrry* nicely."

Lacking the courage to broach the subject of the new chef's Spanish omelettes cooked for six but intended to feed fourteen, or his unthawed frozen quiches served at previous lunches, I opt for the other reason. I'm her ally, so I must speak honestly. "Then I'll tell you. I've been to three parties for Cleavage and Machiavelli already, and I find I have absolutely nothing in common with either of them. Honestly, Gloria, I haven't the energy to fawn over them anymore."

There is a long pause before Gloria speaks again. Her voice is darkly sombre. "I will tell you sometheeng, Leendsay. Not once since they arrived has Cleavage written a note of thanks for a deenner party, or a lunch, or the flowers I have sent her. Not once. I weell not geeve any more parties for her. It is *vehrry* bad manners."

"I can understand how you feel," I offer lamely. "Is Machiavelli getting you what you want?"

Perhaps it's my imagination, but Gloria seems less ebullient about him too. "Not yet. No, I don't suppose we will *ehverr* get those bronzes."

9.

Jumping the Cracks

July 2002

Harry Rogers Foster Hayes came to live with us just before the Quincentenary, bringing a purple blanket and a pillow with him. These were evidently enough to keep him comfortable and he settled into his new life quickly and quietly. Sue (my old ally in the Airport referendum), who made her farewells to him at Villa Le Breton, was beyond speech with grief at leaving him, so I appealed to JJ, who knew him previously, for advice on his character. I had never met Harry before.

"He's dopey," said JJ without preamble. "That cat is always sleeping – he looks only half-alive sometimes."

"I've noticed he's wobbly on his legs. And his tail has a lump as though it's been run over at some stage. Did he have an accident that you know of?"

"As far as I know, he was one of two cats brought out from England by people called Rogers. When their contract was over a new contract family, the Fosters, took them over at Piccolo Hill. But Harry's brother was accidentally run over as they reversed out of their drive. Perhaps Harry was also in the way."

Dear little grey and white Harry with his gentle face, an English cat of indeterminate age, and clearly a survivor. "He's had quite a history then."

"He looks arthritic to me," opined JJ, "though this cat has been fed every vitamin pill on the market. Sue kept him wrapped in cotton wool the whole time she had him and he hardly ever went outside. I think he'll enjoy your big garden."

And the warmth of Jamestown, I added, considering the cold,

damp climes of Piccolo Hill's expatriate compound at Longwood. Before long Harry took to a morning constitutional, at first just a gentle stroll along the garden path to meet us when we returned from shopping, but eventually extending his explorations to encompass the entire half acre. It has never ever occurred to him to leave his strange abode or to rail against transfer to foreign territory. He simply accepts us as his new family and is pleased with us – the easiest cat I have ever adopted.

As time moves on he grows stronger. The back legs have toned up a bit and he sleeps less, watching insect life from the garden shade of certain bushes of his preference. But most of all, he enjoys evening television from the vantage point of my collar bone – a position he habitually gains by a running leap from the sitting room door. Undeterred by food on my lap, he then strings himself lengthways under my chin from shoulder to shoulder and purrs. He is affection itself, and a different cat from the one delivered to us.

Then one night we discover the reason why. Bish joins us at the veranda table after a long supper which has declined into postprandial glasses of Amarula, an outstandingly delicious South African export cream liqueur brewed from the fruit of the marula tree, the berries of which, incidentally, are potent enough to cause drunkenness to elephants who relish them in the wild. And Harry comes running. With a glint of desperation in his eye, he clambers on to the table where he finds instant succour from the Bishop who dips a finger in his glass and offers a lick to our cat. Harry nearly bites his finger off. That's too much for Bish to resist. "Get a saucer," he commands Virginia, and proceeds to pour a small tot into it. Harry falls on it, slurping it up like a first lager after a St Helena beer drought, and when it is finished he looks hopefully for more. But we have come to our senses now. This is a cat, after all – a cat with a drinking problem. He shakes his head to clear the brain, and when he realises no more is forthcoming, retires to a chair to sleep it off, probably for days.

I phone JJ. "This cat of ours is an alcoholic!"

JJ guffaws. "Well, that explains everything! That visiting friend of Sue's, who was unemployed while he was here, did nothing but sit at home all day and drink. He was smashed nearly all the time. Obviously Harry was his boozing companion." So Harry goes back on the wagon, and in due course his temporary stumbling clumsiness once again improves to steady feet and an accurate nightly leap to my chest, good health and, hopefully, several more years of clear-headed happiness.

Not long afterwards, Virginia and I added Mimi Wyn-Ricketts to the household as well – a whole different kettle of fish.

When David and Jacqui Wyn-Ricketts came to the end of their contract, they bequeathed to me their child. Mimi was given to Jacqui as a very young feral kitten whom she tamed to finely-tuned domestication with just enough spirit left in her to lead us a dance. When she moved in, I kept her shut in Richard's vacant bedroom for several days while we grew accustomed to one another, and in no time she was all sweetness and light, placidly licking the butter I smeared on her white paws, purring and *prrmmowing* when I stroked her prettily striped khaki-coloured fur, blinking her exquisite green eyes at me languidly – until, at last, it was time to let her loose in the house.

She was, it seemed, relieved to be freed from her south-facing prison with its view of trees and familiar inland hills, and explored the rest of her new habitat with fervour, prowling up and down the windowsills when she thought I wasn't looking, rubbing against my legs when she knew I was. And all it needed was a chink in a doorway for her to flee. Gone! For a while, I felt sure she was lurking in the garden somewhere, cocking a snook at me. But after forty-eight hours, and several searches in the country on my part, she eventually turned up at her old home, Prospect House, having traversed on foot the roughly three-mile distance uphill through deep guts and forest, across winding roads and utterly foreign terrain. The gardener there phoned me, and for the umpteenth time in two days, I drove up the hill to search for her.

She was less than thrilled to see me and flatly refused to get into the car, explaining in no uncertain terms that this was her house and she would not be returning to That Place in Town. Then she hid. And so the weeks went by. Even Bish, who was supposed to have adopted her in the first place but had to bow out at the last minute, felt beholden to trundle up the hill with me in search of her, and more times than we could count we drove the winding roads to Prospect House in the hopes of coaxing her back, *if* we could spot her. When, occasionally, we actually managed to capture her and headed her back to Jamestown, restrained in a tightly wrapped towel while she noted every stick of the passing scenery, making clear mental notes for return journeys, Bish suggested that our homeward trips should be circuitous, and we drove miles out of our way to confuse her. But once back at Villa Le Breton she would consume a meal, drink a lot of water, purr in a charming manner and, the moment I turned my back, be gone again – totally unconfused by our deviousness, and taking less and less time to return to Prospect with each journey.

Then the process would start again, but by now the Bishop had withdrawn from the hunt, and both the housekeeper and gardener at Prospect no longer worked there. If I caught her, there was no one to hold her, and putting her into a box elicited such shining flashes of wildness, seriously endangering my eyes, that there was no option but to let her roam free in the car. It made for interesting journeys as this furious female stamped back and forth across the dashboard, snarling anger at me, thrashing her tail, winding through the steering wheel even as we descended the treacherous hairpins of Constitution Hill, my shortcut home. Five times I brought her back this way, and five times more she decisively returned to Prospect House, until at last, with her previous home utterly deserted, Mimi finally realised that she was quite alone.

My car was parked in its usual place behind her house that day, in full view of the big field and forest that rose behind it, and though I called and called, she would not answer. It was a huge property, with terraces and orchards in front as well, and I searched all corners diligently without success. Then, just about to climb back into my car and give up the search for the day, I heard her voice. And there she was, emerging daintily from the forest behind, high-stepping through the long grass, talking as she approached, making sure I saw her. Eventually she sat down in the middle of the field, wrapping her tail around her, and looked at me. I sat down too, at the bottom of it, but I didn't look at her, nor did I call. I simply waited. This was crunch-time, I realised. This was the moment that she would decide whether to stay here alone and return to a feral life forever, or whether to receive from my hand a dish of food twice a day for the rest of her life. At length, after considerable thought, she chose the latter and when, eventually, she had made up her mind came quietly tripping down the rest of the field towards me, inviting me to pick her up and put her in the car. This time, sitting demurely on the dashboard all the way home, she surveyed the scenery with diminished interest, no longer noting landmarks for future use. And after that, she never ran away again, and I was eventually able to report to Jacqui that her child was doing well.

Our garden, too, is now flourishing. Fine crops of sweet carrots appear on our table, with beans, bright green small cabbages, potatoes and leeks. The Shrubbery is growing dense, its forest of frangipanis scenting the evening air with pale pink blooms in season, strange-shaped bromeliads in heavenly coral-pink flower, sprouting between rampant geraniums and a tangle of other flowers – a whole quarter tailor-made for cats who hide in it.

Leaning against a veranda pillar with my early morning coffee, I watch fairy terns returning from breakfast at sea, this morning counting forty-five highlighted against the brown cliffs as they fly inland, ethereal in their beauty. Our solitary resident fairy tern – widower of the poor spouse once consumed by a neighbour's cat who left nothing of it but wings laid out like RAF emblems on the lawn – is lazing on his jacaranda branch, occasionally taking off to play with another flutter of fairy terns above the mango trees, while a cardinal lands on the sky-blue plumbago hedge to flaunt his scarlet brilliance like a traffic light. By this point, eighteen months after my Season of Desolation, this garden is a sanctuary and I am immeasurably proud of our property.

It is early July and I am on countdown now, due to sail in two weeks' time on my annual return to our primary home in Cape Town – a developing ritual of our quirky 'double life' that also brings Chris and Richard to St Helena twice a year, while we keep two homes running concurrently. That our far-flung friends find it hard to keep up with our movements is no surprise, but some apprehension among them that a troubled marriage requires such separations, we find truly alarming. The bald facts are, while Chris has business to attend to in Cape Town and our school-going son deserves at least one parent on tap, Villa Le Breton has turned out to be a house that cannot be left empty for white-ants to feast on, and so a continuing presence here is obligatory. And this time, while I resume the reins of our South African life for three months, Virginia will be left in charge of cats and bills in St Helena until October when I return, Annette in charge of house cleaning, and Zander nursing our garden.

Virginia is resolute about coping with this big house while her originally intended six months of gap year now extend to some indeterminate time in the future and, still enjoying her voluntary work at Prince Andrew's, she displays no desire to return to the bright lights of the Outside World. Things are falling beautifully into place. She has her own ancient little Ford Fiesta to get about in, which I bought her in February in order to obviate the use of my own car as a bus for noisy young Saturday night disco revellers, and she is showing every sign of a responsible disposition. I love having her with me.

I've now passed nearly ten months in St Helena – the longest unbroken time I have ever spent here. I refresh my cup of coffee and consider my views on the island now. The physical aspects of living in a remote place, where time and supply are so foreign, are becoming easier. Shopping patterns are at last fathomed out, and hidden treasure troves of a few rarer commodities discovered. New signposts lately erected at far-flung road junctions are a godsend to finding my way around the black countryside at night when I otherwise would get lost, for negligible distinction exists between some country roads and driveways to private houses. The cockroach exterminator works from the end of our road and his telephone number is pasted on the fridge in large figures – though it's harder to raise a plumber or electrician, I have found. We have a doctor living next door, and one up the road, while the hospital is so close I could throw stones through its windows.

By now we even have a tame mechanic who knows my car from its bumps and bruises in Main Street the time I was breathalysed. Indeed he even knows Virginia's tiny Ford Fiesta which she managed to smash within nine hours of insuring it back in February, the very day she took possession. Proud of her new acquisition, and a good driver, she had nipped just around the corner to fetch a friend for their evening out, when, turning back into a link road at St John's Church, a white pet rabbit darted across the road, let loose by its owners for its usual evening run in the street. Rather than hit it, she collided with the church wall, smashing a headlight and buckling the bumper so far into the wheel that it became undrive-able. So, limping into the church's parking bay, she ran the short distance home in a justifiable state of agitation.

"Take my car," I suggested, instinctively getting her back behind the wheel before shock set in. "If there's no damage to the rabbit or the church, there's no need to call the police." I was wrong, of course. I did not know that in St Helena the police are summoned even for your damage to your own property. So a neighbour from St John's Road did it for me.

When the gate bell rang I went into the pitch dark to conduct this surprise interview, endeavouring to prove as helpful as I could to a policeman whose dark skin and black uniform blended perfectly with the night. "You'll probably find her at the Consulate Hotel," I offered, wondering how well that would go down after a motor accident. "She swerved to avoid a rabbit in the street. There are often rabbits around here, some are pets, and wild ones come down the mountain."

"I know, m'am. We still must be have a talk wit' her. An' breat'alyse her."

I swallowed hard, picturing my tender child publicly flushed from the Consulate Bar on a Saturday night and frogmarched away by two stern policemen. "What is your name?" I asked him, preparing some reference for future battles.

And now the invisible man metamorphosed into a Cheshire cat, his row of gleaming white teeth hanging in the sky. A short chuckle was heard. "I is the officer what breat'alyse *you* a few mont's ago, m'am!"

When Virginia returned in the early dawn hours she was fully recovered and unfazed by her brush with the law. "Oh, yes, they took me to police headquarters to breathalyse me, but the reading was clear," she announced casually, perched on my bed. "They couldn't understand it at all, and when I told them I had not drunk alcohol for two weeks they nearly fainted!" She's a rare bird among the local young.

Not long afterwards a different encounter with the law drew amazement. Regarded as a crime-free island, St Helena has long enjoyed a life where car keys remain in the lock, house windows are never closed, front doors never barred, even as that innocence inexorably thins with each passing year. Violence is confined to drunken brawls and domestic fisticuffs, and while the litany of an average week's court cases on the radio news might appear alarmingly long, many are fines meted out merely for a dent in someone's bumper, or for dropping litter.

However, as I drove the twisting bends of rural Gordon's Post Road one Saturday at noon, I suddenly came face to face with a policeman who signalled me to halt. A police sedan was parked on the right-hand side of the road, but drawn up to the hillside ahead of me was a private car from which was now being extricated, by a second officer, a thin and angry civilian, his hands held aloft in submission. From my ringside seat I then observed what I have seen only in American movies: the civilian frogmarched to the police car, spread-eagled across its boot and body-searched. While this was done, the first policeman strolled over to the private car and, before my eyes, removed from the back seat a very large rifle. When the rifle was safely stashed in the police car's boot and the man in its rear seat, I was finally allowed to proceed, driving all the way to Saturday drinks at Hallams with jaw dropped and eyes still goggling, impatient to tell John Beadon everything I'd seen – learning later, with total amazement, that the rifle owner had actually been *en route* to shoot his wife's lover, his unfaithful spouse seated calmly in the front seat of his car throughout the arrest.

There is much to smile at here, often at the island's expense, of course; but islanders themselves laugh over some things, recognising the small idiocies that sometimes occur in the name of officialdom. This being a British Overseas Territory where the sometimes quite irrelevant laws of Britain and the EU apply to the letter, I was astonished to find – on my return from Cape Town last October – that a fight against foot-and-mouth disease was in full swing in St Helena, based on the epidemic being currently rampant four thousand miles away in England. Some precautions understandably had to be exercised against contracting the scourge among our handful of vulnerable far-flung island cattle (who incidentally, are required to suffer so many expensive EU-compliant inoculations, even here, that local farmers now can't afford to produce fresh milk from their cows); but there seemed to be some mysterious gaps in the logic of this operation. Squashed into the rickety blue bus that bore us from Landing Steps to Customs shed, we were barely seated when the shuttle stopped after a few yards' travel and exhorted us to get out again. With the vehicle gate in front of us securely padlocked, I noticed, passengers were summarily herded through a narrow pedestrian gate on foot, crossing a squelching mat as they did so. "Disinfectan' for shoes, ma'am," we were proudly informed. The authorities watched our step carefully, ensuring that no one inadvertently jumped the mat, for this was a major issue, and my thin-soled daytime flatties were saturated by the solution. But the operation struck me as odd for, arriving off a five-day voyage from Cape Town, I had patently not been walking in the diseased fields of England very recently, nor had anyone else on our ship. And surely, if I *had* hiked across English dales during the northern autumn, would I have been wearing the town shoes I presently sported? No passenger at all was invited to unpack and disinfect his dirty trainers or hiking boots. Then I heard that in feisty Ascension things weren't much different. There the authorities made an exerted effort to ensure foot-passage across a mat that was absolutely bone-dry, a friend recounted to me. And when someone asked why this was so, he was told by the Saint in charge: "Well, you see, the disinfectan' ain't arrive yet!"

I can't help laughing. It will take a lifetime to fathom what makes these islands tick; but it will be a lifetime of wry amusement. Frustration too, of course, to those with Outside World habits, for St Helenians habitually stop short of asking salient questions, of making touchy decisions, of getting up and seeing something through to the bitter end – or, in short, of taking responsibility. "History's done everything for them," someone once suggested. "Perhaps it's slavery that drained out initiative."

"How do you feel about St Helena now, now that you're living here?" I am asked.

I look around at my house and garden and my heart beats faster. I gaze on the glories of the island's scenery and I know I am still in love. My blood runs soothingly warm when I hear these lilting accents, when passers-by wave and call to me. I love the awkward lifestyle, the fun, the little irritations of certain shortages about which we make such fuss, the rhythm of the ship's arrival and the stillness when it goes...

Yet I have lately seen a side of St Helena that I never wanted to know, learning it at first-hand. I have myself experienced the island's two great failings: inexplicable and vicious resentment, and an inbuilt prejudice against settlers. Even Deirdre succinctly advised me one day: "Expatriates can't come muscling in here and expect to live normal lives." And somewhat taken aback, I pondered what really constitutes *normal*? Obviously, I decided, I've done the wrong thing by showing willing to give time and energy beyond the call of duty for a bit of fundraising, but my efforts come with genuine interest and I'm not there for accolade. I simply want to help because I love the place. And now I remember wise Father Joe's warnings. "People who come for a week think this place is heaven on earth. After three weeks they begin to see the cracks. After three months they fall into them."

After twenty-eight months since we moved into this house, and ten months of unbroken island life this year, I have indeed seen those cracks, I acknowledge as I drain the coffee in my cup. My recent unhappy experiences regarding the museum have been a devastating eye-opener. I perhaps would have preferred to read them merely as character lines, but I was shocked enough to see them for what they really are. And yes, I have fallen into them.

10.

The Royal Ham

November 2002

It's November. I've been back a month from my annual sojourn in Cape Town, and Virginia is jangling her car keys at me. "You have to see this, Mum. Come with me, I'll drive you to the Wharf. It looks like an ice cream parlour!"

The island is in a fever of 'decorating'. Even the little houses of those who can ill afford the cost are newly dressed, and Market Street has taken on an entirely new aspect in the past few weeks. Certain main roads are frantically being resurfaced, and coloured lights and bunting are strung across Lower Jamestown.

Virginia taxies me past all this industry and then takes a right turn on to the Wharf, driving towards the far end where its narrow lane is lined on one side by ancient buildings honed into the cliffs, and on the other by a seawall. Even this area has not escaped the paint pots. "Look!" She makes a sweeping gesture. "What did I tell you!"

A Neapolitan ice cream is the first thing I think of. Shades of strawberry pink and sickly mint are in predominance on the buildings, with vivid bubble-gum blue doors setting them off, and far too little vanilla around for my tastes. Worse is the shade of green on the seawall, clashing hideously with the mint on some buildings. Virginia then leads me to the Landing Steps where the rise of each broad step is now a puke-worthy danger-yellow. "So what do you think?"

"I think that Princess Anne will have a fit!"

"But not as much of a fit as when she sees the Castle!" Virginia promises, and I see what she means as soon as we backtrack and pass under its dignified arch into the shady cobbled courtyard. The gracious white portico that usually bestows elegance on this important building

– in fact its single vestige of exterior architectural significance – is now dressed in lilac; a pastel shade of lilac, topped by a corrugated iron ceiling of deep purple. I can only gulp in response.

We discover the Bishop luxuriating in the warmth of our veranda when we arrive home, impatiently anticipating coffee. "Dear God," he utters. "Look what scrappy instructions Machiavelli has sent out. This is guidance for those likely to shake the Royal hand." He passes over a sheet of paper bearing a few short paragraphs of instruction for the uninitiated, the directives printed in somewhat incongruous Comic Sans. The Princess, it advises correctly, is to be addressed as *Your Royal Highness* at first greeting, but thereafter followed up with *"Ma'am to rhyme with Ham."*

"I think you'll find that Debrett's – a source of better taste – will suggest that *Ma'am* rhymes with *'Pam'*, an altogether more dignified option," I offer, matching Bish's criticisms.

"It's too late now," he groans. "Everyone's already referring to the Princess as Her Royal Ham!" Despite that, he's visibly excited about the visit, I can see. "I've also received a seating plan for the dinner – twenty-two of us at Plantation including the Princess. Mostly senior office-holders and wives – you know the drill, Speaker, Chief Secretary, Chief Financial Secretary, Sheriff, that sort of crowd, as well as the visiting Chief Justice of the Appeal Court. And I'll be seated on her right, the Governor on her left."

"She'll find you entertaining." I remark, withholding my opinion that the Princess will long-since have run out of lively exchanges with the Governor by then. An encounter with His Excellency in Main Street yesterday showed me a man nervous about the impending visit, even appearing mildly out of touch with proceedings gathering momentum around him. And the planned programme shows that from her first moment, almost to the last of her fifty-hour stay, he will be clamped to the Princess's side. Even her accommodation for those two nights will be passed at Plantation House without the benefit of a woman's ministrations, for Gloria long ago informed me: "I will *not* be here for Princess Anne. I have a doctor's appointment in London which I made a long time ago. And besides, I have nothing to gain from her visit; I've met royalty before, when Duncan was a Consul." And true to her word, she boarded the last ship north. Duncan Hill will carry the can alone, a man of best intentions but limited scintillation.

"I don't know who's drawn up these lists!" the Bishop goes on. "Machiavelli, I suppose. The former Speaker of the House hasn't been invited to the dinner – yet he's one of only two OBEs on the island, and the whole object of the dinner is to entertain people with Honours!" He flings himself back in his chair. "And you won't believe this! Everyone who attends the dinner at Plantation is *barred* from the cocktail party at the Castle the next night!"

"Ah, the Riffraff Party!" Drinks for the hoi-polloi, is the other term around town.

"Not even the Sheriff whose own mother is receiving an MBE from the Princess that night is allowed in – and she's *furious*! What's more, two MBEs awarded are for work in the Church – and even *I*, as Bishop, am not allowed to attend! Protocol's *dead* in this place!"

I rather agree. But the one person on the island who knows how things are properly done has long since fallen foul of Gloria; and so protocol now flounders under her contrary pull in one direction and, regarding the Royal Visit, the tattooed tug of Machiavelli in another. "Then it's not dubbed Riffraff for nothing," I remark. I confess to being a little sour about this affair, since I am not invited to the Castle either. "The funny thing is, half the expats going to the Castle cocktail party don't give a fig for the monarchy."

Yet here is a South African national who does. One whose earliest continuous memories are those of preparations for Queen Elizabeth's coronation, spending weeks dressing up in bed-quilt trains to parade around the house with a rubber-ball orb and walking-stick sceptre, exercising a royal wave from the French windows at startled subjects passing our house. When that was over and the red-white-and-blue ribbons of celebration were dismantled at home, I concentrated on drawing pictures of the Royal Yacht *Britannia* carrying Prince Charles and me away on honeymoon when we eventually grew up. Even the realities of growing up in a South African republic have never diminished my loyalty to the Queen and her close relatives, and since living in St Helena I have, with sincere feeling, attended memorial services on the deaths of Princess Margaret, and of the Queen Mother six weeks later, and a happier occasion to celebrate the Queen Elizabeth's Golden Jubilee – all services at which a massive dearth of British-born expatriates was glaringly obvious. So, since every member of both my immediate family and Christopher's have had reasonably close social encounters with the Royal Family at one time or another, I had hoped that I might, in this insignificant place, enjoy the opportunity to exchange smiles with the Princess Royal. But I am, it turns out, not considered worthy even of riffraff.

With the island now on countdown to the Royal visit, even the brass bands are putting in extra hours at rehearsal, their practises offering free Tuesday night concerts that drift towards my veranda as they blast away in their borrowed shed near the bottom of our road. And when the annual Remembrance Sunday service takes place just five days before the Princess's arrival, we are entertained there by a higher standard of music than has been enjoyed for some years.

Held at the solid white cenotaph on the brink of a surging ocean, this annual wreath-laying ceremony to remember the dead of wars past and present, is set in a deeply emotive place. Against a background of swaying ocean, sometimes swishing amiably and at other times throwing spray indiscriminately over the crowd, hundreds turn out in dark suits and lapel poppies. Fairy terns flutter overhead like doves of peace, spirit-like in their daintiness, while the distinctive *coooorr-roo* of real doves issues gently from the tall trees growing in the moat. Led by the trumpeting bands, the clergy of various denominations take up position to one side of the Cenotaph, sun glinting off the mitre and purple robes of the Anglican Bishop who leads the service. And while the only official to arrive by car is the Governor in full regalia, his habitual earliness – sometimes by a full five minutes – causes annual irritation to the Bishop who times the Service with military precision, designing it to exactly coincide the requisite Two Minute Silence with Greenwich Mean Time. This year, however, His Excellency is obligingly punctual, and even the clock at St James' does not strike the incorrect time because it has been stopped during church renovations finally underway with all the money our charity Scrabble games have earned.

The Service then proceeds, with a certain amount of tear-wiping while Laurence Binyon's immortal words are recited by the Governor:

"They shall not grow old, as we that are left grow old:
Age shall not weary them, nor the years condemn.
At the going down of the sun and in the morning
We will remember them."

We shed a few more after the wreath-laying when the Kohima Epitaph is intoned:

"When you go home
tell them of us and say,
for your tomorrow
we gave our today."

By the end of the ceremony there's a lot of salt water on the Wharf. The wreath for the Territory, St Helena, is laid by the Governor, after whom other representatives remember their own dead: the Honorary French Consul for the President of the French Republic, the Royal Navy, the Army, the Royal Air Force, Merchant Navy (laid by a crew member of the RMS *St Helena*), the St Helena Police Force, the St Helena Fire and Rescue Services, and even the Cable & Wireless company.

Today the weather is calm and co-operative, obligingly avoiding the microphones through which wind often thunders from huge speakers erected for the event, obliterating all meaningful messages. Today we hear everything, yet our minds disobediently stray to the diversions caused last year by a breeze so capricious that it wickedly snatched the feathery purple hat from the head of the Lady Sheriff and whisked it out to sea. It was also on that Remembrance Sunday in 2001 that St Helena chose to again commemorate the dead of the *Darkdale's* sinking in 1941 (a ceremony distinct from the RFA's wreath fiasco that took place at a different time). And so a small boat was designated to the spot where the *Darkdale's* oil still oozes to the sea's surface after rough weather, carrying on board a wreath which, upon a prearranged signal, was to be ceremonially tossed upon the waves. It was a moving moment. With the signal given, the congregation turned seawards against the Wharf railings, quiet in their contemplation. The boat was clearly identifiable among the other small fishing vessels at rest in the bay but... We screwed up our eyes. "Can you see what's happening out there?" I eventually whispered to the person beside me.

He shook his head: "An' I got goo' wision." The late morning sun glistened on the ocean, the boat's outline sharpened into clear focus. "There's two men on board," he advised. Yes, I could see that much myself but was at pains to spot a wreath cast upon the waters near it.

On the shore we still stood in respectful silence, eyes peeled on the sea. And we stood and stood, while minutes dragged by with the slowness of aeons.

"You know what?" my neighbour suddenly hissed. "I believe they done throw that now wreath ower on the next side of that boat, so we can't see nothin'! And no one have arrange a signal to say it done!" That seemed a likely explanation. And in the resigned habit of St Helena we could have stood there all day, waiting fruitlessly, if the Bishop's patience hadn't expired, prompting him to proceed with the service. In fact, the well-intentioned wreath never did appear before the public's eyes; but when we sneaked another look, what we could locate, determinedly setting sail for Brazil, was the Sheriff's little purple hat.

A rebroadcast of the service the same evening on Radio St Helena fortunately did not make much of the floating wreath operation, perhaps because of programming time-constraints. But they dealt with these in their own inimitable fashion. In order to keep within the allocated time frame, the station took the trouble to edit out all but two verses of each moving hymn the congregation had sung – but then delivered over the airwaves a rather tide-surging-cough-and-snuffly-foot-shuffling recording of the full Two Minute Silence.

HRH the Princess Royal is arriving at St Helena on the RMS – the way we all do – with no more than a few minor adjustments to her accommodation. Without state rooms on the ship, only a few cabins offer the luxury of a small sofa, a fridge, and an intercom telephone, and she is installed in one of these. Refurbished with new curtains and carpets before she boards the vessel in Ascension Island, having flown there from Brize Norton RAF airbase near Oxford, the cabin also has a ringing lock fixed to the door. This, we hear, will alert her accompanying PPO and PS (Personal Protection Officer, and Private Secretary) to any comings and goings from her quarters. And the Princess has revelled in the voyage, Captain Martin Smith informs Bish in emailed reports. She has played Bingo, mixed with other passengers, struck up a friendly and somewhat conspiratorial rapport with her St Helenian cabin stewardess, Ursula, who acts as Lady-in-Waiting for the voyage, and lounged around during the day in casual white slacks and a loose striped shirt for comfort, almost assuming an ordinary lifestyle in those unique surroundings.

But from the moment the RMS drops anchor in James Bay at ten in the morning, with a jubilant bellow, Machiavelli's duty-roster propels her into action. "He hasn't even allowed her time for a loo visit!" complains Bish. "She goes flat-out from Friday morning to Sunday noon! She'll be completely exhausted!"

Half the island has turned out to get a glimpse of her and buzzing crowds are eagerly compressed against the railings as the *Gannet Three* ploughs towards the shore. Fluttering police ribbons mark our limits lest we attempt to ambush the princess on arrival, while the Youth Orchestra, awarded wider boundaries for their seating near the Customs gate, scrapes its violins with the verve of the sinking Titanic musicians. Out of our sight, hidden behind a large crane at the end of the Wharf, a prescribed line of besuited government officials are jostling for precedence behind the Bishop who, officially second in status after the Governor, waits in state at the top of the bilious yellow Steps to shake her hand. His Excellency, meanwhile, is personally escorting the Princess from the ship in the ferry. But, before she even steps ashore, one of the Comic Sans directives presents a conundrum. Among such stern warnings as "*The Princess is to be asked no direct questions*", stands out one that affects the boatmen and their helpers at the landing: "*There is to be no bodily contact whatsoever with Her Royal Highness.*" So, with the fear of Zeus instilled into them, not one of the ferrymen dares extend a helping hand to assist her leap to the Steps, and the Princess is abandoned to manoeuvre the landing quite on her own. That no mishap occurs in this tricky operation is undoubtedly thanks to her legendary sporting agility.

Every child on the island, bussed to the Wharf for the occasion, has been given a small Union flag to wave as soon as the Princess is disgorged from the Governor's car at the Customs barrier to begin her walk to the Castle where tea awaits her. Backed by the valiant Youth Orchestra, they also have a song to deliver, written by the pre-school pupils (and staff, I expect) of Half Tree Hollow First School who won a competition with these immortal words and a tune I have forgotten:

"*Welcome, welcome, Princess Anne (repeat twice)*
It's good to have you here
We hope you will enjoy yourself
From beginning to the end
To make this Royal welcome
The best you'll ever spend..."

"Who wrote this song?" the Princess politely inquires of the Governor who is beside her while she pauses and exchanges smiling words with random spectators along her path. But Governor Hill looks nonplussed. "I have no idea," he admits, though the song has lately been emblazoned in the press with showered accolades for the winners. Uncomfortably out of his metier in these circumstances, he appears ill at ease even at this early stage. By the time he reappears with her in the early afternoon to review the troops on parade, he wears a vaguely besieged expression. Perhaps the omnipresence of the Princess's bodyguard around his house unsettles him – a sight so unprecedented in St Helena that we all eye the PPO's watchfulness with fascination. But it does not take long for the man to fathom the absurdity of ultra-diligence in a place where crime is virtually unknown, and where friendliness is what the islanders offer. For right under our gaze, almost in deference, his body language subtly shifts key, shoulders lose their tension, and only his eyes never stop roaming.

Yet another podium has been set up outside the Courthouse, furnished once again with dignitaries in smart hats who enjoy shelter from the mid-November afternoon, to watch the review. Its cost has caused a vociferous outcry after recent discovery that the Q5 platform in use a bare six months ago has bafflingly been commandeered for building wood elsewhere, on the Governor's instruction, and new podium timber has had to be purchased at highly inflated prices. But after a rush, it was finished just in time; and now the Governor, changed from this morning's brown suit into obligatory white uniform, mounts it to read out his official speech of welcome to the Princess. She has changed too, swapping her practical landing slacks and jacket for a stunning pink suit with a matching hat – its arum-lily decoration a gesture to St Helena's national flower that instinctively wins the hearts of the people. She speaks easily in reply, without notes and with an extraordinary memory for detail, making much of her Mother the Queen's fond memory of flourishing wild arums during the 1947 Royal visit, and also of her brother Prince Andrew's warm welcome to St Helena in 1984. Certainly a huge painted message proclaiming exactly that in white letters still adorns the retaining wall of the Ladder Hill Road, as does, elsewhere, a welcome to the Duke of Edinburgh hung over from 1957.

From the Parade review, the Princess is whisked away to further duties. Tea at the General Hospital with ancients transported there from their miserable old-age home, some of whom barely know who she is, is next on the schedule. This takes place on a curious concrete apron at the bleak rear of the building, and for a while from my house I clearly hear the animated chatter of hospital staff and the chink of teacups. Then she's off to Ladder Hill where she lays the cornerstone of a future retirement complex. "And there are even more geriatrics for the poor woman tomorrow," someone comments wryly, "even though her favourite charity is Save the Children! Trust Machiavelli to neglect that little detail!"

By now decorative flowers have joined the coloured lights, bunting and British flags all through Jamestown; and bridges, balconies and banisters are adorned with creamy arums, banana leaves, palm fronds, orange 'Birds of Paradise' (strelitzia), Cape yew, and shiny mango foliage. For sheer brilliance, bougainvillea in scarlet, orange, mauve and pink are a popular choice despite its short life as a cut flower, and generous armloads in all those colours have been cut from my garden, with permission, to tumble over the balconies of the hospital in efforts to cheer up that singularly dreary building. Even the tiny New Bridge across the Run, close to the hospital, has received an artistic swathing of arums, though I am not sure the Princess will actually travel that way. For even without reading her gruelling schedule, her designated routes are easily recognised by the energetic road-resurfacing that has lately taken place around the island, while flouted routes have unashamedly retained their engine-jolting potholes. The surfaces of New Bridge Road have sadly not been improved.

Late in the afternoon, as she is borne back to Plantation House to don evening dress for the Governor's formal dinner for twenty-two, I resume the pattern of my own life, my personal involvement as curious spectator of her visit by now completely satisfied. But by the next evening I am unsuspectingly yanked back into the swirl of the island's exhilaration, at an impromptu and intimate dinner at the Consulate Hotel, hosted by my Caribbean friends, Kurt and Eulie. This is a Sulks' Dinner, I surmise, since none of the five people present was invited to cocktails at the Castle with HRH this evening – the so-dubbed Riffraff Party – and all of us are aggrieved by such a breach of protocol. For, seated around our small table with humble me, are not only our hosts for the evening, the Honourable Attorney General and his wife, but our own Lord Bishop *and* the visiting Lord Chief Justice of the Appeal Court, all inexplicably spurned from that gathering because of their presence at Plantation House last night. Yet, with marvellous humour among us, this evening turns out to be uproarious; and in hilarious post-mortems of recent events, I learn the lowdown that keeps us in stitches all night. "I've never seen such gaucheness!" the Lord Chief Justice exclaims, barely touching his soup as he recalls our Governor's careless indiscretions. "There we were in the grand drawing room at Plantation last night, the ladies looking beautiful in evening gowns, men in dinner-jackets, sipping our aperitifs as we waited for HRH to join us for dinner – and finally His Excellency ushered her in. It's his duty, of course, to introduce her to *everyone* in the room, whether they've met before or not. And so he did – until he came to *us*!" The Judge makes a sweeping gesture that includes the Bishop, the Attorney General and his eminent self, and explains to me, as though all responsibility were mine: "This Governor of yours reached our side of the room, casually waved his arm our way, and announced to Her Royal Highness: 'You've already met those three reprobates over there!' *Reprobates! Us?*" The Judge, hiding white fury under a cloak of cheery wit, keeps us laughing, seconded by the Bishop who advances his own stories while even the quiet Attorney

General and his wife put final flourishes of colour into each tapestry. I am clutching my sides, suddenly inordinately grateful that I am here in the Consulate Hotel dining room with this entertaining group of friends, and not in the crowded Council Chamber at the Castle where the Princess is greeting just one person in every organised group of ten, according to Machiavelli's caveats, before dutifully moving to the next cluster.

The Bishop, seated on her right at dinner last night, achieved much more than a simple greeting, I learn, and by the end of the evening he and the Princess were conspiratorial friends, sharing a sense of humour that served them well through the evening, since His Excellency, on her other side, imbibed too much and soon descended into morose silence. But, Bish laughs, his finest moment of victory arrived when the Princess, learned on the subject of St Helena and also of matters aeronautical, expressed such succinct views on the spectre of St Helena's proposed airport that her government-serving airport-passionate co-diners were sent into shock. "I've looked at all the island's charts," he quoted her, "and I can see by the crosswinds that an airport at Prosperous Bay Plain simply will not work."

"B-but – " stuttered a staunch promoter, "we've had *experts* here!"

"Yes, and that's the kiss of death!" retorted the Princess Royal. A woman after my own heart, I think, who does not hold the majority of visiting experts in high regard.

This morning the Princess went missing, we hear, putting her PPO into a frenzy of agitation. Could HRH have been abducted *here*? The Governor, knowing nothing of her whereabouts, was no help. But the Bishop, if consulted, might have assisted. (Or he might not have.) Over dinner he and HRH had shared some small secrets, and one – it transpires – was her yearning to explore on her own. Simply to be alone. No one can blame her for that. And the Bishop obliged by suggesting that if she rose early enough, she might escape the house through a side door into the garden and soon would find a path heading into the woodland behind. There is a delightful walk there, leading between tall dense trees and surprising stands of bamboo, through ancient gate-posts and across streamlets, to descend into the deep valley where the Butchers lie. Whether he actually mentioned the Butchers' graves I don't know, but deep in the forest their two neat graves lie side by side, one marked by a cleaver, the other by a skull and crossed arrows. Both were slaves, we are told, and though legend has it that one killed the other, they have found an oddly companionable resting place in this quiet forest, and the leafy route provides a favourite walk for Chris and me, enjoying the easy terrain and the tranquillity of the surroundings. To be honest, the faintly spooky atmosphere immediately surrounding the graves puts me off walking there alone, but I'm sure the Princess, if she discovered them, would be less fainthearted.

With a desperate scarcity of restaurants on the island, the only appropriate venue for a princess to lunch would be at Farm Lodge Country House Hotel in the rural heart at Rosemary Plain. So it is no surprise that this elegantly renovated Georgian residence was selected as temporary host to the royal visitor today. Sandwiched between more geriatrics in the morning and an afternoon of judging stalls at the Agricultural Show, the Princess's roster allowed a luxury luncheon for eight prominent guests, devised over months of meticulous planning and dedicated ingredient-storing by the excited proprietors. Crayfish were specially imported through the Cape from Tristan da Cunha for this event, I'd heard, and heaven knows what other delicacies were on the menu. So, intrigued, I question the Lord Chief Justice – currently a resident guest at Farm Lodge himself – about the success of this occasion. But in answer, he growls. I look up in confusion to find our host's eyes twinkling across the table. "I believe lunch is a sore point," he offers cryptically.

The Bishop can't resist input. "Lunch didn't happen, that's why! This week Farm Lodge was told that instead of hosting the Princess and seven prominent guests for a sit-down meal, they could expect a horde of Prince Andrew Secondary School pupils for a buffet!"

There's a stunned pause while we variously picture the horrified faces of the Farm Lodge proprietors, famously choosy about their patrons. *"Teenagers?"* I eventually gasp. "Did *they* get the crayfish?"

The Chief Justice is now smiling wryly. Kurt and Eulie are grinning. "They got teenager fodder. Hamburgers probably."

"Wouldn't HRH have preferred the crayfish herself?"

There's a little hoot of amusement among the others. "HRH didn't share lunch with them at all. Instead she enjoyed the privacy of a bedroom upstairs, taking only an apple, a piece of cheese, and a glass of water for her midday repast!"

"And did you eat the crayfish, or the hamburgers?" I ask the Judge, and he growls again.

"Well, actually," he finally pronounces, "neither the two visiting judges resident at Farm Lodge with me for the duration of Appeal Court Sessions in St Helena – *nor* I – partook of either crayfish or hamburger. In fact the proprietors of the hotel were somewhat inexplicably instructed *to get rid of us* during the Princess's presence in the hotel!"

"Was that written in Comic Sans?" asks Bish facetiously, reading the stamp of Machiavelli in this.

"Worse, it was word of mouth. And *why* were we to be banished from our own hotel?" It's clearly a rhetorical question, for the reasoning is unfathomable. Besides, the Lord Chief Justice of the Appeal Court is enjoying this story in a perverse way, his white hair flicking across his forehead with animation, eyes agleam with sardonic humour. "Let me tell you. It's because our proximity to the Princess Royal could, we were advised, constitute a *security risk!*"

"Of course," murmurs the Attorney General softly. "Why didn't I recognise that terrible danger to her personage?"

We all laugh in disbelief. For the fact that all three, apparently threatening, English judges have very recently spent two days confined on a small ship with Her Royal Highness, does not seem to sway the absurdity of this suspicion in favour of any modicum of common sense... But then, this is St Helena.

Sunday being the day of her departure, she attends the cathedral in the morning, enjoying classic hymns and prayers assembled by the Bishop at her personal request. And as she leaves from there to drive directly to the waiting RMS, it is the last we see of her. But she's smiling and her eyes shine, her attachment to this little island evident in her face, and she has already pledged to return. Hopefully by then someone will have acknowledged her special interest in the island's history, and our fascinating ruined military fortifications in particular which she dearly wished to visit but was allowed no time to do. Perhaps by then, her duty-roster will include a few engagements more scintillating than fifty seemingly successive hours of tea with aged people who are not sure who she is. Perhaps by then, someone familiar with protocol will not exclude our OBEs from dinner, our dignitaries from cocktails, or the Lord Chief Justice of the Appeal Court from remaining in his own hotel as she passes through it…

Perhaps, though I somehow doubt it.

11.

Away in a Supermarket

December 2002 – December 2003

Christmas is coming. Piped carols started in Thorpe's Grocery way back in October, lest we forget, and the festive season in St Helena is getting underway. Inevitably much planning hinges on what the RMS brings from the Cape in mid-December, particularly where Christmas parties or large Christmas dinners are concerned; but most presents have already been purchased from stocks that arrived in October or November. It's the food that really concerns us, and the nagging questions of whether there will be potatoes, onions, or fresh fruit offloaded from the ship in time. We wait and see before planning any menus seriously. At Villa Le Breton we already have our turkey, safely tucked up in our freezer – Chris brought it with him in a freezer box, along with some jars of lumpfish caviar and other rare delights when he and Richard arrived a few days ago. And I have homemade Christmas pudding at the ready, as well as homemade mincemeat for little Christmas pies, when we get around to baking them.

Main Street and the lower reaches of Market Street are strung with coloured lights, the curving seawall along the Wharf also edged with them. On The Bridge (named for The Run that invisibly passes beneath the Market area) the familiar painted Christmas boards annually fixed to the Market building, to Musk's shop, and to the Standard and White Horse bars have already been nailed into position. And this morning, outside the Canister and in pride of place at the head of Main Street, a huge Christmas tree went up, which – because of its immensity – will be only scantily dressed with coloured lights. To South Africans long-accustomed to hot Christmases, it isn't odd that reindeer prance across the tropical sky or that Father Christmas might swelter under his suit of fur, for we also grew up with these northern traditions. But first-timers in these southern climes are visibly thrown. All the shop windows in Jamestown wear flickering lights or shining garlands of tinsel, and even in the residential heights of Upper Market Street, the exteriors of homes – almost universally repainted as Christmas approaches, but in this year of 2002 still wearing their Royal Visit coats – are cheerily lit and adorned with ornamentation. Colour abounds, and some homeowners have been imaginative and generous with their arrangements. Even Half Tree Hollow – a suburb of extraordinary dullness in its scrubby location on the western cliff top of James Valley – is a delight to drive through at Christmas, with vivid Christmas trees and angels, flickering stars, and extravagant strings of fairy lights twinkling all the way up the steep plateau.

Oddly, now that Christmas is so close, Thorpe's has toned down its jaunty carols, though familiar tunes are still discernible in a slow Country-&-Western variation that is less hectic and closer to home here. Passing, I hear melancholy snippets of *Please Daddy Don't Get Drunk This Christmas,* or the lamenting *Gonna be a Blue Christmas Without You.*

The excellent Salvation Army Band is more demure, playing traditional carols outside the Market building, in the Grand Parade, and at various appropriate venues in the country in the lead-up to Christmas, and my personal delight is their post outside the hospital each year. I stand in our garden then, surrounded by the soft light of evening, watching the sunset light up the cliffs as shadows gently creep in elsewhere, and tune my ear to the hidden brass band a hundred yards below us. *Hark the Herald Angels sing...*

Our whole family is happily together again, though mother-in-law Fee is not joining us this time, and nor do we expect other guests. So, relaxed and on our own, we are doing little more in the gentle build-up to Christmas than sipping crisp Cape wines on our pleasant veranda, when Christopher suddenly has an idea.

I am used to his ideas. Though they are generally good, there is a nearly always a disconcerting catch in them: to bring to fruition they entail a great deal of activity from someone *else*. This one's no exception. "It would be nice," he begins, "to have an RSPCA Christmas Tree. A fir tree set up somewhere public, for people to notice and remember their pets at Christmastime. Perhaps they could buy something for it, to raise some money. Like the lights they sell for the hospice tree in Cape Town."

My heart is sinking already, but I recognise it for a brilliant suggestion. Putting the Heritage Society firmly behind me, I had finally joined the RSPCA (the Royal Society for the Prevention of Cruelty to Animals) St Helena Branch last June, soon after Q5, and for my sins he's dropped this right into my lap. My mind begins to tick. "Ribbons?"

"Ribbons would be good. People could buy a ribbon… and tie it on themselves… and make a wish…" He's thinking aloud.

I'm already at the phone. "JJ, Chris has had an idea." I outline the thought.

An expletive issues from the other end of the line. JJ and I have been elected to a two-man subcommittee in charge of RSPCA fundraising. Him and me. "Do you know what the date is? It's barely ten days to Christmas!"

"I'll order a tree and buy the ribbons. We could start on Tuesday."

"Tell Chris it's a brilliant idea, but he'd better help! I'll run it by the Chairman."

Michel, the RSPCA Chairman gives his blessing at three o'clock. The men at A&NRD are just knocking off for an early Christmas Friday when I catch them by telephone. "We need a Christmas tree," I announce, knowing full well it should have been ordered in November, "and we would *really* like it to be ten feet tall and delivered to the Jamestown Spar first thing on Tuesday morning. And we would be thrilled if you'd donate it." I have already ascertained that the Spar supermarket has a space for us.

"Donate it?"

"It's in aid of the RSPCA – the animals. It's to raise money for them." I am chancing my arm. The RSPCA, for some reason, does not rate top of the pops on the island, especially not with the A&NRD. Animals are just animals, after all.

But I have reached a genuine Saint here. "For the animals? Ah, that a excellen' thing, ma'am. I see what I can do." *Oh bless you, bless you, whoever you are!* "We'll deliver Toosday mornin'."

Next morning, Saturday, Chris and I go ribbon buying. The

London Gift Shop has just one kind, but this is special – broad white satin decorated with line-drawn red candles. We buy it all. The Emporium has nothing, but the Victoria thankfully turns up a treasure trove of ribbon in all colours. We buy what we perceive to be more than enough of the brightest and broadest, and bear them off home to cut into half-metre lengths. The rest of the weekend I spend on the computer, drawing up flyers, placards, and explanatory notices. Chris's idea is evolving, and JJ and I already have a title for the tree – *The RSPCA Tree of Celebration, Remembrance & Hope* – which, while it certainly is a little fundraising effort, will also hold the essence of Christmas. It will, we hope, give the public pause to consider the less commercial aspects of the season, if only for a few moments, and so we offer a plethora of reasons why the harassed shopper should stray over to our corner and donate some money towards the pleasure of tying a colourful bow on a fir tree. It's up to the customer to tie the bow herself (preferably), for whatever sentiment she privately prefers; but a prompt-sheet nearby will offer such reminders as: *Because you're missing absent loved ones; To help an injured animal; With thoughts for the sick or lonely; To make a special wish...* And so we have plenty to do.

JJ takes one look at the broad white ribbon and singles it out. "We'll charge £1 for that – it's different, it's broader, and it's special. The rest will be 50p. The white one will be our Elizabeth Scholtz Memorial Ribbon." I like working with JJ. He doesn't waste time debating.

So the white ribbon with red candles on it gets a box of its own, and a price tag of £1.00 each. I don't know how many people will spend a whole £1 on tying a ribbon, but it does remember a quite extraordinary woman. Elizabeth Scholtz was a South African who worked as a voluntary vet in St Helena for nineteen years. A theatre nurse by profession, she taught herself veterinary medicine as soon as she discovered that St Helena is afforded no qualified veterinary services, and then launched forth to work tirelessly for the animals of the island until the very day before her death from cancer just over two years ago. Her energy, knowledge, fire, and perseverance were legend, and while the wellbeing of all the island's animals came first in her life, she did not suffer human fools gladly. Her business-like brusqueness was sometimes intimidating to the meek, yet others adored her. Perhaps those few of the latter will buy the ribbons, I think.

Elizabeth's great bequest to the island was the knowledge she passed on to assistants while she was still alive, and since her death they have endeavoured, to the best of their ability, to keep her work going for as long as they can. It is difficult for them, working as volunteers in such an intense role while holding down full-time jobs in other fields. And with the onus of veterinary care now solely upon those few, they already are struggling to find time for their families, and soon will start disengaging themselves from a demanding public panicked by the absence of Elizabeth and a lack of reliable alternative facilities. Last June, after persuasive nagging, a veterinary trainer was brought from the UK by the government to teach employees of the Agricultural department the rudiments of veterinary care. But the course sadly turned out to be insufficient, and the new practitioners, more comfortable with livestock than domestic pets, are known occasionally to flounder. But though the RSPCA's chief remit is to campaign hard for a qualified permanent vet for the island, the government isn't interested. There is still ceaseless work to be done.

It is Monday afternoon when the phone jangles in my kitchen. Spar is on the line. "Ma'am, there one big tree lyin' in our storeroom – it in our way."

My turn for expletives now; we're all geared for Tuesday morning. I lift the phone. "JJ, you've got to come to town!"

The tree that we find in the storeroom is huge. Handsome, freshly hewn, well-shaped – but immense. It takes the full strength of Chris and JJ and me to drag it from between the crates of the storeroom, through the length of the supermarket itself, leaving a long carpet of dust and needles behind us on the pristine floor, to the space we have been allocated near the street window. It is an excellent spot, and the tree will be visible from outside, if we ever get it standing, but so far we don't even have a tub for it, or rocks to stabilise the tub. That had been this afternoon's mission.

It also takes all three of us to raise it to a standing position, only to discover that the large garden bucket we grabbed from home – the one usually supporting our own tree – is too small for this generous donation from the A&NRD. So Christopher is dispatched to the nearby Solomon's DIY store, where he soon appears to have taken the afternoon off, for he simply doesn't return. Eventually I follow to find him standing utterly perplexed by a simple matter of choice. This is indeed an unusual plight in this place, and Chris, I think, is in shock.

"The biggest one!" I command briskly, without lingering to perplex myself, and abandon him to pay for it while I rush back to assist JJ who's been left to support the beast on his own. The tree, too big to rest on the floor at this place just inside the supermarket entrance while Christmas shoppers are coming and going, is leaning dangerously, and I cannot see JJ at all. "Are you there?" I venture, and a stifled voice comes back at me from the thicket: "Dooley obble blarraf Ω¿!∂ξΞж Chris? Floofly xzzhin bbblit this ∂Θξж§Ω tree anymore! Help, for ∂ξ*ж sake!" And I plunge into undergrowth again, at least affecting some show of support despite my flimsy back.

When Chris, saviour of our souls, finally arrives with the new garden tub, the tree is doing a line-dance of sorts. Three steps this way, three totters forward, bow to your partner, four steps back. And a customer at the till has his hands on his hips, his head on one side, and an expression of advanced mirth on his face. "If you take much longer with that tree," he takes the trouble to shout across the shop, supposedly to those of us buried within it, "I am going home to fetch my video camera!" At this stage we don't give a damn if he airs his film on BBC World; we are barely recognisable for the pine needles protruding from our hair, our mouths, nostrils and ears, and gummed to our clothes like the coarse hair of warthogs. But the tree is in its box at last, stabilised with stones hurriedly collected from the hillside behind the supermarket, and carrier bags of good earth brought from our garden, which all add weight. And now it stands tall and straight, quite splendidly.

JJ blows down his nose. "I'm going home now, to clean up. While I'm gone, Chris, don't get any more Ω¿!∂ξΞж bright ideas."

And Chris doesn't. Not yet anyway. But he does help me sell an amazing £44 worth of ribbons in just the remaining two hours of the afternoon. I am utterly staggered. All the customers have come to look at the tall real tree standing naked in the supermarket, and as they've read the placards, they have dug into their pockets. We have sold a 50p ribbon each for all the past pets of an animal-lover, for sons and daughters off-island for Christmas, for private wishes, for a sick relative in hospital, for a beloved dog that died last month. St Helenian reserve does not often invite others into personal thoughts, but many of these people are choosing a ribbon colour carefully, searching out a perfect spot on a prickly branch, and occasionally we are told: "That's for my son. I'll remember where I tied this one." One man tells me, "I want to tie ribbons with my wife – we'll come together at lunchtime tomorrow." This man is a friend of ours and I know he'll keep his word, and that he and his wife will in fact tie Christmas ribbons together on our tree for as long as we set one up. Some customers have been pleased to simply make a donation, but one of the first to twig the real message behind our tree, informed me as she scuttled to its more private side: "Us recently done had a family berea'ment, see. An' now I tyin' this ribbon for you, Uncle," she announced to the tree aloud as she perfected her bow, "because us all still miss you so." And I was so touched for Uncle's sake, that I couldn't even see her ribbon through my watery eyes.

But even during these first two hours, it is the white memorial ribbons that dominate. Broad and gleaming like beacons against the dark green fir needles, the *Elizabeth Scholtz Memorial Ribbon* seems to signify a national confidence that Elizabeth is now sitting comfortably by the side of St Francis of Assisi. We have nearly sold out of it already, on this our first afternoon, with four more selling days to come. I must buy more coloured ribbons tomorrow, which are running low as well, but there are only a few white ones left in all of Jamestown. I wish we could have bought more, for something wonderful has happened here today: for just a moment thoughts have turned away from food and parties and presents, and whether cargo will arrive in time; and someone else has been remembered. Pets and people, sick and departed – and with it all, money is gathering for the RSPCA.

The Spar's manager catches us as we're packing up at closing time, his eye falling with a twinkle of pleasure on the small notice propped at the tree's base: *The RSPCA is grateful to Spar for this space, and to the A&NRD for donating the Christmas Tree.* "You'll be very welcome next year as well," he says. "Our girls are over-the-moon at having a real live tree in the shop, and it's already looking absolutely beautiful."

Feeling satisfied but exhausted and sharing some of JJ's sentiments, I look at Chris. "This is a success – but please don't have any more good ideas."

Following hot on the heels of Christmas 2002, Virginia and Chris have made a lightning three week round trip to the Cape, and now are back laden with good things to eat and drink. It's been a shopping spree with gastronomic purpose and they've brought back treats for a Silver Wedding party – twenty-five good years of marriage – which Chris and I have chosen to celebrate on the island.

Donny's is the selected venue, largely for the flaming summer sunset he will provide over cocktails from his broad wooden deck beside the ocean, and a starry sky above us later as guests relax in the warm summer night after dinner. The sit-down meal will be held inside so as to allow free-flow outside during the cocktail hour, and for weeks Donny and I have agonised over whether to use the attached ground-level disco hall for this, or the more atmospheric basement area with its built-in bar counter. Up and down the stairs we've traipsed, finally deciding upon the novelty of the downstairs venue which is rarely used. And so, when I greet Chris and Virginia returning from Cape Town just four days before this event, I straightaway lead them off to show them our plans. Great, Chris says in full agreement.

The catering gets underway, mostly commandeered by excellent Millie, Donny's cook, while Virginia and I add to the menu with great fillets of South African beef, lemon-chicken casseroles, rum-soaked chocolate soufflé cakes and mixed-berry confections. Chris gloats over his wines, carefully selected from the Cape's finest vineyards, which we deliver to Donny the evening before the party for long chilling against the projected heat of the next day. The sky is cloudless, the sea azure. "The weather will be *parfect* tomorrow, you'll see," promises Keith the barman, who is wise with years. Everything is going swimmingly, everyone is happy... And then the day itself dawns.

Tuesday morning, February, the very peak of summer, 9am Donny is on the phone. "I think we should move the dining room upstairs," he announces at this eleventh hour. "It's – er – raining a bit down here, and the steps might be slippery for guests going up and down to the toilets. I think you'd better come down and see for yourselves."

JJ, who has offered to help with decorations is there when we arrive, already assessing the sodden situation. The deck is slippery with water, and Donny, perched on a pergola in pouring rain, is frantically hammering a vast white tarpaulin to its wooden struts for shelter while Keith the barman, wringing his hands, is looking personally responsible for the deluge. Chris and I inspect the steep tiled stairs descending to the basement and see at once why we dare not put our guests at peril in these conditions. So the disco hall it has to be. JJ shrugs in his inimitable way. "We'll make it nice."

And he does. By the time Donny has finished securing tarpaulins as far across the deck as they will reach and is standing back to watch, with misgiving, their accumulated dams periodically vented over the sides like a local Niagara Falls, JJ has arranged, as a focal point inside, a giant display of the cactus, flax flowers, dried agapanthus heads, and sundry vegetation that we have pillaged from the countryside during the weekend. Then, as Donny also moves indoors to start dismantling all the disco lights, wiring, and sound-system appendages above the little platform at the far end of the hall, JJ rolls up his sleeves and smothers the arrangement with silver spray paint. Delegated to lay tables, we meekly do our job, striving not to get underfoot. JJ in charge is like wildfire, sweeping about with his spray can, silvering smaller arrangements he's fixed to the platform balustrade, hanging long silvered sheets of paper and giant silver-crepe bows along black-painted walls to brighten the scene, strewing paper-glitter over the white tablecloths that will wink and tremble in the light of the silver candles brought from Cape Town, a gentle movement in the room created by wafting helium-filled silver balloons that are attached to chairs-backs. An extraordinary transformation has taken place by the end of the morning, and such an aura of festivity now furnishes the former disco hall, that we are almost entirely able to overlook the multi-coloured plastic chairs and the inevitable plastic cloths that come with the territory. This recreated dining room is almost elegant!

Guests are expected at six o'clock, and at five it stops raining. A watery sun emerges between the clouds, and dapples the sea with flecks of silver, highlighting the fishing boats moored in the bay. My beautiful Roland electric piano is plugged into one corner of the deck and we are lavished with *real* cocktail-hour music by a St Helenian friend who plays professionally at a Cape Town bar – such a novelty on the island that a fresh scene is set even as the first guests arrive. Expatriates Bill and Jill Bolton are among the first, having taken seriously our invitation suggestion to wear *a frivolous silver decoration*. Contriving gigantic Elton John glasses silvered with glitter, and a jaunty silver wig, they are greeted with inevitable laughter, a proffered tray of champagne, and platters of delicious cocktail snacks wielded by bow-tied stewards on home-leave from the RMS – a brilliant detail organised by Donny without our knowledge. Behind them come varieties of silver feelers that tremble and glitter above the heads of the crowd, huge silver flowers in the hair, massive pectoral crosses (to tease the party-loving Bishop), tinsel boas, and a couple wearing large matching silver hearts on their heads. Shy guests note the fun and delve into handbags for little silver corsages they were too timid to arrive in. "You could have done better than *that*, Bishop!" exclaim the Boltons when Bish arrives with only faint glitter creaming his cheeks. "Look at the effort the rest of us made!" There are silver shawls, silver tops, silver bow ties, and laughter bubbling across the seafront. When the sun sets at seven, the sky stripes itself with gold and platinum in order to join the party.

After dinner, Donny – who has already leapt well beyond the bounds of duty with his tarpaulins, the dismantling of his disco, and the secret provision of professional waiters – pulls a final surprise from his copious hat. Coffee... *Real coffee?* Instant powder is the accepted norm on this island, and we have not made further provision than Nescafé granules for our eighty guests. Donny grins mischievously, slanted eyes crinkling with laughter into his Asian-spun features: "Not just real coffee either. *St Helena Coffee!*"

"*How...?*"

Jill Bolton soon lets us know. "We're outraged! We're *supposed* to be guests!" she teases. "As a guest I did not expect to have to work at your party!"

"We didn't know a thing about this!"

"That's your story!" she retorts, somehow conveying the likelihood that we'll be reminded of this social infraction for years to come.

"I asked them," Donny admits. "I've just sold Jill and Bill all my coffee equipment for starting their new coffee shop, so I couldn't make any myself. I thought that real local coffee to end a lovely evening would be the crowning touch. And a surprise for you."

A crowning touch, definitely, and the evening has been full of surprises, and of accolades for Millie's catering and our own, and of amazement at JJ's transformation of that dull venue into something special. It's been huge fun, and now that guests are dancing on the deck to a livelier cycle of tunes from the piano, real silver stars have finally burst through the thinning clouds overhead.

Jill and Bill's coffee shop is the talk of the town. With wooden bench-tables topped by large cream umbrellas, it has not only breathed a welcome puff of life into the lacklustre Leisure Park at the seafront, but is the first of its kind ever to grace the shores of St Helena. The scent of fresh roast beans now wafts from one of the abysmal 'bus shelters' that has magically metamorphosed into a kitchen, and Chris and I are drawn like moths to a flame. The first coffee in St Helena arrived in 1733, introduced by the English East India Company at a time when the Dutch were already industriously growing plantations of it in Djakarta (Java), and the French in Ile Bourbon (Reunion). The English had some plantations in East Africa with which they supplied the coffee houses of London, popular in the late 1600s; but by the mid-1700s they were experiencing such difficulty procuring actual plants from Mocha (Al-Muktā) in southwest Yemen, source of the best coffee, that their appointed cargo for St Helena arrived as berries. Though the Green Tipped Bourbon berries are delicate travellers, these seeds promised good crops, yet, typically, were not altogether welcomed by the farmers of St Helena who did not expend adequate energy in nursing them, and despite all the effort taken by the EEIC, in a short time the delicious crop entirely disappeared from St Helena. However coffee plants, once rooted, are quite sturdy and have a propensity for growing in some unlikely places; so it was with delight that, in 1814, the eminent botanist William Roxburgh, on a visit to St Helena from Calcutta, came upon it growing wild at Bamboo Hedge in Sandy Bay. This happy find also allowed Napoleon to enjoy this island's coffee soon after his exile to St Helena in 1815, evidently provoking his unsubstantiated remark that *"the only good thing about St Helena is the coffee"*, though a rather poignant account remains of him begging for a few spoons of it just days before his death. St Helena coffee – having been declared *"very superior"* in London in 1839 – seems to have thrived until 1845 before fizzling out like so many St Helena projects. Making a fleeting reappearance at the Great Exhibition in 1851 where it won a Premier Award, it then vanished completely. Few present-day islanders have ever had the opportunity to savour it, however, since the excellent quality berries of new trees planted in 1994 in an ambitious private venture, are now so swiftly exported for exploitation as one of the most exotic (and expensive) coffees in the world, that none of it is available in St Helena itself. Its foreign success is indeed laudable, but our instincts warn that this seemingly over-extended local production cannot stay the course for much longer and that all these currently thriving bushes will, in the St Helena way, soon wither and die.

The expatriate Boltons, with their own Rosemary Plain estate lush with coffee trees, looking for a hobby for Jill in Bill's retirement, hit on something that is as strange to this island as a high-rise building: a coffee shop selling real coffee – *St Helena* coffee – of that same old Yemeni strain now more generally known as Arabica *(coffea arabica)*. But 'retirement' does not feature strongly in this little enterprise. While Jill cooks and brews in her tiny kiosk kitchen, it is Bill who organises pickers and sorters during harvesting season. It is Bill who dries the berries, then roasts them. It is Bill who grinds and bags the beans, and then rushes up and down the lawn of the coffee shop serving steaming cups of his own magic and, like his much younger wife, dispensing the good cheer that makes all their products taste so good.

"Of course, nobody drinks real coffee on the island," asserts Bish sagely. He is suffering a strange mood of petulance lately, which I trust is temporary. "And anyway, no islander can afford to waste a whole £1 on a cup of coffee. It will only attract tourists and other expats, you'll see."

It certainly attracts Chris and me. We wander in after shopping and try their filter coffee, cappuccinos, and coffee milkshakes. We tuck into fresh-baked chocolate cake, carrot cake or Bakewell tart. Sometimes we lunch on cottage pie, lasagne, or tuna-mayo toasties and salad, all foreign foods in St Helena. This is a rebirth. This is something quite unutterably extraordinary. With the introduction of this coffee shop comes hope for the future.

"We're going to have to gear up with restaurants if we get an airport," I remind Bish. "Tourists have to eat."

"We won't get an airport. You know as well as I do that SHELCO has mysteriously fallen foul of the government, so *they* won't be building it now – even if they're still standing by the door with hotel plans clutched in their hands, waiting for the first airport sod to be turned at Prosperous Bay Plain." True enough. A full year has passed since the airport referendum, and only rumours fly. Among them is SHELCO's unexpected fall from grace, based on an outrageous untruth that as one executive may once have been a fairground barker he must be considered socially unfit for any airport dealings. The truly disturbing factor here is that government officials have swallowed this. And the notion of that gullibility is just as unsettling as the *real* exodus of young people from St Helena since British citizenship was restored at Q5 last year. For, grasping their new British passports, first the school-leavers went, then the late twenty- and thirty-somethings – some of the island's sharpest talent departing with them. And already the first of whole families have sold up and gone. Today I look at the town on a busy shopping day and see only pensioners and the older middle-aged. Who will be left to man an airport? From a steady population of 5 500 for decades, we have dropped almost overnight to 4 500… 4 300… 3 800… going … going…

Yet talk of air-tourism doggedly persists. And St Helena, with little notion of real-world tourism, does nothing towards it. At present there is really nowhere to eat out. Ann's Place – situated in a far corner of the Castle Gardens – is well-known to yachtsmen who have hung their flags from her ceiling, their posters on her walls, and have traipsed to her with their dirty laundry for decades, but the island fare on offer is mainly fishcakes or mild St Helena curry, attractive only for a quick, light lunch if you're starving. Other options are home-cooking guesthouses where pre-arranged parties are preferred to a couple casually popping in for a night out, while the more sophisticated Farm Lodge Country House Hotel has such an exacting booking system that few diners bother to visit. Even Donny's pub-style meals concentrate on Fridays, though the pub opens (in the preferred habit of St Helena) from Thursday to Saturday.

And so we watch the new St Helena Coffee Shop with interest. Is Bish correct in assuming that Saints don't drink real coffee and won't patronise this place? "I think you're wrong," I argue. "At a League of

Friends fundraising coffee morning at Maldivia House last week, I was one of the tray bearers, offering jugs of boiling water for that god-awful powdered instant everyone serves, and pots of real coffee ready-brewed. And of the sixty-four cups filled that morning, exactly *four* were instant powder!"

"And look!" I add, dragging him off to the Coffee Shop at the first opportunity. "Saints *do* drink real coffee when they're offered it. Look at that table crammed with firemen – they come here *every* Thursday. They don't look like expats to me."

There's a lesson here somewhere, I feel sure, and perhaps one day we'll even know the sublime joy of a proper restaurant.

Time flies in this small place, despite the repeated references of an ignorant wide-world friend to my lazy days of holiday here. It is already June 2003, and JJ and I must raise more money for the RSPCA. So we plan an Event. Purposely different from St Helena's habitual coffee mornings, it must take place before I swan off for my annual three months in Cape Town, and so we roll up our sleeves and get to work. It's a Fashion Luncheon. JJ has the professional background, but I can cook, plan a party, and follow his thought processes.

First we take a quantum leap from local tradition and instead of sending out invitations we *advertise* the event in the *St Helena Herald* – a full-page ad in the quarto-sized newspaper, impossible to miss. It's a stylish, illustrated advertisement, describing the attractions of enjoying a variety of soups and homemade breads in the elegance of the newly-opened General's Apartments at Longwood House which few islanders have seen yet – a venue generously donated to us by the RSPCA stalwart, Michel the French Consul. The Fashion Talk afterwards will brim with useful tips on colour co-ordination, dressing up and dressing down, and the fashion no-nos you wish you'd always known. The entrance fee is a whopping £10 per head all-inclusive, and women are invited to dress smartly. As we can accommodate no more than thirty-five for lunch, early booking is essential.

So the first person I run into after publication of the ad, is St Helenian Ilva. "Are you coming to the Fashion Lunch?" I inquire, since

I peg her for a likely candidate, well-groomed, savvy, always keen to be seen in a social setting.

She snorts at me derisively. "Why do I need to go to a Fashion Talk? I wouldn't learn anything there." I glance at the white shoes she is wearing with her dark navy dress, and think she probably could. One of the outspoken JJ's pet castigations is that of wearing shoes paler than the hemline.

"I think you'd enjoy it," I offer, "and there'll be a good lunch."

"It's a waste of time for people like me. And expensive."

Then I bump into well-heeled Rachel, another social St Helenian. She is buying fresh bread at Spar and finds me in the queue. "I don't suppose you've sold any tickets yet for your Fashion Luncheon," she cruelly surmises. "No one on the island is going to spend £10 on a bowl of *soup!*"

"There's a variety of excellent soups, lovely breads, and a talk afterwards. It will be well worth it."

"Well, I'm certainly not spending £10 on anything like that."

Even Bish puts in his crusty oar. "You realise no Saint is going to spend £10 on soup and bread and a lecture afterwards? You won't sell any tickets at all at that price, mark my words. And if you do, your only guests will be a few expats."

I let him expel all the steam he wants before I respond. "Actually, the ad appeared on Friday evening. By lunchtime Tuesday we had sold *all* thirty-five tickets – seventeen to expats, *eighteen* to Saints. And I'm still getting calls from disappointed hopefuls."

"Well, I'm glad I'm not going," he retorts.

"So am I. Men aren't invited."

I leave him smouldering on our veranda while I answer the phone. It's Radio St Helena, offering to push the event even though we're fully booked. "I'll just keep mentioning the RSPCA," suggests the young interviewer, "so that people know you're out there and raising money – we're all so desperate for a vet on the island. And this Fashion Talk sounds like so much fun." I outline some of our plans for Saturday, and next morning, as I put my breakfast together to the radio's chitchat, I'm pole-axed to learn that among the many delicious dishes we will serve at the Fashion Lunch, we are also greeting arriving guests with glasses of warm "glue".

It is deluging with rain at Longwood and a cold winter's day when guests arrive, every one smart and groomed and eager for something different; and glasses of spicy *gluhwein* are what we actually offer them to warm up before lunch. The tables are set with unusual centre-pieces and petals are prettily strewn on the floor of the dining room and sun room where a seated lunch is in store. Each place has a cardboard mat, hand-cut by JJ, with a pencil slotted into one corner, and after lunch he will show the women how to fold the mat into a small notebook in which they can jot down tips that take their fancy.

In the meantime they stand chatting over their spiced wine, wandering through these unfamiliar rooms, admiring Michel's collection of Napoleonic prints on the deep red walls, the display cases of old china and antique glass, the heavy Napoleonic furnishings that are so elegant in these illustrious surroundings. Virginia and I are uncovering great tureens of soup and bringing in trays of oven-hot home-baked breads and muffins. It isn't a bad selection, all in all. JJ has made a creamy crayfish bisque, tomato and basil bread and farmhouse loaves. I've brought the spicy butternut and orange soup for which I am famous, a curried almond soup, and piles of courgette muffins – all of them steaming in the wintry air. As the women settle down to their feast, JJ and I know we've done a good thing here. There is animated chatter at every table, and when Virginia and I offer seconds – and even third helpings for those who try all three – we know that Ilva and Rachel, who disdained this fun affair, will regret their snobbishness.

The fashion talk is everything it promised, and more. And before the afternoon is over, a deputation advances upon the two of us. "We want you please to hold an event like this again. Something like flower arranging or table-setting next time, perhaps. It's been *such* fun – we wouldn't have missed this for the world!"

Hah, my Lord Bishop! Wrong again!

It must be something he eats that prompts these blinding inspirations, or perhaps it's just the resounding success of his RSPCA Christmas Tree idea that yet swirls his self-satisfaction. It is the early southern summer now and I am back on the island from another annual South

African visit, but Chris is still in Cape Town when he phones to announce a new Good Idea. "I was at the local vet's this week, buying cat food," he informs me, "when it struck me that, in the five years that our two cats here have been fed on these Scientific Diet pellets, they have never needed medical attention. I mentioned it to the vet, and he says it's common with many of his patients who are, more usually, injured animals. As there's no vet in St Helena, we must introduce this food to the island to keep the cats and dogs healthy."

I am silent at the other end of the phone for so long that he wonders if I've abandoned him. *Good idea, that I grant you,* I am thinking, *but this will mean a lot of WORK. For me.*

"I've already spoken to the Cape Town rep for the Diet," he offers more meekly, "and he's laid a ground-plan. It's a bit complicated because this stuff is not sold through retailers, only through veterinary clinics. But he's run it by his head office overseas and they were so horrified to learn that the island has no vet that they're delighted to help us help the island." The figures for 2003 stand at 500 licenced dogs, and an assessed 1 500 to 2 000 cats, though for some reason our feline friends (and our 150 donkeys) are not incorporated into the Official Census of 10 000 animals. Chris has quoted these numbers to the rep who registered visible shock at such statistics, and he adds now: "Richard and I will bring the first consignment when we arrive for Christmas."

I ring JJ and have barely said hallo when he exclaims, "∂Θξж§Ω! I can tell by your voice, Chris has had another Good Idea!"

I explain, and I hear that JJ is forgiving, because his mind spontaneously clicks into overdrive before creating a chance to argue: "Here's what we'll do. We'll arrange a procession down Market Street with marching bands, and banners, and dogs on leads… We'll arrange freebies for kids and pets, and centre the whole thing on a Saturday morning in the Market building…"

Then the dampers descend. Because we are not licensed vendors we're barred from hiring any part of the Market, we learn. Even for charity. And besides, the Gettogethers Band is growing too elderly and infirm to march and blow brass at the same time, especially as the annual Christmas concert, *Let the People Sing*, will come up around that time and they must save their puff. Scratch them off the list.

JJ shifts gear. "We'll use the Leisure Park, on the grass opposite the Coffee Shop. The RMS will arrive from Ascension that day, and everyone will be streaming past to meet family coming for Christmas. We'll make a big noise and they'll notice us."

So Christopher arrives bearing goods again. There are pallets of bulging bags for mature dogs, mature cats, middle-aged pets, puppies, kittens – and there are T-shirts, flyers, posters, and sample packets galore. Unexpected promotional videos, describing the assets of Diet, entail a mad rush to install video screens where the shows will run continuously in one of the empty bus shelters for the benefit of passers-by, and time and energy are donated to the cause by an ever-increasing number of animal enthusiasts. Even by RSPCA members who declined to help with our Christmas Tree.

The chosen Saturday dawns iffy. Our spell of good weather has broken and rain hurries us and all our displays into the bus shelters, and out again, in again and out, lugging about the heavy bags until we are ready to drop. But by midmorning the sun has decided to shine after all, and we leave the tables set up in the generous shade of a tree near the coffee shop, watched by curious patrons across the path. All the helpers – including Chris, Richard, and Virginia who are dragooned into service as well – are wearing logo-emblazoned T-shirts, another first for such a promotion, and with rhythmic Latin-American music blaring from lusty speakers, we spontaneously start jigging. Soon even pedestrians on their way to the Wharf are picking up the beat as they pass – and the public is pouring in.

Policewoman Julie, animal-lover of note and devoted parent of three cats and a dog, is watching the activity. "My animals are so fussy they'll never eat this," she says almost wistfully, as customers stagger away under the weight of the bags they are buying. I shove a couple of samples at her, which she is reluctant to take. "I swear, they won't try anything new," she protests. But she takes the packets anyway, and before close of business at lunchtime, she is back. "I hadn't even opened the samples yet," she says, "and they were fighting to get at them! I'd better buy some bags."

Our friend Ursula stops by to announce: "Our cat has never ever eaten if anyone is in the room. But when I opened my sample she wolfed it down with me standing right next to her!" We must, I decide, be doing something right.

By one o'clock we have sold all of our substantial supplies and are directing customers to the Spar for more. Our tables are bare. The helpers are flopped on the grass with exhaustion. "This has been absolutely amazing!" says JJ. "Half the island's been here today. There're going to be a lot of healthy animals now." Yes, and that's a very good thing. But to keep them that way is going to employ JJ and me in hours and hours of ordering and hefting for years ahead, I can see. I make skinny eyes at Chris, but he doesn't notice. His mental cogs are probably already turning towards the Next Good Idea.

12.

The Dusty Purlieus of the Law

May 2004

Youth, no matter how far above suspicion it might reign, has an inimitable housesitting style of its own; one not necessarily coinciding with parental traditions. And though forewarned by experienced expat friends who return home annually to re-carpet their Scottish home after their trusted young adult children have housesat, for me this has been a new lesson learned over the past two years, since Virginia – after being invited to enrol in a local Teacher Training Course – now seems to be settling on the island for good. In truth, after Annette's various accounts of my dear child's curatorship, I appreciate why our motherly housekeeper has resolved upon a job in commerce instead.

But on this bright May morning in 2004, four years after establishment of this beloved second home, the front door opens and I smell polish and flowers! There are no shrouds of penicillin on dishes in the kitchen sink, no spills of blue-tinted Curaçao cocktails on the yellow sofa. Instead there is crisp, ironed linen on my bed. Floors are shining, windows sparkle, and even the white balustrades of the veranda are cleanly scrubbed of muddy paw-marks. In every room reposes a welcoming posy, freshly-picked from the garden. In undisguised amazement I stare at Virginia and see that, suddenly, she's all grown-up. Something has vastly changed in her life in the four months of my latest absence. She knows what I am thinking, and flushes, her blue eyes alight with joy. "I have a photograph of him," she tells me. "I'll show you later."

This May has slipped into its sweet new rhythm, quieter than previous years, but a tempo of my own choosing. This May my nose has been in books, ears tuned to music, senses drawn to the flittering distractions of birdlife in a colourful garden and nuances of light on the mountains. Taking my coffee to the rusty old bench on the middle lawn terrace, I lazily watch life trundling up Side Path above us, lorry engines groaning painfully under the weight of their cargo, small cars whining shrilly behind them, long-wheel-base vans hooting warningly at the numerous hairpin bends. Now and then an unidentifiable pedestrian will rest at the retaining wall to gaze on the miniature town strung out far below him, and I will wave just for fun. I know he can study my garden from there, watching its gentle development from his lofty heights, just as he could be entertained by toenail-painting on our upper veranda when Virginia and I indulge in girlie afternoons. Later, when sunset brightens the two green pudding-basin hillocks at the head of the valley, and the brown cliffs are thrown into shadow, the bleat of goats from a smallholding high up on the hillside echo plaintively into the evening glimmer, and the snowy fairy terns fly in from the sea to settle in their chosen roosts. Our own lonely tern still sleeps in our jacaranda, widower of the poor spouse relished by the neighbour's cat some time ago. The mate has never remarried, sad to say, though we hope for such an event, and watch with interest when sometimes he entertains a friend on his branch in the evening.

The strutting, bossy mynahs are a far cry from the dainty fairy terns with their slanting black eyes and graceful wings. The mynahs screech and whistle without finesse, aiming their yellow beaks at competition, sizing up everyone with evil yellow-lined eyes, in general owning the road. They have profoundly long memories, it seems, and hearts of small forgiveness, for Mimi must once have done them ill. Whatever it was, they will not forget it; and each day as Mimi steps forth about her leisure, her progress through the garden is marked by swoopings and the strident curses of harpies. Miss Phoebe Moss who, in 1885, released five imported common mynahs near the Briars at the top of James Valley, never dreamed, I suppose, that her once-caged entertainment would, over time, spawn with quite such robustness throughout the island.

The bright male breast of the also numerous Madeiran canaries sparkle through the garden with luminous flashes of gold, their females dowdier by far, like the drab little female Madagascar fody (known here as cardinal, or even as *Robin Redbreast*) who is not entitled to the splendid scarlet cassock of her mate that gleams with such exotic brilliance in summer. Then there are the disarming Java sparrows, tiny and dove-grey with neat black helmets, round white cheeks, and red beaks, doing everything by joint decision, *en masse*. "And now we will all drink!" suggests one among the row lined up along the rainwater gutter, and a dozen small heads dip forward. "And now we'll turn around!" and, as one, they all swivel on the perch. For a while they are happy to kiss and cuddle, and then with a decisive tweet they are all off again, their sudden decorative arrivals and swift impulsive departures flurrying the air with exuberance. By comparison, the feral pigeons that forage for our carefully sown garden seeds are a lot more staid, and the little brown common waxbills – erroneously called *avadavats* here – that also pass through the garden, are almost overlooked. The peaceful dove, a New South Wales import, shows no fear even in the throbbing heart of Jamestown, unconcernedly pecking around feet at the Coffee Shop, sometimes plucking cake-crumbs off our plates, wandering dreamily along the pavements or unconcernedly settling down in the sun in our garden even as Harry and Mimi stroll by.

The only surviving endemic of St Helena's birds is seldom seen, except on high open land in the far corners of the island. Of the plover family, long-legged, masked, shy and semi-flightless, the wirebird *(Charadrius sanctaehelenae)* is almost an endangered species, currently numbering around four hundred individuals only, living on beetles and other invertebrates, and nesting in shallow hollows on the ground. They do not much inhabit the beaten path and, generally speaking, strong binoculars are a useful aid to seeing them at all. Yet history tells us that in the centuries before the first explorers unthinkingly introduced predators to St Helena, the land bird population was probably made up entirely of endemic species. From great numbers of bones unearthed in certain areas of the island, we already know about two species of flightless rail, a flightless pigeon, a plover, a nearly flightless hoopoe, and a cuckoo. So try to imagine, for a moment, the consternation of this defenceless population when unexpectedly approached by pigs and goats left to roam free to provide meat for passing sailors, and cats, dogs, and rats that had slunk ashore from ships. Massive colonies of seabirds also nested here at that time, among them three endemic members of the petrel family – the St Helena gadfly petrel *(Pterodroma rupinarum)*, the St Helena Bulweria petrel *(Bulweria bifax)*, and the St Helena shearwater *(Puffinus pacificoides)*, none of which still survive. Later, a merciless reaping of eggs and guano during British colonisation saw to the sorry demise of all these seabird colonies around the cliffs.

Once, in the late 1800s, I read somewhere, blackbirds, larks, sparrows and starlings were all imported into the island, but none survived. And occasionally, unseasonably strong winds have brought in the odd migrating bird, sometimes with its mate. In 1886, a crane that had survived here for two years, was shot dead *(why?)*, and more than once a pair of white storks has shown up on the island, presumably blown off-course on the annual migration from Europe to southern Africa. There is something both tragic and romantic in the vision of their confusion as they find themselves adrift over the wide ocean, and also something blessed in their landfall of this place. Yet, as far as I have been able to ascertain, not many – if any – have survived their visit here, and certainly none has ever bred here. For even the handsome lone white stork that arrived in December a year or two ago, desultorily feeding in an empty corner of the island while we admired his great dignity, did not live to continue his journey. On Christmas Day he flew into a power line and was killed.

In a way it's been doomed from the start; this particular evening. Certainly my heart is not in it, but it seemed churlish, at this point, to refuse Giles's desire for a small celebration of farewell. Youthful Giles has been a guest at Villa Le Breton for the past six weeks, but in the light of his imminent departure from our lives, I could hardly refuse him that minor request. His wants are few and his guest list small; but the particular weariness I am suffering at present, the pain in my back, and my strong personal reservations towards Giles himself, make the effort rather more onerous than usual. And into the midst of these laborious and somewhat stoic afternoon preparations, the telephone rings. It's my next door neighbour.

"There's a young yachtie here from Cape Town, waiting for repair work on his boat," she says, "and he's dying to meet some young people. I thought at once of Virginia."

I think at once of the new photograph propped up beside Virginia's bed. "Well," I utter cautiously, knowing exactly how the island would interpret her public appearance with Someone Else while the new love of her life is languishing many thousands of miles away in the Falkland Islands, "he could come round for supper tonight. Giles is still here, and some friends of his are coming."

"Also," continues my neighbour, "for some reason there's no ferry running tonight, and I wondered if he could spend the night with you."

That's fine too. I'll stick him in the vacant little bachelor flat attached to the house, which we dub the Cottage. No problem. He'll add spice to the evening ahead.

And so Guy duly arrives, a well-mannered, well-educated, highly-personable young South African, easy to talk to. And for some time I am happily entertained by a remarkable story of his forty-five minute swim with a ten metre-long whale shark in James Bay. This extraordinary creature *(Rhincodin typus)* is not unknown to St Helena waters, yet is not especially commonplace. Often weighing around fifteen tons and classified as the world's largest fish, the gentle giant – dark-coloured with white spots – is more usually found in the Indian Ocean, or off the coasts of Queensland and New Guinea. It possesses a daunting three hundred rows of tiny teeth but, fortunately, prefers to feed off plankton and the occasional tuna rather than human body parts, which knowledge no doubt afforded Guy a unique experience as he stroked it and even rode on its back while it played in our bay.

Guy is pretty much the only asset of the evening, as it turns out. For Virginia, yawning and drowsy from too much sun during a fishing expedition with her new boyfriend's father, is a less than sparkling hostess, even to the poor newcomer. And when our guests appear, Dane comes hobbling in on crutches, a broken toe causing such great pain that he sits in anguished muteness throughout the evening except to request two Nurofen tablets. Ed develops hay fever from our cats, and under our gaze his eyes swell and water, his nose streams, he sneezes and coughs copiously around the garden where he divorces himself from the group on the veranda, and gains a clearly crashing headache after which he too requires Nurofen tablets. He badly wants to go home, but his wife is in party mood. She has been watching the end-of-season cricket match at Francis Plain and has consumed great quantities of homemade loquat wine there, and now nothing is budging her. Besides, she reminds us, they can't leave yet because Giles, the guest of honour, hasn't arrived.

And indeed his absence is noted, but when he does make his tardy appearance, he is bouncing off the wall. He played cricket all morning, he tells us, and at the celebratory barbecue afterwards managed to consume very liberal quantities of Windhoek beer, champagne, gin and tonic, and loquat wine to name but a few of the delights he savoured. And now he wants a shower. We start eating without him, but Giles never returns; for, after falling asleep in the shower where he was lucky enough to awaken before he drowned, he has put himself to bed. This means that, thank goodness, as soon as supper is done everyone can go home. It's been a hell of a party. Guy must be having a ball!

Giles is finally moving house. He has packed his bags, gnashed his teeth a great deal, and smoked up the island's supply of *555s* today. Donning a neat blue shirt and tie, he has this afternoon dramatically retrogressed from a cocky lad into a frightened boy facing his first day of boarding school. The Headmaster is an unknown quantity to him who, with a reputation as a hardliner, has assumed the power of Zeus in his eyes. Giles looks pale and fearful as he stands in the Supreme Court dock with hands tensely folded before him.

Over these past few weeks – with Giles living in my house – I have long pondered why a supposedly-intelligent newcomer to the island, employed by the government as a Secondary School teacher, should be reckless enough to seduce into bed not just one but *two* young local girls below legal age. That Giles is wondrously immature for his late twenties has some bearing, of course, but he is also entirely devoid of respect for St Helena's laws, it seems. Of course underage sex is not a rare crime in St Helena, in fact quite the contrary, but that law is more commonly infringed by local people. I regard him with mixed emotions as he stands there now looking so pathetic, more sorry for his distant family in England than I am for him, and angry that he has brought censure to my daughter who has acted, on his behalf, with a maturity far beyond her twenty-one years.

When the first misdemeanour was discovered and Giles's brief magistrate's hearing allowed him out on bail, he had nowhere to go. Summarily dispossessed of both his government-supplied house in the country and his teaching post, he was then required to be placed under curfew between the dark hours of 7pm to 7am, which entailed new lodgings. As might be supposed, local anger against an expatriate school teacher in these circumstances was marked; and so it fell to Virginia – herself an outsider – to volunteer responsibility for him. She was never close to Giles but since both were involved in teaching they moved in the same circles, and at first she sympathised with his distance from home and family at such a traumatic time. Vaguely familiar with the first of his victims – a girl who, it transpired much later, had promiscuously entertained innumerable lovers before Giles, and was possessed of a worldliness that showed – Virginia, like him, had long mistakenly assessed her age at a legal sixteen or seventeen. Under such circumstances, she could almost forgive him his foolhardiness. "At least she wasn't your pupil," she commented while reluctantly ensconcing Giles in her brother's bedroom. And Giles uttered a horrified gasp: "God, no, I would *never* do that with a *pupil!*" But just a few days later she and her boyfriend arrived home to find a note propped up on the stairs: *I'm in gaol again.* This time the more innocent victim of Giles's profligate philandering, newly come to light, indeed *was* a pupil; one substantially younger than the first, and far less worldly.

Virginia was outraged. One bout of silliness she could vaguely overlook; but his *grooming*, in legal terminology, of a respectable teenager, and his lies coupled with such flagrant disrespect for her own solicitude, was trust abused in the direst way. She was hurt to the core; but by now the court had registered her offer of responsibility for him and it was too late to change course. She hid her rage from Giles, but it seethed below the surface all the time that he continued under our roof, even after I had arrived back on the island from a holiday in Italy and publicly shown support for her actions.

We went through the mill during May, Virginia and I, reaping both spoken criticism and censorious looks from a variety of dignitaries in the local legal fraternity, education fields, and even the Church. Forewarned, on the ship, of disapprobation even before I had set foot back on St Helena, a teacher travelling with me – already more familiar with details of the scandal than I – had offered an earful of terrible warnings that my daughter's "public support of a paedophile" would not only likely bring a swift end to her Teaching Course but certainly an end to her credibility. I was stunned. If the educators of St Helena could not teach moral courage and loyalty to their youth through the example of their teachers, there was little hope for the future of this island, I felt, and with the fury of a mother tigress had flown to her side.

But Virginia, through the passage of time, was not invited to abandon her classes. And so it is that, without her presence beside me because she is at lectures, I now find myself awaiting the trial of this boy who has pleaded guilty to five counts of indecent acts. Marie, the comfortably down-to-earth wife of the Lord Chief Justice of St Helena who visits annually from England – his appointment distinct from the Appeal Court Judge with whom I shared such hilarity during the visit of the Princess Royal last November – is sitting beside me on one of the hard public benches that have drawn an interested gathering of spectators to the small Supreme Court this afternoon. Properly separating our friendship from the business at hand, neither of us has so far breathed acknowledgment of this case since her arrival with the Judge a few days ago. No phone calls of *hallo*, no invitations to tea. But she is nonetheless a forthright person with definite views; and with the Judge out of earshot as he prepares to enter the courtroom from the antechamber, she deems it safe to speak. "I very much admire you and your daughter for what you have done for this boy," she announces in a stage whisper, and her words fall into my lap like stardust. Nearby, one of my loudest critics flinches visibly.

"Thank you," I croak, suddenly so swelled with emotional gratitude on Virginia's behalf that I can barely breathe. It's the first supportive word I have heard in the three weeks since I returned. The tension seeps from my shoulders, and suddenly the sun comes out and blazes through the courtroom window. In less than an hour this will all be over, and my daughter and I will pick up our old lives again.

I look around the cream-walled room with its large Union flag and a very youthful Queen Elizabeth II hanging on the wall, and decide that it has changed little in the thirty-four years since the last court case I attended here. That civil case had raged for days, consuming the island with intrigue, and was not to be missed. So, with my friend Anne who was travelling with me then, I was here each day, riveted. Progeny of a stout line of South African lawyers, with two Attorneys General in my immediate family, I was particularly interested in observing, for the first time, English law enacted. Yet it was not the law alone that brought us forth punctually each morning, but something more bizarre – the hats of the expatriate defendant's wife, a different one each day, and each worse than the last. A veritable pageant of imaginatively hideous headgear was paraded before the assembled court that year, culminating on the final day in a pixie-pointed cap, shimmering and glistening in entirety with virulent green sequins, which, even all these years later, is impossible to forget. We couldn't stir our gaze. For even as she breathed, so each little light twinkled and trembled, sending shards of colour darting around laps and shoulders in her vicinity as she moved her head, effecting a horrible hypnosis.

We had a new Chief of Police that year. A deep-voiced mountainous Scot named Robert, recently arrived on the island and still feeling his way when we first met him. He held sixteen offices, he gravely informed us, entailing everything from Governor's aide-de-camp to Controller of Weights and Measures and, sandwiched somewhere between Fire Chief and head of Customs & Excise, was also the job of Court Registrar. This was as alien to him as many of the other offices he held, though he was not alone in his bemusement. At that time St Helena was rarely drawn into the purlieus of the law, and before these particular sessions the island had seen no judge at all for nearly seventy years – not since 1904 when someone was murdered at Prosperous Bay Plain. There was no such drama on offer back in 1970, but the intriguing civil contest at hand had brought to St Helena – out of quite long retirement – an elderly English Judge to hear the cases. A respected and learned man; bewigged, begowned – and very deaf indeed.

Travelling with Anne and me on our voyage from Cape Town had also come – specifically for this milestone court case – a youngish English solicitor, to play his part in these hearings. A sort of country-town lawyer perhaps, quite bright but, as my grandmother might have remarked, unlikely to set the Thames on fire. However, his moment was sweet. For before he even set foot ashore in St Helena, he was acknowledged as London's Most Brilliant Barrister, and so did his dazzling fame run before him. He rose to the occasion, strutting before the scribbling Judge who, despite the presence in court of both a stenographer and a working tape recorder, doggedly insisted on writing in long-hand each pearl of utterance from the Brilliant Barrister, frequently stemming the flow in mid-sentence with an ill-timed "And hah doo yoo spell thet?" Back and forth strode the Brilliant Barrister, focussed on his arguments, choosing his words with precision, playing to the gallery, every few minutes checked by a booming command from the Bench: "Kayndly repeat thet!" until eventually the Brilliant Barrister's patience frayed. Annunciating with sarcastic emphasis, he turned to face his Lordship: "And in the famous case of Bezzick & Bezzick – SPELT, m'lord, Bes-WICK and Bes-WICK...!" The Judge glowered at him. "Ay know thet," he said curtly. "Ay can hear yoo perfectly well."

Nor was Robert the Registrar having the time of his life while Anne and I secretly split our sides at this comic-opera. For, arriving on the island quite unprepared for these ancient rites, he had searched an old trunk in the courthouse and finally come up with a gown and a Court Registrar's wig. The gown was in ribbons, worn with the passage of time to a frondy garment that floated seaweed-like around his mammoth frame, while on the very apex of his head perched the little white toupee, ill at ease on such an expansive crown and giddy with height, tangling with the strung wires of the tape recorder each time that Robert stood, and hanging suspended for a few chagrined moments until it was hastily replaced on his head, often awry.

The gown, however, was dealt with in its own way. Adjourning for lunch meant that Robert retired for a strong gin at the Consulate Hotel where Anne and I were staying. And during that fevered break, it fell to me to cobble together (by hand) as many of its ribbons as I could accomplish in the given time. The next day the chore was continued, so that by the end of the week – perfectly synchronised with the closing of the case – the gown at last appeared intact. I fully expect it then finally met a dustbin, together with Exhibit A from a long-previous case, which, in the temporary mislaying of a real gavel, was used to pound ear-shatteringly upon the courtroom door at each entrance of the Judge.

I smile as I remember Robert now, recalling the afternoon that his car drew up beside me as I stood in the sun watching crabs on the stony beach below the Wharf, before the modern seawall was built. I still feel the stillness of that day, a visiting Royal Navy ship lying quietly at anchor in the bay, the sound of the restless sea. Back then the surf had a different voice from the steady roar of today, and the whoosh of incoming waves would precede the distinctive stone-rattling that marked their retreat. It was as mesmerising a sound as was the spectacle of myriad tiny black crabs washed up the narrow beach and their persistent racing back to the sea before the waves carried them up once more; and in the lazy atmosphere of that time I could watch them for hours. "You've talked a lot about Sandy Bay," said Robert, shouting to me from the driver's seat as he leaned across to open the passenger door. "But I've never seen it. Jump in and tell me how to get there. I have an hour to spare before my next appointment."

I leapt in beside him, and he drove like a maniac up the narrow and winding country roads towards the Ridges, not stopping the car until we reached the far end of this scenic drive. A family of chattering St Helenian picnickers were settled on the hillside just below us, and beyond them the amphitheatre of Sandy Bay lay blue and purple in the late afternoon light and was beautiful. "Wow!" said Robert, climbing out of the car to take it in from the edge of the road. "I can see why you like this."

We stood for five minutes or less, feasting our eyes on the view, before he looked at his watch. "There's a party for the Royal Navy at Plantation House tonight, and I'll be late if we don't get back to town soon," he said, giving a cursory wave of farewell to the picnickers. Waving too, I climbed in beside him.

Back down the twisting roads we roared, the Chief of Police hazardously exceeding the creeping speed limits of the island, and when we reached the hotel, he briskly paused to let me out. "Sorry to rush you," he apologised, "but I have to change into Mess Dress with spurs and all for this do at Plantation, and as ADC to the Governor I can't afford to be late!" And off he zoomed.

The next day he was laughing. "I arrived at Plantation all booted and spurred last night," he said, "and the first person I saw was the captain of the visiting navy ship. He came bounding across the room to me and immediately shook my hand. 'I believe congratulations are in order,' he said. 'His Excellency told me you got engaged this afternoon!'"

Did he? The only people who glimpsed us on that speedy tour to the countryside were the picnickers, and they had witnessed no touch between us, nor any intimate glance. But I learned early, from that diverting anecdote, that if there is no story to tell about you in St Helena, certainly one will be invented. For Robert, for all his blustery amiability, was the very last person on earth that I might have contemplated marrying.

Today, waiting for Giles's hearing, the three knocks on the door that announce the entrance of the present Judge into court are softer than Robert's lusty thrashings, and I assume a proper gavel might be used now. The Bench is seated. The Court is ready. The prosecution gets going, fiery and energetic, followed by a lay defence that has no hope of winning its case. And still, all I can think of is Giles's poor mother back home in England. I have scant sympathy for the accused himself, and when at last the Judge, after admonishing Giles for his manipulative nature, sentences him to two years' imprisonment in HM Prison, St Helena, I am frankly amazed. This is no hardliner after all. Two years, serving maybe fifteen months before he is released from a tiny gaol where life is publicly deemed reasonably comfortable, is small penance for an irresponsible school teacher who should have known better than to coerce teenagers into sex with him. Our Judge, even on the Bench, is a gentle man with a gentle heart.

I stand on the Courthouse steps afterwards and watch Giles being escorted across the square to the gaol, a very lucky man. "Phew!" I exclaim to Marie, the Judge's wife. "Thank God that's over!"

"Yes," she says. "We can get together for tea at last. Come to Judges' Lodge tomorrow afternoon."

Tea with her tomorrow will be really pleasant. But a strong drink now is necessary.

13.

The Old Order Changeth

June 2004

Virginia is beside herself. The new boyfriend, a St Helenian employed in the Falklands for the past seven years, is coming home to stay. But the RMS *St Helena,* completing his second leg of the journey, from Ascension, has been delayed.

They met last March when Stuart was home on holiday and Chris and I were off-island; and on return to the far south he had lost no time in resigning his lucrative plumbing contract there to come whistling back to her side. This is it, my bones tell me, this is *The One.* And though intrigued to meet him, I'm not half as frantic to see him as Virginia is, who has diligently kept Cable & Wireless in business with nightly hour-long overseas calls ever since he left her. I await the next bill with mounting trepidation but hold my peace, since I myself still look forward to Chris's twice-weekly calls with the same flush of youth as she who now pips me to the phone at every tell-tale double-ring of an overseas call to St Helena. They have a system, I soon realise: Stuart alerts her on a £10 phone-card that lasts about half a second, then she calls him back through one of the most notoriously expensive telephone monopolies in the world – my landline. But at least, now that he's flown to Ascension from the Falklands this early June, and is already waiting there to catch the RMS home, the calls are becoming marginally cheaper.

News from the shipping office is dire. With a huge tropical storm brewing off the bulge of Africa (marked as a vast black blot on BBC World's weather news, so we know it's really there and that, in truth, the ship has not broken down), the RAF station in Ascension believes conditions might worsen. Already their sea is so high that the RMS, tossing about off-shore, cannot safely disembark the passengers she brought north from St Helena on this shuttle-voyage. So embarking southbound travellers for her return to St Helena in these circumstances is out of the question.

On shore in Ascension, we hear, St Helena-bound passengers are exhorted to congregate at their landing steps every hour, hopeful of a go-ahead. They dare not stray from the precincts in case a decision is made, even while the ship itself cruises away to explore the vain possibility of landing passengers at English Bay along their coast.

The RMS was originally due here next Wednesday. Now it's due...*when?* Already the air in Jamestown is zinging with rumour, the heartbeat of our only ship pumping, as always, the very blood through the island's veins. Perhaps, we hear, she might return to St Helena without disgorging her current passengers at Ascension at all, or taking on new ones. Perhaps Stuart won't arrive here for several weeks. Virginia's face is drawn, long blonde hair straggly with anxiety. She is not far from tears, and Sandra, a co-student at the Teacher Education Centre, awaiting her own boyfriend, is in the same state. At Villa Le Breton, the phone barely stops ringing: the editor of the *St Helena Herald* calls in with updates; Sandra agitates at frequent intervals; Stuart's mother, Margaret, begs for news, as does his father, his cousin, his sister, his niece. I am fielding the radio broadcasts, the phone calls, the rumours, the updates, the agitations, and simultaneously trying to locate Virginia who now seems to have vanished altogether.

And then there's a breakthrough. Finally, from the shipping office comes the joyful news that all St Helena-bound passengers have actually embarked. The ship has left Ascension, racing south at a hell-bent 15.9 knots, and will arrive on Friday. Stuart, thank God, is on his way. I rush outside to proclaim this fact when Virginia eventually saunters home, triumphant bearer that I am of Great Good Tidings, anticipating squeals of delight and sighs of relief from my lovelorn child. "Yeah," she shrugs impassively, her face rather mask-like. "I heard it down the street." It's all been too stressful, I decide. Completely wrung out now, she will only recover when she actually sees him.

The winter weather has been wild. Wind has lashed us, rain deluged down, and I find the temperature cold. Not Arctic cold but unreasonably chilly for the tropics. I am extraordinarily tired – perhaps at last reacting to the suppressed stresses of the Giles debacle just ended, as I slowly regain control of my life. And I have a massively sore throat. Losing the battle of self-medication in this instance, I reluctantly walk it down to the hospital to be interviewed by one of the island's four doctors; this man a brilliant surgeon but such a devout Indian Muslim that he cannot venture closer to me than his desk's width. From across files and folders, a lamp and sundry other bric-a-brac, he aims a small torch into my gaping maw, confirms that I really do have an inflamed throat, and hands me Panadol, a much milder pill than I've been swallowing at home for several days past. When I inquire whether an antibiotic might be helpful at this stage, he informs me that he can only prescribe that once a swab has been taken. I wait expectantly, but he briskly furthers the distance between me and his wheeled desk chair – I am, after all, a married woman alone in his office with him – and directs me to the lab upstairs. Hauling myself wearily up the steep wooden staircase, I cannot but reflect how removed from a *femme fatale* I feel at this present juncture, and am nearly certain the poor man would have been safe in my proximity.

The lab technician looks mystified when I explain my presence: "But the doctors have to take the swab!" she exclaims. "We can't do it, so you'd better take your own." And thus I am offered a secluded corner of the upstairs landing, where I shove a stick rather clumsily down my gullet, seal up the evidence for analysis, and then take myself home to await the results. By the time they come through, if they ever do, my throat will undoubtedly be better.

Still sorry for myself, I have spent the past few days holed up, reading, and cosseting myself. Virginia has brought me cold jellies and ice cream, the very newly resident boyfriend, Stuart (whom I immediately liked), has cooked creamy chicken curry and rice, and I – with less success – have levered myself from my downy couch to make a smooth leek and potato soup, carelessly allowing the lid to fly off the blender midway through and then having to mop up every corner of the kitchen. Job done, I surrender to the sofa once more to watch successively a televised 60th anniversary of D-Day, the transit of Venus, the funeral of Ronald Reagan, and eventually, rather more cheerfully, Trooping the Colour 2004. On this last day, from my prone position I eventually stagger up, don a suit (and yea, even a hat to hide my unkempt hair!) and set forth with Virginia for Plantation House to celebrate another Queen's Birthday in this forgotten outpost of Empire.

Wearing neither the Uniform, Medal nor Decoration decreed on the large gold-crested black-printed invitation, but looking appropriately formal nonetheless, Virginia and I arrive, according to protocol, neither one minute late nor early, having tottered on high heels across the soggy field where we have once again been directed to park the car. This field is normally the territory of three of Plantation's famous giant tortoises, the oldest and largest of whom is Jonathan, assessed to be around 170 years of age, and originally a native of Aldabra in the Seychelles. A hearteningly feisty character, despite encroaching blindness, he still enjoys his female company enough to fill the night air with noisily lustful grunting, I am told by Gloria who adores them all, especially Speedy, the fourth, who lives in the house's small courtyard. As none are in sight today, I trust they have been moved to safety from the parking cars. Virginia and I, reaching the tarmac, discreetly shake mud and grass off our stilettos and join the queue of guests outside the marquee, waiting to shake the Governor's hand. At least it is not raining today.

This year, invited under cover, the Gettogethers Band with gleaming brass and red jackets is blowing full blast to one side of the marquee, cheering up a slightly stilted atmosphere. Governor Hill, in white uniform and plumed hat for the last time before his extended term finally ends in September, is fielding this throng alone since Gloria has not yet returned from preparing their new London flat for retirement. Speeches are made, toasts raised to the Queen, and Her Majesty's Birthday Honours read out. But for all its familiar ritual, this year's party is an historic event. The incoming Governor-Designate, due in October, has already announced that he will *not* be wearing the uniform during his three-year term of office. This is sad news, many of us feel; for though ostensibly outmoded in a modern world, the quaint uniform still sits unusually well with this time-warped island. Like everything else, its demise has financial reasons; for, following the FCO's announcement that it will no longer foot the bill for British Overseas Territories' uniforms, the onus would fall to our next Governor to buy his own. Costing up to £6 000 (including the expensive general's Mameluke sword for which he would have scant use in later years), the Governor-Designate justifiably suggests that the uniform is not essential to his work here. And while his decision caused an initial flurry of agitation on the island, it was notable that the pain subsided immediately upon the suggestion, originally the FCO's intention, that St Helena itself might pay for the suit. The Governor of the Falklands still wears one – two in fact, both winter and summer versions – willingly paid for by the Falkland islanders. And so does the Governor of Bermuda. And since St Helena's single most valuable asset is its old-world charm, many are upset that such a tradition should have been so lightly discarded. Especially as there sits, in the new museum, a perfectly good former Governor's sword from the last decade, just itching to symbolise all St Helena's future dress swords; but as usual, the decision wasn't quite thoroughly thought through. *"If you are standing under the Union Jack with a lounge suit rather than the uniform,"* comments Robert Gieve of Gieves & Hawkes, the Savile Row tailors who have made uniforms for the past 200 years, *"somehow it presents the nation as second best..."*

Nostalgically, I imprint the crisp white uniform on my mind now, noting for the last poignant time its high embroidered collar and embroidered cuffs, the epaulettes, white gloves and shoes, sword standing awkwardly at the hip, the tall white hat draped with its flamboyant tea cosy of fluttering swan's feathers.

Without discernible national characteristics in dress, music, dance or food, this uniform is ironically the nearest thing to a culture that St Helena can boast, its particular outmodedness representing a history of British colonialism, which, however non-politically correct it might be regarded in these pedantic times, is a fact that cannot be forgotten. This uniform speaks to the existence of St Helena in the past; for all her people who were never endemic to this island; for her wealth of historic buildings and military batteries for which this island is famous; for the island's own English patois which includes words and intonations imported from the colonial East Indies and colonial Africa. It speaks to the existence of St Helena in the present day, wholly supported as it is by the British taxpayer who, I am convinced, will unwittingly continue to pay for the island's upkeep long after the airport has been built and air-access is found to be wanting because St Helena still cannot financially support itself. Therefore it speaks to the future too, as this small place – no longer one of the most remote inhabited islands in the world once tourists can access it in four hours – grapples to offer something better than its non-existent charms of golden beaches, wild nightlife, and warm weather for tourists. In quaintness value, the cost of a white uniform, with a sword borrowed from the museum, would have been cheap at the price.

Virginia and I have been socially peripatetic for the requisite two hours stipulated on our invitations, and I am ready to leave now, taking my poor throat home to rest before a dinner party at Jill and Bill Bolton's tonight. But protocol again dictates that none of us may move before the Lord Bishop has gone, and I search the crowd for him now. I have seen little of him since his return from overseas leave on the same delayed voyage that finally brought Stuart home, but in time will no doubt catch up with tales of his recent adventures in Rome, his audience with the Pope, his happy reuniting with the Princess Royal, and all the news not exchanged during the months that I was away... And I quickly locate the robust figure in his bright new purple cassock, weaving between guests with jovial remarks as he bustles towards the exit. He shakes hands with the Governor, takes his leave, and finally he is gone. "Come!" I command Virginia. "We're free to leave now!" And we line up once again. My feet hurt terribly in the too-high heels, tonsils screaming blue murder, head reeling from over-generous whisky dispensed by Plantation staff in the absence of Gloria, and all I can think of is bed.

We shake His Excellency's hand formally. "Thank you very much," I utter, eager to move on. But the Governor leaps after us, catching Virginia's sleeve before she disappears. "I just wanted to say," he hisses, "thank you for what you did for that young Giles! It was a very kind act."

Virginia and I stare at each other in gratified amazement all the way across the soggy field to the car. His Excellency needn't have remembered, and he wasn't at all obliged to comment. But he did. We are deeply, deeply touched.

✳

Chris hates email. He sent me one once, some years ago, but I heard so much about the length of time it took to type it that I suggested he never send another. He's a promoter of the ancient world of *facsimile*; and while I can't deny some of its advantages and am pleased to send him faxed shopping lists, I communicate with the rest of the known world by email. Best of all, though – in the absence of Skype in our house – is the old-fashioned telephone. We chat about this and that, and over the wire I actually *hear* him laughing. Today he is telling me – just to elaborate upon his loathing of computers and especially email – that, within the past two weeks since his PC came back from the repairers, he has received 7 600 spam emails. "Well," I counter, "I have received the Cable & Wireless phone bill."

The amount at the bottom of the page that dries my mouth is £772. A lot of money for phone calls. Of course, it is really Virginia's bill for all those lovelorn chats with Stuart that I knew would catch up with us. But Virginia simply does not earn enough to produce that sort of cash in one fell swoop, and though I have plans to bleed repayments from her over the course of a lifetime, I will still have to pay it now. However, something about it makes me smile. Two days after the bill's arrival, when I am still faint with shock, a sealed envelope from Cable & Wireless comes winging in after it, by personal delivery. This is a typed personal letter, signed by the company's managing director who, in verbal terms, is prostrating himself over a mistake in our latest bill. It seems they've overcharged me, and I am truly enchanted to hear this. As I relish the apologies which follow swiftly, one after another, I grow ever more appreciative of that honest establishment. Yes, indeed (I decide), of course I will forgive the company... *And so,* their letter continues, *when you next call at our office, will you kindly deduct the error from the total amount shown on the bill in hand?* Yes, gladly I will. This will certainly ease the load on my pocket at the end of the month... My eye falls eagerly to the last paragraph. The error amounts to 55p.

Inevitably Chris asks about the Airport. He knows of the dejection felt among some around the island when SHELCO fell from grace, and of DfID's bumbling efforts afterwards to *test the market* and recruit alternative private sector interest in handling this questionable project. He knows what we all knew immediately, that no one except

SHELCO, which was the only company to demonstrate *compliance* with their demands, was going to show much interest. But now SHELCO is evidently *persona non grata* again. He knows of DfID's rethink of the whole contracting invitation idea earlier this year, and their start a few months ago on *feasibility* tests. He knows, as we all do, just where this is leading. To confusion. I tell him that on the front page of a recent *St Helena Herald* blared the certain reassurance that: *"DfID/FCO aide memoire reconfirms the UK Government commitment to provide access to St Helena."* Yet on the very same front page, following the week he has just spent here, the visiting DfID Air Access Project Manager himself announces: *"There is no commitment from Ministers in our Government to develop Air Access".* Is it any wonder that everyone shrugs at mention of the Airport now?

I also tell Chris about the Queen's Birthday Party at Plantation on Saturday, and about that night's dinner with Bill and Jill and how, when I arrived home from it after 1am, a protective Virginia and Stuart were wearily waiting up for me, as worried as two anxious parents even though St Helena is the safest place in the world to drive alone at night. Then I tell him that my happy trio of decorators – Pat, Gibby and Growler – are back at work on our house at last, with their radio and their laughter, and he cheers on my behalf.

I have waited eight months – since October last year – for further renovations to the kitchen, and now improvements are finally under way. An unused outside door to the yard has already been blocked up, leaving a lovely deep alcove in the thick old walls for future shelves, and shabby plastic floor tiles have been lifted, making way for earthy terracotta tiles from Cape Town – and except for the fact that the whole house is now six inches under dust and resonant with hammering, I am ecstatic. The large kitchen table and its six mismatched chairs are crammed onto the already-furnished veranda, while the chest-freezer has been ousted to the yard; and according to the state of the undressed kitchen floor, the awful old fridge and gas cooker that came with the house shift position every day, soon to be exchanged for more modern appliances. We're at pains to retain this kitchen's comforting country atmosphere, with its tongue-and-groove woodwork and dark ceiling beams; but the new look will accommodate beautiful, extended wooden counters to fill the gaps where there were none before, and the dream is finally taking shape – especially the new alcove which will eventually be a focal point with moulded architraves and shelves of cookbooks and pretty bowls.

Chris and I conclude our call eventually, and as I replace the receiver I remember half a dozen added things to chat about. But the phone is already jangling again, another double-ring overseas call, and this time it's for Stuart. He takes it in the hall, and when his conversation is over, he returns to the sitting room wide-eyed with shock. "That was my brother in Ascension," he says. "He's just heard that two hours ago our St Helena police found a body in Jamestown's moat, near the Honeymoon Chair!"

Virginia and I digest this enlightenment with open mouths. *A dead body in the moat...*

"And the police suspect foul play."

"That's impossible!" exclaims Virginia incredulously. *Foul play? Not here!* "It must have been an accident, someone drunk falling over the railing into the moat." We're so stunned we don't even question why the news has reached us first from Ascension, when the empty moat that edges the city walls along the seafront lies only a mile from our house. *Perhaps it isn't really true!*

But after a speedy drive up the mountain pass to the head of the Ladder with its bird's eye view of the seafront, the incorrigibly inquisitive Stuart confirms that police are indeed swarming all over the Wharf, and there's a concentration of officialdom just around the bougainvillea-swathed white stone seat known as the Honeymoon Chair. So it is true. Murder most foul.

The next morning, waking just before seven I turn on the radio. According to local convention, we are served no news bulletins on Monday mornings or the day after a Bank Holiday. But after yesterday's dramatic events surely there'll be an exception...? I listen patiently through the distinctive nursery-anthem call-sign of the BBC World Service signing off, and then a bright young local voice reminds us that, having spent the night with the BBC, we are now tuned to Radio St Helena. She wishes us all a very good Tuesday morning despite the grey skies, and hopes we've had a wonderful long weekend. "Well, there's no news today," she adds, "so we will go right into our first song..." *No news?* The island is reeling with agitation! There's been a murder – an actual *murder* – in crime-free St Helena! Everyone's in deep shock.

The body was young, a boy of nineteen named Ryan Thomas, whose blood was copiously spilt on the tarmac around the Honeymoon Chair before he was apparently tipped through the brittle roof of a disused shooting range in the dry moat below. Already rumours are sweeping the island, and so far, from general conjecture, we have heard that part of his head was crushed, that his throat was slit, that he was frequently stabbed; that only his throat was slit and there was no damage to the head; that his injuries were sustained as he fell; that his injuries were sustained *before* he fell. But whatever the true version, the boy is dead, and this is definitely foul play. Few facts are known, except that Ryan Thomas was last seen around midnight on Friday night and, living on his own, was not missed until Monday's Bank Holiday morning. When his body was discovered at 10am, the area was immediately cordoned off while a fevered hunt for a working police camera delayed its removal from the scene for some hours. People shake their heads and smile sardonically at this, in the time-honoured St Helena way: "Batteries dead, prob'ly. Nobody never check 'em." However, it was not long before two arrests were made and the plot thickened. The suspects were also boys, eighteen and seventeen years old respectively, both relatives of the victim. So what was the motive? Nobody knows anything at present, and those who might are saying nothing. But everything is suddenly all different. The Wharf is deserted except for those men elected to fix rain-proof tarpaulins over the smashed roof of the shooting range crime scene, and an almost tangible pall of disbelief hangs over the island. In one mightily devastating blow, St Helena has lost its innocence, and now we must come to terms with this.

To all intents and purposes life trundles along as normal, with a charity dinner taking place as planned at the end of the week, which I attend with friends. But the violent death of young Ryan still weighs upon us, and in the shops our voices are tempered, our shouted hallos in the street a little restrained. At the Coffee Shop, fount of all knowledge,

I hear that a forensic scientist is already on her way to St Helena but physically cannot arrive here for another two and a half weeks because of our geographical remoteness. Actually there are *two* forensic people coming, the errant Giles tells us when he phones from the prison to complain that he is bored there. I pass this insider knowledge on. "I don't know why anyone's coming at all," retorts someone, "because I heard that the government workers who put up the tarpaulin crushed all the evidence underfoot."

At home, I have suffered my own little dramas – those that loom disproportionately large whenever men are at work in your sanctuary. Most of the banging has ceased for the time-being, and the dust is settling a bit, but I can't enter the kitchen. I can't hang washing in the yard except at weekends when they are absent. I can't move on the veranda for all the kitchen furniture housed there. And so I have taken myself into the guest cottage to clean cockroach-droppings out of drawers, cupboards and hidden corners.

Cockroaches? Yes, indeed. Perhaps I've not made clear that while gentle St Helena is entirely devoid of snakes, low on poisonous spiders and scorpions, and even quite sparing with centipedes who give the nastiest bite of all, Jamestown is home to the world's mother-lode of cockroaches. They come in all sizes. Tiny, busy things that hatch between the bristles of a nail brush and then do the wall-of-death around the hand-basin when the tap is turned on. Bigger ones that scurry in panic when you ferret for clean table napkins in a cupboard. There are those that wave long feelers at you from the invoice drawer; and even bigger chaps that – having inadvertently passed across a *Dyroach* zone – lie down to die on the kitchen floor, pathetically waving arms in the air for gruesome hours until they eventually run out of steam. I can't stomp on those, of course, as I can't bear the crunch, so I simply avoid the kitchen for six to eight hours until they die, or until Stuart comes home and does it for me. And last of all are the worst – those the size of zeppelins, flying like brick-red buzz-bombs through open windows on a hot January night, grazing your nose as you watch television, occasionally landing in your hair. I do not like cockroaches. So it is bold of me to spend a day with their droppings.

Then Pat looms in the doorway. "We got a problem," he says. Can things get worse than the pass they are at, when all I can find to do is clean up cockroach crap? "We've run out of floor tiles in the kitchen."

The gong of doom clangs in my head. Somewhere in the depths of my throat I am scrabbling to find a voice. It comes in a squeak, eventually. "How many?"

"About twenty will do it."

Twenty. These beautiful terracotta floor tiles were bought from a massive Cape Town warehouse ten months ago. I am now expected to pop down to Jamestown and find twenty identical matches just-like-that. I draw a steadying breath, but my voice is still in shocked soprano. "Do you think I might find the same *size* tile here, even if it's not remotely the same colour?"

Pat shrugs disarmingly and grins his infectious, toothy grin. "We jus' can hope so." And so I set off downtown.

The Emporium at the base of Napoleon Street is a little like Queen Mary Stores without the food. It mostly sells hardware, but stationery and shoes and rolls of fabric vie for position beside pots of paints, saucepans, washing-machines, and children's toys. I have my required measurement written on a slip of paper, and at the tile rack I delve into my bag for a tape-measure. There is a generous choice of *five* designs here, but one has already caught my eye. It's bigger than all the rest, and shade wise relates vaguely enough to my terracotta end of the colour spectrum to raise my hopes. I hardly dare look at the answer as I stretch the tape against it...

Clearly my hours of penance in the cockroach drawers have smiled on me, and now I am faint with good fortune. "I'll have twenty of these," I say largely to the assistant who has to cross the road and trudge some way uphill to a crumbling termite-infested storeroom to fetch them for me. The measurement is exact! How much will it matter that the colour is definitely not? This, after all, is St Helena and we are grateful for small mercies.

"And there's something else," says Pat when I get home with my booty. "This pole that stands at the bottom of the green stairs – what's it for?"

"You tell me," I suggest. It's a peculiar thing, a metal pipe ascending from the kitchen floor to the ceiling of the landing above the green stairs. This is an old house, where electricity wires still run visibly along walls and corners, so I have never actually queried the uses of this pole. It's simply another quirk. But it is now posing a problem in the laying of floor tiles just there, and Growler would like to remove it. He is kicking and thumping it viciously, perhaps in the hope that it might collapse. But it looks pretty strong to me. Pat is shaking his head doubtfully, knowing that if the house falls down upon the pole's removal, it will be his responsibility to stick it all together again. Gibby has joined us too to consider the risks with thoughtful visage, and suggests in his dry manner: "Well, if the house falls down, then we'll know it was important, won't we?"

"What if there's wiring in there, or gas or something?" I ask. We are in a semi-circle around the pole, deliberating, all with arms akimbo and puzzled frowns. Growler badly wants me to risk it; I see it in his eyes. And I am too weary to worry anymore, actually too tired to care. If the house falls down, we'll somehow deal with it. If it blows up or catches fire things will be a bit more awkward, but the pipe sounds hollow. Why it was ever put there we cannot imagine.

"Oh, take it down," I say in a wild moment, and Growler whoops. He doesn't seem to mind the idea of an upper storey collapsing on him, whereas I do. "Let me know when it's safe to return," I say, and retreat back to the relative comfort of my cockroach droppings. As far as the floor goes, I haven't dared compare the darkly disparate shades of the Emporium tiles with the richly earthy Cape Town ones.

But at the end of the day Pat finds me once more. "I lifted some Cape Town tiles and put them to one side. All the darker Emporium tiles are now laid out of sight under the dishwasher and the oven and behind the fridge. Tomorrow the whole visible floor will be matchin' tiles." He is grinning broadly. "And by the way, the house is still standing even though Growler cut down the pole."

"Phew!" I sigh, sinking into a chair with relief. I'm rather fond of my house. I'd really hoped it would not fall down.

We don't exactly know when this house was born, but we know something of its history and the land on which it stands. We start in the Indian Ocean, around 1735, when the vessel *Drake*, under Captain Pelly, paused in its voyage to rescue ten natives of the Maldive Islands found mid-ocean in a drifting boat. These poor people – three of whom subsequently died on board the *Drake* – had been swept 450 miles from their land and were in an advanced state of exhaustion when discovered. But five men, one woman and a boy survived to be landed in an altogether different ocean, on faraway St Helena, as slaves, very likely to their disappointment. The men were immediately put to work in the Government Plantation near the top of James Valley which, not unexpectedly, quickly became known as the Maldivia Gardens, and which comprised a large area for such a narrow neck in the valley. It was a fertile plot fed by fresh waters from Chubb's Spring that ran down the valley beside it, and their plants thrived. Today, in the grounds of Maldivia House, assigned home of successive Senior Medical Officers, there still remain remnants of their handiwork, and that garden, perhaps above all others on the island, retains more isolated examples of exotic trees and fruits than even the old Castle Gardens in Jamestown.

Fifty-nine years later, in 1794, the Gardens were eventually divided into separate plots for sale, and one that measured 110 feet in width and 240 feet in length was acquired for the sum of £40 *"current money"* by a certain John Newton, plumber for the Honourable East India Company (plumbers presumably dealing with lead lines for ships in those days). The only attached obligation to this purchase was to pay the Honourable East India Company, *"on the Feast of St Michael the Arch Angel"*, the annual sum of £7 sterling for their loss of income from *"the yams, plantains, etcetera"* previously grown on this land. Not long after the purchase, a house rose on the property, and on 21 March 1808, it was signed over as a wedding gift to John Newton's 16-year-old daughter, Elizabeth, upon her marriage that year to a dashing sea captain of Guernsey, named John Le Breton.

Captain Le Breton and his bride whooshed off to London immediately after the wedding, and too soon afterwards for the comfort of a loving father, *"a Commission of Bankruptcy was issued out against the Estate and Effects of him the said John Le Breton"*, which immediately prompted Elizabeth's irate father to slap his daughter's St Helena property into a Trust. All rents accrued from the lease of the house during his daughter's absence from the island were, he instructed the trustees, to be paid to her *"without any manner of control by or from her husband"*. In fact, he stressed, should Elizabeth demise without issue living, the house and premises were in no way to fall to her errant spouse, but to revert instead to her dear sister Matilda Carrol.

I wish we knew more of John Newton, evidently quite a prosperous figure around town, whose friends and business associates seem to have comprised many highly-respected names that frequently pop up in Records of that period. But he himself numbers among the historically anonymous, but for the papers in my possession that tell me what little is known of this man. His will, dated 1815 (the year that Napoleon arrived on St Helena), when Newton by then described himself as a shopkeeper, tells us more than is otherwise known. And we see from it, to our wry amusement, that his hostility towards the thriftless son-in-law had subsided enough to bequeath to Captain John Le Breton his gold fob watch.

What is really interesting, though, was the surprise discovery of just how much land of the old Maldivia Gardens John Newton had actually bought. For from that will, we learn that the property immediately behind Elizabeth's house (by then known as Le Bretons), was to be left to his son Andrew. This would be Cambrian House onto whose gardens our own south-facing kitchen windows open at ground level. To his daughter Caroline Blunden, he left the house and property adjoining us to the east – our next-door neighbours' house still known as Blundens. And at the foot of our garden, two small houses were bequeathed to his daughter Matilda, married to the then American Consul William Carrol. The Carrol's two little houses have since disappeared, probably under the foundations of a later house called St John's Villa which is now part of the hospital, but I have often pondered whether some of the shards of old blue and white china dug from the lower end of my garden when we first moved in, rather than being ships' ballast as suggested, perhaps once had pride of place in Matilda Carrol's kitchen.

An excerpt given to me by a friend from an unidentified book published in 1873, describes the Upper Jamestown of the writer's wanderings: *"Just above the Hospitals* (there were two then, Military and Civilian) *there is a pretty House with a small garden attached to it called 'St John's Villa'... And immediately above this and joining 'Cambrian Cottage' is a fine large house which could be converted into a Sanatorium, and I think no better site offers in Jamestown, it being eligibly situated and has a good garden attached to it."* Reading it, even now, gives me a glow in the stomach, for when that piece was written Elizabeth Le Breton was still living here. After her marriage finally foundered, she returned to St Helena and lived out the rest of her life in this *"fine large house"*. Apparently she had only given birth to her first child by John Le Breton a full five years after her marriage, and though she then went on to mother five more children, few Records remain regarding descendants from her legitimate male issue – just one son who died aged twenty-seven, and a query-marked older son, who died aged thirty-two. She did, however, not halt her descendible line on the cessation of her marriage; and, according to some history in my possession, it is suggested that even in middle age she conceived three more children who took the Le Breton name. For all that, it is to me quite poignant that only one male Le Breton survives in St Helena today.

Upon Elizabeth's death on 4 January 1875, at the venerable age of eighty-three, a deferential obituary citing her death as a *"melancholy catastrophe"* was published in the *St Helena Guardian,* the local paper of the time, telling us that following a large funeral, she was buried in St Paul's Churchyard in the country – a cemetery I have hopefully, but fruitlessly, prowled around for many hours in search of her grave. I am, however, quite convinced that the woman who (reputedly) wanders our garden sometimes on moonlight nights, is Elizabeth Le Breton. And though I have never seen her myself, I feel she has every right to be here.

14.

Stairway to the Stars

July 2004

It's only a week since Ryan Thomas's body was found, and the air still hangs heavy over the island. In this tight community there has been an instinctive drawing together in the shared pain of such tragedy. Everyone is now related, St Helenians and expats together, confined by limited space and geographical seclusion to one family, like it or not. And because we are here, flung away in mid-ocean on this calm, famously crime-free, island we cannot shake our distress. Now the reality of it comes even closer to our household as our telephone rings. The call is again for Stuart.

Once more he returns from the phone looking mildly shell-shocked. Stuart's plumbing qualifications are advanced, and for fifteen years he has never worked at anything else. But now, he informs us – because he has been home barely two weeks so isn't yet employed – his services as a prison guard are urgently required. Would he please report to HM Prison first thing in the morning? "It's only temporary," he keeps repeating, trying to get his head around this unusual request. "But they're frantic. They have only six wardens for 16 prisoners in a fourteen-bed prison – and the two boys arrested for Ryan's death each have to be watched twenty-four hours a day! I'll just be helping out for a few weeks until the court case comes up."

He reports in at 8.30 the next morning, and we don't see him again till five in the evening when he flings himself on to the sofa, exhausted. "I've been assigned to the older boy," he says. "And I sit outside his cell all day, recording everything he says and does in a logbook for the benefit of his defence counsel. I bring him meals and coffee and escort him to the lavatory. He's forbidden to talk to anyone else, especially not to the younger boy who has his own twenty-four-hour suicide watch, but he is allowed family visitors at any time, any number of letters, and can smoke as much as he likes." Stuart adds a whistle of amazement: "But the rest of those prisoners – they live in a first-class hotel!"

Over the following weeks I gradually pick up bits about life *inside* in St Helena that make me wonder why the great unemployed don't strive harder to get in there. Breakfasts are of the prisoners' own desiring, I have learned – a full English breakfast produced, if requested. And on Saturday nights, when Cyril's Fast Foods opens in the square, the wardens are dispatched to buy takeaway steak dinners or hamburgers for those who spurn the prison's lavish offerings. Stuart declines to do that because, he exclaims, usual prison meals offer choices of gammon and fishcakes with mounds of vegetables, and even the island's popular pumpkin fritters are available at the self-service table where dinners are laid out. The cook with a soft heart occasionally even makes cupcakes for them. Most prisoners walk freely inside the area by day, helping themselves to coffee at all hours, some playing games on the communal computer set up for their amusement, while others are driven to the cool air of the country to feed pigs and dig potatoes on the prison farm. A woman inmate sometimes helps out in the kitchen, chopping onions with a murderously large knife, says Stuart, while one of the men with a talent for mechanics is restoring a car, free to wield hammers at will. This man appears at the desk from time to time to beg a few pounds from his own cash envelope, the latch on the outside door is sprung by the desk officer, and out goes the inmate to buy his small car part from Solomon's DIY shop in Main Street. The cash envelope is fuelled by the £1 a day that prisoners are paid while interned, ostensibly to cover their cigarettes, video hire and other delights. It sounds like a good life to me – one pleasurably lacking in any form of responsibility from the criminals, while family members left at home struggle to make ends meet during the absence of their breadwinner. But a human rights man once came here and told the island how important it is to nurture prisoners and keep them happy and so, we presume, this must be right way to punish them.

I very much like this man of Virginia's. Wearing a beguiling smile, his jeans are rolled up to the knee, sleeves pushed above the elbows and, unbidden, he is spending his day off cleaning my house. To a blaring background of Louis Armstrong he is vacuuming floors, washing stairs, shining windows, scrubbing muddy pawmarks off windowsills. The sight of him with mops and scrubbing brushes dissolves Pat into screams of laughter when he calls in to hand me his kitchen-renovation bill. Pat is secretly laughing at me too, I think. I acknowledge that he has not often witnessed me beating cushions with such verve, nor dusting and tidying with such dedication. I can vouch that he has never seen me covered in Goddard smudges as I carry trays of gleaming silver back into the dining room. But the house has been feet deep in dust from the kitchen work and, without Annette here anymore, something radical has had to be done. It's his fault, after all. Pat veritably clutches his sides, splutters out something about "Hey, Stewey, she really got you goin' now!" and then deems it time to depart. I mop my brow, and sit down to investigate his invoice.

It's not bad, really it isn't. It could have been much larger considering the high standards they set, the way they tidy up each night, the cheerful banter between them, Gibby's humorous repartee, Growler's whistling, and the atmosphere of comforting jollity that pervades their working hours. They moved out a week ago, but I still miss them. "Let's go and admire the kitchen again," I say to Stuart, which is a pretext for making another pot of coffee. And he says, as a matter of course: "I don't mind the different coloured counters."

"Are you sure?"

"Yes, definitely sure."

"You know, I actually *like* the different coloured counters," Virginia will say when she returns from her lectures. And inevitably I will ask her too, "Are you *sure*?"

The counters that Pat has just built are golden, you see, whereas the kitchen counter that he fitted in our first year here is red – a glorious, rich red full-bodied specimen of *real* tree. Something to caress and talk to, even if it only surrounds a sink. I am so deeply in love with that particular wood that when the newer counters were planned, we ordered the same again – from the same supplier in Cape Town – and large planks were duly shipped to the island months ago after which it lay safely under wraps on the upper veranda until Pat was ready to build. Finally, up it went, its beautiful grain swirling around the new cooking hobs, floating on deep shelves that now ornament the disused door he'd blocked up, making a striking feature on that wall... Then came crisis. No one could find the brilliant *Woodoc25* sealant that we used for the old sink counter. I searched the tool shed, Pat the store room, Gibby double-checked both of them, and I checked behind him and searched the house as well. And yet we all could remember that plenty was left over from last time. I looked at the virgin wood surrounding both new cooking work-stations – gas hob and electric hob in opposite corners – and thought of oil marks, tomato stains, burn marks and scratches on those pristine surfaces while I wait *weeks* for more to come from Cape Town. And I looked at four years of invisible hot-water proofing on my beautiful red counter and wanted no other sealant but that one. Hysteria rose. One does not simply go out and buy your favourite sealant in St Helena.

For a full day, progress ceased in the kitchen. Pat turned his attention to the cottage's shower outlet that had suddenly taken to swishing soapy water all around the perimeter of the cottage to puddle and bubble at its front doorstep. Growler did not whistle as he dug the new French drain for it. Gibby morosely applied himself to other small details around the house. And then – eureka! The sealant appeared. "Disguised as a pot of white paint," said Growler modestly, after actually *moving* things in the store room to find it. Crisis over, thank heavens. The first coat went on, looking thin and pale. Then the second. When the third was down, Pat called me. "This colour alright?" he inquired carefully. "It the same wood, the same sealant, but this colour look rather light." Anaemic golden, in fact. Not rich or red or living at all. We shook our heads in disbelief, and shook them in puzzlement. *Why* did we have two different coloured woods... and what was to be done about it? Finally we shook our heads decisively at the option of staining, and resolved to live with the contrast. At no time did we consider ripping anything out and waiting months to start again. Light gold is not the end of the world, after all; just an adjustment of priorities.

However, the rest of the kitchen looks great – new terracotta tiles on the floor; walls and painted cupboards all creamy soft; new electric oven built in as well as new hobs, and a dishwasher installed. The room looks larger and brighter without losing its farm-like feel at all. We christened it last weekend with a celebratory Sunday lunch of butternut soup, roast fillet of beef, and baked lemon pudding (after we had scooped the dust from the drawers and washed every receptacle in the house), and found it to be a vastly more efficient place to work. Though still utterly mystified about the blonde counters, I'm slowly getting used to them…

And then I open a document drawer and a large paper flaps at me. When I draw it out, it tells me quite specifically that the lovely red-coloured sink unit was dark Cape Yellowwood, and the new counters are… *Oregon pine!* Mystery over. No one's fault but my own. I ordered these in person. I *have* to like them now. "Don't they look odd, different colours like that, different woods side by side?" I ask each new viewer of my quaint old kitchen.

They probably read the warning in my eyes before they dare to venture the truth. "Not at all," they offer comfortingly. "Besides, you'll soon get used to them."

The handsome invitation to a mid-July Bastille Day cocktail party at Longwood House is all in French, except for the dress-code which is in English for public benefit. *Semi Formal*, it states decisively, reflecting the natural dignity of the incumbent Honorary French Consul who does justice to his status – a distant cry, unfortunately, from the ubiquitously slapdash *Smart Casual* suggested on invitations to Plantation House. St Helenians, by and large, enjoy dressing up, and tonight men are handsome in dark suits or blazers, all with ties, their women elegant. There is a buzz of celebration in the room although Michel is the only French national here. Tall, gracious, very good-looking, he is standing at the door, himself dressed in a suit and tie, kissing us on both cheeks in Gallic greeting, a tray of sparkling wine at the ready behind him, making us truly welcome.

Longwood House, a strange building of jutting wings and arbitrary extensions, was home-in-exile to Napoleon Bonaparte for the six years, from 1815 to his death in 1821, after dispatch to St Helena as a prisoner of the English. Today the house and its substantial grounds on one of the chillier plains of the island, flies the French flag – as do the site of Napoleon's Tomb in the Sane Valley, and the Briars Pavilion where he spent several weeks as the guest of an English family while he waited for completion of renovations at Longwood. Tonight Michel has thrown open the General's Apartments again – the wing in which JJ and I held our Fashion Lunch last year – but many first-time guests to these quarters are enjoying the opportunity to admire this interesting museum extension. When they were opened for the very first time, the guests of honour were a select group of visiting French dignitaries, themselves nearly all descended from such devoted Napoleonic Household staff as Marshal and Countess Bertrand, Count and Countess Montholon, General Gourgaud, and Count Las Cases and his son; and the very charming couple with whom I happily conversed for some time during that celebration turned out to be descendants of Napoleon himself. The rare presence that evening of people whose forbears actually lived here in exile with the French Emperor somehow added poignancy to the formal opening of this elegant wing.

Michel Dancoisne-Martineau is one of my local heroes. In his late thirties, he has run the French Domaine in St Helena as Honorary Consul since his father died in this post not far off twenty years ago, and his work at Longwood, the Briars Pavilion and the Tomb, reaps accolade after accolade. Like his predecessor, he is a masterful writer; and his artistic talent is prodigious. Self-taught in watercolours and oils, his paintings range from meticulous botanical studies of extraordinary texture to lifelike human figures, his portraiture simply breathtaking. He is a serious collector of books and antiques, and a social visit to his newly-built home in the Briars Valley requires added time to absorb the wonders both of his accumulated African bronzes and of his own works of art, and is a feast for the senses. So it is small wonder that he has lately been named *Chevalier*, the French equivalent of a Knighthood, in the Order of Arts and Literature – a gesture of recognition that quietly pleases him but which he modestly does not flaunt.

The front area of Longwood House, where the Emperor's own rooms were situated, is (and has been for decades) a purely Napoleonic Museum for the general public, packed in equal amounts with *objets* and atmosphere, where dynamic and knowledgeable guided tours are delivered by JJ. As talented in his own line of arts as Michel is in his, JJ has catered for the event tonight, and I am anxious to try everything on offer, knowing that his food will be innovative and refreshingly different from the standard fare we find everywhere else. In the meantime I grab a tiny satay, take a sip of whisky, and survey the guests. There are a lot of islanders here, notably many who are not often seen at Plantation House where Gloria still avoids entertaining locals if she can, and I observe that they are not breaking furniture, destroying antiques, or getting drunk at all, as she suggests. They are pillars of society, in fact, many of them our personal friends, relaxed in these surroundings and making interesting cocktail party conversation without monopolising the show, while the Hills are... *Where are they?*

The jacketless Governor and his Lady make a noisy entrance a full hour late, visibly irked to find that the French Consul, now tending to more polite guests, is no longer posted at the door waiting to greet their illustrious personages. And they have barely settled in before Gloria catches me nearby and pins me into conversation. She's in one of her feisty moods tonight, so I deem it prudent to steer her straight into the safe arena of history, upon which she happily alights. Tonight the preferred subject is Queen Victoria's grandchildren in Europe, and specifically the biography I am reading about Vicky, her eldest daughter, so my contributions are fresh and detailed. But it soon becomes clear that Gloria's formidable knowledge wildly outweighs any gems I have mustered from my bedside book, so, thwarted, I tremulously descend into mediaeval times – soon discovering that era to be another of her particular areas of expertise. Too soon my input dwindles to quavering comments—which she scores through dismissively, clearly irritated by my ignorance tonight. Her flow falters, and she looks around at a tempting plate of snacks on offer. "My God! What sort of food is *thees*? I can't eat thees! I shall be *eell*!" she exclaims in resonant tones, and I wince, offering the suggestion that they are actually delicious. She casts me a disparaging look. Then a waiter drops a glass which tinkles to bits on the floor right behind her. Gloria tosses her head, long hair girlishly loose, and sniffs pointedly. "What sort of inferior staff do they employ here?" she demands, pleased to find a point for loud criticism in the French Domaine. "At Plantation House the staff is *trained* not to drop glasses!" Unlike His Excellency the Governor, part of whose job it is to entertain frequently and generously – and so he has staff employed for that purpose – the French Consul in St Helena entertains officially only once a year, on Bastille Day, often out of his own pocket, and it is his property workmen who rise to the occasion. Quite admirably, I think. I catch the eye of Annette's son, Bradley, a young gardener here, smart in black pants and white shirt tonight, who, like his colleagues, is doing a sterling job as waiter. He grins conspiratorially, like everyone else familiar with these foreign-accented criticisms, and helps his friend sweep up the shards of glass. Both then swiftly move from her air.

So do I eventually, anxious to escape to less dominant company. And I find my neighbour, Dr Derek, reminiscing over a much-loved character on the island, recently died. Dot Leo, maker of the world's best fishcakes, was an institution for years, operating from a corner of the Market where a frying pan sizzled flat out and her lusty laugh and *Dahlin'*-spiced chatter kept pace, notwithstanding the cigarette permanently fixed in the corner of her mouth and its fallen ash in the cooking. "Dot once went to Cape Town on a medical referral," Derek is saying, "and came back with two overwhelming impressions of that city – one positive, one negative. Firstly, she was amazed that in Cape Town she could enter a restaurant at ten o'clock at night and order spare ribs – and even more amazed that they were served up at her table! But, on the down side, she was very much aggrieved that the South African national news made no mention of the RMS *St Helena's* arrival and departure times!"

It has been noted, of course, that even our own Radio St Helena occasionally forgets to furnish these details – more vital to the island than in the mayhem of an average South African newscast – and will be happy to announce a departure from Cape Town but makes no further mention of the ship's anticipated arrival at home. Yet mostly the news is right on the spot. Last week, when the Wharf seethed with activity after a second forensics scientist had been urgently carried to our Crime Scene, first by RAF flight to Ascension and then by RMS running at full throttle for two days, and the Wharf was transformed into a scene from a crime movie, Radio St Helena news gave us a detailed description of the felling of a Norfolk Island Pine near White Gate. It was evidently vital knowledge for us, and an interview with the actual tree-feller did not let us down. He informed us, for our enlightenment, which side of the tree he had dug holes, where he placed the wedges, how he used the gouge, and what happened after that. Then the newscaster continued with a full account of what the tree *might* have hit had it fallen this or the *"next way"*. Yet the Bishop, who lives not far from the offending tree, says succinctly, "There was no need to fell it anyway. All it wanted was a few heavy branches lopped off."

I ventured near the Crime Scene while the forensics woman was here; at least, as close as I could get. The policewoman on traffic duty at the Parade allowed me the last remaining *park* on the western end of the Wharf, and I triumphantly sailed through the Arch to grab the space. Parking was at a premium that day, for the entire eastern half of the Wharf was barred to traffic and strung with breeze-snapping *Police*-emblazoned blue ribbon. Pedestrians were not allowed near either, and though I squinted as hard as possible, nothing of interest could be seen – probably because the business took place in the moat, below eye-level.

But Stuart, collecting a box from Customs on the far side of the action, was allowed to drive past, and his eyes are young and quick. "Everyone's wearing white overalls," he announced when he got home, "just like they do in the movies, slippers and caps and all. But how they can find evidence down there after all the rain and wind of the past few weeks, and the footmarks of the workers who threw up the tarpaulin three weeks ago when the body was found, I don't know." Still, the scene was alien to St Helena, the atmosphere shivering with tension, even from the distance at which I stood. The town remains numbed. Even on weekend nights and with the ship in the bay, there are few cars outside the Consulate Hotel during happy-hour and nobody on the street at all. The murder has wrought a profound effect on this island.

Nevertheless there are still small rituals to observe; and Donny's is one of them, our Friday evening constant down on the Wharf, even in these shaken times. By five-thirty the working traffic has emptied from Market Street, clearing out of town at four to leave only a few late shoppers straggling home up the uneven pavements at this hour. The buildings are mellow in this light, wearing the soft colours of late afternoon as shadows lengthen under the pink mountainside, and the world here is surprisingly still. I wave at chubby Scrabble champion Freddie 'Hog' as I pass, a corpulent chocolate-skinned fisherman who spends all his rest-hours leaning bare-topped over his cottage wall watching the world pass as he smokes, and he lazily flicks his hand in reply. Just below his house, opposite the Rose & Crown Shop in the upper reaches of the retail hub, sits the derelict Duke of Edinburgh playground shaded by 200-year-old trees that are regularly the cause of hot tempers between those who wish them cut down and those who don't. The subject of the myriad mynah birds who call these trees home never seems to arise, however, but as I pass, their deafening bedtime cacophony surges through the open windows of my car. Passing the Stand lower down, I get a wave from Stedson's wife, Joyce, as she loads her car with carrier bags of shopping before joining us at Donny's, throwing me her delightful toothy grin that lights up her face so radiantly. "I'll be down to join you in a minute!" she calls out.

Tonight, because of the calm weather, I park my car on the Parade to enjoy the short walk along the seafront. Scores of little fishing boats bobbing at anchor are starting to catch the westerly sun, the water beneath them glinting with diamonds. My target is a four-seat plastic table sporting a handwritten *Reserved - Stedson G* sticker plastered to it, where I find the man himself reading the just published weekly *St Helena Herald* while he waits for the rest of us to arrive. He rises to kiss me hallo, places my order for a whisky and water with Michael the barman, and then stabs at the newspaper indignantly. "This thing's still printed in blue," he complains. "Look at it, you can hardly read it in this colour. More black ink won't arrive until the next ship."

"I haven't read my copy yet," I reply, settling myself for a view of the winter sunset that soon will light up the bay in awesome magnificence. "Any news this week?"

Stedson grunts. "We're getting a sniffer dog. They're sending a policeman to England for a six-week course in Drug Dog Training – costing £21 000 from Good Governance funds – as though we have a drug problem here!" Cannabis is our greatest threat, grown on the island in the past and in the present, and occasionally smuggled in on the RMS or passing yachts. We once had Ecstasy actually but officially that's all. Drugs, as the rest of the world knows them, are not an issue here. All the same I rather like the idea of a busy little police dog snuffling around. "And the straw poll in Jamestown shows that nobody's interested in a New Constitution," he continues. "People say they have no faith in the Councillors, there's not enough information from the Castle, too many big words are used, and the whole subject is pretty boring. Cheers!" He raises his glass, flashes his amazing grin, and tosses the *Herald* aside. "Ah, good, here's Joyce."

Joyce is still smiling, stopping to chat sociably at each table on the way as friends hail her. "I'm starving, Steds," she announces. "Anything new on the menu tonight?" Dear God, this is St Helena, we know the menus backwards! As Joyce and I optimistically investigate, Millie screws up her face when she lists the steaks, a coded warning that they're tough tonight. "But there's fresh grouper," she confides in a conspiratorial whisper, with wide-open eyes, and our problem is solved. She'll keep our fish aside until Bish arrives.

I sometimes wonder how we appear to other tables, this happy little Friday group of ours – the laughter at Bish's brand of humour that bursts like Roman candles from our corner, the lively debates dominated by Stedson's famously booming voice, and the sudden drawing together of our four heads in what we call *The Venus Flytrap* when a gem of insider knowledge is divulged into our midst. But this evening's a bit different with Stedson not in the mood for politics. Locally dubbed the Astronomer Royal, he is deeply preoccupied with the sky tonight and, growing visibly restless as the sun sets, he eventually rises to lean against the wooden railing of Donny's deck to gaze out to sea. We know he is watching for a green flash, often served to St Helena at that fractured second when the sun disappears below the horizon, and his keenness is infectious. Bish and I spontaneously rise too to squint into the crimson orb of the sinking sun, and behind us other heads have turned and now are also watching. Down it goes, halfway, three-quarters, nine-tenths – "Now!" And to our delight a luminous and fleeting green light replaces the red. Stedson's smile is just as luminous as he turns back to our table, his alabaster-white teeth gleaming from an espresso skin darker than the average St Helenian. "Who will see the first star?" he challenges us.

Notwithstanding that St Helena reputedly enjoys only seven cloudless days a year, so I was once told, this has been a choice planetary viewpoint for many noted astronomers. Edmund Halley was the first, arriving here in 1677, aged twenty; having acquired King Charles II's blessing for free passage on an East India Company ship. His intention, I understand, was to *"correct certain defects in the theories of Jupiter and Saturn and to supplement in the southern hemisphere the labours of Flamsteed and Herelius"*. In the age-old tradition of St Helena where no two stories quite tally, one history tells me that he also came here to observe the transit of Venus, but another states that in St Helena he actually observed the transit of Mercury. Stedson, whose alternate collection of histories leans towards Mercury, says that Halley's own letters home in fact never mentioned this at all, though he did mention observing, during his time here, both an eclipse of the sun and one of the moon. In any event, we know that, despite the clouds hovering over the hilltop observatory that he built – on Halley's Mount at the eastern end of the high Ridges – this young man did succeed in mapping out the stars of the southern hemisphere.

Nearly a century later, King George III, showing particular interest in the anticipated transit of Venus in 1761, was graciously pleased to encourage the Royal Society to send two astronomers to the distant Island of St Helena for purposes of observing this phenomenon. These were Dr Nevil Maskelyne, the future Astronomer Royal, and Mr Robert Waddington, who were supplied with an observatory behind Alarm House, *"half a mile higher than the surface of the sea"*. But, as luck would have it, on the appointed day, they *"could not see the contracts, the day being very rainy and cloudy"*. Ironically it was quite clearly observed by several people far below in Jamestown.

In 1826, the Governor – then the innovative Brigadier-General Alexander Walker, anxious for his men to learn sciences other than military – saw to the establishing of a well-equipped observatory on Ladder Hill. In theory this was an ideal site for observation, and when it was completed in 1828, Manuel Johnson (afterwards Radcliffe Observer at Oxford) arrived in St Helena to make a catalogue of 606 southern stars from this vantage point. But, like so many clever introductions to the island, this fine observatory was allowed to fall into ruin as soon as the Crown took over the island from the East India Company in April 1834, and two years later the expensive instruments were dismantled. Most of these – excluding two clocks, two sidereal clocks, a transit instrument and a chronometer which remained with the local Time Office until their own various demises over the next hundred years – were forthwith packed off to Canada. When, in 1877, Professor David Gill and his wife were dispatched to Ascension Island to measure the sun's distance and make observations of the planet Mars, they first did a tour of St Helena; but at Ladder Hill, fifty years on from Johnson's successful cataloguing, Mrs Gill was horrified to discover that the previously excellent observatory built there at such expense by the East India Company, was now no more than an artillery mess room. And at Halley's Mount, two hundred years on from Edmund Halley's visit, all that remained of his observatory was a piece of low wall.

Stedson can't prise his eyes from the horizon. The tropical sunset retains the shortest of twilights, and now the last glimmer is playing on a calm ocean ahead of us. In this continuing spell of unseasonably clear, sunny July weather, the sun's lime-green legacy has swiftly turned to palest turquoise, to blue-grey, to navy. And we can feel a palpable excitement as Stedson watches for Mercury to appear. He acquired this passion at the age of four, riding home across the country in the dark on his father's shoulders and gazing at an eclipse of the moon, an occurrence that ignited his lifelong curiosity about the night sky. "There he is!" he booms jubilantly. More or less above the sunken sun, a faint light glimmers. This is ours. This is the planet that is hardly ever visible in the northern hemisphere. (So how, I wonder, did the Greeks come to name it? I am, however, too shy to ask Stedson such an elementary question!) A little later, as the night closes in and we attend to our fillets of grouper, Mars appears. "Just three or four fingers below Mercury," is where we find it, and Stedson is now on a roll. "Venus is close to the Earth at present," he informs us, "and is at her brightest today. She looked *magnificent* at five-thirty this morning! Did any of you see her?" Of course none of us had. My house is too low in the valley to see her, or I might have risen in time. But Bish claims sleep as his excuse. Joyce just smiles. She has lived for many years with Stedson's stars.

We all separate at around eight o'clock, early enough to catch television or an indulgent early night with a good book, or Friday's specially long and pampering bath that Joyce enjoys, and we find our cars. I walk back along the seafront towards mine, caught as always by the romance of this scene at night – the tiny lights marking moored fishing boats, or the occasional yacht mast swaying at anchor in the quiet bay, perhaps one single busy light moving westwards for some night fishing. Where the seawall curves past the centuries-old Customs House and Captain Wade's House that are pressed into the far cliff face, the lights illuminating the working Wharf are brighter. And down at the pier head itself, there is a whole cluster. But I turn right to cross the bridge over the moat. Floodlights are on at the tennis court behind Donny's, and a few young people are rather desultorily playing basket-ball there, forcefully dragging themselves out of the social mire that the murder has caused. Then I am through the Arch and in a universe of my own. These stars I recognise: two lamps gleaming outside Police Station and Supreme Court. A gentle glow, like moonshine, from the recessed Castle courtyard. The lighted clock face on St James' church might be the moon itself, and beyond it the streetlights of Main Street forming their own little galaxy. I unlock my car, and as I do so the double string of Ladder lights catches my eye and takes my gaze soaring upwards – two, by two, by two, by two… Like fairy lights they fly skywards, sweeping up the now-invisible cliff face apparently of their own volition. And when they are very small and closely-paired against the black sky, one or two fly off their rails and become real stars and planets a million miles above them. Those are Stedson's passion, those ones beyond; but these down here are mine. They are part of my new home, and I *feel* at home here. I climb into my car, smiling, happy with my Friday night.

Top: Approaching Jamestown
Bottom: The Ladder; and Ladder Hill Road

a story of St Helena

Top: Castle entrance at night; Cardinal
Bottom: RMS at anchor, through the Arch

Top: *Main Street from the Arch*
Bottom: *Upper Jamestown*

a story of St Helena

Top: The rattling blue bus; Fairy Tern
Bottom: View over the Coffee Shop and Cenotaph

Top: Munden's cliff landing place
Bottom: Christmastime buskers

a story of St Helena

Top: Inland scenery
Bottom: Ball Alley, Sandy Bay

Top: Sandy Bay Battlements; Endemic Wirebird; and endemic Gumwoods
Bottom: Lot at Sandy Bay

a story of St Helena

Top: View from the Peaks
Bottom: Tessa & Louise; the Heart Shape Waterfall

15.

Coming of Age

July 2004

When my friend Anne and I travelled to St Helena together on one of my earliest visits, way back in the early '70s, the personable captain of the 12-passenger MV *Good Hope Castle* on which we sailed, taking a liking to us, announced his wish to introduce us to his cousin recently retired to St Helena. The elderly cousin was John Beadon who, with his Scottish wife Jean, soon became friends for life.

We were first introduced when John and Jean came aboard the *Good Hope Castle* to greet the captain on our arrival in James Bay, and they immediately assailed us with invitations to visit them at their house in the country, Hallams, as soon as we could find our way there. This was, of course, also dependent upon finding a car to carry us.

Self-drive hire cars weren't easy to find in St Helena back then, but we eventually procured a 1946 Ford Anglia – an ancient green-painted upright box of rattles and wild idiosyncrasies, with an added propensity for uncouth backfiring – whom we named Alexander. Anne drove; ears folded back, hair standing on end with the stress of coaxing this recalcitrant machine up the 1:3 gradient of Side Path, breasting its nerve-wracking hairpins and manoeuvring past oncoming traffic on roads even narrower than they are now. But she managed, and when at last we located Hallams in the midst of velvet fields, dark forests, and sweeping panoramas over High Knoll Fort to the wide Atlantic beyond, we decided to take up the Beadons' invitation. But the car remained at the gate. Looking up the long steep drive to the house, Anne's nerve finally failed. We abandoned Alexander on the road below, and set off uphill on foot.

As a general rule, in St Helena, one does not venture into the country without warm covering. This is an island where four seasons may hit in as many hours, and almost certainly the weather in the country will bear little relation to the climate in town. We had already been primed, so brought cardigans with us. Yet it happened that this particular day was exceedingly warm all across the island, so Anne and I, trudging up the drive, carelessly slung our cardigans over our arms as we laboured forth. Doors and windows were flung wide at the house, the place looking hospitable, and John himself could be seen working a vegetable patch behind the building. He turned at the crucial moment, and greeted us with a welcoming wave, immediately abandoning his cabbages to run down the drive towards us and usher us on to the veranda. He seemed pleased that we had called, and announced that Jean would soon be joining us with coffee.

But Jean did not appear. There were whisperings in the back of the house, and we had glimpsed her at a window as we had made our way uphill, so we knew she was home, but neither Jean nor coffee came our way. John began to shuffle his feet, sliding uncomfortable glances towards the door, and after what seemed a very long time, he leapt from his chair and disappeared indoors, leaving Anne and me wondering whether to depart despite John's warm welcome.

Inside there were more whispers, then a stifled guffaw, a giggle, and a sudden hectic clattering of cups. And like champagne bubbles, Jean exploded from the house. Her cheeks were pink with embarrassment, but her lovely weather-beaten face was wreathed in smiles as she seized us both up in hugs. Then she sat down and laughed. "I saw you two at the gate," she explained, "but I couldn't make out who you were. So I asked the maid, 'Who are those people coming up here?' and she said, 'Jehovah's Witnesses, ma'am, carrying cardigans over their arms like they always do.'" Jean rolled her eyes. "Well, when I saw John run down to meet you, I left him to it. I didn't want a lecture on religion, and I certainly wasn't giving them coffee!" And now, all these years later, John and I still laugh about my first visit to Hallams – and I have, assuredly, never draped a cardigan over my arm again, anywhere.

John, widowered since 1986, has long presided over his Saturday Open House. But today there are not many of us there – only the stalwarts who dare not absent themselves without a cast-iron excuse.

Even so, there is much laughter at Hallams. Today it's John himself who is entertaining us. We have often enjoyed colourful tales of his escapades in the East as a young bank manager for what is now well known as HSBC, and have frequently relived his romance with the young Scottish nurse, Jean, who one day during the Second World War fortuitously turned up at Kuala Lipis – a small dead-end town in the deepest jungles of Malaya – whom he subsequently married. My family and I, on holiday in Malaysia once, sought out this place, partly out of intrigue and partly on John's behalf, and John is now pleased to share this extra bond with us, recalling with refreshed memories the town's crushed streets of Chinese shops where his small bank was situated, the great square British Governor's residency on the hill, the wide river Lipis slouching along its way, the dense and suffocating jungle pressing in on all sides – a town still redolent of that past colonial era that was John and Jean's youth. We have also heard, with wry amusement, of Jean's circuitous voyage from England to the Caribbean, undertaken in her wartime efforts to meet him in India, and his stories bring a lost world to life.

But today he is recalling the time he was best man at a wedding at Westminster Abbey – a confusing tale that takes us from Calais via Budapest to Paris, quite literally, and brings us belatedly to London to stand at the altar beside his best friend. We are in stitches, almost unable to drink our beer for laughing, and John is in high spirits. After so many subdued weeks the laughter is a tonic for us all.

But next morning my mood is very different. Richard, in Cape Town, turns eighteen today, and I am 1 700 miles away. I awake feeling guilty and missing him badly; and when I deem it late enough for a teenager to have roused himself on a Sunday morning away from boarding school, I telephone home. "Happy Birthday, sweetheart!" I sing merrily (even though Bish, in disgust, once chastised me for calling a grown boy *sweetheart*.)

"Thanks," says a deep, sleepy voice at the end of the line. Richard is a man of minimal words on a telephone, and this explosion is followed by total silence.

"How are you celebrating today?"

"I went out last night."

"Where?"

"Out with Craig and Alistair. That was my celebration. Dad told you."

Oh God, how do I forget something like that? I begin to gush. "I'm really missing you, poppet!" (Don't let Bish hear that one!) "I really *wish* I were there to celebrate with you today."

"Yeah," he says pointedly, his voice still heavy with despond. "This is the first birthday of mine you've ever missed!" *And it's your eighteenth, your unofficial coming of age, and I am nowhere near you, and I can't even hug you, and soon you will leave the nest and...* Far away across the ocean, he clears his throat, his voice unexpectedly throwing off its weight and suddenly all cheerful and forcedly bright: "But you shared the other seventeen." *Dear heaven, now he is being brave...*

I go through the rest of the day with a burdensome yoke of guilt pressing on my shoulders, and no matter how much I reason with myself, I am feeling weighed down. I am a bad, bad mother, I decide. We should have sold this house the moment we realised it was not a lock-up-and-go, and should have given up our adventure here immediately, and long ago resumed our old humdrum suburban existence in Cape Town... I am wracked with remorse, and bleat pitifully to Virginia. "He'll get over it, he's *eighteen*," she points out matter-of-factly. "I got over it when you and Dad *both* weren't here for my twenty-first." She borrows Richard's pregnant pause. "And I was in *hospital*!"

Indeed she was, unbeknownst to us. Chris and I, due to circumstances beyond our control, were both in Cape Town when she turned twenty-one alone in St Helena, though before I departed I had left careful plans for a celebratory dinner and suitable luxuries in the freezer for that event; for, to all intents and purposes, she would have *fiesta* with her friends here and wouldn't miss us at all. Nevertheless, on the day, we rang her – Chris and I with heads pressed together, singing *Happy Birthday* lustily and somewhat tunelessly down the wires, and after some following moments' silence, an utterly strange female voice answered us: "Virginia's not here, she's in hospital."

Embarrassment was swiftly overridden by panic. *Why?* Her friend wasn't quite sure, so I immediately rang her doctor. Dr André's South African voice, mellow across the miles, was familiar and soothing. She had suffered a series of bad "attacks", he told us – those frightful abdominal agonies she had recently begun to suffer that were, as yet, undiagnosed – and now was on a drip. But she might go home tomorrow or the next day. "It's her twenty-first birthday!" was all I could say, and now, reminded of that absence too, by her cruel, cruel tongue, I have no recourse but to wail: "But I don't know how to be in two places at once."

"Richard will get over it," she says again, as indeed she professes to have done herself. And I have to stop bleating.

My mood of fragility is not improved by attending Ryan Thomas's public memorial service on the Wharf that same Sunday morning. His family has purposely requested this gathering at the Honeymoon Chair, not only to respect the place where Ryan died but also somehow to exorcise the area where no islanders will sit any more, or gather, or even pass by if it can be avoided. And indeed it is a sobering sight to see his bloodstains still marking the tarmac where they have been brightly encircled, as evidence, with rings of paint.

This boy was nineteen, barely older than Richard, and his mother is here and all the rest of his family, and I feel the deepest compassion for them. Because the official funeral has already been held at the cathedral (finally permitted after a full month of forensic investigations), this service is short and simple. And the Bishop, standing under the bright bougainvillea awning of the haunted Honeymoon Chair, his feet surrounded by the blood-marks and casually using the seat for his books, is striving to return normality to this unhappy place. Those closest to Ryan's family are dressed in black, many clutching posies to leave on the Chair or, now that tarpaulins and all signs of the forensics have been removed, cast into the moat where he fell through the roof of the shooting gallery. They are strung in an informal arc before the Bishop, while the rest of us, not closely involved, quietly line the seawall railings behind them, where the tide crackles the stones of the narrow beach below.

There is not a huge crowd, and I recognise many present. Yet it takes me some time to realise, to my sadness and some distaste, that apart from the Bishop presiding, the only expatriates here are ancient John Beadon, confined to his car parked a little to one side, and Virginia and me. There is no Governor present – indeed he didn't even respect the formal funeral. No Chief Secretary. In fact, no British representative in any degree of office is here, making an effort to demonstrate sympathy with an island in so great a state of shock as ours. As an expatriate, I am abashed. And then I remember that John Beadon and Virginia and I are not *paid* to be in St Helena like those others. We are on the Wharf out of respect for our adopted compatriots, and on the island for sheer love of the place. Therefore, the island's pain is ours, and even if we have never known Ryan or his family, we are suffering with them. I go home with small lumps in my throat, one for the tragic loss of a virile young life, and one for love of another who celebrates his eighteenth birthday without his agonised mother anywhere near him.

Over a feast of fresh broccoli soufflé, and a salad of rare delight considering St Helena's culinary limitations, Virginia looks at me: "I've been thinking," she says slowly, "the RMS reached Cape Town yesterday – and leaves again tomorrow, doesn't it?"

"Don't say it!" I shriek.

"So you *could* have been there for his birthday, after all."

Now I am not only feeling sad and very guilty for my son, but also murderous toward my darling daughter. Sometimes I wonder why we even *like* our children.

A whole year ago, when our attached 'guest cottage' still appeared on the Tourist Accommodation list, I was asked by the Tourist Office to make a booking for a South African visitor arriving in July. I was given only her surname, nothing more, and as her arrival now approaches and I have had to prise Virginia and Stuart out of their new lodgings to make way for this stranger, I grow ever more apprehensive. For some reason I have a clear picture in my mind of this woman. She is ninety-eight, hideously thin, vegetarian, not very mobile, and extremely critical of everything. She will complain about the distance to town, about the unevenness of Jamestown's pavements, about the lack of teashops, especially about the island's lack of vegetables, and she will find no humour here. She will die, literally, if the cockroach that lives in her cutlery drawer continues to evade my pursuit and waves its feelers at her upon arrival. As the ship approaches, I dread her more and more.

The licence to take in tourists on a self-catering basis in our Cottage (really a one-room bedsit) was actually awarded to Christopher by dint of his revered British citizenship. So he is allowed to scrub and clean the flat, to wash and iron its bed-linen and dirty towels, to shop for bread, butter, eggs, cheese, coffee, tea and other expensive fodder for a Starter Pack, to rise at dawn to await complete unknowns at the Wharf, to carry their heavy seagoing suitcases in and out of our car which serves as their taxi, and then to reap the rewards of their remuneration for a week's stay. But he is 1 700 miles away when we (rarely) take in guests. So I do the work.

Anyway, for the past year the cottage has been my private art studio, where the light was right and my work could be left without interference from feline paws. Until Stuart's advent, that is, when he and Virginia moved into it, putting a welcome lid on housing tourists on my property, and I explain this to the Tourist Office with a measure of glee. The bottom line is, I suppose, that while I am delighted to nurture invited friends, I push the comforts-boat out so far for tourists that in the end the fee barely covers the cost of my time, cash output or labours. So why I ever agreed to accept this crotchety ancient from South Africa, I don't know.

Her voyage, arriving from Cape Town, is having teething troubles with the recently-introduced ISPS code – the beefed-up International Ship and Port Facility Security Code – which, thanks to 9/11, is guaranteed to delay and confuse all maritime travel for the foreseeable future. The RMS drops anchor punctually at nine in the morning, but because of the new red tape nobody gets ashore until ten-thirty. By then, my feet are agony and I am chilly and wet from the sudden winter downpour inflicted upon us. A few people huddle under umbrellas sensibly brought along, others simply stand there getting soaked. I am one of the latter. I can't wear my waterproof jacket, even in the open air, because it has been so thoroughly sprayed on by the stray cat who sneaks in at night to enjoy Harry and Mimi's upmarket Scientific cat pellets, that people around me would collapse from asphyxiation. I am desperate for strong coffee at the Coffee Shop which is open for business even on this Sunday morning, but I daren't leave the Wharf. I am going to *hate* this week.

Eventually, I recognise someone I know alighting from the

first rattling bus from the Steps, and ask him to describe this crone of mine. "Just look for a polar bear," he says, and moves off to greet his friends. *Snow-white hair. Oh God, she's probably even older than I thought. A hundred and three!* The bus turns and goes back to the Steps for another lot. It does this many times, arrivals coming thick and fast, the welcoming crowds around me dwindling, yet I see no polar bear.

She's on the very last bus. Unmistakable. Short white-blonde hair. A large jolly-faced woman about my own age, with sky-blue eyes and pink cheeks (like all polar bears). I shout out her surname and a beam of good cheer illuminates her face. "It's Norleen!" she shouts back lustily. "Let's forget formality!"

Formality takes flight immediately, and somehow I get her and her luggage into the car. But we jabber so much on the mile-long drive home that I entirely forget to point out Jamestown's world-famous landmarks along the way. Nonetheless, she is entranced by the view through the big black slatted gate of our great white house resting behind it, and the garden and – "Let me know if there's anything else you need," I offer as we heft her bags into the cottage. There are fresh flowers and a few precious vegetables in a basket for her nourishment, new-laid duck eggs (because there is not a single hen egg on the island at present), some precious fruit, the best I could muster to make her week comfortable, and the tiny accommodation with its blue and cream theme, is looking as pretty as it can. "All I can think of is coffee," she announces. "I'd *kill* for a cup right now!"

Heavens, so would I. And so my impulsive mouth opens again, even fully aware that her kettle works and her cupboard harbours Nescafé Gold and a new box of long-life milk for her convenience: "I'm going to make a pot of filter coffee next door. Would you like to share it with me on the veranda?"

Not surprisingly, she follows me into my kitchen, both of us yakking away like old friends. And I have not yet switched on the coffee machine before I learn that her late husband's best friend was *my* mother's godson, and later over fruit cake, that her niece was in Virginia's class at school. Things really take off from here. We laugh, complain, confide, gossip, and laugh some more. She says what she thinks, which makes me comfortable. And within the first half-hour of arrival she has requested to eat all her evening meals with us, for which she offers to pay but I refuse to allow it because we're already friends. Meals provide times of great hilarity, and Virginia and Stuart collapse with laughter as Norleen and I reminisce over our comparable adolescence of iron-mesh hair lacquer, board-stiff petticoats, pungent jasmine-scented talcum powder and Cliff Richard. Around the sociable kitchen table, hearty non-vegetarian meals are followed by perishing hours of chatter on the veranda late into the winter night, while cigarettes keep her warm and I roll myself tightly in a duvet to keep my teeth from jangling from cold. After her first full day took her on a round-island tour in the old 1929 charabanc, and an introduction from a mutual friend accorded her tea with the French Consul at Longwood House on her second, she announces that she's now seen enough of the island and will be totally happy just sitting on my veranda for the rest of the week, enjoying the garden, the birds, and the hilarity. And that she does.

My sister back in Cape Town, meanwhile, finds people to send to me. Not only friends of her friends, but even friends of vague associates; persons for whom I am supplied only a name but no further information. They could be axe-killers for all I know. "I've no idea what he looks like or where he's staying," she writes helpfully, evidently under the misapprehension that time hangs heavy on my hands here. "But maybe you'll spot him at the Wharf. You can give him dinner." If she comprehended how hard it is to *find* dinner here, she wouldn't do it. And nor is she alone in recommending this St Helena connection, the mutual-friend syndrome. Two passengers on Norleen's voyage have tracked me down, courtesy of my sister, and I have given them a great and glorious tea. Then a voluntary school librarian who once worked at Richard's prep school with someone I know finds the house herself and pops in. Two others, from that same voyage, come for drinks because their daughter, twenty-odd years ago, attended a nursery school run by a friend of mine in Cape Town. And just before the ship departs again, I bump into two total strangers who fall on me with cries of recognition: "It's *you*! We got your name from someone in Cape Town who's a friend of your friend in England. We'd have visited you, but we ran out of time!" No, dear sister, time does not hang heavy on my hands here.

Meanwhile, St James' Church at the Grand Parade is ready for rededication. After closure for several months, the extensive interior refurbishment is finished, thanks to all those charity Scrabble games, and as it is Norleen's only Sunday here, she wants to attend this evening's service to get the feel of St Helena through its church community. I go with her, for a rather different reason. Our dearly loved friend, Tommy Dunne – gentlest of gentlemen, and artist not only of the exquisitely refurbished new museum but also of this restored church – died in England two days ago, and the wound of that news is still raw. Though an Irish Catholic himself, I know his presence will be with us tonight at St James' where his unstinting work will stand as his monument for many years to come, and I feel sure that this particular service of celebration and rededication will also serve as a kind of memorial service for him.

Not unexpectedly, the church is packed; front rows reserved for invited dignitaries, those behind crammed with press-ganged Scouts, Guides, Cubs and Brownies who would patently prefer to be home watching DVDs on this Sunday night. The rest of the congregation is designated seats elsewhere, and Norleen and I seat ourselves behind a packed pew of Brownies in the middle of the two-aisled church, from where I can see Tommy's woodwork legacy and the other restoration works. All the historic memorial plaques have been carefully replaced on the walls in their proper place, and the stained-glass window behind the altar has lately been hand-painted by a young local artist who had never worked on glass before. The colours are fresh and vibrant, showing tantalising flashes of brilliance as wind, lashing the trees behind them, briefly exposes their magic with the lights from the Police Headquarters across the square.

The Bishop is taking the service tonight, and while happily celebrating this rededication ceremony on the Feast day of St James, he also talks at length about Tommy's energetic contributions to both church and museum, and then we hold a poignant minute's silence in his memory. But the little girls in front of Norleen and me are not much interested. They begin to wriggle and whisper, and the further the service proceeds the more restless they become. There's an awkward swapping of seats along the row, and much giggling, followed by some sort of game starting up between the two immediately in front of us. Norleen and I discreetly blow through our noses with irritation, but they're such pretty little things we can't be cross. As the congregation prays, there's accelerated hissing among the friends and then, as we all rise for a hymn, a row of songbooks is pressed against faces to disguise further conversation. But Norleen is not taken in. "Hey, you lot," she protests, looming over them from the rear and placing powerful hands on thin shoulders. "I want to hear you sing the hymns, as loudly as you can without screeching."

A string of widened brown eyes turn to stare at her with some surprise, but concentration is nonetheless applied to the challenge at hand. For a blissful three verses we hear actual juvenile voices raised in praise, and order reigns in St James' Church; but when the singing ends, the fidgeting starts again. "Sit still!" orders Norleen in a stage whisper, and I, who must continue to live with these children after Norleen has gone home, bestow on them my indulgently-kindly-with-a-warning-scowl smile, which is utterly confusing, even though I am aching to prod one particularly hyperactive girl sharply between the shoulder blades with my red fingernail. However, Norleen is the one who has gained respect. Even when she leans forward again and in commanding tones admonishes the Brownies to follow the prayers in their prayer book, one small spokesperson turns to appraise her seriously. "You is a very *importan'* person, ma'am?" the little girl inquires politely, and I stifle an urge to guffaw. Norleen falters, but only for a millisecond. "Yes, of course I am," she replies imperiously, and there is no more trouble in the pew ahead of us.

16.

Going Nowhere

August 2004

We had a friend once who used to phone me on a weekly basis: "If my husband and I emigrate to New Zealand, will you and Chris come with us?" This was during a period when seemingly half of white South Africa was leaving the country, first because of its white government or later because of its black one. "No," I would say, emphatically. But the following week, she asked again: "If we emigrate to Australia, will you and Chris come with us?" And so it went, every week – New Zealand, Australia, England, Canada by turn, round and round, for years. And always our answer was No. "Think carefully before you act," I warned her once. "It will never work well if you move because you want to *leave* where you are. You must *want to be* where you're going."

That was several years ago and, strangely enough, she is still in Cape Town and I am in mid-Atlantic, as far from publicised strife as one can be. Without turning my back on South Africa – a country so vibrant, so scenically breathtaking, so diverse in population and colourful in spirit, and so exciting to live in that I wonder why anyone should want to leave – I have simply created a double life between my beautiful real home and where I also want to be, drawn by that inexplicable pull of the heart that forms the strangest liaisons. However, this minuscule paradise is like a microcosm of the Outside World, I am discovering; with the same frustrations and failures, except they're crammed into a tiny space. And they're inescapable.

"It's a microcosm of Africa, actually," says Bish in a mood of doom today, probably suffering from some form of cabin fever as people occasionally do this far from the world. On this sunny evening he's ensconced on my veranda with Harry on his lap and a

244

whisky and soda in his hand – the last soda water in St Helena in fact, which happened to be in my fridge. "Look at the place. Nothing works. Everything's done on the cheap. The engines that power our electricity are ferry engines – the same kind that keep breaking down on the RMS, so they seize up here too and our freezers thaw. Since the manufacturers went bang years ago, they're now repaired with little more than sticky tape and rubber bands."

When he pauses I say nothing because I know there's more. "The new wind turbines at Deadwood Plain are also second-hand, of course, so there's always something wrong with two of them. If all three worked together we'd at least see a cut in our electricity bills. Even the tar used on our roads is a cheap option, so when summer comes it melts and they have to close the roads until they've spread that frightful grit all over the place. Have you ever turned on a tap at Red Hill?"

I haven't. Turning on a tap in Jamestown issues crisp, clear water above suspicion, except that it tastes revoltingly of chlorine and dries the natural oils from my hair in frequent washing.

"Huh," grunts Bish. "Count yourself lucky. All my white shirts are brown now, but no one's doing anything about the water there." He rubs gentle Harry vigorously. "And DfID is only interested in sending us experts."

His is a typical expatriate opinion, coming across harshly, and I am sanctimoniously about to chide his negativity when I remember the dinner party I recently attended for a visiting South African borehole expert. This man clearly knew what he was doing, and for weeks had been pacing the arid wastes of Prosperous Bay Plain, studying the lie of the land to pinpoint underground catchments. Then he was joined for a week by a woman hydrologist, also dispatched by DfID, who carried a sheaf of research with her from previous hydrology investigations showing all the island's dykes where underground water has formed good lenses. Since they coincided exactly with the borehole man's own findings, these would have been obvious places to bore. But no! Since London's latest orders decreed boring in sites under recommendation by someone at a desk 4 000 miles distant, the two professionals were obliged to spend valuable time putting down sophisticated equipment with no results at all. On their second-last day before departure, however, they found themselves with a little time in hand, and the hydrologist opted for boring at one of her own chosen sites. And there, just as they guessed, was deep, wonderful water. At the dinner, the borehole man shrugged wearily. "If that's the way the British government wastes time and money, there's nothing we can do. What's worse is the wreck of a special bore-machine that I found here, designed to drill sideways into a mountainside; it cost a fortune a few years ago, but it's just lying in a field now, all rusted. That will also happen to the new expensive bore I brought to St Helena on this trip. Nobody here will maintain it, because it wasn't the island that paid for it." He's right, of course. So I refrain from chiding Bish. Instead I try to jolly up his mood.

"The new speed bumps work." They've slowed the traffic to a dead-stop.

He snorts, half with derision, half with the same amusement with which I regard this major new installation. At least I've coaxed a crooked smile from him.

The new speed bumps that grace Market Street are a first in St Helena, and have greatly excited the local News. And though I have lived long in the Outside World with the nuisance of such devices, I had never learned before about the laying of them. I am much wiser now, for Radio St Helena news has taken trouble to inform me in finest detail about the digging of trenches during the quiet times when commerce closes down on Wednesday afternoons, about the pouring of cement into the trenches, and how long the cement will take to dry. Then, we learn how the rubber cowls are fixed over them, and that their luminescent strips will shine in the dark, and that our cars will suffer a "nasty jolt" if they are crossed too fast.

There are two of them, strategically placed in the region of Pilling Middle School, halfway down Market Street. Which, of course, at once bring the traffic to a grinding halt since these two phenomena straddling the road are a clear source of wonderment to some who have never seen the like in their lives.

I was driving towards them on their first afternoon, at the very moment when school ended and pupils were released to freedom. And a state of chaos was reigning – an ironic condition since the entire project was devised for the sparing of these children from the speeding traffic of Market Street (usually constituting 30 mph, and a lollipop man on duty). But, caught up myself in the mêlée of parked parents collecting precious offspring, it rapidly became obvious that no one cared a hoot about the children anymore, and everyone was far more concerned about that prospective "nasty jolt". My own tough vehicle, when I finally crossed them, shrieked in protest and I knew, without any checks under the car, that motor repair shops will soon make a fortune from these speed bumps, at the expense of the private car owner.

Bish clinks his glass to show that it's empty, and settles for whisky and water in the absence of another soda. When I return from the kitchen, he's still on a roll. "The trouble is, no one takes responsibility here. Probably a hangover from slave days when the masters supplied everything and the people paid for nothing." Harry, clearly unsettled by such peroration, jumps off his knee, and Bish beats down his now grey-haired black trousers. "But if you said that in public, you'd get run off the island. You must be careful what you say here." It doesn't occur to him that *he's* doing the talking, and he's really trying to scare me. It's a game he plays when he's tired. "Have you applied for St Helenian Status yet?"

This curious conferment is conditional to five years' residence on the island, with sundry other stipulations to which I conscientiously adhere. But because of a late start in calculations, I'll only be eligible to apply in a year or two. "I'm still on countdown."

He takes a huge slug of his drink. "You'd better hurry up with that application," he advises, as though there's anything I can do about the slow march of time. "If they bring in a new Constitution the waiting time might be seven years…"

The sun has set. I'm hungry. But do I have the strength to invite this black-mooded Jonah to stay for supper, and so suffer continuing dreariness? The phone suddenly blares into the quiet evening – salvation! – and Bish abruptly rises. "I must go home," he announces. "Thanks for the whisky. By the way, there's still soda water at the little shop in Blue Hill. You'd better get over there and buy more before it's gone." Even though he is the only one here who drinks it.

"Have they got cooking oil? Or cake flour?" Stuart has driven me to every home shop on the island, fruitlessly in search of cake flour.

"No, you're too late for that; also for potatoes and salt. No one has those left."

"And onions?" I call after him as I reach to answer the phone. I have three onions to last until the ship returns in two weeks' time. But Bish is almost at the gate and I don't hear his response. It's probably negative.

Negativity seems contagious at present. And it is especially marked in response from foreign companies towards *Designing, Building, and Operating* our airport – a curious concept soon abbreviated to DBO – when DfID starts calling for new tenders for the Airport. Disinterest is blatant, yet the egocentric island seems faintly surprised that the world is not clamouring to do this for them.

And so, five years on from our Governor Hill's gung-ho promises of 1999, nothing concrete has yet developed. Slowly, slowly airport talk dwindles again, smothered perhaps by remembrance that though St Helena was first surveyed for an airport in the 1940s (and several times since then), the island is still without one. Already the British consultancy firm handling the latest feasibility studies has earned £5 million from this project, yet there's absolutely nothing to show for it. And these millions, the people feel, are excessive earnings for announcing that we have three alternatives: a long runway, a short runway, or a replacement RMS (meaning no runway at all), as though this is rocket science. "At least the island is becoming more realistic while the government still floats in cloud cuckoo land," says Bish when I bump into him in Thorpe's Grocery. "You know what the Governor's saying now? 'I promise you, the island will have an airport up-and-running *within the next five years*.' Didn't he say that to you in 1999?"

"He did. Named after himself."

"Well," says Bish complacently, "it's 2004 now. I hope he accepts that if the airport ever arrives, it won't be named after him." To earn that, Duncan Hill must turn the first sod himself, and his already extended term of office ends in just a couple of months.

The Chief Justice is back on the island, and I find him at John Beadon's Saturday drinks. It's been a quick turnaround back in England for him, since he was last here barely two months ago for Giles's case, and much time since then has been spent in travelling to and fro. This time Marie is not with him, but he's in high spirits nonetheless, and after extending a dinner invitation to me at Farm Lodge Country House Hotel for later in the week, settles down to inform us that the Murder Trial will definitely not happen this year. Analysis of the forensic evidence in England is taking a long time, and the logistics of sending out two barristers to argue the case in this godforsaken outpost must be appreciated. It will probably be set for the middle of next year, 2005, he says.

Ah, so that's why Stuart has been invited to take on permanent employment at the prison and has, accordingly, been fitted with a new smart uniform. So, what's happened to his plumbing profession, I inquire, since he's one of the most highly qualified plumbers on the island? "I promised to stay with the prison until the trial is over," he tells me. "And, because Virginia and I want to holiday in Cape Town in two years' time, I'll probably make a move then. Maybe I'll start my own plumbing business after that." There's lots of scope for that here, I agree. For all that the population has plunged so radically since British citizenship was restored twenty-seven months ago, the building of houses has not ceased. New dwellings continue to spring up over the countryside, and the suburban sprawl of Half Tree Hollow is speckled with homes half-built, all awaiting continued construction or further finance from owners earning good salaries in Ascension or the Falklands.

A few days later the Judge and I converge again, this time at a concert as guests of Joyce who is a Friend of the Ladies' Orchestra. While she weaves between tables, seeing to programmes and seating, our party enjoys pre-show drinks at our table. Stedson is there, of course, and the Bishop who is Master of Ceremonies, and other friends. And conversation unsurprisingly turns to the murder trial. But when Stedson hears about the two barristers coming next year he flings himself back in his chair. "That trial is going to cost a *fortune*! *Imagine* the bill for two barristers coming all the way from England!" he exclaims in resonant tones.

The gentle Judge looks faintly abashed. "And me too," he reminds Stedson. "I'll be coming back. And also, with us, two solicitors to accompany the barristers."

Stedson is doing sums in his head. "This murder is turning out to be *very* expensive!"

"Yes," someone adds sagely. "And it's already cost a life."

A moment later Joyce is seated with us, announcing that the concert is ready to begin, and from the back of the crowded ballroom, the Ladies now appear, filing through the crowd to their podium in black skirts, white shirts, and the clef-imprinted chiffon scarves that bring visual cohesion to a group which – as one orchestra member admitted to me – "sometimes lacks aural harmony". They do improve, these amateur musicians, as time plods on. But sometimes it's hard to appreciate a frequently wilful recorder bounding through Abba's *Mamma Mia* while the rest of the orchestra is reading *Greensleeves*. A little discordant, certainly, from time to time, but Joyce gets cross when we smile at their falterings. "They're just amateurs, and they're very brave to play in public," she argues.

"We're brave to listen," someone mutters in my ear.

Someone announced that Jamestown received 53mm of rain this past August, over double the average for our wettest month. But we have little else to complain about. Though this island's subtropical climate hardly offers the stuff of popular travel brochures, we suffer no extremes. Strong summer winds are the norm, with brisk upland temperatures, ever-present cloud, heavy rain in winter, and stifling January humidity in Jamestown. But so far no calamity of climate has indisposed our daily lives. Occasionally strong gales fell trees in the country and put out lights, as a backlash from Caribbean hurricanes that start from the Bulge of Africa, though we are not feeling any effects from this September's North Atlantic ravages. Not even the ocean, reputedly swelling at Ascension five days after the birth of those seasonal hurricanes and at St Helena seven days after it, seems affected, for the sea here is presently quite demure. Thunderstorms are so rare in St Helena that they are mentioned in the Records where I see there once was a thirteen-year gap between them; so the distant storm that brought residents of Ladder Hill from their beds to witness flashes of lightning out to sea one night this month, justifiably frightened the children. The September air, too, has lately been blessedly calm, and we can't help feeling that spring, such as occurs in the tropics, is on its way. Male canaries are sprucing up their mating yellow, and cardinals' breasts growing pink, while in the central island swathes of white arum lilies are burgeoning at the roadsides. The roaring winds and downpours of *Scruffy Ogus* have been soothed into occasional drizzle, light clouds split by bursts of sunshine and, unusually, there is almost no wind.

Zander has brought us a huge bunch of stocks, and broccoli and cauliflower from his own garden, and in mine he is picking beans again and pulling baby carrots for us. He has also pointed out to me the two plump aubergines hanging in expectation of the frying pan, and fat broad beans emerging. Tiny clumps of sage and thyme and sorrel are finally taking off, basil thrives, and there is almost too much rocket though I make mounds of it into pesto. The lemon balm I planted in a pot is slowly spreading at last, and catmint growing around our youngest mango tree brings unchecked joy to the hearts of Harry and Mimi – and gales of laughter to us as both cats leap and roll and caress it without self-consciousness.

This afternoon JJ is here, his lively imagination in hyperactive mode. He is wandering around my estate, mentally ripping up my garden, and as he speaks my eyes widen in dismay. Evidently he is planning Virginia's wedding here – a strictly *potential* occasion that she and Stuart have not themselves yet considered. But JJ already has it taped. "You will get in a team to lift the top lawn," he commands. "They will roll it up and put it in the corner over there, and *you* will water it regularly. Then they'll level out this terrace before they roll down the lawn again." I splutter a bit. This thing is feasible in Cape Town where actual garden services are available – *but in St Helena?* Where does one find *a team* to start with? After four years of residence I can barely find an electrician, though, thank God, we now have, by default, acquired a live-in plumber. "You will build a gazebo on the hardstanding under the jacaranda, which will be draped with fabric," he continues. "That's where the ceremony will take place because Virginia won't want to be married in church, which is boring! And then, later in the evening, the band will play there for dancing."

"Dancing? *Where?*"

"You'll build a dance floor on the new level part. And tables and chairs will be set up in a marquee here…" *An actual intact marquee? Where do I get that from?* The ideas flow like white-water rapids.

No party is easily thrown in this place. Months of planning and hording are involved. Spinach, for the tiny popular Greek *spinotkas* I like to make, for instance, is accumulated for weeks, seizing a bunch when I find one, cooking it and freezing it, and adding to it until I finally have enough for forty-eight mini-cigars. The same level of hording is followed with eggs, tomatoes, cheese, cream, lemons, garlic, yoghurt, peppers, apples, tonic water…

The size of the party also has a bearing on stress levels during planning. If the numbers exceed the nineteen dinner plates I own, I must resort to hiring crockery. But without a catering hire service here, only Ann's Place will oblige, as long as that establishment isn't hosting an event on the same evening. Cutlery also comes from Ann, but glasses that used to come from the Malabar wholesalers where we buy our drinks, now come from the Consulate Hotel. Again, we must hold our breath and pray while Noelene at the hotel reception desk pages through her diary. If dates clash I don't get glasses. God help me if we were ever to throw a really large event – JJ's planned garden wedding, for example! – for the anguish of hiring chairs, tables, linen cloths, and marquees would collapse me before I even began on champagne flutes, virtually unknown in the land where bridal couples are generally toasted with Chamdor sparkling grape juice sipped from flat plastic bowls. The treasured flutes I found at the time of our Silver Wedding party – their box labelled *Red Wine Glasses* – have disappeared along with the Malabar, and I must have been regarded as a rarity for wanting them, because for a year afterwards I was enthusiastically offered them each time I crossed the warehouse threshold, perhaps the only person ever to have hired them before. That lesson was quickly learned, and on my next visit to Cape Town I procured a quantity of my own flutes – but not enough for a wedding.

He phones me two days later. "I've decided what Virginia's going to wear."

In a panic, still locked into the conundrum of *The Team* that will roll-off-roll-on my hard-won precious lawn, I can't contain this secret anymore. "Are you two planning a wedding?" I ask Virginia.

She looks at me rather oddly. "Not any time soon. It's still too early to get married, especially as I have another two years of my course before I even get a job! Why?"

I tell her about the Lawn, the Gazebo, the Dance Floor, and the Dress that JJ has designed for her. I even tell her – though I quail at the vision of Zander's face if I were to suggest this to him! – that JJ wants *all* the vegetable plants to be lifted for the event, stuck away in individual pots, and that section of the garden levelled too, in case we need to lay a dance floor there instead. She's looking sorry for me, knowing that this is strictly mother-of-the-bride territory and that she will not be so foolish as to rush in where angels fear to tread. But she does say, about three hours later: "You know, I'd be really interested to see what dress JJ has in mind." Dear God, this is chicken-or-the-egg stuff. Surely the dress doesn't come before the decision to marry?

Anything JJ suggests after this will be tamer. He pops in again for Coca-Cola and fruitcake and sits on my veranda, surveying my thriving and colourful border flowers and bloom-laden hibiscus running alongside the path. "I think you should pull all those things out," he announces dismissively. "Put the hibiscuses in a few big pots, get rid of the rest, and grow the lawn right up to the bricks. Then cut down the hibiscus hedge between the top and middle terraces and open out the garden."

I take a few shaky moments to reply. I have a natural reticence towards arbitrarily cutting down plants that have taken years to grow. I weep when trees are felled. And did I not just a few years ago expend great effort trying to save the very hedge now under discussion?

But if I screw up my eyes, I can see the hedge gone, as well as a few of its neighbouring bushes, and the garden is suddenly made wide and gracious. I nod agreement, and JJ nearly faints with amazement that, for once, I have not seen a lion in the path of his inspiration. The truth of the matter is not that JJ's ideas aren't brilliant, but that he is substantially fitter than me and outstrips my energy levels by about five generations. Or so I sometimes feel. Nonetheless, I am not the one required to physically dig out the hedge. Zander is. And when I pass on JJ's idea he smiles tolerantly. "That's no trouble," he says soothingly, "no trouble at all." It will ultimately mean one less hedge for him to trim.

Anyway, though the garden is happy, the rest of us are not balls of fire at present. Suffering from both writers' block this week and a tendency to fiddle with paintings long since completed, seldom to their advantage, I dab at finished watercolour portraits so that whole personalities change with a glint of an eye, the twitch of a smile, and Virginia, like a mother hen, incessantly clucks: "I told you to leave that picture alone!" She did. But I'm restless and feeling thwarted by my drained creativity, so eventually descend into mindless TV mode, kept company by Stuart who, because of his graveyard shift at the prison, has mustered two hours' real rest in the last forty-eight. By Saturday evening we are all three glassily staring at a BBC documentary, when the phone rings. "I've got to go on duty again!" Stuart exclaims, swiftly rousing us. "Georgie Smoke's escaped."

Georgie Smoke is the prisoner who waters the flowers outside St James' Church. Tonight he went out at five-thirty as usual – and didn't come back. Prison break, St Helena-style.

Stuart eventually returns at midday Sunday to grab some sleep, describing how he and a colleague, in civvies and driving a hastily-hired car (undercover, of course!), searched all through Saturday night, exploring the dark Run, the moat, the mountainside above Maldivia Road, and even Donny's where Georgie Smoke's friends were playing in a rock band. In the country they visited pubs, Georgie's friends and relatives, but still found no sign of him. Since Georgie's lately shown signs of depression, suggestions of suicide begin to surface – a particularly depressing notion so hot on the heels of June's murder. And by now everyone knows of the escape, and even at a Sunday lunch party that Virginia and I attend, abandoning Stuart to sleep, the escape is a hot topic.

Eventually comes Day Eleven of the search. The police have been relentless in their hunt, and even the Sea Rescue boat has kept up a diligent, almost daily, shoreline patrol along cliffs and bays. He's been mentioned on most news bulletins, smiling pictures of him are posted around the town, and the Chief of Police has urgently appealed to the public for information in a rarely-utilised government half-hour slot on television. But nothing comes up. Hopes of his survival are fading.

Meanwhile, in the basement of an empty house in Market Street, Georgie Smoke is growing bored with freedom. He has visited his mother in China Lane at night, and during daylight hours has kept a low profile, amusing himself for ten days watching the search without ever leaving Jamestown. So, on Wednesday, he takes a last look around the place where he has been camping since he abandoned the plants of St James' Church to thirst (for no one else has taken over the watering in his absence), pockets the cutlery that has aided his meals there, and resolutely sets off downtown towards HM Prison, wearing a crisp change of clothes. He is in no particular rush though, and the heat of midday attracts him to rest for a while under the shade of a mango tree in the Old Brewery Yard about halfway down the hill. He is still there when a police van cruises by, so Georgie pops up his head, and *shakes* his hand at it. "Hey, you lookin' for me?" he calls, and with broad smiles climbs into the van. He's healthy and relaxed. "I ready goin' back now," he informs the authorities, "even for extend sentence. I just was need to be by myself awhile." Next day in court his sentence is indeed extended and he is regraded from a mild Category D to a more serious Category B prisoner. The radio news bulletin later announces that, following a tip-off, the police "discovered the escaped prisoner" in Jamestown and immediately "apprehended" him. Our streets are surely safer now.

The following day, while Virginia and I lay the table for her birthday dinner party tomorrow and Stuart, up to his ankles in soap-suds, is scrubbing down the veranda with a stiff broom, he utters a shout of surprise. Running down our garden path is another of Her Majesty's Prisoners, brandishing an envelope. It's Giles. "Just popped in to deliver a birthday card to Virginia!" He looks at me: "Hey, I saw you in the Emporium yesterday when I was buying this card, but you didn't see me. Can't stay, we're on our way to the farm. Cheers!" And off he runs again.

"Are the inmates ever behind lock and key?" I ask Stuart facetiously, and he laughs.

"Sometimes."

The prison bus is parked in our drive, and a whole line of miscreants have clambered out of it to gaze at our garden, their heads in a neat row above our garden wall. We wave, and they all *shake* back cheerily with shouted greetings before continuing on their way to feed the pigs upcountry. No wonder Georgie Smoke returned to gaol.

Within days, Giles is on the phone. "Stuart, when you come to work tomorrow, bring overalls and a fork with you to help me dig potatoes."

We hear the quick chill in Stuart's response, a timbre as completely strange as his usual deep-voiced laughter is familiar. "First of all, Giles," he annunciates clearly, "I have no overalls or fork. Secondly, you are the prisoner, and I am the guard. I do *not* dig potatoes with *you*."

The more I learn of HM Prison, St Helena, the stronger I support the whip and the gallows. Well, not really, but you know what I mean. I am laughing at Stuart's furious face, as perplexed as the rest of us by prison liberties. For Giles, after serving only three months of his two year sentence, is already – by virtue of his IT knowledge – more or less manning the prison's front desk and its computers. Where does his punishment lie?

17.

Bad Go...

August to October 2004

Gloria is on the phone. "We are going ahead with a Casino Night at Plantation. I want to give one last event for the League of Friends before Duncan and I leave next month, at the end of September."

My mouth, unseen by her, falls slightly open in surprise. As I stifle my spontaneous "Oh!" she forges ahead. "I would like Virgeenia and her friends to be croupiers again. Pretty girls – dressed sexy but not tarty. They did a *vehr-ry* good job of it last time."

"Oh," I utter again, and point out that this will have to be run by Virginia first. Indeed, last time this kind of charity event was held for the League of Friends, she and her friends proved great assets to the evening after a crash course from an old hand at such things, who turned my veranda into a croupier workshop for an afternoon.

But a wild night of gambling at the residency is not the germ of my surprise, since recent troubles at both Plantation and the Castle have prompted assumptions that the long-suggested event would be cancelled. The Governor is ill, awkwardly ill, with a malaise that promotes violent rages, wild accusations and a rather irrational instability. And while, officially, we're informed that he's suffering from stress and soaring high blood pressure, I hear that his rash behaviour could indicate possible diabetic schizophrenia. Circulating talk is always lurid, this time embroidered with tales of abusive language and threats of violence; and for some time before hospitalisation, our Governor walked Jamestown unkempt and unshaven, in uncharacteristically crumpled clothes. Alarmed, the island is now requesting the Foreign & Commonwealth Office to recall him on grounds of ill health, and has suggested he be embarked on the RMS that will soon depart directly for the UK. But the recall never comes. "What is London *thinking*?" the public exclaims, outraged and bewildered. "The man's too ill to govern!" And so the rare RMS voyage to England arrives and departs without him.

And yet Casino Night is going ahead? "Duncan will be allowed out of hospital for two hours to attend Casino Night – he's much improved," Gloria apprises me nearer the time. And so, on the chosen Saturday, players duly assemble beneath the sparkling chandeliers of Plantation House, less formally attired than on the previous fun-filled gambling orgy held there, I notice, and with markedly fewer people present. Saints are voting with their feet now, weary of these incumbents at Plantation House who have been in office five years already, two years beyond their original contract.

We go through the motions at roulette and golden spin, blackjack, poker, and crazy dice, mostly borrowed from the RMS whose officers also are conspicuous by their absence, while the smiling young croupiers – sexy but not tarty – manage the players. Only I observe that Virginia wears a sub-epidermal face like thunder, and suffers a crashing headache with feverish desire to be nursing her cold at home in bed; and therefore it is not long before her enticing décolletage is entirely obscured by an all-encompassing coat that almost buries her ears. "You won't ever have to do this again," I whisper reassuringly in a quiet moment. "We just couldn't say no to Gloria." She replies with a spasm of coughing.

When His Excellency makes an appearance during the course of the evening, he is freshly-shaved, neatened up, and chatting benignly with a few guests, even laughing a little self-deprecatingly that he's been "allowed out" for two hours. But this remission seems short-lived. Within days, stories are circulating again. We hear that his official appearance at a farewell tea party thrown for him by the Corona Society, on countdown to his departure next month, was attended in jeans and a shabby T-shirt; and though pleased to accept the many gifts they bestowed upon him, he departed without thanks for anything, utterly outraging these ultraconservative ladies.

When I bump into him outside Thorpe's Grocery soon after Casino Night, he is back to his grunge look in faded jeans, a fulminating beard, and a faintly frantic timbre in his voice. He clutches my arm as

I greet him, and looks deep into my eyes. "I don't want to leave the island," he almost beseeches me. "All I want is to build a tiny house in Longwood and live there for the rest of my days."

As I grope for a mental picture of this – unable to place Gloria there – he adds another restraining hand to my arm. "I've been a good Governor. You know Sammy 'Pot'? Sammy 'Pot' told me: 'Governor, you're the best we've ever had!' And I believe that's true."

"I know Sammy 'Pot'," I reply noncommittally. The well-known smoker Sammy is not nicknamed 'Pot' for nothing.

He mentions another name, famous for drunkenness. "And *he* told me as well, 'You're a *very* good Governor'. You do agree, don't you, Lindsay? You've owned your house as long as I've been Governor here – you do agree that the island has taken quantum leaps during my tenure?"

I honestly don't know how to respond to that. I know that his projected airport is not yet physically in the works, as guaranteed by him five years ago. And I know he has conscientiously ignored the RSPCA's desperate appeals for a vet, and... I mumble something that seems to satisfy him, and by the time Duncan releases my arm, I am feeling shaken. Somehow my shock at his current situation has given way to intense sadness, to a terrible regret that during the past five years the island has not sometimes met the unconventional Hills with kinder tolerance. Mostly, though, it has given way to anger that the FCO, explicitly informed of matters here, has not spared this sick man the island's pity and public derision by recalling him early under an acceptable excuse of ill health.

"I've asked the authorities," announces newish expat Ed, blowing his nose from cat hay-fever, "what form the Governor's departure will take?" It's well past midnight and, despite a downturn in the weather, we are on the veranda enjoying single malt, coffee and cake after a four-course meal that has amply celebrated Virginia's twenty-second birthday. Ed and his gregarious Saint wife Bea, with Bill and Jill Bolton, are her invited guests. I was chief cook tonight, with Stuart in charge of drinks, dispensing with efficiency and generosity, and it's been a wonderful evening. "I asked if we can expect march-pasts and brass bands? Are there farewell parties, and will there be flags flying down at the Wharf as he and his wife walk through the crowd? Will he wear the feathers?"

My eyes pop at the imagined spectacle, while the faint possibility of his being drummed off the island nudges the picture aside. "And what was the answer?"

"I gather that nothing is planned," Ed informs us flatly. "Of course I never expected anything. I just asked."

"I'm not surprised either," comments Bea. "The Hills are a disaster, and it would be appreciated if the FCO sent us a better Governor next time."

"*Bad go, worse come,*" puts in Jill. "You know the old island saying."

"I don't think we can get worse," says Ed drearily. He does not brim with humour at this advanced hour. "Right up to the last moment, staff have been leaving Plantation House, unable to stick it out even for these remaining few days."

Bill Bolton refills his glass. "That's a bit foolhardy. They'll want those jobs back when the new Governor arrives next month. He was Chief Sec here a few years back, and was well-liked, I think."

"The island should do *something* about a formal send-off for the Hills," I offer vaguely. "As Governor in such a colonial place he should be afforded some ceremony, surely?"

Ed looks as though I've departed from my senses. "Do you *know* how the island feels about them? Can you honestly *see* marching bands and H.E. dressed in feathers, and Gloria kissing old women and kids?"

Poor Hills. They've made their own bed and so, I suppose, must lie on it. But I'll miss the lively exchanges with Gloria, a spirited horse even as she's galloped roughshod over all measure of intellect, breeding, or status lying in her path – not so much jumping the hurdles as trampling them underfoot as she passes through. Many in her path have not been brazen enough to reset the hurdles behind her, and perhaps that's been to their disadvantage; but while I refuse to condone her often-public rudeness, I can't deny that she's probably the most dynamic, intelligent and *alive* person we'll see in Plantation House for decades. It was just her great misfortune that Duncan got St

Helena instead of Rome.

Five days later, we hear that the departing RMS will board passengers at four o'clock. But how the Governor and his lady will be acknowledged as they pass through the lingering crowd is an absolute unknown. I am not at the seafront to witness the moment, but hear about it soon enough, from Bish.

"It was eerie. The Wharf was almost deserted. Everyone who had come to see off friends left as fast as possible in case they bumped into the Hills. They were in no danger of bumping into Gloria, however, because she came down by car, driven straight to the Steps, looking neither to right nor left." No smile? No gracious wave?

"At least the Governor did the right thing, by deciding to leave on foot through the cheering crowds," Bish goes on. "But he did it in shorts and a crumpled shirt. It looked *awful*! He came belting around the corner from the Arch, anticipating crowds – and there were *eight* people waiting to wish him farewell, four from the public sector, four from the private sector. It was terribly sad."

I hand him a whisky and soda. He looks as if he needs it, even though he's come here by way of Donny's who opened on this Wednesday especially for the ship's departure. "It gets worse, too. As I was passing the Castle, before Hill appeared, I heard this terrible raging, raining down audibly over the Wharf! Apparently he had some dispute with the councillors over the swearing in of an Acting Governor before he was out of territorial waters, and became so abusive they refused to see him off. It's frightful."

Though not the timid type, Bish looks somewhat shaken. "Once he was safely on board, the crowd from the Castle came to Donny's which was already packed with all those people who had hidden there to avoid saying goodbye to him. But when the RMS finally blew its whistle, everyone – led by the Chief Secretary – rose up, cheering and clapping and shouting 'Good riddance'. I'm sure they could hear it from the ship!" Duncan Hill, in the addled clouds of his present health, probably did not notice the roar from Donny's, but perhaps Gloria heard. Almost certainly, behind the wall of bitterness she erected here through her unhappy five-year tenure, lives, I am sure, a still warm heart that would really have loved to be loved.

By the time bedtime comes I am wrung out myself, for no clear reason except that I still have a sour taste in my mouth from Bish's story. And a remorseful sense that I myself could have been a better friend to them lately. But I've been a coward, I know, fearing the brutal ostracism of an island people who are quick to shun the enemy camp. I have leapt Father Joe's imaginary cracks often enough in the past few years, and fallen into their dank depths quite a few times. But I don't want to do it again.

Down Main Street, in the Grand Parade, another platform is going up. Men are huddled over wooden beams and struts, hammering and measuring, and the sudden activity causes the oddest lurch of excitement. The new Governor arrives next week, and this will be his induction platform. Already the island has shaken off the Hills like a clammy raincoat, and spirits have visibly lifted. Faces are turned to the sunlight and the old island adage that *Bad go, worse come* seems to have been forgotten today. The new Governor, completing his former term as Chief Secretary only five years ago, knows what to expect of this island, just as he is already a familiar figure in government circles. That, in itself is a consoling start. And if there are people who seem apprehensive of how he will govern, there are others swift to recall his previous administrative efficiency and give rise to even greater hope. The island is clinging to that hope. "Worse not comin' this time," someone says with absolute conviction. "We already done had that Worse!"

On the new Governor's ship from Cape Town, is arriving a tourist I've never met – another of my sister's third-hand contacts. So I resolve to nip to the Wharf and sneak a look at him before extending any lavish invitations, and also look at our new Commander-in-Chief. I am up early, listening for the usual cheery hallo of the RMS, and it sounds off at a manageable 8am, faintly trembling the old windowpanes and echoing through the house with its inimitable familiarity.

The new Governor's welcoming crowd is only moderate, I notice. And for all I know the majority of adults are really here to meet passengers. But schools have closed for the day and hordes of children, bussed to the Wharf, give a reassuring indication that the island has moved forward since the unhappy exit of Duncan and Gloria two weeks ago and now is prepared to present a clean slate. The miniature Union flags last waved at the Princess Royal have been hauled out of mothballs and are again obligatorily aflutter in small hands, amid an undeniable air of expectancy.

I take up a good position in time to get a cheery wave from the Bishop and the new Attorney General as they walk past. Following the recent departure of my friends Kurt and Eulie at the end of their contract, the new AG is another old hand at St Helena, returning to the same post after nearly twenty years' absence, coinciding also with a changeover of Staff Officer (goodbye to Machiavelli) and Financial Secretary. I still find this new peripatetic world of hallos and goodbyes in which I have placed myself, takes some getting used to, even though each new arrival presents a fresh journey of discovery.

The two pass through the Customs barrier where the rest of us are halted, and continue on their way to the Landing Steps to form the usual official line up while the Chief Secretary, in his capacity as Acting Governor, has already gone on board the RMS to escort the designated Governor ashore.

There's a lengthy wait for us, the public, who can't see the officials at the Steps from where we stand, but eventually the Governor's sleek black official car, pennant flying, comes whistling round the bend and screams to a halt outside the awful plywood Customs shed. As the car stops, two rear doors fly open and out step a slim, prematurely white-haired man and a pretty woman in the smartest of navy pants suits. This is a good start, I decide, watching them both immediately plunge into the business of shaking hands and happily reuniting with old acquaintances. He's taller than I remember from our brief meeting when buying our house while he was Chief Secretary; but his wife is completely new to me. They are smiling and chatting, an air of warmth and grace about the way they are diplomatically greeting everyone, making slow progress along the Wharf like royalty. Before turning across the moat for a short reception at the Castle they even dart towards the Coffee Shop for sociable greetings there, I hear later, and am oddly reassured by this detail. Somehow, my bones proclaim, this Governor's first priority will not be the naming of an airport after himself, yet I have no doubt that his official remit from London is still to get us one, come hell or high water.

When the other passengers come ashore, I study them carefully. I was told this stranger of mine has distinctive red hair, so it's not long before I pinpoint him. He's about four feet tall and holds the sort of expression that has never smiled. As he searches faces when he comes through the barrier, I know instinctively he is looking for me, and despite my reluctance to put aside time in my schedule for an unsmiling unknown, I dutifully present myself to him.

He delves in his pocket on introduction, and pulls out a piece of paper showing four all-too-familiar digits. "Is this your telephone number?" he inquires in sole response to my welcome. "I want to make sure it's correct."

"It's correct," I assure him, and can see where this is leading. I am trapped into this association, willy-nilly, but am still wriggling to escape. "Just phone me if you need any advice or tips while you're here."

"You live at the top end of Jamestown. I'll find the house."

Escape is out of the question now. "I'll give you a ring at the hotel. Perhaps you'd like to pop up for a drink at Villa Le Breton before you leave the island?"

He nods, picks up his hand-luggage and disappears along the Wharf.

In the afternoon crowds gather again, this time on a Grand Parade that is fairly bristling with cameras. Two television travel documentary crews arrived on this morning's ship, and they are bustling about finding good vantage points for their shots, aware that the last-outpost-of-Empire ceremony they are about to witness is a rare thing in these times. But how much rarer, I think – and more splendid – it would have been if our new Governor were dressed in whites and feathers. How much we will miss it, even as history is made here today – the first time ever that a Queen's Representative in St Helena has not donned a uniform for his inauguration.

The local uniformed contingents are still in fine fettle, however, with polished brass and knife-creased pants, advancing joyfully down Main Street with precision timing and a blast of stirring music. The bands have seldom played so well, nor the marchers ever looked so smart, and suddenly everyone is smiling. The brigades take up position on the square in straight, stiff formation as the last of the seated dignitaries finds his place on the wooden platform, and the crowd awaits the Governor's car once more. And here they come – our new royalty, at ease, dignified, and both with gratifying presence.

They're a good-looking couple, and with a woman's eye I at once examine the stunningly feminine suit worn by the Governor-Designate's wife this afternoon as she alights from the car. Her taste is impeccable and I decide at once that she will do good things on the island, even though rumour has it that she will only be here for three weeks before scuttling back to her high-powered job in Britain. Then I turn my attention to the man who will actually govern. His suit is dark and beautifully cut, smarter than anything Governor Hill ever wore. He is elegant, his height adding to an air of reassuring capability. And yes, I admit as we get on with the business of the inauguration, this man has managed to get away without the uniform and still look good, even if future Governors might not wear civvies quite so well. I still wish, though, that we might have decreed something a little more dignified. Like morning dress, perhaps.

I have to rush into Thorpe's on the way home after the ceremony, and am delving in the ice cream freezer when a voice behind me makes me jump. "I've been thinking," says the red-haired stranger. "Tomorrow evening will suit me very well to have dinner with you. I'll take a taxi to your house at seven o'clock."

I almost fall into the chest, but haul myself upright to nod in hopeless acquiescence. By the time I have made it back to my car, I have formed a mental help-list of other guests who simply *have* to come too, to support me. With Virginia stuck into study and Stuart on shift, I *can't* spend a whole evening alone with someone who has never smiled.

"Don't do this again!" I implore my sister in an email. "At least send people you *know*!"

But her response is quick. "Everyone has a friend with a friend who knows you're there. I can't not give out your number."

Oh-but-you-can. *Please.*

Within the three weeks since inauguration, all the innumerable social duties of the new Governor's role have been dealt with – the dinners, cocktails, uncountable teas for the aged, the infirm, the disabled – and almost every business and institution known to St Helena has been visited. But tonight, everything revolves around *fun*. Lights blaze from Plantation House as they have never shone before and the building itself – as we obediently queue to shake the Excellent hand just inside the front door – fairly trembles with dance music. We are dressed to the hilt, men in dinner jackets, women in evening gowns, and chatter hums from inside as guests are proffered baskets of masks for this splendid charity Ball. We have not, ourselves, even had to agonise over making disguises, for that's been taken care of by Girl Guides and Brownies, beneficiaries of this event, who have made bright little visors of cardboard – men's secured with elastic tape, ladies' attached to quizzing sticks. I *love* this!

An old friend of the Governor's wife, JJ has been at work again, seldom able to control his design flow or his fingers, and her mask has the stamp of professionalism about it – almost flouncing in black lace and gold, a fetching, femininely seductive bit of handiwork that at once distinguishes her from the crowd. What JJ never knew, was that her chosen ball gown for the evening just happened to be black lace and gold, and she looks gorgeous as she floats easily and with natural warmth among her 250 guests. It's aeons since we saw such grace here – and it sits well with this beautiful residency.

With the exception of the sloping paddock in front of it, this handsome Georgian mansion sits squarely amid thick trees. According to scant Records for the time, the forest dates back to 1673 – just fourteen years after the English East India Company first settled St Helena in 1659 – and was planted by the English when they realised that already the natural forests of the island were being too quickly denuded for fuel and building material. The house, however, is a hundred and twenty years younger, completed in 1792 but added to by Governors Wilks and Lowe respectively between 1813 and 1821 to complete a very fine abode of about thirty-five rooms – twenty-four of which are living rooms of one kind or another, while bathrooms and store rooms make up the balance. While it is not exactly clear what improvements were wrought by Colonel Wilks, we know that

Sir Hudson Lowe (whose term covered the captivity of Napoleon) added – among an unprepossessing billiard room, a nursery above it nicknamed Chaos, offices, a coach house, and stables – the beautiful library with its splendid skylight, which is the nicest room in the house. In the attached courtyard Speedy, one of Plantation's famous giant tortoises, may be seen on a quiet day placidly munching outside the library window.

It is the 33-foot dining room at Plantation House that sees most of the action at social functions, and tonight it is our Ballroom. A band I've never heard before is playing with gusto at one end, offering a toe-tapping mix of everything from a sedate minuet, through the jive to the contemporary jerking of present-day dance, and I am mesmerised by the rhythm emanating from this simple combo of keyboard, drums and spell-binding saxophone. Dumbstruck, in fact, for this is undoubtedly the most professional and sophisticated set of musicians I've heard on the island, and I can't fathom why we don't hear them publicly. I could happily spend all evening watching them; but here in the dining room, with the large furniture and chairs removed from the room and the French doors flung open to the cool night air, is where dancers are doing their thing, and it's churlish to use their precious space for staring.

In the entrance hall, the exquisite round Regency table with pretty brass inlays of leaves and birds that usually graces this room, and on which we sign the Visitor's Book when attending dinners here, has also been removed for this event. And now guests circulate under the royal eyes of King Edward VII and his lovely Queen Alexandra, whose large full-length portraits in oil hang opposite one another. On the left side of the hall is the formal drawing room where enough sofas and comfortable chairs have been arranged for conversational guests to relax. So I, rather boringly, spend most of the evening here, in apprehension of having to refuse an invitation to dance and look like a stick-in-the-mud.

The truth of the matter – beyond the fact that I am not a fairy-foot at the best of times – is that I'm in pronounced pain, strapped to the hilt in corsets and moving with the flexibility of a telegraph pole since the old troublesome ligament in my back is threatening to rip again at any moment. It has been bothering me for a while, and I live in abject terror of it tearing on me before Chris and Richard arrive from Cape Town at the end of this month. Without any successor to the departed Annette at home, I have been applying myself rather too rigorously to scrubbing and rubbing in anticipation of my men's illustrious arrival for Christmas, and this is the price I pay for a clean house. And so I find an upright chair, and with the aid of my mask, quiz others in the room, certain in the knowledge that concealed behind a token of silver-glittered red cardboard I am utterly unrecognisable to others until I deign to lower it! Though I enjoy interaction with those who sit beside me, also revelling in the comparative quiet of this less boisterous room, it is probably not the most sociable way of passing an evening at a Ball unless, indeed, I were playing the role of a chaperone-matron to some Regency virgin. But the atmosphere is such fun and the idea of a Masked Ball here so novel, that I would have hated to miss it.

My back grows weaker as the evening progresses, and with some gritting of teeth I manage to hang on until midnight. But as the clock strikes twelve I take my leave, and though JJ was gracious enough to provide me with masculine escort upon arrival, I am permitted to leave on my own and now make my way across the tarmac drive, through the little paddock gate, and down the grassy slope to my car parked on the pitch-black field below.

I look back at the house as I reach my car. Lights are still blazing everywhere, and the building seems almost to be dancing on its own foundations as the mellow sax oozes down the slope. The rhythmic drums keep illuminated heads bobbing and swirling on the far side of the long dining room windows, and from all three front reception rooms laughter rings out into the quiet country air in great spontaneous bursts. There is something magical about Plantation tonight, and I check once again to make sure that my carriage has not turned into a pumpkin as the long hand of my watch moves past the twelve. But it is still my familiar motorised workhorse and I gingerly hoist myself into it, kicking off my high heels in exchange for user-friendly driving shoes, wryly smiling at the fact that I have just eased myself all the way down that dew-damp slope in the dark without so much as one glass slipper dropped!

18.

Deck the Halls

November 2004 to January 2005

The ballroom at the Consulate Hotel is a distant cry from that at Plantation House, but we're gathered here once more for another festival of music. Arranged in orderly rows on plastic chairs (as it is done here), we await an evening of wartime music pre-empting November's Remembrance Day – a concert that will clearly be different from the light-hearted version offered by the Gettogethers Orchestra last year, a performance of well-played music and a merry sing-along of wartime tunes that everyone knew. This one, organised by a former major in the Scots Guards, threatens to be altogether more sombre, since there are already slides flashed on the wall depicting war scenes of some poignancy, and the Bishop has been requested not only to conduct prayers at this event, but to hold a two-minute silence – a detail that puzzles him, since he will be holding prayers and a two-minute silence at the formal cenotaph Remembrance Service next Sunday. For the rest of the evening our stars will be the Ladies' Orchestra, who take their places with smiles, a number of new faces among them tonight.

For all its limited facilities for formal music study, the island holds a buried wealth of natural musicality. And though lacking in ethnic originality, such as the steel drums of the Caribbean or pennywhistle of South Africa, one of its finest demonstrations emerged at a Quincentenary concert when the incandescent star of the evening was the St Helena String Band – a jolly, rollicking, floor-thumping, eclectic group of fiddle, accordion, banjo and guitar players playing old-time music. Hastily cobbled together from across the island, this was real country music – toe-tapping Irish reel and hoedown stuff that made one wish to dance in the aisles and indeed did get a few islanders on their feet, even in the staid Consulate ballroom. With irresistible charm, the love of the music showed in the animated faces of the musicians as the clock was turned back before our eyes. Long before electric keyboards and disco apparatus came to dominate St Helena's homogeneous present-day offerings, this was the music played at Saturday dances attended by my island contemporaries in their youth, either at local gathering points or spontaneously in cottage homes. It was the norm when the pleasures of life were simple and fun, and it's sad that the only remnant of those days now survives in the nickname for the sustenance of note that came around at those pleasurable get-togethers: *Bread-and-dance*, a sandwich of traditional chilli-spiced St Helena tomato paste that is still in evidence at every local gathering.

Nowadays, except for a rare occasion when guests might bring an accordion or fiddle to a private party, background music in the home is supplied by CD. But one of the most memorable local parties that Chris and I have attended was in a remote country cottage to which several guests had brought instruments; and after a feast of curry, roast pork and barbecued chicken legs, we sat in the garden with the night sky above us and all of Prosperous Bay Plain below, and sang our voices hoarse.

And then there is dancing. It is doubtful that a single St Helenian is born without this natural aptitude, and to watch the grace and footwork with which islanders, young and old, prance through waltzes, foxtrots and the pretty Boston two-step, offers me far more delight than futilely attempting to emulate them. The faraway Blue Hill Community Centre is a favourite place for dancing, set as it is in a conservative farming area somewhat removed, and in some ways self-protected, from the outside influences of Jamestown. The once-a-month Invitation Dance held there (except during Lent, a self-imposed abstinence) is one of the most popular events on the island – one that no charity event would dare to clash with for it hosts a healthy list of regulars who would not miss the night for anything. Such dances are the nearest one might come to old-style St Helena, and the only thing missing from real tradition in the present day is the former custom of offering bananas to signal the end of the evening. One for the road, so to speak.

So what was life like when my Saint friends were growing

up? Less complicated, perhaps, but hard. A hankering for self-improvement certainly took scores of young women to England where, at that time, St Helenians were offered initial employment only in domestic service, though from there many moved into teaching or nursing professions before they eventually returned home. The crash of the island's flax market in the mid-1960s, when the post offices of Great Britain ceased using string (made from flax) and switched to nylon for tying parcels, had changed the face of St Helena overnight, as all the local flax mills closed down and an entire industry found itself out of work, with nothing to export. By the end of the '60s, one-third of the island's income was generated by the sale of postage stamps, mainly to collectors – the other two-thirds handed over by the British government. When my island friends were very young, St Helenians were poor; yet today's smart clothes and well-kitted houses belie the fact that many who now run successful businesses, teach, nurse, and hold office in government, never owned a pair of shoes as a child.

The locals now laugh about their youthful deprivations – about the hand-me-down dresses, shoes that did the rounds of each sibling, holes cut in too-small sizes with falsely-bandaged toes protruding (fake injuries), in order to be smart for church on Sunday. At a small tea party recently, as a group of women friends started reminiscing they rocked with laughter at memories of the old cow-grass mattresses they shared as children, high and soft and at first as puffy as great feather pillows, then hard and flat as the grass grew old, remembering how they helped to cut the cow-grass and stuff the mattresses themselves. Notes were compared about setting off from home in early mornings after chores were completed, walking all the long country miles from distant Blue Hill to school in the central island, and walking back when school was over to carry out more chores until the light faded and a candle took them to bed.

The town girls had other chores. Audrey went down to the Steps every evening when the fishing boats returned, and from a clothesline on which fresh fish were strung, selected enough for her family's meal that night, free from the sea in days before the modern fish export factory monopoly started eking out small quantities of fish for local consumption at hefty prices. She poignantly remembers captured turtles trapped on their backs in the Market, sometimes for days, until enough shoppers had placed orders to warrant killing them, sobs and little tears dropping from their eyes as they awaited death. (Wisely, turtles rarely call at St Helena anymore). Audrey also recalls the man who served the Ladder Hill community and the burgeoning Half Tree Hollow with fresh fish, by swinging in rhythmic gait up the Ladder with a yoke on his shoulders and baskets of fish hung from it. But today his successor drives a fish van whose cheery horn, at seven-thirty in the morning two or three times a week, jauntily sounds the opening bars of the William Tell Overture across James Valley as he makes his way into the country with fresh-caught offerings.

Old crafts have disappeared. Pretty copper candle-lamps bought on my early visits have given way to occasional brass lamps beaten especially for tourists, while the exquisite endemic wooden inlay work I have treasured for years has never been matched since the death of talented Bert Nicholls decades ago. Traditional old banana-weave sunhats only appear when elderly Daisy Grey demonstrates the laborious art of peeling, soaking and intertwining strips of banana palm bark to fashion them at rare crafts fairs. And even St Helena's famous lace is sometimes, blasphemously, machine produced now, unless hard-won by special order from the ageing Jessica March who is one of the last remaining really fine lace makers still flicking bobbins in her distant country cottage.

The craft of lacemaking was not an indigenous art, but came to St Helena through the prodigious energies of a school teacher named Emily Louise Warren who was sent out from England for three years to head up the Girls' School in 1898. In between teaching singing and maypole dancing, producing concerts with the children and marrying a chemist named Thomas Jackson, she developed a passion for lacemaking which detained her in England for eight months during one of her visits home, while she set herself to perfect the finer qualities of Honiton, Torchon and Bucks. On her return to St Helena, lacemaking caught on swiftly as she gathered together other expatriate women skilled in the craft who helped her to teach, and her art soon broadened to incorporate lace patterns even from Madagascar, India and China.

When the home government thought to assist by sending out a Miss Penderel Moody, a lace expert who brought a weaving loom with her, this was curtly brushed aside by the students who had swiftly adapted to hand-lace and vastly favoured bobbins. By then Mrs Jackson (formerly Warren), procuring a donated lathe, had anyway already set about teaching the boys to make bobbins for the girls at a nominal price, and to make fillets for them to work on. Miss Moody's influence, however, was one that set a very high standard for work produced, refusing to allow any sample of lace to leave the island before being passed through a panel of scrutineers. The great sadness of modern St Helena is all the more poignant then, for the resolute refusal of young people to learn these arts – even for future posterity – while they can still be demonstrated.

And so, because of the local propensity for too-long concerts, my mind has wandered years away as the Scots Guard major continues to put the Ladies' Orchestra through its Remembrance Day paces. But the evening is finally drawing to a close, and I have enjoyed it, finding it not half as "dire" as one participant had warned me after a rehearsal. In fact it was not dire at all. The energetic conductor did a marvellous job with her contingent of non-professional musicians, and tonight's gusto and smiles from the platform have gone great lengths to inspire us, the audience, with their own infectious verve. I am slowly coming to admire them.

With the official Remembrance Sunday Service over at the Cenotaph, the crowd disperses from the Wharf and drifts, chatting, across the moat and through the Arch to take up casual positions on the Parade where the new Governor, the Bishop, the French Consul and the Chief of Police, leading the way, have already reached the stoop of the Courthouse. Now we wait for a music-heralded march-past from the uniformed bands to follow us – and here they come, blaring trumpets, booming drums, one-two, one-two, past the Courthouse, eyes left to acknowledge the Commander-in-Chief. No salute this year, because now there is no uniform; another small detail gone. Behind them, as always, trail out-of-step teenage Scouts, less than enthusiastic about giving up Sunday sleep for this event, Guides, Brownies, little Rainbows skipping or flagging according to their whim. Finally, when all the contingents have vanished up the slope of Main Street, Virginia and I are freed to race home and put finishing touches to a birthday celebration for me, with seventeen lunch guests hot on our heels.

November's weather grins with sunshine on Zander's newly manicured lawns, smooth and inviting, and gloriously bordered by the brilliance of Stuart's blooming zinnias. For one who has never gardened before, Stuart has discovered green fingers, and the dahlia, zinnia, snapdragon and cornflower plants he has scrounged from friends and family over the past few months, have shot to prodigious heights alongside our yellow-brick path. Our big apricot-pink canvas hammock is invitingly slung between two mango trees, a peachy glow in this dark-leafed glade, with Gay gently swaying in it, watching a hilarious – if not exactly skilled – game of *boulle* being played across the path on a bumpy middle terrace. With his wife sadly returned to the portals of her high-powered career, the new Governor, Michael Clancy – showing a sharply competitive streak – is joshing Bill and his team about cheating at sports, while Stedson and Joyce, having completed an exploration of the entire property, now stand on the sidelines hooting with laughter at the exhibition. Those less energetic are lounging in chairs on the veranda or smoking on the little lawn below, and regular bursts of laughter bubble through the still afternoon heat. Lunch is long-since over now, food served buffet-style from the dining room – a Moroccan lamb stew, chicken with rosemary, large salads, a rich chocolate tart, summer pudding (from frozen berries, of course), and sliced oranges steeped in liqueur – all of which sounds ordinary enough in a normal world but here have constituted a feat of accumulation. And the mother-lode of credit for all this lies at Virginia's feet, for while my nagging backache – shrieking abuse when I bend or lift – has plagued me for weeks, she has handled the physical aspects of this party almost single-handedly. Even Stuart, on duty at the prison today, is not here to help spread the load.

And so, while guests are urged to help themselves to wine or beer from a large ice-box placed close at hand, I float about from group to group enjoying the company, relaxed and watching the sun which was overhead when my guests arrived now tint the garden in its late afternoon light, and eventually slowly move behind the towering slopes of Ladder Hill to lengthen shadows across the valley. When the sun has set completely, the last guests leave.

This month is packed with activity – barbecues, a charity supper (with movie!), cocktails with the new Attorney General, a visiting surgeon for us to entertain at Villa Le Breton, and continuing spit-and-polish around our aged dusty-creviced cockroach-rampant house in frantic preparation for the arrival of Chris and Richard from Cape Town a week from today. All that – and a big RSPCA conundrum taking up a lot of precious time.

It's a pet food problem. JJ and I picked up the first notes of discord nearly three months ago but there's a rising crescendo now. Something to do with an accountant for Solomon & Co., which manages the Spar Supermarket franchise, aiming to profit from selling our Scientific Diet themselves, and refusing to acknowledge the stumbling blocks here. This special brand, we repeatedly explain in exasperation, is only on the island because of an arrangement exclusively drawn up between the Diet suppliers and the RSPCA (St Helena Branch) who foots bills for it strictly as non-profit charitable funding. The Diet is expensive, and while we would be delighted to have someone else spend the money, shoulder the responsibility, and keep the island pets supplied with good health, the accountant in question will certainly not sell the pet food at cost-plus-freight as we are doing. Greed has seeped into the equation ever since the retail business noticed how popular the product is. Our Diet pellets have been an extraordinary asset to local pets in the eleven months since we launched it, and those lucky dogs and cats whose owners diligently top up their bowls when fresh stocks arrive are recognisable by shining coats and bright eyes. In fact, the greatest accolade for our labours comes from one of Elizabeth Scholtz's own protégées, one who sees to the micro-chipping of puppies. "We can look at litters," he says, "and tell at a glance which ones are fed on the Diet. They're all bigger, stronger, and healthier." That's exactly what we want to hear in a land with no vet, and why we've gone to all this trouble. It's also why we are now nervous that this meddling in RSPCA affairs might upset the supplying applecart.

But the retail ankle-biting is not going away. Like an errand-boy, the RSPCA Treasurer runs messages between us and his friend, Solomon's accountant, as we each doggedly stick to our guns. And so it's crunch-time. The intricacies of this business must be sorted out once and for all in a meeting between the four operatives – the RSPCA Chairman, its recalcitrant Treasurer, JJ and me. We arrange a breakfast meeting at my house for 9am on Monday morning.

Notwithstanding the heavy sweeping and polishing that have enslaved me over the past couple of weeks – try as I might I can't find another Annette! – my troublesome back has obligingly taken a turn for the better and I've been much more mobile through the past three days. This is good, because on this very day, Chris and Richard are boarding the RMS in Cape Town and will be here this time next week. Things are looking up. The house is shining. I am feeling strong. And now I am preparing a really nice breakfast for the meeting – a large jug of chilled (boxed) orange juice, chilled creamy porridge with (frozen) raspberries, a full offering of eggs, bacon, grilled tomatoes (real!), sausages, and (canned) mushrooms; toast, hot homemade (frozen) cranberry muffins, and pots of Guatemalan coffee to end with. I deem it adequate sustenance for thrashing out a bit of unpleasant business and set to work with verve.

The porridge is finished and chilling in the fridge, along with the orange juice. I have laid the table in the kitchen for ease of conversation, and have cut the tomatoes and prepared them with generous herbs from the garden. Everything is right on cue at the moment, carefully timed to least disrupt our verbal thrashings once they start, and as long as everything is ready to cook as soon as they get here, this will be easy. I bend to flick a baking tray from its cubbyhole and – THWANG ~ ~ ~ !!

Oh, God. Oh, God. Keep your wits about you. Before you pass out, phone someone – "JJ!" I bleat into the telephone, my voice in mezzosoprano, "I've torn a ligament in my back. Please rush down and cook breakfast!"

And like all good friends, JJ comes running, swiftly followed by the new Chairman (the Bishop) and Treasurer arriving on time, who find me pinned to an upright kitchen chair, supportive staff in one hand, powerful painkillers in the other, wearing a frighteningly pallid complexion. I smile bravely, aware that I look the martyr – and am feeling the martyr too. I'm *in extremis*. Barely able to speak, I certainly can't think. And I have very little interest left in breakfast, in Committees, or indeed in our Scientific pet food. "Where do I find a spatula?" asks JJ who has never cooked in my kitchen before. "How do you turn this oven on? Which coffee do you want?" I can think only of my bed, and the longer I sit here, the more rigidly my shocked and shrieking frame will set in the shape of this chair; I fear I might evermore be moulded into a half-swastika. Meanwhile the humourless Treasurer supportively offers me a verbal directory of apparatus suited to fragile beings like me, and though they sound useful I cannot possibly take them in right now. I'm also striving to be helpful to JJ who is, after all, being very helpful to me, but am hardly able myself to direct him around my own kitchen. An uncharacteristically sympathetic expression passes through Bish's eyes as he observes my misery. "I've never seen you look so *old*," he remarks.

I want to cry, great plopping tears of pain and self-pity, instead of trying to act the responsible committee member and good hostess. Not only am I experiencing agony, but I have precisely one week in which to mend before Chris and Richard arrive. This is not the first time they will find me at the Wharf leaning on a stick. This is the third time since the Season of Desolation four years ago, that I have injured my back on the very day they have set sail to join me. It is no longer a joke. I must stop shining the house for them.

JJ produces a laudably fulsome breakfast, though the chilled porridge with raspberries is omitted because I've forgotten to tell him about it; and I can't even be bothered to mention the muffins, so toast suffices. But by the time we get to second cups of coffee some sort of agreement has been reached about the pet food. An ultimatum to the avaricious accountant, I think, to accept the *status quo*, stop meddling in our affairs, quit going behind our backs to the Diet suppliers who are alarmed by his behaviour. In fact, like our system or lump it; meaning, we'll find other distributors.... *I want this all to be over. I want to lie down...*

And eventually I do. I lie down for six whole days, struggling to raise myself enough to eat or drink, while a simple journey down and up steps to the bathroom becomes a test of strength like conquering Everest. But on the seventh day I heave myself up, put aside the walking stick, wash my hair, paint a smile on my lips and gingerly set forth for the Wharf. Virginia, now on holiday from her teacher's course, drives me there, just as excited as I am to welcome Chris and Richard. But

Stuart is mysteriously absent…

The RMS has glided into happy view around the bluff of Munden's and is dropping anchor as Bill Bolton places two cups in front of us. In the light of an open Coffee Shop on these early ship-day mornings, our old tradition of coffee and blueberry muffins or ginger biscuits dispensed from the boot of my car has given way to frothy cappuccinos as we mark time till passengers come ashore. Now we sit in comfort on one of their benches, lazily sipping coffee as we hear that heart-lurching rich-voiced call of greeting from the RMS, watch the Immigration people ploughing out towards it on *Gannet Three*, and the lighters hitch up alongside the ship to start immediately with the unloading of freight. A good while later, when all the formalities have been seen to in the Main Lounge of the RMS, when passports have been stamped and overnight bags slung over shoulders, when tickets have been issued for a place in the ferry and DfID dignitaries ushered to the head of the queue, then the little *Gannet Three* will come charging back with our passengers.

"Stuart's not *seriously* frightened of meeting Dad?" I ask Virginia as we watch the activity.

"Terrified. I happened to mention that Dad's a big man. I called him a Gentle Giant, but Stewey's still nervous. All men are frightened of meeting girlfriends' fathers for the first time!"

"But Stuart's been living with us for six months already. Surely he knows he's accepted as part of the family now?"

"He'll only be sure once today is over." Poor Stuart. Running the gauntlet of not only The Father, but also The Brother, is quite tough.

"He didn't seem nervous when he met *me* for the first time," I comment, and Virginia simply guffaws.

"You totally confused him!" she laughs. "You ran right past him as though he wasn't there!"

Well, it wasn't exactly like that. True, I was returning from Friday at Donny's when I found the two of them waiting for me on the veranda, just hours on from Stuart's long-awaited and fraught homecoming voyage from Ascension. But I was absolutely *desperate* to see an imminent television documentary, so my greeting, though warm, was on the short side of brief since I was late for it. I did rather rush past him, I suppose, and so he was spared the anticipated parental

Third Degree. But I saw immediately that he was the possessor of gorgeous almond-shaped eyes that looked directly at me, and a warm white-toothed smile that lit up the whole of his dark face, and worked on the premise that he was probably here to stay anyway, judging by Virginia's build-up descriptions. So what was the hurry in interrogating him? Time would show if he was a good guy or not.

And time has shown that he's fabulous – information that I have diligently passed on to The Father who is already prepared to like him too. Neither Stuart nor Virginia should have anything to fear from Christopher. I rather think The Brother will be the real test.

As the *Gannet* butts back to shore with the first load of passengers, Virginia and I wander along the seafront, past our strategically-parked car, through gossiping groups of other greeters and the many locals who have come to the Wharf out of curiosity just to see who is arriving. And we take up position as close to the Customs barrier as possible. Everyone is chatting, the air of expectancy infectious, especially as this early December ship will also bring Christmas mail and the precious summer soft fruits that we see only once a year. Already the red Royal Mail van has beeped and edged its way through the crowd and disappeared towards the Steps to collect the mailbags, and as we reach the barrier we are just in time to spot the rickety blue passenger transport starting towards us from the far end of the Wharf.

Chris and Richard have got themselves into an early bus, a pleasant departure from their usual habit of keeping us waiting for hours at the railing, craning our necks to spot them as passengers clamber from busload after busload to be consumed by the monstrous Customs shed. They have both pulled finger this time, and as soon as the Customs officers have satisfied themselves that no contraband has come with them, they tumble forth across the tarmac between us.

"Where's Stuart?" demands Richard, searching the crowd for a likely face.

Virginia laughs. "He's run for the hills. He heard *you* were coming." Sibling banter is back in our lives.

"He's scared of Dad," retorts Richard. "But he'll have to meet us eventually."

And eventually he does, discovering that neither The Father nor The Brother is an object to be feared. Chris's acceptance is immediate and warm, and Richard simply hijacks this new family member.

A few days later Virginia is grumbling. "Since Richard arrived, I've hardly seen Stuart at all. They're always out together – down at the Consulate, off to the Wharf, out in the car. Don't they remember I'm here?"

"You wanted Richard to like him," I point out, "and they're brothers now. You can't beat that!"

"Hmph," she grunts.

The old Chevrolet Charabanc is a wondrous thing. Long, square-backed and high off the ground, seats designed for the very slim and redolent with the scent of old leather, it is an almost-British-Racing-Green colour with a pull-up hood against the intemperate climes of the central island. And though it's a bus that cries out for passengers in period dress, or at the very least the grace of pretty driving-hats and baskets of champagne as company, beer and modern sunhats suffice on the day that Chris and I are invited to join an outing in it. It's a pleasant gathering, fourteen of us, hosted by two expatriates whose contract is ending, and this is their farewell.

We meet at Longwood Green at ten o'clock on this Saturday morning, and from there, securely protected from harmful rays by sunblock, and from chill by coats and cardigans, we settle ourselves for the drive past the wide Devil's Punchbowl to the main road fork at Hutt's Gate where an ancient white-washed former inn still marks the divides, and then we turn east. The sun is shining here, and the tall flax cloaking Halley's Mount on our right reflects the light in rippling silver and green as it climbs up towards the island's beautiful cloud forest on Diana and Actæon peaks above us. Proclaimed St Helena's first national park in 1996, conservation teams have taken pains to preserve the ancient tree ferns that still valiantly fight for survival among their alien neighbours up there, and the three marked trails across the peaks – one path named for the tiny endemic blushing snail who still finds a home there – offer a beautiful hike on a clear day.

After Halley's Mount we enter shaded avenues past the sad ruin of Teutonic Hall. This large late 18ᵗʰ Century country house, deriving its name from the German-descended Janisch family who once lived there, has long been a bone of contention on the island. Lusted after by many, wept over by both the National Trust and the Heritage Society, privately-owned by a local family who can neither afford to restore it nor will drop the outrageous price they ask for selling it, this beautiful landmark has, over the past ten years, disintegrated before our eyes. Now it's too late to save it. The building is condemned and falling down. Like Willowbank and historic Walbro nearby, which have already gone. Like ancient Rock Rose a little further on from here, once an atmospheric structure that now has *Danger* signs plastered on its few remaining walls. Like romantic Rose Cottage at Sandy Bay, a decaying house of magical enchantment when I first saw it, but now so utterly lost to the climbers of the forest that have smothered it, that it's hard to find at all. They are the real treasures of St Helena, these Georgian country houses, for each has had a life and a tale to tell that is a vital part of this island's historical tapestry – a story of such vibrancy and colour that the heart bleeds with every stone that falls.

Like jewels and sequins set in the cloth of St Helena's brilliant history, are the characters who have added to this distant island's depiction – those men of the sea already mentioned, 16th Century circumnavigator Sir Thomas Cavendish and Elizabethan sailor, pirate and explorer, wild Edward Fenton. The 16th Century Arctic explorer John Davis visited and Dutch traveller John Huyghen van Linschoten who gave us such fine descriptions of the St Helena that he saw around 1629. The 17th Century circumnavigator and buccaneer William Dampier followed and, as previously described, Captain Bligh of the *Bounty* who brought fruit and vegetable plants for us. Captain James Cook came twice, once on the *Endeavour* in 1771, and four years later on the *Resolution*, and the naturalist Charles Darwin stepped off the *Beagle* here in July 1836, to study fauna and flora. Another naturalist, and a fine artist, who taught here before going on to greater things in southern Africa, was William Burchell, after whom the Burchell's zebra is named.

There were warriors too: Lord Cornwallis, Sir George Elphinstone, and Admiral Sir Charles Elliot, a Governor here. Robert Jenkins actually lived here for a while, better known for the American War of Jenkins' Ear than for his stint as Governor of St Helena, but his little house, Lemon Grove, still stands halfway down the zigzagging road to Sandy Bay Beach. And Lord Roberts visited. We have talked about General Cronje of Anglo-Boer War fame, who was a prisoner-of-war here, and also Prince Dinizulu, captured twenty years earlier in 1879, during the Zulu Wars. But better known than all of those was Arthur Wellesley (the future Duke of Wellington) who visited the island for the first time in 1799. Legend has it that when he came for a second visit, in 1805, his first night ashore from the *Trident* was passed at Porteous House in Jamestown, which, by curious coincidence, was the same boarding house that exactly ten years later put up his famous foe, Napoleon Bonaparte, on the French Emperor's first night ashore.

The astronomers came, as mentioned earlier – Edmund Halley in 1677, followed in the next century by Dr Nevil Maskelyne, later Astronomer Royal, and the century after that by the busy Professor and Mrs David Gill. And writers came: William Hickey, in 1793, "Who," says the historian Philip Gosse quite bluntly, *"made up for an ill-spent life by leaving behind him one of the most entertaining books of memoirs in the English language."* An evidently seasick Hickey's delight at seeing St Helena hove over the horizon of an exceptionally stormy sea is marked; yet he does not tell us much about the passing of his week ashore other than to mention a large sum of two thousand rupees that he managed to spend while here. W.M. Thackeray, on the other hand, was six years old when he passed through on his way from Calcutta to England in 1817, but he clearly remembered having Bonaparte pointed out to him by his Indian servant with the horrible warning that: *"He eats three sheep every day, and all the little children he can lay his hands on!"*

Twenty years later came the fascinating Dr James Barry, taking up a position as Principal Medical Officer in St Helena and moving into a cottage in Jamestown *"with a mango tree in the garden".* However, the good doctor left again, quite suddenly, within the year, after – claims one doubtful account – refusing to duel with another officer even though Dr Barry was known as a dab hand at swordsmanship. A more reliable document states that the slight, red-haired doctor, ever a feisty and somewhat formidable personality, fell so far foul of his military colleagues on the island that he was ordered home, under arrest, by General Middlemore, Governor of St Helena at that time.

The good doctor's rise to Inspector General, the highest rank in the Army Medical Service, and a trail of colourful tales that accompanied the illustrious career through thirteen years at the Cape, in Mauritius, and in the West Indies, makes for fascinating reading. But what was assiduously hidden from the world until death occurred in London in 1865, when all was revealed, was that Dr Barry was no man at all, but a *woman* masquerading as a man through all her professional life.

Of the royals who have made their way here, most have already been mentioned, with the exception of the French Prince de Joinville who journeyed here in 1840 specifically to fetch Napoleon's body back to Les Invalides in Paris, after the French Emperor had lain for nineteen years in his sylvan and far more emotive resting place in the Sane Valley. Twenty years later, however, the visit of Prince Alfred, son of Queen Victoria, was much jollier. Legend has it that he made so merry at a Castle Ball held in his honour that an alarmingly short time afterwards the ballroom floor collapsed.

The uninvited termites that came from Brazil in 1840 on a slave ship are perhaps – even more than the human neglect that, where history is concerned, seems endemic in St Helena – responsible for many ruins around the island. The termites are almost everywhere – disdaining, for reasons best known to their wily little ways, only the fortunate area of Blue Hill – and they hide themselves from view until it's almost too late for salvation. Resembling minute grains of rice, they bore tiny holes into the very heart of a table leg, a door frame, floorboards, ceilings, or the bamboo and mud walls that support many of the old houses, and there they live, chewing their way to improved health from the inside outwards. Within a few years of their unanticipated arrival, they had munched up papers, furniture, clothes, books, and once, when the large bible was opened at St James' Church for the reading of a lesson, the reader was shocked to find that only the frame of the pages remained while all the text had been neatly chewed away. Then they started in on the bigger stuff, and by the late 1860s, with the island's mother-church almost in ruins, other buildings around Jamestown were so unstable that pedestrians reputedly took their lives into their hands when walking the pavements, for fear of a house toppling over them. So it is small wonder that old houses are still decaying before our eyes. The tragedy is, their stories die with them.

The charabanc is still winding along the pretty inland road, heading towards Woody Ridge where we can look eastwards and see distant Deadwood Plain with Flag Staff and the great grey hulk of the Barn – volcanic origin of St Helena – looming behind it, and then the semi-desert Prosperous Bay Plain lying in wait for an Airport that yet remains little more than rumour. The charabanc pauses in the narrow road near rolling pastures to allow right of way to a truck loaded down with St Joseph lilies on their way to Jamestown, and from our open vehicle we are momentarily heady with their deeply sensuous perfume. A short way further on, we spot the source of the flowers – a field luxuriantly white with exquisite blooms, better known here as *Christmas lilies*. Through the curves and bounces, the deep valley and vertiginous slopes of paradoxically-named Levelwood we drive. And close to a signpost to the Bellstone – a large trachyandesite rock that clangs when hit with a stone – we turn toward the southern passes of the island. Here is the rise in the road that I eagerly await; a short but steep incline, and at the top, displayed dead ahead, all the massive height of St Helena's glorious green peaks soaring skywards, and then falling to the ocean, such monumental distance between hilltop and valley floor that it arrives as a breathtaking surprise each time we come here.

But the bus is soon over the breast of the hill and we enter the spectacular Sandy Bay area that surprises at every bend – except today it's all obscured by fog. But because all fourteen passengers are old hands at St Helena's views, this doesn't faze us. We are relaxed and chatting, enjoying beer or cool drinks as we drive along, now reaching for our coats because despite the summer season in the tropics, the chill wind in the open bus is perishing. This too shall pass, I reassure myself through chattering teeth, and eventually we turn up and up and conquer another hill which, in moments, places us as if by magic, on the opposite side of the island where the sunshine is radiant. There's no telling in this place what weather you'll find as you turn the smallest of bends.

Lunch at Farm Lodge Country House Hotel is new to Chris and me. We've enjoyed several dinner parties here, and once spent a night in this beautifully renovated house just for fun; but lunch is served only by special request. It turns out to be cold meat and salad, but welcome nonetheless. The bus has spat us out here to arrange ourselves at tables on the veranda and the grass below, and afterwards we wander, admiring the manicured lawns and the purple brilliance of jacaranda trees that embrace the scene, and the surrounding forest. It is a quiet rural setting whose silence is broken only by the fat quacking of ducks behind the house and the occasional bleat of a sheep. Doris the donkey is in her stall today and so does not rise up to place front hooves on shoulders in her characteristic greeting, but we visit her nonetheless. Then on we all go, and it is as we pass the abattoir up the road that I make my defining assessment of the likable new Governor, a judgement I have carefully reserved for some two months since he arrived. Notwithstanding the fact that it is a Saturday afternoon, it is close enough to Christmas for the butcher to be working overtime. And this afternoon, at the very instant that the charabanc passes his farm shed, an extremely large pig is being manhandled through the door towards extinction. He is shrieking fit to bust, a high-pitched scream of abject terror, and all the soft hearts in the bus immediately cover faces with hands in horror. The Governor is sitting alongside me, since Chris has found a more expansive long seat at the back that welcomes his frame more easily, and my shock is easily recognisable. He casts a sympathetic eye at me. "I know for a fact that the process is very humane on the island," he says; and it's good of him to reassure me from the expert knowledge of his rank, even though I already know that from my involvement with the RSPCA. Yet I cannot be so easily comforted. All I can hear is that terrible, terrible sound echoing in my head, and my watery eyes are precariously close to overflowing.

"I'm sure it is," I manage to utter. "But it is the animal's *terror* of where he going that is so ghastly..."

This man is my age, but he lowers his voice and speaks soothingly, like a kind village vicar to the very young child he has just seen in me. "I don't think it's terror at all," he explains gently, "but rather a protesting that he's leaving his friends."

I can't help smiling at that. It's a charming thought, and his effort has given me the impetus to pull myself together. "Thank you, that's kind," I say, recovering. And I mean it. I've seen who on the bus was affected by that momentary incident – and who wasn't. It confirms much about those I don't care for a lot. And it tells me that, however he turns out in the end, our new Governor is a soft-hearted man.

God Rest Ye Merry, Gentlemen on pan-pipes is once again the seasonal offering by the time Chris, JJ and I hit the Jamestown Spar – a message hardly appropriate to our present dispositions. Just twelve days before Christmas and, neither resting nor merry, we have spent much of this week heaving weighty packages of pet food about. The last straw of that nagging Diet saga finally broke the camel's back and a decision was made. We're changing businesses – physically hefting all the heavy Diet bags from the current stores, and shifting them to the Rose & Crown shop in Market Street. Larry 'Nails', at least, is savvy enough to see a useful loss-leader when delivered to his door, and has welcomed the Diet with open arms. But this is time-consuming work. In addition to physical removal, there's a mass of paperwork involved. While ads have gone out explaining the change of supplier, Radio St Helena has been quick to question our move. And we've answered as diplomatically as possible under the circumstances, submitting a similar statement to their sister-in-print, the *St Helena Herald*. But tensions are now running high with our own Treasurer and his greedy buddy. Furthermore, though we have no quarrel with any other aspect of Spar St Helena, we're left feeling like the guilty party. The floor girls, always helpful and co-operative to us, are watching us balefully as we fill huge cartons with pet food, stocktaking as we go. And the floor manager, who has turned himself inside out for us on occasion, now strolls across to loom over us, hands in pockets, expression bland and unreadable.

"What exactly did you mean by 'management' in your statement?" he asks. "I am management. I've had nothing to do with all this."

Well, someone was going to get upset, but this is the last man to deserve criticism. We explain about the accountant, he nods knowingly, and then laughs. "I suppose you still want your RSPCA Christmas Tree in here next week?"

"Of course," says JJ without hesitation.

"Well, you're still welcome. That Tree is always welcome, in fact.

The girls love it and it brings a lot of customers in here. Like the pet food did."

JJ doesn't mince words. "Tell that to your Ω¿!∂ξΞж accounting department. Those customers are going to Larry's now. And yes, the Tree will be here by Tuesday." To me he grumbles, in his cheerily familiar style: "And next week's another whole ∂Θξж§Ω week given over to the ∂ξ*жΘ RSPCA, selling ribbons!"

The particular rigours of catering for Christmas in a far-flung place have been solved in inimitable island fashion, notwithstanding the inconvenience of a full refrigerated container of Christmas goods, destined for the Spar supermarkets, left languishing at Cape Town docks by the current RMS voyage. Another full container of fruit, destined for Thorpe's, also has suffered misadventure, having been carried on by mistake to Ascension Island where it was unlocked and opened and very briefly exposed to that island's seaside atmosphere. And because of that tiny inadvertent act, all of it was inexplicably condemned by the authorities so that neither island enjoyed, in the end, the peaches or plums we rarely see. However, somewhat understandably, the fury of fire and brimstone exuded by Thorpe's Grocery is still felt as white heat all through St Helena.

So Christmas this year was, generally, faced without fresh summer fruits, fresh vegetables, yoghurt, paté, charcuterie, or any interesting cheeses – the last of which included the cream cheese necessary to the pastry of my spectacular traditional mince pies. But, along with the sense of humour vital to survival in St Helena, comes a measure of resourcefulness. So this hurdle was neatly overcome when I drew from the freezer at Villa Le Breton a large pack of Bulgarian yoghurt (whose label had expressly exhorted me *not* to freeze it) which we drained through a muslin cloth until we had made our own cheese, delivering such a load of the finished product that once Virginia and I had completed the baking of quantities of delicious and crispy mince pies, we then spent valuable extra time potting small balls of cheese rolled with every flavour from sundried tomato to flaked almonds, to use up what was left. Making the cheese was worth the effort for the pastry, though, because my homemade mincemeat had, in some extremity of mid-year generosity, been virtually drowned in single malt Highland Park whisky which was, I determined, not going to be wasted on stodgy pastry.

The island-wide need for some fresh summer fruits was, however, fortuitously solved by a rare prior delivery on the RMS voyage that had brought Chris and Richard for their holidays. And we had gained it through the annual free-for-all that occurs on these occasions. Chris and I had lurked around Jamestown Spar for most of a morning, waiting for crates to arrive from the Wharf, not daring to go home in case we missed them. But eventually we cracked under a yearning for coffee, so headed to the Coffee Shop for a quick cappuccino. As may have been expected, it was just as Bill placed our rich and enticingly frothy cups before us that the Bishop, an inveterate shopper, came scurrying through the Arch with tidings of joy: "There are peaches at Horse's! If you run you may still get some. The plums have already gone!"

Cappuccinos abandoned, Chris and I set off at a brisk trot up Main Street in the mounting heat of the day, and when we reached Horse's (the Queen Mary Stores), panting with exertion, there were six peaches left, two bruised beyond recognition. I scooped up the remaining four like trophies. "I wish we'd got here earlier," I wailed to the assistant as I handed over pounds for them. "We've been waiting in town all morning for fruit."

"If you run to Spar now, very quick, I think they openin' their crates," she offered. And so we ran hell-for-leather – only a minute's walk away; and there was the entire population already grappling over plums and nectarines, peaches, grapes, kiwi fruit –

"Strawberries! Grab them!" I yelled to Chris at the far end of the cooler, and he leapt for the last punnet. I gathered whatever I could reach, women leaning across me, short ones burrowing up from below, arms entwined by accident, hand clutching foreign hand on the same avocado as the odd elbow hit ribs. But nothing was vindictive, for when all was said and done, all we wanted was nutrition. We grabbed what we could reach and then queued an hour to pay for it.

At home great garlands of juniper from John Beadon's property hang on our huge black-painted front door and the Cottage door. And a little fir tree, delivered by the A&NRD – a tiny sample of the huge tree they have again donated to the RSPCA at the Spar for charity ribbons which Chris and JJ and I have sold in abundance – holds pride of place at one end of our veranda. As is our family's tradition, an entire afternoon was given over to the tree-dressing project, accompanied by frustrated mutterings over tangled threads and lost glass-ball clips, an inevitable debate about the pros and cons of tinsel, and sharp directives to hold the ladder steady; accompanied also by our old Christmas CD collection jauntily blaring out spurring songs about sleigh-rides and winter wonderlands, notwithstanding the heat of the day. With Richard, in the way of a teenaged youth, more or less flinging decorations into place – a little loop here, a casual drape there – Stuart was allowed the honour of fixing the top star this year, his first Christmas shared with us. Essentially an English Christmas which we hoped he would enjoy, since we have not yet accustomed ourselves to the favoured goat-meat curry of the island's preferred festive traditions.

But in every other sense, we have joined in all the island celebrations and the December diary has been chock-a-block. With the stressful pet food saga costing us busy days, followed by a hectic week of ribbon-selling without aid from any Saint RSPCA members (all of whom begged off helping "because of Christmas preparations"), evenings have been occupied with annual carol-gatherings, concerts and parties, and popular parades down Market Street ranging from school events to the lusty Christmas Eve parade that comprises loud music, kaleidoscopic costumes and Santas *en masse*. Chris and I have even attended a lavish party thrown by SHELCO; for since the new Governor's arrival the dreaded Airport issue has quickly been roused from months of apparent slumber.

What a start to a new year! World news, as 2005 slides into place, has been dire enough; but it is a tabloid article of local interest that has Bish yammering about the British *Mail on Sunday* as he races down our path. One look at him suggests that a late-morning whisky seems justified and we settle him on the veranda.

He has hauled the article off the internet and evidently emailed the transcript to us in full, complete with downloaded photograph of the original newspaper spread, and on arrival he bullies me to the computer to read it. I can barely breathe as I carry the printed copy downstairs to show to the family. It's jaw-dropping, somewhat horrifying. It's very, very sad. Fresh from London, its headline spanning its double-page spread, blares in the characteristic fashion of Sunday tabloids: *Good Riddance, Your Excellency!* The centre sports a full-length photograph of our former Governor Hill in white uniform and feathers, plus some smaller pictures. One of the two contributing journalists fairly recently visited St Helena on a tourist assignment, but the uniform, evidently, was not what caught his attention.

Before the body of the text takes shape, there's a plethora of eye-catching subtitles designed to draw the attention of a lazy Sunday reader, followed by a rough geographic explanation about remote St Helena and its relationship with the Foreign & Commonwealth Office. The bones of the article get going with an unprepossessing description of our former Governor, interviewed at a pub close to his London flat, before the interviewee himself starts committing verbal *hara-kiri*. We are stunned. Duncan Hill was ill when he finally departed St Helena, and we knew that his illness caused an irrational state. But here he is, three months later, going public with irreverent nonchalance about his crush on island girls; yet he touches long enough on his marriage only to suggest that St Helenians are too uneducated to have been worthy of socialising with his wife. I'm reading this aloud but Bish, who already knows it by heart, interjects: "I bet a few of the several Saints who hold Master's degrees in Education will take issue with that!" When I'm allowed to continue, we learn about Hill's psychopathic hatred for certain critics on the island, naming the Lord Bishop of St Helena specifically, and we now comprehend Bish's wrath. Obscenities, also, are strewn like birdseed throughout the article, and more than once there are threats of physical violence made against named island dignitaries, just as there are against the very journalists interviewing him. The article shows direct quotes, so there's no possible libel action involved in this outrageous publication. Chris and I are so flabbergasted we are silenced, but Bish readily retrieves his voice: "He threatens to *knee-*

cap one of the journalists interviewing him! Imagine that! He's done *himself* more damage than the most vicious tabloid journalist could!"

Omitting any hint that illness was involved, the result is tragic in its publicity. We pour ourselves wine to keep company with Bish's soothing Scotch, reading and rereading the article, still in shock. But the angry Bishop is now smiling a little smugly. "This is so sensational that people will run for their atlases. But it's not this island that should blush – it's the FCO who ignored our call for help. We *warned* them of his illness." So we did.

On the death of Johnny Drummond, the former feisty Editor of the *St Helena Herald* who never baulked at challenging the government who sponsored his paper, his bequest was a sum of money intended to set up an independent radio station in St Helena, specifically to be headed up by his friend and equally spirited assistant editor, Mikael Olsson, a Swedish immigrant. And now, with equipment purchased and a few local staff already trained at small radio stations in South Africa, the new station has been officially launched from the renovated Association Hall at the bottom of Main Street, squarely in the heart of Jamestown. SaintFM is in business.

During the final months of preparation for live broadcasting, the new station has served the island with twenty-four hours of music a day, during which time we've grown accustomed to finding its mark on the dial. But now we are also offered informative news bulletins, fresh and updated, even delivered at weekends. This vibrant competition has inevitably rubbed off on the old station tucked away on its country hill, but though no dramatic changes have appeared in Radio St Helena's age-old timetable, we detect a sudden new verve in bulletins which lately cover more than their previously prescribed three stories.

"Now the *St Helena Herald* needs a kick up the rear," proclaims Bish a few Fridays later at Donny's, casting a challenging eye over his spectacles at Stedson, a member of the Media Board. "That publication is no more than sheets of A4 masquerading as a newspaper!"

Certainly the inertia in which the old *Herald* presently dwells does not make for thrall, and this month's four weekly editions have produced no headlines more riveting than:

Water Main Dries Up in Longwood
Still no Word on Access
Budgetary Aid Mission Dates Fixed

The *Herald* appears at midday on Fridays, but I take it to bed with me, with good reason... Well, let's just say, we actually buy it for the television schedule. For pertinent information, the *Government Gazette* would be more exciting.

Though the headlines don't reflect them, there have been several happenings this month worthy of reporting. The embarrassing *Mail on Sunday* article, for instance. And there, in the horrified and reverberating wake of its publication, sits on page eight of our only print media, a careful little reference to it entitled: *Unflattering Article on ex-Governor. Unflattering?* It was shocking, appalling, damning in every degree! This was, after all, His Excellency *our* Governor – and half the island who saw it is still in shock! The other half, however, are patronisingly spared any quotes from it, even as the *Herald* conversely publishes all the emails of aghast reaction that have winged in from England, Canada, Australia, the United States, South Africa and Europe where the article has already been circulated. Despite this, all that our island is fed is a blurry photograph of the *Mail on Sunday* article with its blazing headline, and a tame comment purporting to paint our former Governor *"in very unattractive colours"*!

In the meantime, an admirable effort has been made by St Helenians to collect monies for survivors of the horrific South East Asian tsunami that stunned the world just after Christmas, and the *Herald* devotes one and a half pages to this, which perhaps makes up for the previous week when the nation was served three pages of graphs on water consumption in the Longwood area. Whatever happened, I wonder, to the good old days when community matters spiced the weekly news, when births, marriages and deaths were properly announced, when we even got to know who was expected on an incoming RMS, when enthusiastic contributors wrote diverse articles about subjects ranging from Russian athletes to antiperspirants?

It is Friday night again and, with our group having dispersed from Donny's, I am again in bed with the *Herald,* ready to cast my weekly opiate aside, when a headline catches my eye: *Drug dog gives second demonstration,* with a sweet picture of Buzz the Sniffer Dog. Buzz, an amiable brown and white cocker spaniel who arrived here from the Somerset & Avon Police a few months ago, is looking unutterably bored, but the article – which is quite interesting – informs me that over the past two years the police have received 106 drug-related reports. Ninety-three led the police on successful operations that recovered large amounts of cannabis. During the eight weeks of Operation Bust which was carried out the year before last by an expatriate Acting Chief of Police, since departed the island, they had recovered 1 375 grams of cannabis, fourteen plants, and eighteen joints, amounting to a street value of £13 750. (Which leads me to ponder why Buzz is here at all, since they evidently managed quite well before the dog arrived). Nonetheless he's now regarded as a member of the Police Force and, according to the *Herald*, has recently much impressed *"the Governor, elected members and other personnel"* with a demonstration of his skills after some cannabis was (purposely, I trust) hidden in a computer printer in the courthouse, which took him *"5-8 minutes"* to locate. Later in the day he was let loose on the luggage arriving on the RMS from Ascension, but there are no further reports on that... I put out the light, fluff up my pillows, cuddling them to me now that Chris is back in Cape Town, and think some more about the *Herald* until... well...

19.

Innocents Abroad

January 2005

The humidity of this late January is excruciating, worse than usual, and everyone is melting. Stuart looks ill when he returns from work and flops into a veranda chair, too tired even to change from his uniform. He has spent the whole day in the stifling, oven-hot courthouse, accompanying the imprisoned two boys who have now been formally charged with murder. When I remark that I thought this had happened some time ago, as it's already seven months since Ryan was killed, he explains that the earlier charge had been merely Suspicion of Murder. But today the court got down to the nitty-gritty of business, he explains, suffering a somewhat perplexing moment when one of them, against the express advice of his lay lawyers, requested a jury hearing when the case finally comes up. "A *jury*?" I exclaim. "*Where* in a place this small will they find an *unprejudiced* jury?"

Stuart shrugs. "That boy's been difficult all along. Even his lawyer looked shocked! Anyway, the case is set for late May, so it seems that the forensic evidence must be in at last." He gratefully accepts a cold beer from Virginia and pours it down his throat. Stuart is a conservative drinker and I have never seen him absorb liquor so fast.

It effects instantaneous revival, and he starts chatting with renewed energy and enthusiasm, quickly casting aside all talk of murders, recalcitrant youths and legal ramifications. And it's not long before his story takes us flying with him on an RAF Tri-Star between Ascension and the Falkland Islands. This was seven years ago, and Stuart was taking up a plumbing contract with Turners International who were sponsoring this journey – his first-ever adventure away from home.

Now pause for a moment. Stuart had seen television and plenty of videos, so he wasn't ignorant of the Outside World. But up to this point he had never, in reality, seen a plane, a train, a high-rise building, a lift, an escalator, traffic-lights, dual-lane highways, pushing crowds, big stores, real menus in big restaurants, beggars in the streets... And suddenly he was informed, mid-way to the Falklands, that bad weather would divert their flight. They put down in the metropolis of Montevideo, Uruguay.

The hotel that Turners had chosen for its diverted employees was a high-rise of some luxury, with marble foyers and patrons dressed to the nines. There was bustle all around, lots of glass, and a bewildering enough array of new experiences just around the reception desk to befuddle any stranger. But he and his equally raw young colleagues were then directed to their rooms via an escalator. This was a contraption of great fascination, and they spent some time working out the principles of it before daring to approach. Timing had to be gauged, after all, and they each made several attempts before finding themselves gliding upwards. For a few glorious moments this was fun. But then suddenly, before their eyes, the steps they were standing on melted away, causing a flurry of consternation and a line of young Saints tightly backed up at the top of the escalator, all nervous of making the leap to stability. Out went one tentative foot after another, hastily withdrawn as the steps-dissolved beneath them and they clung desperately to the moving handrails, performing a sort of dance in the middle of this plush hotel of fur coats and elegant hats, until one by one they eventually lunged forward to safety. In their rooms they found minibars which were soon emptied, with heavy and unanticipated tolls exacted on their pockets later, but Stuart was far more fascinated by watching, through the zoom lens of his camera, a beggar woman in the street below, rummaging through litter bins; a sight quite unknown in St Helena.

After working in the Falklands for some years, Stuart was eventually offered three months leave, and once again he boarded an RAF flight back to Ascension Island, intending to come home to St Helena to see his parents. But while on stopover there, impulse put him on a plane to England instead of the ship south. He was not sure why, but simply thought it might be fun. And so it was that he first set foot in England's green and pleasant land on a military airfield at Brize Norton in Oxfordshire, and was left wondering where to go next. *Swindon*, announces a nearby coach, and since the name was vaguely familiar, he climbed aboard and went to Swindon, where he was delivered to a row of black taxis parked outside the railway station. Well, he's no fool, our Stuart. Determined not to be taken for a financial ride by any young twerp, he walked up and down the row, studying all the drivers until he found the oldest and wisest-looking of them, and together they began the hunt for accommodation.

By now it's clear to me that Stuart always lands on his feet. For the lodging that he found was run by an ex-RAF man who, knowing the Falklands well, promptly cut Stuart's daily B&B rate by half. And so he was tempted to stay two weeks in Swindon, walking the streets, gazing at shops and the horrible crowds of people, until eventually he bumped into a Saint who recognised him (Swindon is not nicknamed *Swindhelena* for nothing!). This cheered him up a little, but he still didn't much care for the town, so eventually he took himself by train to central London where, still inside Paddington station, he spent fifteen minutes bemusedly observing all the people purposefully heading somewhere while he had no clue where to go, before climbing back on the train and returning to the familiar safety of Swindon.

Virginia and I are nearly hysterical with laughter as we hear his story. "But that's not all," says Stuart who had now seen both Swindon and a London station and condemned all of England. He wanted out of there. So he walked Swindon again until he found a travel agency that listed destinations in the window – and in he went. Los Angeles was one name on the list. This was two months after 9/11 and nobody was going to the US; so the travel agent offered to get him on a plane to LA the next night for £550 return. Great, he said, he'd take that and go for two and a half months. The following day he went by bus to Heathrow, an airport overwhelming even to seasoned travellers, and was delivered into the mêlée of Terminal Four. "Well, I wandered up and down a bit," explains Stuart matter-of-factly, "but the stuff was all written on my ticket, so I just looked for the right desk and the right gate and so on." And then the check-in girl inquired: "Would you like to travel First Class?" Would he? He shrugged. "Why not?" He was wearing rough jeans, a sweater and a baseball cap. His co-passengers were in designer wear. But he found the seats comfortable, the champagne refreshing and the food good, the private television obliging, and he was much taken with the bag of socks, shades, and male beauty products handed to him.

During his short sojourn in the British Isles he hadn't carried the phone number of any relatives in England, but he did have the number of a brother-in-law in San Diego, California, and once he landed at Los Angeles, a short call clinched matters there. His sister was surprised but welcoming, and she and her American husband promptly drove three hours to LA to fetch him, and three hours back to San Diego. And so, after two months in America, Stuart was now quite worldly. He had ridden exterior glass elevators, survived freeway driving at 85mph, four-lane traffic weaving at speed and switching lanes. He had seen stars in Hollywood and their houses, driven across the deserts of Arizona, travelled to the bottom of the Grand Canyon, visited theme-parks and baseball stadiums, and eaten American takeaways on Christmas Day.

He is open to travelling again someday, especially to visiting Cape Town and diving with Great White sharks off the South African coast, he says. But don't try and lure him back to Swindon.

The Bishop has an ulterior motive. He's wearing that particular smile that I know presages some scheme or other. "I met these lovely people," he tells me. "They're visiting the island for a month, and I know you'd like them. They're living right behind you, at Cambrian House."

I have met a lot of passing visitors over recent months and I'm not really looking for fresh company. "Oh?" I respond, with limited enthusiasm.

"They're really *very* nice. They're keen to attend Jack Horner's Ordination at the cathedral on Sunday." I am not meeting his eyes because now I know what lies behind them, and I have no particular desire to attend the Ordination myself. "They're looking for a lift."

I smile my own particular smile, and he knows that I'm being bolshie and saying *No*. I am not a taxi service. I don't want to go to the cathedral on Sunday. He can surely find them passage with someone else. Yet I know him so well that I'm certain he won't try. On the other hand, he knows me well too. He's pretty confident I'll come round eventually. But at the moment I'm digging in my heels. I'm not interested and I'm making it plain.

Three days later, at Friday drinks at Donny's he affects a wistful voice: "Those nice visitors at Cambrian House, the Shuttleworths, they're *still* looking for a lift to the cathedral on Sunday."

I really don't feel like being used. I am still disinterested. I shrug and change the subject.

But the following day, on Saturday, something changes. I am at the Coffee Shop with Virginia, enjoying a chicken-tikka enchilada when I happen to notice an unfamiliar couple at the next table. They are enthusiastically chatting to someone else, and there is something charmingly ebullient about them. They both have smiling faces. I like them immediately and instinctively know who they are. Feeling remorse at my earlier stubbornness to help them, I am instantly on my feet beside them. "You must be the Shuttleworths," I declare. "The Bishop said you were looking for a lift to St Paul's tomorrow morning. I can take you, if you like."

The woman smiles up at me with one of the softest and merriest faces I've seen. "That's so kind of you to offer," she says, "but the Bishop has already arranged a lift for us. It's with someone called Lindsay at Villa Le Breton." I might have known.

"About tomorrow – " Bish begins cautiously on the phone that evening, a note of faintest apprehension in his voice as the Ordination draws ever closer.

"It's all arranged," I say officiously. "I met them today, I liked them, and I offered them a lift." Bish is dying to say *I told you so*, but doesn't dare or I'd cancel. Instead he says, "I've invited them for a picnic on Monday. If you're free, why don't you come too?"

Now I'm smiling. I like picnics, and it will be fun to show these people some parts of the island they wouldn't normally see. We meet next morning, and get on so easily in the ten-minute drive up Ladder Hill, through the suburban sprawl of Half Tree Hollow and past the great brooding fort of High Knoll to the cathedral, that I am now very glad I was roped into this favour.

However, for the immediate present, we have the ceremonial

business of an Ordination to attend. With eleven Anglican churches strung across the island, St Paul's Anglican Church, for all its cathedral status, sits fair and square in the rural heart of the island, surrounded by tall trees, with well-tended graves inexorably climbing the green slope behind it towards boundaries marked by a school and the Radio St Helena broadcasting station. Birdcalls resonate, along with the occasional bleating of lambs, and at certain hours the shrill decibels of school break times. Ahead of the church, across a valley, sits High Knoll. And away in the distance, beyond rolling fields and more lush valleys, the swirling colours of Flag Staff's distinctive peak form another focal point. But it is the graves that dominate the surroundings, the hillside crammed with them. Past Governors and Bishops rest here, soldiers, visitors, progenitors of family names, beloved wives by the hundred, and far too many children – whole groups of family members some time afflicted by epidemics of measles or 'flu that once cut swathes through this sheltered population. Among the children buried in this very English churchyard are even two baby Zulus far from home – children of the Chief Dinizulu captured by the British during the Zulu Wars of the late 1800s and exiled to St Helena in 1890. Arriving here with an escort of several wives, some servants, and two rather grim uncles who did not emulate his congeniality, the friendly Dinizulu – shrugging off the image of his own notorious warrior father, Cetewayo – promptly set about adapting to English ways. He learned to read and write English, to play hymns on the piano, to dress in English clothes and, most particularly, to submit to the beliefs of Christianity, soon pressing to be baptised into the Anglican faith. This, of course, presented a little poser for the local church at the time, since their passionate new convert was a polygamist. But after some conjecture, it was agreed that just one of Dinizulu's wives was to be officially recognised, while the others were designated 'attendants' upon his several children, and this did not seem to deter him from procreating either with them or with at least one local woman – the St Helenian descendants of whom are still proud of their royal Zulu heritage.

After moving house a few times until the new captive was satisfied by climatic conditions at Francis Plain House (now part of Prince Andrew Secondary School, in the valley below the cathedral), Dinizulu settled down to relaxed enjoyment of this new life. Developing a taste for serious fashion, he ordered his suits from Savile Row, and by 1896, when he played host to the Bishop of Zululand, had acquired enough other English affectations to serve his visitor tea and cucumber sandwiches on the lawn outside his house. His uncles, however, were not so adaptable. They refused to convert to Christianity, to sit on chairs or use tables or beds, or even to eat western food. And though they were forced to wear European clothing when they walked out in the country (lest they trouble the sensibilities of English ladies, presumably), they refused to do so within the boundaries of their home. And the mental vision of two disgruntled warriors in loincloths and animal hides, sprawled in such a prosaic setting, exercises the imagination.

Built in 1850 on the site of an earlier wooden church which, as early as 1691, was described as "much decayed", the former St Paul's Country Church holds its dignity well as a cathedral. It is an unassuming grey stone structure of good proportions, and inside, a light interior shows off old memorial plaques which, like the headstones in the cemetery, tell so much of the island's story. On the east wall, splendid stained-glass windows depict St Peter and St Paul who, on this sunny morning, cast their colourful blessings upon a congregation poised to see Father Jack, a late middle-aged Irishman, ordained a community priest. Shopping where the Pope shops, the Bishop is resplendent in his new robes, and the choir is in full voice, led by an exuberantly-pounded organ. Candles glow, and the air is redolent with incense and perfumed oils. Brilliant-hued posies are dotted about in the St Helena way, and video cameras roll – all of this summoned by one lone bell that jauntily swings in its grand three-bell turret.

The Shuttleworths are all smiles as we emerge from the church into the noonday heat when the service is over. "What a lovely service!" they exclaim with their customary enthusiasm. "And oh, look at that view!"

"I'll take you home on a more scenic route," I suggest, thinking of the sylvan drive past Knollcombes where the Boer prisoners lie, pretty Bishop's Bridge where Bishop Welby fell off his horse, the verdant hairpins of the "W" Road that zigzag across the stunning central island to emerge at the head of Side Path. "And by then we'll be ready for gin-and-tonic at Villa Le Breton."

"Marvellous!" they cry. And soon, as ice clinks in our glasses and we sit back comfortably on our veranda's wicker chairs, we feel that somehow – though we've barely met – we've long been friends.

Early in the afternoon, Bish is on the phone again. "About tomorrow's picnic, I have a lovely basket set up with glasses and plates and everything we'll need. The Shuttleworths are bringing beer and wine. I *suppose* I could make some sandwiches…"

And so the voice that lurks inside me and occasionally speaks unbidden, promptly makes an announcement about which I have not been forewarned: "*I'll* make the sandwiches, if you like, and I'll see what else I can put together." In fact this means that the rest of my Sunday will be passed in the kitchen, for the voice is now uttering: *Spinach and Haddock Roulade – sliced roast pork – homemade bread – fresh salad – almond tart –*

I spend much of Monday morning packing these delicacies into cool-boxes and baskets, and adding anything else I can think of – savoury biscuits to accompany drinks, fruit, chocolates, a thermos of filter coffee and all the bits that go with that. I collect jerseys against the chill, camera, binoculars, sun cream, sunhat, dark-glasses, walking shoes, reading glasses – in fact everything I could possibly require for an expedition to the Arctic that might accidentally land up in the Sahara. I just about find space for the Shuttleworths in my roomy car by the time I have stocked it.

At Bishopsholme, Bish is looking very relaxed. "You're sure you don't want me to bring anything except the basket?" he checks at this late hour.

"Nothing." There is nothing edible left on earth that I haven't already packed myself. "The Shuttleworths' drinks are in my cool-box. Everything's set for transfer to your car."

"Then let's go," says Bish bracingly. But as he reaches his car he stops. "Actually – I don't think I have enough petrol in mine – "

There are three petrol stations in the whole of St Helena. One down the hill in Half Tree Hollow. One in the city hub of Jamestown. One in far distant Longwood. All of them are in the diametrically opposite direction of that in which we are headed. I turn to glance at the Shuttleworths who are discreetly clutching their sides with laughter, and Bish knows as well as I do that I will not only offer my own car now, but be expected to drive it. I wait till he is ensconced in the passenger seat and deliver him a wry grin. "And whose picnic was this?" I inquire. The Shuttleworths are bubbling with audible humour by now.

"Just drive," Bish commands. "I'll tell you where to go."

Sure enough, we go where he bids me drive, directing my car south from his house, past deep grassy pastures and arum-white gullies, across the great flax-covered ridges of the island's central mountain spine, and down the winding descent into the huge amphitheatre of Sandy Bay. Here is some of the most stupendous scenery on earth, and it takes your breath away. The Shuttleworths, looking and observing and questioning with the keen curiosity of inveterate travellers, make it all seem new to us too. Through their eyes the wild roadside nasturtiums and ageratum suddenly seem more prolific, the gnarled trunks of old thorn trees more of an art-form, the deep foliage of others thicker and more varied. Below us, I freshly observe that some of the island cottages are far older than I'd previously noticed, and above us the ascending sweep of the shimmering flax-covered mountain higher than I've ever calculated. We pass elevated views of the great grey volcanic finger of Lot rising from the turmoil of its gully, and beyond it the dramatic pink and blue skyline of Lot's Wife and the Asses Ears. Somewhere in between, buried in forest, we can just detect the old house called Mount Pleasant, which once belonged to an elderly dignitary named Sir William Doveton, and I point it out.

This house was selected by the exiled Napoleon Bonaparte as a suitable destination for a breakfast picnic on the last occasion that the Emperor ever took a meal outside the grounds of Longwood House, and therefore has a faintly poignant historical attachment. In those days, October 1820, Napoleon, though already ill, was still able to ride out within certain bounds; and that Mount Pleasant and the hospitable Sir William fell within that area was fortuitous. But Napoleon, not wishing to impose upon his hosts, brought his own meal which, I confess, was rather grander than the locally scrounged-together picnic now reposing in the boot of my car. Potted meats and cold pie, cold turkey and curried fowl, pork and *"a very fine salad"*, dates, almonds, and oranges, all washed down with a little champagne and some delicious island coffee – together with a somewhat questionable homebrewed liqueur of fermented fruit in alcohol, proffered by Sir William. These he ate under the oak trees on Doveton's lawn, together with Count Montholon, Count Bertrand and others of his household who had come for the ride, and shared them with Sir William and his daughter, Mrs Greentree. He appears from accounts of that visit to have been as affable a guest as Sir William was the surprised host to this so-called tyrant who arrived at his residence, unbidden, that October morning. And Napoleon seemed happy to make the acquaintance of Mrs Greentree's young children, to whom he dispensed pieces of liquorice after he had affectionately tweaked their noses. I cannot ever view Mount Pleasant now without this scene in my mind.

We descend by more twists and turns, until Bish suddenly directs: "Here! This leads to St Peter's," and my car climbs a muddy drive up a short hill. I park beside a bell-post and piles of planks and woodwork machinery, and out of the car we climb, pausing to take in a different astounding aspect of Lot and the valley below. Tiny St Peter's church was originally built on this steep slope as a schoolhouse, but in 1917 was dedicated as a church, and is a simple place whose rusticity in these surroundings constitutes its special charm. We wander about, absorbing the atmosphere, even while workmen hammer at window frames around us. The place has been riddled with white ant, and they've had to pull out almost all the old timber in the building and replace it – a costly venture in St Helena where expensive imported iroko hardwood is the only antidote to termites. A small flat attached to the church is also being renovated and Bish talks excitedly about thinning some of the tall surrounding trees. He does not have to explain to us what an amazing view will be enjoyed from the upper storey once this is done. This is a beautiful, beautiful area – often misty and damp, but indescribably gorgeous on a sunny day. Yet for all this, I'm nearly always inexplicably beset by a curious weight of spirit when I come to this side of the island – a ghostly, faintly haunted feeling which I don't mention now. We're having too much of a good time.

Back up the mountain we drive, my trusty tough car pulling up those hairpin bends with admirable aplomb, eventually swinging left along the Ridges towards the western end of the island. And if the Shuttleworths think they've seen all our beauty already, they have another experience awaiting them. This is mostly farmland here, grassy rolling pastures bordered by deep valleys or sudden green peaks. We pass the roadside donkey pound where hosts of retired asses turn to watch our passage with lazy interest, while cattle grazing deeper in the valley don't bother to look up. We follow a sharp curve in the road that takes us past High Peak, and a hard gust of wind momentarily rocks the car. Someone once told me that a wind turbine set here to make use of the constant breeze was barely raised when it was completely blown away by the force of the wind, rendering the project useless. But as soon as we are round the corner, past High Peak, we are sheltered. And suddenly we find ourselves driving along the narrow col where we always stop to gasp at the verdant pastures falling into dark pine forest on one side, which, like the phoenix rising, swell into the great, charcoal-grey, hunched massif of High Hill that borders the coast. On the southern side, of course, lies the dramatic Sandy Bay basin again, with a very different aspect of the same lush hillsides we have just left, and from here I can look down the sharp slopes, somewhat ruefully, towards that infamous muddy road where we were once stuck in mud at Peakdale Cottage. One or two faint paths of green mark uncertain streambeds moving down the basin to the sea, but otherwise much of the scene is coloured in blues and browns and pinks and greys today, terminating at the little white rim of sea-froth around Sandy Bay Beach in the distance. It is, without a doubt, one of the most breathtaking scenes I know, made even more magical on a sunny day when clouds shift the colours of this extraordinary landscape from moment to moment; or when the mist that roars in from this southern coast beats against High Peak on our left, and then jumps and swirls back from it like a thousand outraged genies.

I describe to the Shuttleworths the scene at Sandy Bay Beach at the base of this eroded amphitheatre, which involves a steep switchback descent to reach it and a seriously tricky drive back up. It is a place of barren wilderness. A brown place, dusty and dry within the rocky walls of its gut, except where a diligent farmer has captured the waters of a small stream and fed it to a plantation of banana trees and a few date palms that lend his smallholding a curiously lush air. An angry place, where the sea rages against a black volcanic shore, and the cliffs that form the little bay are knife-sharp and threatening. Around the corner, where the outer surges of the Atlantic's cold Benguela Current beat against the south-eastern island, a repetitive cannon-like booming can be heard as waves crash into some unseen cavity. And the teeth of the tall reef on the opposite side of the bay, where spray leaps metres high into the air, are sharp and uninviting.

There is almost no vegetation around except, if you look carefully, a few examples of a puffy green succulent locally known as Babies' Toes (*Hydrodea cryptantha*, a member of the *mesembryanthemum* family), but in an effort to make this area tourist-friendly the Nature Conservation Group has planted some endemic saplings which hopefully will provide some shade in the future. Godforsaken though the place appears, it possesses the only real beach on the island, albeit black with a vicious undertow and the area wears a certain historic charm as an old lime-kiln nearby dates back to 1708, and a curtain-wall fortification threads across the mouth of the valley, where a few original cannon have lately been propped into position. Over the high hill on one side of the beach, a dust track worms its way upwards, eventually disappearing over the brow of the skyline. And along this road tread the fittest of the fit. Lot's Wife's Ponds are their destination – a fine collection of deserted rock pools at the base of a vertiginous cliff, that invite swimming and joyous floundering about in order to cool down after the mammoth exertion of reaching them.

Having imprinted this panorama on our minds we continue westwards along our road – past the turning down to Blue Hill (which sits in a valley), and onwards to Thompson's Wood (which is a meadow). And here Bish, thank goodness, is content to share with the Shuttleworths the quiet charms of the smooth hills at Thompson's Wood, stopping short of the rough track that would carry my car once again past Old Luffkins, the Gates of Chaos and Peakdale, to Fairyland... Today, on the meadow, nothing is heard but a softly sighing breeze, the occasional conversational lowing of cows, a far-off birdcall, sparing us the pressure of absolute silence. But this place, though part of St Helena, is not part of it. There is nothing visible here to remind us of any other area – no familiar peak or fort, historic country house or landmark – and for a few glorious minutes we are released from the constraints of living on such a small island.

By the time we drive back along the route we have come, almost as far as the car-spotting donkeys, we have grown hungry. And I am very, very thirsty. I could kill for one of those beers now, and just beyond the little church of St Helena and the Cross, Bish reads my mind. "There's a lovely spot just here," he declares, far more familiar with this locale than I am, and I pull to the side of the road. On the grassy slope above, there are two long bench-tables placed end to end, a richly leafy bough leaning down from its tree to keep the sun away, a natural forest behind, and in front a view of emerald green fields and blue ocean. Within minutes he has laid a cloth, brought out glasses from his bottomless picnic basket, produced plates and knives and a bottle-opener. Scrimmaging in cool-bags, the rest of us bring out the Shuttleworths' drinks and the food I have assembled, and finally we settle ourselves to feast. It is a Monday and there is one passing car all the time we sit there. And we sit for hours. The food and drinks hold out, the view is gorgeous, and our laughter bubbles easily. How is it that we four have not known one another all our lives?

It's close to seven o'clock by the time I drive the visitors home. We've come from Blue Hill by way of Horse Pasture, miles off the beaten track, to view from that drier area the crinkled mass of our forty-seven square miles with its landmarks crushed into such puzzling proximity, and the cliff faces folding one behind another all along the northern coast, noting that for all our seeming distance from home, Jamestown is little more than two cliff-folds away. So near – yet far enough to earn us a cool gin-and-tonic at Bishopsholme after the long and winding way back. It's been a lovely day.

"What about coming here to dinner on Saturday night?" Bish asks the Shuttleworths as he packs them back into my car for the final leg to Jamestown. "And you too, Lindsay, of course."

Of course. I will play taxi again, naturally. I know that I am free, but I don't immediately say so. Instead I give him a mock-glower. "Am *I* going to cook the dinner?" I ask, though he is a good cook. And he actually flushes. The Shuttleworths are hooting with mirth.

"No," he concedes. "You can come here and relax. You've done very well today." He pats me patronisingly on the shoulder, and the Shuttleworths chuckle about him all the way home.

"It's far too hot for coffee." I slump exhaustedly against the Coffee Shop counter. "Give me an orange juice instead, and a cheese and onion toastie."

"Coming up," Jill says cheerfully. "But the orange juice is pineapple until the RMS comes back. And there are no onions on the island. I'll give you tomato, with mild cheddar because the shops are out of mature. By the way, did you hear about the fuel crisis, just broadcast on the radio?"

Thank God for the Coffee Shop. Without it – and sometimes Bish – I would hear nothing. "*Our* fuel crisis?"

"Only one fuel storage tank is working at present, and we're running low. It's just been announced. The petrol ship is delayed in Ghana and each car on the island is restricted to ten litres of fuel a week until it gets here," she reports. "You'd better get yours today – you know what the siege mentality is like here!"

Bill is far less interested in running out of fuel than keeping up with stores for his lunch patrons. "Have you seen any lettuces in your travels around town? Or potatoes?"

"The island's completely out of potatoes, and there're no lettuces either," I tell him on good authority. "I saw a cabbage at the Market, if you're interested. I was looking for lemons."

"Sophy's hens are laying again, by the way," Jill butts in, and I give a shriek of delight: "EGGS!"

"We are no strangers to deprivation, are we?" remarks Bill.

I quickly pay the assisting Sophy for half a dozen luxuriously fresh eggs and snatch them to my bosom. "Hold the sandwich and juice, Jill. I'll come back for those *after* I've got my petrol!" With shopping bags bouncing and eggs in dire danger, I run to my car on the Wharf. Behind the wheel, turn the key, foot on the gas. Up Main Street I roar, turn right to reach the petrol station down Back Way (which should read Narrabacks, but the wrong notice was hung there years ago). There is already a queue waiting, and a tired assistant behind the till. "Ten litres, seven pound fifty," he says. "This till already don't know no other number but seven pound fifty." At least my gauge now tells me my tank's nearly full. I sigh with relief and drive back to the Coffee Shop to enjoy my orange juice that is pineapple, and my toasted cheese and onion that is tomato. The RMS is not due for a week. Who knows when the fuel ship will come?

It is so hot we're all exhausted. Saints and South Africans alike are gasping from the heat, enervated by the high humidity, sweating shamelessly while English visitors wonder why we are so feeble in this 'wonderful weather'. I should drive into the country for cooler temperatures (even taking a light jacket with me), but I can't find the impetus for it. My days are wasted by lack of energy and nothing is getting done. Chores must be finished by ten or I start melting, so I rush them and by ten am completely exhausted anyway. I am planning no dinner parties until the next Ice Age. It's simply too *steamy* to think.

But JJ knows me well. He knows that once I grow socially silent I tend to remain so until he snaps me out of it. "It's Marine Environment Week," he informs me on the phone. "And there's a dolphin trip tomorrow. I've never done the trip before, so I've booked a place on the boat. It's only about two hours. You must come too."

Really? Every fibre of me has fought such suggestions in the past, not because of disinterest in dolphins but, more practically, because my stomach abhors the sea. My mind argues the toss. This is hot February, there is no wind, there are no February Rollers evident this year, and I'll be with friends. One friend, at least. And then Stuart announces that he and Virginia will come too. I am quite looking forward to this now. I make the requisite bookings and go in search of my seasick pills.

The boat that takes us out is the *Gannet Three*, the same one that is our ferry on arrival and departure on the RMS, but I can offer no more technical detail about it than to describe it as red with a little wheel-house where the skipper handles matters with some expertise. With equal expertise, an assistant boatman hands us down the Steps and guides my leap into the swaying boat. Virginia and Stuart and I soon take up a position in the bows where the breeze cools our faces and the spray exhilaratingly stings our skin. JJ is somewhere else, battling with an unfamiliar camera, commanded in jest to take a picture for Michel of "the whole island with a dolphin leaping over it." *Gannet Three* can carry forty people, but there are only about thirty on it today. The sea is calm and everyone is looking relaxed. Even me. I'm glad JJ ordered me out.

The daunting cliffs rise almost a thousand feet above us in our little boat, and it's impossible now to imagine the verdant scene that evidently met our Portuguese discoverers. At that time, too, the shores proliferated with sea lions, seals, turtles and endemic seabirds. But now, with basalt cliffs brown and bare, and those sea animals gone, even our indigenous seabirds are fewer.

We putter along the shoreline, passing plunging precipices at Breakneck Valley with the dusty flats of Donkey Plain above, and one wonders at the colourful word-picture once painted of this island by Jan Huygen van Linschoten after his visit in 1589: *"When the Portingales first discovered it, there was not any beastes, nor fruite, but onely great store of fresh water, which is excellent good, and falleth downe from the mountaines, and so runneth in great abundance into the valley where the Church standeth... The Portingales have by little and little brought many beastes into it, and in the valleys planted all sorts of fruites: which have growne there in so great abundance, that it is almost incredible. For it is...full of Goates, Buckes, wild Hogges, Hennes, Partridges, and Doves, by thousands... Now for fruites, as Portingall Figges, Pomgranets, Oranges, Lemons, Citrons, and such like fruites, there are so many...that all the valleys are full of them, which is a great pleasure to beholde, for it seemeth to bee an earthly Paradise."*

Lemon Valley looks marginally more hospitable than Breakneck Valley, with an old disused Quarantine Station still nestling near the shore and some indeterminate greenery lining its long, steep gully from its start near the infamous Crack Plain near High Peak. Lemon Valley Bay is popular for picnics under the natural cave there, and for swimming in its tiny rock-sheltered pool, and on Bank Holidays great parties are organised for this. But by and large, picnickers travel there and back by boat, more sensibly than the crowd of madmen Chris and I once accompanied on foot, many years ago, for our first foray up and down this toilsome valley. We won't be doing that again.

Our *Gannet Three* is moving on, past the plateau of Horse Pasture with Egg Island below, and the mouth of Thompson's Valley. And suddenly our focus changes as the boat swings away from the shore – and all around us, leaping and flashing, twisting and dancing, are the silver-black streaks of dolphins cavorting for our pleasure. There are hundreds. Three, maybe four hundred of them, everywhere we look, and the boatman points out the different species among them. The most common, he says, are the pantropical spotted dolphins (downgraded locally to *porpoises*) who swim in average groups of two hundred, and they're showing off for us now, bow-riding and performing such acrobatic leaps out of the water that we are all entranced and are laughing like children at a circus. Playing among them today are bottlenose dolphins – the species that more commonly inhabits the other side of the island and sometimes welcomes the arriving RMS in pods of fifteen or twenty; though in the winter months bottlenose dolphins are also seen in James Bay, chasing flying fish on to the Landing Steps. Today we even see rough-toothed dolphins, similar to the bottlenose but with a sloping head and blotches on the skin, and are interested to learn that these were first recorded at St Helena just two years ago. We watch in fascination, enmeshed in the magic woven by these extraordinary creatures, and can almost touch the glistening backs of those playing at the bows of the boat, diving and leaping, crisscrossing each other right under us and sending a myriad diamond sparkles of frothing water into the air beside us. I am not sure that I have ever before been part of such complete freedom and delight.

Eventually the dolphins move off, and the *Gannet* turns to adventure. We are rounding a massive headland and dramatic Speery Island looms into view, those needle-sharp rocks beyond South West Point. This is where the sea changes, notoriously rough no matter what the weather, and both blood and euphoria drain from my face. Giving up our viewpoint in the bows, Virginia and Stuart and I return to the bench seats in the stern where our balance is not so precarious. JJ is there, still battling with the camera in his attempts to shoot the unshootable, for a dolphin is almost impossible to capture on digital stills. I let him battle in peace and stay quiet, having ceased smiling as soon as we rounded that headland. Now I want to be sick, notwithstanding the pills I have shovelled down my throat, and am heartily gratefully that I brought with me a collection of stout non-transparent plastic bags for that purpose. When the time comes to use them, I will not be at all embarrassed by the presence of friends and strangers observing that demeaning exercise. I will merely wish to die.

The reverse trip to Jamestown, after turning back from those mighty swells, takes the boat close up to Egg Island. And this is fascinating in a different way. Once described in rather poor verse as a *"guano-shrouded throne"*, we can indeed reap the full benefit of its shroud as we approach. The guano is thick, glowing in many colours, rich and pungent, not the best remedy for seasickness; but the inhabitants of that towering egg-shaped rock divert attention as we idle so close to the islet that we can almost touch the rock. Sea birds are here *en masse*, swooping and diving through the air with the same verve as the dolphins played in the sea, and now we're being entertained by Madeiran storm petrels, Arctic skuas, Pomarine skuas, and both brown and black noddies. One particular black noddy, among thousands, has taken a fancy to us and inquisitively hovers just above JJ and me, eyeing us up, its black-brown body and white cap starkly outlined against the sky, and I wonder what it wants from us. Then it decides that we are not of great interest after all and smoothly lifts away to rejoin the higher black cloud of its brothers swirling above the boat. Trespassing in this craggy corner of St Helena is a different sort of magic from sailing with the dolphins, but for a brief few minutes as we drift quietly around Egg Island and slide right under the massive dark cliffs that leap behind it, we are transported into a world that isn't ours but is, rather, a domain reminiscent of dreams and childhood bedtime mysteries. This jaunt, despite its brief and humiliating discomforts, has been worth every minute of its good company, its happy passage, and the revelations that nature has offered us. What a wonderful island this is.

20.

Flights of Fancy

February 2005

Little children take Fancy Dress seriously. Tiny boys especially, who are ludicrously dolled up in fulfilment of matronly fantasies, while the child is dimly aware that he pays penance for he-knows-not-what. I am guilty of this myself, of course, and have in the past sent my own small son into the world as a pair of glasses (*Making a Spectacle of Myself*), and various other restrictive uniforms, though the worst thing I ever did was turn him into a sulky ox (with powerful *papier mâché* horns) for a nativity play. He has yet to forgive me for that. He wanted to be a Wise Man. My young daughter, likewise, once suffered first prize as a Christmas parcel, incarcerated in a large glitter-wrapped and beribboned cardboard box that did not make the mounting of steps to the platform easy for her, and she has also appeared in public variously as an autumn leaf, an angel, and a hippopotamus. She, too, prefers to forget the last.

I now look around the hall of Jamestown First School and see the competitive glint in the eyes of the mothers ranged along the wall, hands neatly folded in their laps, heads leaning languidly against the wall, a half-smile of satisfaction playing at their lips as they wait for the show to begin. Each is confident that her child will win. Even placed beside a peacock of inestimable grandeur, her plain little owl is – like the subject of Brian Wildsmith's wonderful children's book – the Most Beautiful Child, and the Judges' Decision will bear that out.

I am one of the judges, flanked by secondary-school teacher Brenda Moors and journalist Paul George of the *St Helena Herald*, and this is not the first time I have been roped in to judge a fancy dress competition in St Helena. I have already judged two Christmas

Parades at this school, one Valentine Parade at Half Tree Hollow First, the Best Hat at the Agricultural Show, and the Miss May Queen at the Quincentenary, as I serve great purpose as a 'neutral' person on this island, with no special affiliation to a cousin's wife's daughter or the grandson of Aunty Maisie's best friend. I simply do not know Who's Who in the world of preschool children.

Today, facing us with solemn visage from across the room, are the participants of the *Miss Valentine and Master Valentine Competition*, and the dominant colour is necessarily red. They line up nervously, receive their numbered placards, and walk towards us like Joan of Arc to the stake. We are a fearsome trio, Brenda, Paul and me, wreaking terror into those small hearts. We smile and smile and try to look like friendly witches, but the children are not convinced. Their eyes are wide with apprehension, and they do not smile at all.

Some are better togged up than others, it must be said, and I make up my mind instantaneously. One little girl's mother has gone to town with hearts on the skirt, and bows and frills, and the child really looks the part, while my chosen boy has been metamorphosed into a king with an equal number of hearts pasted over trousers and shirt. They look splendid together and have certainly won my heart as a triumphing pair. But when the dreaded moment arrives for the judges to retire and make their final decision, I am outvoted by Paul and Brenda on the boy's side. My selected Miss Valentine has gained a unanimous vote, but the Master Valentine they prefer is a solemn page-boy-cut three-year-old wearing a man's suit with a red bow tie; a sweet little chap, certainly, but bizarrely young for the role.

We have tea and biscuits and a relaxed chat with the teachers afterwards, perhaps as protection against angry mothers following us out with knives and spears, and I learn that Muriel, Head Teacher here, is, like my friend Joyce who is Head Teacher of Half Tree Hollow First, retiring in April. That brings to seven the number of teachers retiring on the island this year. It is a worry, as schools are already amalgamating for lack of staff and pupils since the great exodus after citizenship was restored. I wonder vaguely if there will still be schools left on the island when Virginia eventually qualifies as a teacher.

And thinking of Virginia, I suddenly remember that I am not supposed to be sitting here, chatting and nibbling biscuits. I have a

Dinner to cook. It is Valentine's Day not only for the very young but, more pertinently, for lovers. I take my leave and rush back home.

It is an indictment on St Helena that there is nowhere to go for a celebration on Valentine's Day. And without Chris here I am a very awkward gooseberry attached to Virginia and Stuart's first Valentine's together. Having long wracked my brains for a solution, I have come up with nothing. There is no cinema here for me to hide in. No cosy bistro where I can eat alone and not be noticed. There is no library late-opening where I can lose myself in research for a few evening hours. And no friends I can think of who are not a couple on this romantic evening. I begin to agonise over it, and wonder if Bish would share a video with me at his house on this evening; then I realise what wing that would give to rumour in a place like this – a married woman *celebrating* Valentine's night with the Lord Bishop, Superior of a celibate Order? I promptly cancel that idea, and phone JJ instead on the off-chance that he is free. But he's invited to a dinner party, so that rules him out and leaves me trying to find just one single-woman friend here with whom I might hide for a couple of hours. There is not one available. So I turn to Plan B. I will happily subsidise a special dinner out for Stuart and Virginia – if there is somewhere to go. The Consulate Hotel dining room is closed this Monday night (as on most nights), and so are Donny's and Ann's Place, despite the occasion. Harris Guesthouse only caters to groups, and so does Farm Lodge. What about a splendid luxury picnic in the country? That might be an option if it was not pouring with rain inland…

And by now I have reached Plan C. "I will cook dinner for you – anything you like – and I will eat in the kitchen while you set up a special table for two on the veranda," I suggest. Stuart turns faint with horror, appalled that I might dine alone in the kitchen. But I am adamant, and extract from Virginia a menu of their desiring. Smoked salmon, roast pork and veg, rich coffee-chocolate frozen mousse for pudding. And now I must get to work.

The perspiration is splashing off me in the heat of the kitchen, but I do not begrudge them a moment of my discomfort. At least we have finally reached some solution in this godforsaken wasteland of culinary arts. I shovel the mousses into the freezer, and pull out smoked salmon with sundry bits to jazz it up. Thank heavens I am well-stocked with Cape Town supplies and Chris's excellent choice of wines! I start on preparing vegetables (I have actually *saved* our dwindling potatoes to roast for this event), and weigh the pork which is locally produced and – now, here's a thing! – has a finer flavour than any pork I have eaten elsewhere. I iron a table cloth and drape it over the little garden table for two that they will use. The three exquisite roses presented to me for judging this morning's event are arranged in a vase with frangipani from the garden, the roses' rarity on this island warranting their special place on this table. And when Virginia arrives home from her course, she adds candles and ribbons to the decorations and lays the table with champagne glasses and good cutlery. It looks pretty, and she is pleased with the arrangement.

At seven, with the sun setting and dusk gathering gently in our garden, the two of them pop a champagne cork and drink from a small cocktail table set on the lawn below the veranda while romantic jazz plays softly in the background. They have both dressed up – Stuart in a smart long-sleeved shirt, Virginia in a new dress she bought from The Hive last week. And I have changed too. I am now wearing the obligatory white shirt and black skirt of a restaurant waitron, and have produced a bell for them to ring when they desire my services from the distant kitchen. Stuart, if he was ever in doubt before, now knows for sure that this new family of his is quite mad.

The evening has gone smoothly; the meal good, their exchanged gifts mutually well-received, the weather perfect, and they are looking happy. I am exhausted, and once my duties have been properly executed I retire gratefully to bed, selfishly relieved that I am not, in fact, sitting out endless hours alone in some little café somewhere. I am just snuggling down in bed when Virginia calls up the stairs: "Mum, I know those roses were given to *you*, but would you mind if we pressed one as a souvenir to put in a frame?" It is a while before I can answer, the sudden lump in my throat interfering with my voice. "Of course you can!" I croak eventually. I have never been so touched in my life. Their evening – their very first Valentine's celebration together – was, after all my agonising, clearly worth remembering.

The Airport question has stirred like a waking giant. From the deep slumber of the past two years, interspersed only by restless snorts elicited by the mystifying appointment of a local Air Access Co-ordinator, it has lain so dormant for so long that sometimes we thought it had finally died. We were almost certain of that fact when this same Air Access Co-ordinator was unexpectedly retitled Air & Sea Access Co-ordinator, and there was suddenly more talk of shipping than flying. But now we are in the thick of Airport talk again. Three SHELCO bigwigs have lately been over from the UK, including Sir Nigel Thompson, the biggest wig of all, spending three days in St Helena on this visit, stepping from the RMS on a Sunday evening to closet themselves immediately in meetings with Governor Clancy at Plantation House. Fresh field trips were made to the sites in question – Prosperous Bay Plain to see the airport site, and Broad Bottom to visualise their proposed 5-star hotel and golf course among those rolling verdant hills. They also met with Legco, the Legislative Council. And on the following Wednesday they left again, departing on a calling cruise ship to fly home from Walvis Bay.

Only on Radio St Helena's Thursday evening's *Prime Time* programme did the public learn what actually transpired – and it all sounded upbeat. Joe Terry, the SHELCO representative who has made a home on the island, has been smiling for weeks and is clearly infected by Sir Nigel's ingenuous optimism. The radio interviews also came over positively, with Sir Nigel stressing that he has accomplished more in a few hours with our new Governor than he'd achieved in the previous five years. The original 'three-legged stool' appears to have been brought from the attic and dusted down – offering airport, airline, and eco-friendly upmarket hotel, all with emphasis on high-value low-volume tourism which will not ruin the charm of St Helena, he promised – and he and the Governor hoped for a final go-ahead from DfID within four weeks.

So, after all these years of conjecture, it's finally come down to four short weeks. Suddenly there's a buzz in the air. If there's a *yes* from DfID, the Governor will meet again with SHELCO in London to tie up ends when he goes to England for the Governors' Conference in April. And then, says Sir Nigel, it should not be much more than three years before the airport is up and running – despite the massive logistical difficulties the entire project entails. This is no simple airstrip smoothed out across flat land. Here there is a hill to flatten, a gorge to fill in, sheer drops to consider at the end of the runway, up-draughts, prevailing winds that scream across this semi-desert site, frequent fogs and, according to SHELCO's prospectus, a thousand almost sheer feet to climb from Prosperous Bay before the first piece of earthmoving equipment arrives on the Plain. There will have to be accommodation for workers, food for workers, water and electricity (in substantial quantity) piped out to this arid landscape. And fuel – more fuel than the population has ever required before – simply to feed the equipment. It's a daunting challenge.

Though it is clear that St Helena needs an injection of change to keep her alive following her blood loss of the past three years, I still cannot accept an airport as the remedy. For a start, St Helena is not a natural contender against Ibiza or Mauritius in the tourism stakes. We have no beaches, no palm trees, no expansive facilities for wind surfing, high-volume water sports or resort shopping, not even shoreline space for resort condos or glitzy hotels catering to patrons of the package holiday. But what I fear most is the ignorant traveller automatically associating tropical islands with beach boys and leis. Stuart echoes my misgivings. "Do you know," he offers morosely, "that nearly 80 percent of British package-travellers can't place their destination on a map? I heard that on BBC World." Yes, well, those are the very people I fear, all running down the aircraft stairs in shorts and bikini tops, ready for a good tan-catching on a golden beach.

I voice this apprehension to Christopher when next we speak on the phone. "Cheap tourists won't be able to afford flights to St Helena!" he exclaims. "Four years ago SHELCO's projected fares for a four hour flight from Cape Town were equal to the second-most expensive cabins on the RMS – and the RMS has always been outrageously expensive. Imagine what that fare would be now! Besides they can't use a bigger aircraft than a modified BBJ, really a Boeing 737, and once modified to carry compulsory extra fuel, no more than fifty seats will be available!"

"You forgot to mention all the sick people going for 'medical'," I remind him teasingly. Flying sick people out has been DfID's pro-airport argument for years – for this reason alone, it would appear, the island *must* accept air access. But the Senior Medical Officer looks bemused. "I was never consulted about this," he says. "First of all, you can't fly out stroke patients, heart patients, patients with extreme hypertension, or very pregnant women, so that cuts out half the medical evacuees. Secondly, while a quite sick patient can travel alone on the RMS because there's a resident doctor on board, we will not only have to fly out a nurse, but also a doctor, with each serious patient. If the patient is on a stretcher, seats will have to be removed to make room. It's absolutely unfeasible – both in expense and in time. Besides we don't have enough staff in the hospital to spare them anyway. A new, faster, and more efficient, ship would really help us."

A new, faster, and more efficient ship is what the tourists are asking for too. They don't want to fly to the last outpost of Empire. They want to enjoy an Expedition on a new RMS. It's part of the fun, part of the adventure, part of that unique clique, the St Helena Family.

I turned off the radio at the end of *Prime Time* and pondered the implications of all that had been divulged. Sir Nigel was sanguine, our quiet and reserved Governor clearly hopeful but infinitely more restrained, the SHELCO Financial Director gushing about everything, and Ralph Peters' voice was tinged with excitement. I decided eventually, it's not the Airport *per se* that was suddenly rejuvenating, but the thought of the island taking one step forward to anywhere, out of the mire.

And now, those four short weeks later, His Excellency is mysteriously absent from an important commitment. He has sent a belated message of apology together with advice that the annual Queen's Commonwealth Day message will be presented by his Staff Officer – not even by his official deputy, the Chief Secretary. In the room, eyes roll at this dastardly breach of protocol. Furthermore, even the subordinate Staff Officer – successor to Machiavelli who departed the island with Cleavage some months ago – is unacceptably late. The organisers huddle together, peering outside from time to time, checking the Teacher Education Centre wall clock anxiously, wondering whether to proceed without him. The strangest air of expectancy pervades the hall, but what has stalled the Governor's obligation to represent the Queen on this Commonwealth Day, the audience has no idea. Neither does the Bishop, it seems, for he is checking his own watch frequently while his shoulders speak of advanced impatience with the delays. The

Head of Education glances at him in the front row, and he nods: "Go ahead, we can't wait any longer."

"My Lord Bishop, Ladies and Gentlemen…"

I'm here by invitation of Virginia who, since this year's Commonwealth theme is Education (reason enough to hold it in the Teacher Education Centre) has been requested to speak on why she chose to take up teaching. Why, indeed? Starting with a casual gap year amusement, she's now hooked on teaching, on St Helena, on its people, its way of life, the community spirit of such a small and remote place… And, to the amazement of many, she still thrashes against the current while her local contemporaries, one after another, depart the island clutching their new British passports to greener pastures.

She's nervous about speech-making. Still only a trainee teacher, she is faced this morning by everyone in Education, as well as certain Legislative Councillors concerned with that cause. Her files are on display for public perusal, she has also had much to do with the displays that bravely cheer up these dreary walls, and suddenly she feels conspicuous.

There's a long wait until her card comes up. We sit through speech after speech, some good, many long-winded. But after she's delivered her own, telling her story simply and without drama, a former Chief Education Officer leans over and compliments me on the excellent impression she has made, causing me to beam. But by now the organisers are running out of steam. We've had the presentations, the motions of thanks to various worthies, and are looking forward to tea with the pink coconut fingers and *bread-and-dance* that await us in the next room. But the Staff Officer has not yet arrived…

And suddenly, in he struts, blatantly reluctant to be here, offering only cursory apologies before hauling out the Queen's Commonwealth message for which we are specifically gathered today. It's read impatiently, he is thanked, and while everyone is invited to stay for tea, he disappears more readily than he arrived. And a hunch is creeping through my bones. I glance at the Bishop, wondering if he knows anything, but before I can ask, someone whispers: "Turn on your television when you get home." And then I'm certain my bones are right. I skip tea too, and speed home.

And there, sure enough, as I flick the remote in my sitting

room a view of Plantation House fills the screen. BBC World has been neatly shoved aside by Cable & Wireless St Helena to make way for a rare live local television broadcast, and a camera now pans the Governor's residence where, I observe, the entire dining room is filled with seated dignitaries. The crowd positively shivers with anticipation, and a close-up of His Excellency reveals that this is his shining hour. "An agreement has *finally* been reached in London this morning," he informs us after lengthy preamble about DfID's recent soul-searching, "and I'm happy to tell you that *within five years* St Helena will have its own Airport..." So. The promised four weeks have already flown.

I slump back in my chair. Five years. That will be 2010, and six years on from the previous Governor's promised Airport. Perhaps, becoming more familiar with this island's machinations and those of its masters, I am growing too cynical to accept that St Helena will be flying any time soon, and I just can't imagine it happening. The exorbitant expense of building it, for one thing, will be unjustified by the tourism it serves unless huge planes several times a week gush visitors. Yet we don't have the space for large planes, or food, water, electricity, fuel or manpower to cope with crowds. We don't have a hospital Intensive Care Unit for islanders, let alone the near-the-airport unit reputedly demanded by IATA. We don't have adequate Fire and Rescue units to cope with a major crisis and our single small rotting Sea Rescue boat with its team of volunteers will be useless in such an event. We don't have a good maintenance record at all; witness the historic ruins, the condition of roads, some dubious water supplies, the troublesome power plant, unstable rocks over Jamestown. So will we bother about aviation safety? What if a plane blows a tyre on landing? We'd have neither the crane to lift it (none has *ever* been suggested) nor space to make way for external help, and I suspect the plane would simply rot on the runway like the expensive water-drilling equipment that dots the countryside. The negative lists are endless.

But if there is a real positive here, it is hope and incentive enough derived from this announcement for St Helenians to lift themselves out of the Slough of Despond into which our recent devastating emigration has sucked everyone. It offers something to look forward to – if you actually want the Airport – and for the moment there is euphoria. With reassurance that the island is remembered after all, the fear of starvation seems to dissolve along with the fear of growing old in a community with depleting medical services and no young families left to nurse their parents. No longer need people fear the demise of the ageing RMS which, DfID announces, will serve only another five years (retiring in 2010) and will be our last passenger ship. And gone is that most terrible of fears: obligatory transfer of everyone to resettlement in Britain – a cheaper option for the British government, we have cruelly been advised, than to maintain this small rapidly ageing Dependency *ad infinitum*. Of course, we *know* Britain has done this before, in the Indian Ocean's Diego Garcia, rendering the mere suggestion more unbearable. But now, with the Airport in sight, everything changes. Psychologically the island has been given a leg-up over the metaphorical stile, for poor little St Helena is indeed, at the moment, a very lame dog. I hear the TV's cheering and clapping at Plantation House, smiling faces all around, back-slapping and chatter, and I'm happy for the island's people. Give them Air Access if that is what they truly want, but my gut still whispers that it won't necessarily lead to a better life.

When Stuart returns from work I sound him out as a true-blue Saint. He shrugs almost disinterestedly. "We'll see if it's really here in five years."

I ask JJ what he thinks. "I can't wait," he exclaims exuberantly, never a fan of the ship.

Bish is unmoved by the turn of events. "The government has to do something to cheer the place up and an announcement is the cheapest solution. I've told you before; their Airport can't possibly work here. It will be financial suicide for everyone concerned – most of all the British government. Everybody but the fools who come promoting it can see that."

"Even SHELCO?"

"In the end SHELCO will either pull out or the government will get rid of them, even though they're the hope of the side. There'll be years of wrangling before anything starts rolling with anyone else, the project will get more expensive every year they delay, and by the time someone actually makes up his mind about it, the price will be exorbitant."

"You're always a voice of such good cheer," I tease.

"I've lived here as long as you have," he says, "and you know that I'm right."

Sheba is beautiful. Long-legged, long-haired, blonde. She follows the teenage Ricco everywhere, lolloping after him as he feeds the chickens and checks on the goats, flopping close beside him when he lies on the grass near the barbecue fire. He teases her and she rolls over obligingly, the scar of her operation now visible to all. The Agriculture department has finally, recently, learned how to spay bitches, and she displays her scar like a medal. As I watch her, an embryonic idea takes root in my psyche.

The whole afternoon they sit together, the boy and this pretty mongrel, and as we lazily down beers against the cloying humidity of late summer – intense even in these elevated climes at Pouncey's where fields and forests give way beneath us to cool-blue Atlantic as far as the eye can see – our attention is captivated by the bond between them. She's a well-trained dog, friendly and obedient to the limits set for her. And even when mounds of sizzling chops and sausages, steaks and pork ribs are passed around, she merely watches Ricco eat and doesn't beg.

And so the hot afternoon passes in the way of true St Helenian hospitality. Drinks flow generously, country music lilts and whines in the background, and replenished trays of meat fresh from the coals are accompanied by rice salads, potato salads, rolls, baked beans, corn, peas, puddings, and we eat and eat. One of Stuart's sisters has returned home from Ascension on holiday, and today we are at her in-laws' home, a typical 'island cottage', low-slung with every room opening to the narrow veranda stringing them all together. In front of it is a garden of rare floral delight, bounteous with English blooms and vegetables set against the wide ocean backdrop, and we are settled in chairs on the lawn to one side of the cottage, relaxed and feeling welcomed. So in the general stupor of this warm afternoon, with so many beers and so much food inside us, with lazy conversation among warm-hearted people, with hens clucking sleepily nearby and goats scrounging for snacks up the hill behind the cottage, mynah birds today whistling prettily from banana palms across the road and scarlet cardinals flitting around the flower-garden, and with a boy and a dog lying side by side on the grass under a blazing late summer sun, my tiny embryonic idea slowly but surely becomes a firm decision.

I look over at Virginia and Stuart and wonder what they will think of my idea. But even as I resolve to sleep on it before acting on impulse, or even letting them into my suddenly irrepressible broodiness, I know their answer. They too have been watching Sheba all afternoon.

The next day I phone Julie of the RSPCA, who knows all the animals on the island, or seems to. "You're too late," she informs me. "There's recently been a whole bunch of puppies born on the island, but they've all gone to homes now. Except for one. She had some sort of injury soon after her birth and has a problem with her legs, I think. Go and see how she's doing." She gives me the address at Deadwood, and Virginia and Stuart and I resolve to visit this small girl anyway. We are not expecting to bring her home.

We choose a Saturday morning when the owner is at home, and head for the country, Stuart sliding down just a little in the driver's seat as he approaches Deadwood. Longwood Gate, like the Pillars of Hercules, looms on the right, marking entrance to the long straight avenue that slices residential Longwood, but he by-passes them and carries on along the narrow road that skirts the head of Rupert's Valley and overlooks the plunging guts fanning out below. Now on our right is the sweeping expanse of Deadwood Plain that once accommodated all those Boer prisoners, stretching like a baize sheet from the roadside to the peak of Flag Staff and then away past the Barn to the Golf Course on the far side of Longwood's settlement. "This is dangerous territory," he teases. "We town boys used to call this area Texas, the people here are so rough." The people here sometimes appear a little different from many other country people, I concede. Notable are some tardy greetings, aggressive driving habits, and sometimes an obvious reticence towards expatriates in this corner of the island. Hostility would not be the best word – especially as some of the gentlest people I know live here – but it so happens that every murderer in the past one hundred years has hailed from around here – as did also that gun-toting individual once encountered on my way to John Beadon's.

"So are the dogs around here also vicious?" I ask apprehensively. Stewey doesn't know. "We'll go and find out."

The house where he stops has a couple of hamsters in a hutch by the garage, and fat fowls contentedly scratching under the banana palms. The small girl who skips out to investigate our arrival appears hospitable enough, and nothing about the place looks rough at all. In fact the woman inhabitant greets us like old friends, already an acquaintance of Virginia's from her Prince Andrew School days. She's a teacher with a gentle face and a soft heart, and for the past two weeks has been nursing the tiny injured puppy whom she inherited from her son.

We are shown into her yard, stepping over a small puppy barricade, and there she is. Seven weeks old. Brown and black body, white chest, white-tipped tail, floppy brown ears, with – unquestionably – the most beautiful dog face in the world! The little thing pounces on Stuart's shoelaces and unties them, and I notice that after just one look, Virginia's big blue eyes have become threateningly watery. Stuart is suddenly silent too. It has taken a moment to realise that this totally lovable bundle of enthusiasm cannot raise her hind legs at all. Lame from the waist down, she is probably doomed.

I struggle to find my voice. We've all fallen in love, one can see that at first glance. But we cannot possibly take on a dog that can't walk, will probably be incontinent all her days, and suffer pain and frustration as she grows older. I shake my head sadly, and the woman tells us, with a catch in her voice, that she has already had her examined by the veterinary people at the Agriculture department, but they can neither diagnose nor solve the problem. So really there's nothing left but to say a tender goodbye to the playful puppy, the soft-hearted woman, and the little skipping girl, and drive home in heavy gloom. The woman can't keep her any more than we can, but is prepared to spare her a few more weeks before a final decision must be made. Poor, beautiful, precious little doomed puppy. If only we had a vet who could *do* something to mend her. We file away thoughts of adopting a dog for the moment; since none is available we'll have to wait for new litters.

But the image of the puppy doesn't go away. We don't speak about her at home, but it eventually transpires that all three of us have dreamt of her, and her beautiful face persistently pops into our minds. Stuart is commissioned to make another phone call. I couldn't bear to hear the worst, nor could Virginia. He clears his throat into the mouthpiece. "That puppy we came to look at…?" It is two weeks since we drove out to Deadwood. By now she might be dead, for euthanasia is within the scope of our limited veterinary capabilities.

I hardly dare listen any further. Then Stuart reappears, grinning. "They say she's doing great! And we can come and see for ourselves tomorrow morning."

So tomorrow it is. Easter Saturday. We are barely down the slope to the Deadwood house before a black-and-tan bundle hurtles towards us, flopping now and then, but with hind-legs bravely shoving along. She is so much improved, this little thing, that we know she will grow up to be stronger. She will probably always have a weakness in her hips, unless a visiting vet can someday operate to right it, but at least she can get around. She's not in pain and is obviously happy. Stuart seizes her up and clutches her to him. "We're going to take her home," I now say to the woman, and she bites her lip. Her husband has disappeared altogether, unable to watch the departure of this adorable creature. "I've really grown to love her," she says softly, "but I think she'll have a good home with y'all."

And so Tessa enters our lives, a little island all-sorts of friendly disposition and humorous gait. It is only one hip that is really troubled, we discover, and occasionally it gives in beneath her, slewing her around quite unexpectedly to face the direction she has just come from, but not once does she complain in frustration at this annoying disability. She has brought a familiar rug with her in case she's homesick, but she is more intent on the new grip of lawn beneath her feet, and starts to run. She smiles and licks us, terrorises elderly set-in-his-ways Harry, while accepting stern advice from Mimi that *Dogs Drool and Cats Rule* (at least in Mimi's case) and seems to be content with that. Then at night, wearing an almost fluorescent pink cat's collar acquired during a hurried Saturday night shopping spree in the pet section of Solomon's DIY and at Larry's Rose & Crown, she flops into her massive new dog basket lined with a yellow blanket, a couple of toys around her and a tummy full of nutritious Diet pellets for puppies, and falls fast asleep in the cottage with Virginia and Stuart.

This is, undoubtedly, The Most Beautiful Dog in the World.

21.

Bright Lights and Dark Nights

April to May 2005

"Stuart's just phoned with a major message for us," Virginia warns as she prepares to leave for work. "It's really important. Whatever you do, do NOT look at the sea between 9am and noon today. There's a mini-submarine in the bay and it's doing some tests – if they hit a 'ping', a very bright light will be let off that could permanently damage your eyes."

"With the RMS just arrived this morning and all the population fetching luggage and containers, that's going to be difficult to prevent, and there's an American military supply ship in the bay as well," I observe. I spent last evening seated beside the Chief Secretary at the Governor's birthday dinner party, with the Chief Information Officer also present – and *nobody* mentioned this warning. "Do you really believe that?"

She shrugs. "Stuart seemed serious. The police were talking about it last night. Anyway I wouldn't risk looking at the sea if I were you, it's not worth it." She sweeps out with her books, her *hurrumph* telling me that I should not doubt Stuart in any degree, and I'm left alone with a violent urge to sit at the seaside all morning. I trust there will not be too many blinded people around the island by this afternoon.

When Bish phones later to tell me that rough seas have cancelled the Charity event to be held on the RMS tonight, I check with him: "I hope you haven't been looking at the sea?"

"Because of the submarine, you mean?"

"Yes," I reply, fishing. "What exactly is happening out there?"

"I don't really know. The radio said there's a little submarine out there and we mustn't look at the sea – but, of course, what they really mean is, we're not allowed to take photographs."

Later Stedson rings up. "Have you been looking at the sea?" I inquire, since his house commands a vast oceanscape.

"I thought it was *tomorrow* that we're not allowed to look. I can't think why it's a visiting *American* supply ship that tells us about a submarine when they're anchored in British waters!"

"Can't you?" I'm grinning at my end of the phone. "You don't think it has anything to do with April Fool's Day?"

I can hear Stedson slap his forehead with sudden realisation. "Of *course!*" he exclaims, laughing too. "I'd quite forgotten the date!"

And now Stuart walks in. "You heard about the submarine?" he asks, and I relate my morning's preoccupation with the subject.

"Well," says Stuart, "it came on the radio that we weren't allowed to look, and definitely not allowed to take photographs. But up on Ladder Hill, the cliff is lined with half the population gazing out to sea. They all claim they can see a tiny sub, but it looks to me like a fishing boat. Besides," he adds, thoughtfully, "if it is a sub as small as that, it would have to be attached to a mother ship nearby, and the Royal Navy isn't expected here for another two weeks…"

Real news comes to Donny's during the latter part of our Friday evening drinks. Ladder Hill Road has been closed. There's been a rockfall near China Lane, and police are allowing no traffic past it.

Around us all the people who use Ladder Hill to reach home are sighing with frustration, since this now entails a circuitous route home *round by the country* – a deviation of many miles that they do not smile upon after a long week's work and several beers. I, however, am suddenly cognisant of just how close this fall has been to my own home, since China Lane lies only a few hundred feet from Villa Le Breton. If the area is closed, can I get home at all? I am supposing that Virginia and Stuart, playing cards on the veranda when I left, have heard the fall and will eagerly regale me with the blood-chill of that rattle. But to tell the truth, I too am suddenly feeling a little unnerved by the high hills above us, since there's been a plethora of natural rockfalls in the past few weeks. April is often the season for them, I'm told, following the great heat of summer and the sudden chill of rain that cracks them. We live in perilous times.

With our southern autumn drawing in and the sunset long-since admired, the night is already dark as my car climbs towards home through the upper reaches of Jamestown. And here, at the top of Market Street, where little China Lane links it with the Ladder Hill pass, groups of tense onlookers are gathered in the street. Police are dotted about. I slow down. Even in the mild street-lighting I can tell that at least one boulder has swept down the mountain with force enough to bounce *over* the houses to my right of Market Street and slam into the solid gateposts of historic Palm Villa across the road on my left. As my car creeps past, I notice the great bite taken from one of them, and their slight shift of position, and realise that the force of the impact must have trembled the whole house. Someone says another rock leapt the wall to land in the garden, and the owner is badly shaken by fright.

The policeman at the corner of St John's Road, the next link above China Lane, recognises my car as I flash indicators, and obligingly waves me through to Maldivia Road. Then I pass the slight curve of the cliff to our drive and am safe home, praying that no rocks will land on us tonight.

By morning we learn that all the houses below the hospital were evacuated overnight, and the top end of Market Street is still cordoned off. I am not affected by the closures this Saturday morning but am headed into the country as usual, so once I've breached the hairpins of Constitution Hill, am away and free. Today's a celebration of John Beadon's ninety-fifth birthday, an event he has planned for the past eleven months. His birthday parties are cheerful annual events – a generous upgrade from our usual Saturday open-house crisps and beer – with trays of catered savouries circulating and drinks flowing, and attended by a substantially swelled collection of once-a-year guests. At John's great age, these birthday parties present an annual goal, and this year's event was no less eagerly anticipated last Saturday when he laughingly reminded us: "Of course, my real birthday is next Tuesday. But I can't celebrate it ahead of time in case something happens."

And tempted Fate took her cue. The very next day he had a fall and so passed his Tuesday birthday in hospital, pale and tired. "But he'll be allowed home for a few hours for his party on Saturday," his doctor told me, "because he will hate to miss it." And so here we are now, perhaps thirty of us gathered in his sitting room while he holds court from a favourite chair as he has done for so many years. But he looks very frail.

Ann Sim has prepared snacks for us, and two of her grandchildren are proffering platters of tomato-paste tartlets, chicken bites, pizza squares, sausage rolls, battered onion rings, Vienna sausages – common island cocktail fare – while champagne and beer do the rounds. And then comes the cake, iced in electric-blue and white, with candles, and John grips the knife that cuts it and makes a wish. Ann is kneeling beside him, cheerful as ever, bringing him into the talkative throng: "And what is the deal we made?" she demands.

"That you'll be here for my ninety-sixth," says John promptly.

"Of course so!" exclaims Ann impatiently. "But you know that not what I talkin' about, Mr Beadon. I talkin' about the party that I throwin' for *you* when you turn *one hundred*!"

John grins. He and Ann made that deal years ago, and we are frequently reminded of it. From weak and tired at the start of the party, he seems to have perked up, and though the noise in the room is fearsome with party chatter, and someone has rather oddly produced a boxful of rowdy party-poppers, loud enough to wobble the statue of Nelson at Trafalgar Square, he appears to be surviving. Bish is trying out his new digital camera with lots of photographs of John and, peering over his shoulder, I can see that there are good ones in the making. But even as I watch those images on the tiny screen, I am suddenly overtaken by a wave of presentiment that we won't be seeing John for much longer.

I move off into the crowd and am deep in a conversation about bee-keeping when I suddenly sense disruption behind me. As I turn, John is being lifted from his chair and quickly borne away. His old friend Harry Legg, with his business secretary, the new Reverend Jack, the Bishop, two nurses among the guests, and his two male carers have vanished into a bedroom and the door is firmly closed behind them. The Attorney General and I, now the only two of the regular Saturday group left in the room, try to read one another's thoughts. Our eyes, I know, are dark with concern. The air vibrates with anxiety, all celebration gone from the room, and slowly the other guests sense that it is time to leave and quietly slip away. After a while the Bishop emerges from John's bedside to inform us that John is exhausted and the ambulance is on its way. A few minutes later it pulls up outside the house.

John, laid on a stretcher, is trundled past, eyes closed, face white and strained. My heart becomes leaden, suffering an overpowering sense that an era is ending, that there will be no one-hundredth birthday. No ninety-sixth, in fact. And perhaps not even ever another Saturday gathering here around John's chair with our gossip and our tankards of beer while he smiles and his watchful eyes assess us all. I look around the room which has been so much part of my island ritual, and take in all the details of it, perhaps for the last time.

"You're not sitting in your special chair today," John had remarked when I chatted to him earlier on, and I'd glanced over at the little yellow velvet tub chair pushed back against the wall where it lives until, every Saturday, ritualistically, I haul it forward into the circle as soon as I arrive.

"Not today," I'd replied, since I hate to sit at cocktail parties. "Today I'll stay on my feet in order to mingle."

Now I look again at the familiar yellow chair with a special poignancy. I wish I had sat in it one last time.

The view in the bay is different today, with two Royal Naval ships breaking the line of the flat horizon – HMS *Portland* and RFA *Grey Rover* – sleek, efficient-looking vessels paying a social call and lying pleasantly at ease in our calm waters. This tail-end of the southern hemisphere summer brings in a small surge of cruise ships, heading from here to Ascension or Dakar or ports in Brazil as they work their way home to the summer routes of the north. Stately liners arrive, as exotic to us as quinqueremes of Nineveh, oozing luxury and sporting their wealth, tossing in their wake the tiny grey former Russian ice-breakers that follow with their own passenger loads of adventurers, fresh from the rugged shores of southern Chile, South Georgia, and the Antarctic. But while tourist ships come and go, creating a brief flurry of activity on the island for six hours or so, these two naval ships are being useful.

It's fortuitous that their call is so timely, and the men – probably anticipating rest at St Helena – find themselves instead knuckling down to manual labour. But we really need the help, for Jamestown has had more rockfalls.

"The island's falling to pieces," says Virginia only half-jokingly, as the news does the rounds, for we're truly vulnerable in our narrow valley. The slightest sound wakes us at night and we cower in our beds, planning hopeful escape if our own section of mountain starts tossing down boulders.

On two consecutive nights there have been violent rockfalls at the Wharf, yet the more alarming danger-zone is again at China Lane, a stone's-throw from our home. Dwellings below us are evacuated once more, though Villa Le Breton is deemed safe and we're not ordered to move. All of Upper Jamestown is closed to traffic, so I spend the best part of Thursday on our upper veranda with binoculars, wincing at the reverberating crash of old containers being set up as a barricade along the base of the Ladder Hill Road. These are intended to catch rocks before they demolish the block of flats below them, during the massive Controlled Rockfall Operation set for tomorrow. But behind the crashing of the containers lies an eerie and unnatural silence. No cars go about their regular business at this upper end of Jamestown; the trucks, motorbikes and boom-boxes that scatter pigeons in New Bridge are all somewhere else today. The only people about are those working with the containers, and traffic police monitoring the road blocks. Even the birds in my garden seem to have been silenced, and the air shivers with tension.

Then, at five-thirty in the afternoon, sirens cut the stillness. Police. From my elevated vantage point I scan the area, and high above me a flashing blue light on Side Path signals some sort of hubbub up there. A truck turned over, it looks like. Three or four policemen are hovering around, but I can't make out details. And a full hour later they're still there, now lounging against the retaining wall and chatting conversationally, their voices singing out in the new silence of evening since the container-crashing has stopped for the day. But their words are unclear. I ache to know what's happened, so I ring the Police Station with twofold questions. There's a meeting I'd like to attend tonight halfway down Market Street, but with the uptown roads closed and Side Path blocked by an accident, I probably can't get there. I query possible access, but the woman on the phone sounds confused. "I'll just ask around the office here," she offers, and I hear several voices conjecturing in the background. When she returns to the phone she sounds amazed. "Ma'am," she inquires, "you up Maldiwia Road? I ask aroun' here, but there are no way out for you tonight. China Lane and St John's Road is block' off, and Ladder Hill and Market Street. And now Side Pat' after a truck that carryin' gabions to China Lane just owerturn there. You better be jus' stay home tonight, ma'am."

"Anybody injured up there?"

"Driver got a broke collarbone, ma'am. They's waitin' on the ambulance."

"But the police have been there since five-thirty – what's taking so long? The ambulance would take five minutes to reach him up Constitution."

"Ma'am, the ambulance instruct' to go by the country, for safety."

Really? The ambulance is housed above the danger line, with a shortcut up Constitution Hill at its doorstep. But it's been instructed to drive *through* the road closures to the bottom of Jamestown and access Ladder Hill Road by narrow Shy Road, and then travel halfway round the island to reach the man with the broken collarbone. Not funny for him at all, but definitely one of those wry-smile occasions by which we live in St Helena.

Friday morning, and in the sunshine of a bright new day the men in blue (who halted the ambulance access last night) have seen fit to release Stuart and me – inveterate investigators – from the confines of Maldivia Road to scoot up Constitution Hill and observe the Controlled Rockfall operation from across the valley. We pick a seat on a rock among prickly pear cacti (known locally as *tungi*) along the high ridge's rough path, and look down on the most endangered homes huddled together in their special vulnerability – a few blocks of flats, some tiny cottages, houses layered behind them – while parked police cars mark off the areas of greatest danger. Many of those residents are also in the watching crowd gathered on this mountain, stoically reserved in the way of St Helenians, showing nothing of their trepidation, yet the atmosphere around us is electric.

No rocks are rolling yet because the exhausted Rock Guards, after completing their container barricade this morning, are still slogging up the steep slope to the massif of menace. So I look down lovingly with a bird's eye view upon my own peaceful bright-white house reigning over its green half-acre below, and thank God that it's deemed out of harm's way at present. It is five years and a month since our family moved into this new home, and it is part of each of us. I wish nothing to injure it.

"Look," someone announces eventually. "They gattin' ready to roll." And yes, across the deep valley and high up on the great outcrop objective, the Rock Guards are moving into position. They're all linked by rope, and those climbing down the rock face are harnessed. It's not the outcrop itself that is the problem, the binoculars show, but aeons-worth of loose rock and boulders that have accumulated in its deep vertical crevices, tall pipes of them waiting only for the skittering of a bird or a mouse to start an avalanche. Perhaps a rabbit started the latest onslaught.

"And there they go!" A sharp intake of breath wheezes through the crowd. One large boulder has been let loose. It swishes the undergrowth as it starts, then tumbles and bumps. And then as it gathers momentum down its steep descent, cracking cuts the air, heard even where we stand a thousand feet up and almost that distance across the valley. Near the bottom of its run it collides with another rock, splits, and its cloud of dust swirls like fire. Then there is a final leap as it crosses the bottom of Ladder Hill Road, and with a reverberating crash hits a container, its satellites coming behind it like meteor debris. One rock down. Twenty-two tons to go.

By the time the midday sun has got to me and my cool home calls, the roadside public lavatories at China Lane have been razed. One container has a gaping hole from the force of a single rock passing through it like a bullet, and another boulder has pushed an entire container through a stone wall and across a garden to leave it resting against the rear wall of the block of flats.

By nightfall, when the job is done and a team of exhausted men is 'sweeping' the last loose stones from the rockfall's swathe down the mountainside, the bottom of Ladder Hill Road is dense with stones.

They'll be left there tonight, blocking the road, for it's too dark now to start cleaning up. The Rock Guards deserve their rest, after all; hot baths, hot soup, and a strong drink at the very least. They have worked hard and can afford to relax for a while, for tomorrow the Royal Navy will come in and take away the mess, just as they have already cleared the Wharf of the Old Customs House debris. They offered, the island gratefully accepted, and we could not be gladder of their timing.

The little church of St Andrew in Half Tree Hollow is one I've never visited before. I am staring wistfully at the pretty stained-glass window donated to it by John Beadon when his Jean died, and she, if I remember correctly, donated its font some years before that. Obviously John had a special affection for this place and I can see why he requested a Requiem Mass to be said for him here this morning, preceding his cathedral funeral this afternoon. Just a faithful few are here, the closest of his Saturday Gang and one or two others, while the Bishop, both friend and senior cleric for this most beloved of old settlers, conducts the service. John's era has died with him. He is the last of the past world of Old Colonials, the British Army veterans, the pensioners from the East or from Africa, the wandering Old Etonians, retired diplomats, and eccentrics, all educated fascinating people with tales to tell, who chose St Helena as their final home. For all my youth at the time, I met many on my early visits to the island and some became dearest friends to the end. But there aren't any left now, and the new breed of settler – among which I include ourselves – can't compare. I am mourning an age as much as a friend.

Christopher is back with us, managing on average to make two two-month-long trips a year to join us, while I annually make one southbound return so that we spend at least half of each year together. And I'm particularly glad he's here now, sharing this little sadness, arriving just in time to bid John goodbye as he faded away in hospital. In the afternoon we progress to St Paul's together. This, too, is a funeral rather than a memorial service and the coffin, black-draped in velvet, is shoulder-borne by pall-bearers who have themselves dug his grave. The Bishop is looking a little wild-eyed about that, I discover, because the site allocated for John beside his beloved Jean has proved so rocky they almost couldn't dig a hole large enough to take his slim box. But in the end pickaxes and hard labour prepared the site in the nick of time.

There is a huge turnout, the church crowded with dark suits and sombre dresses. Funerals are big in St Helena, and John's is no different from a typical Saint send-off. Lots of traditional English hymns, a little humour thrown in by the Bishop to levitate the solemnity if the dear departed was known to him, a eulogy and sometimes fleets of emails from distant lands read out by the organist. Everyone remains for the committal afterwards, proceeding from church to gravesite to quaver, rather more tunelessly, a few unaccompanied hymns while the hard-working gravediggers set about the business of covering the interred coffin.

John and Jean lie not far from an old enclave of military graves, whose headstones make for interesting reading. But any wander over the grassy hillside of St Paul's will turn up similar insights into past times. There is the bizarre tale of a young woman dying on a vessel bound for St Helena, and buried at sea. But the story goes that her coffin, inadvertently unweighted, floated off on the current and she arrived at St Helena before the ship did, to be properly buried at St Paul's. Most headstones have weathered well over the centuries, while others are broken or smoothed by rain, and I am still immensely disappointed that there is no sign of the grave of Elizabeth Le Breton, true chatelaine of our historic home, despite newspaper evidence that she was interred here.

Well, John Beadon, you reached the age of ninety-five and it was a good innings. We'll miss you but we don't begrudge your going. It's just so unbearably poignant that you have taken a whole era with you, as the new era certainly does not promise the same grace or good manners, the colourful stories, or the unsung generosities of your generation.

Already the new Airport era is not boding well, and for months I've been in a fever about tourism – ever since last Christmas's Block Leave when every shop closed in St Helena for ten days' holiday, bizarrely leaving all the invited Governor's Cup yachtsmen hungry until after New Year. In fact, just weeks before the Airport announcement in March, I was moved to write a letter to the press about the lack of hospitality the island affords its visitors; and the subject is doubly pertinent now, since DfID's main objective in pressing Air Access upon us is to encourage self-sufficiency through tourism and thus make St Helena financially independent of the British government. Anyone can see their point, but I hear the Bishop's emphatic rejoinder: "That will never happen! Saints are too lazy."

My letter was, I confess, upbraiding but to the point, and I was heartened by the number of people who stopped me in the street after publication to commend me on it. A frighteningly fragile line exists between tourist exploitation and preserving charm, and tourism here must be monitored with extra care. But St Helena still has light years to travel in that department, according to many tourists who air their views on the RMS after a visit to the island, heaping compliments on a Saint for his beautiful geography, but to expatriates like Chris or me voicing the whole truth. Food, not unexpectedly, is at the crux of every criticism. Saints indeed are charming, gentle, friendly – they agree – but physical comforts during their stay are deeply wanting.

Basic tourism expects ready access to restaurants, imaginative cooking attractively presented, linen napkins, quiet places for pre-prandial drinks without thumping pop music… Self-catering visitors require the convenience of tasty home-cooked frozen dinners to heat up in a microwave – and to this end a young Welshmen with a gift for cooking spotted a niche to fill; but when he applied for a licence to prepare such meals for tourists, it was denied him because he did not work out of a stainless steel kitchen as EU regulations decree. Eventually, frustrated to desperation point by a partner who ate only St Helenian food, the budding chef turned to the Consulate Hotel where he offered to cook for free, for the joy of it. But there he was informed that, except for breakfast, this flagship hotel would prefer not to serve food at all, and his offers were turned away. He once cooked a superb three-course dinner for us at Villa Le Breton at his own request and we can vouch for his talents, but of course, by now thoroughly defeated by the system, he is back in Wales.

The spark that really sets me alight is a small advertisement in the *St Helena Herald*, appearing hot on the heels of the Airport announcement. A relatively new government department is seeking suggestions for upgrading tourism in view of our imminent air access. Since I'm already fired-up enough about the issue to have had a letter published in the paper – and now they're actually asking for *ideas*! – I can't let this go by. I sit up late into the night scribbling suggestions. In the light of day I start asking around, descending upon friends, both Saint and expat, family, tourists, anyone I can think of who has imagination, collecting their ideas. And then I start writing. By the time I have exhausted my energies, I've compiled twenty-two pages of viable tourism suggestions for an emerging St Helena, each listed in categorised point form with descriptive details and methods of execution. Some ideas will cost nothing, others are expensive, all of them are cognisant of that fragile charm-preserving line, and many can save the dereliction of already crumbling historic properties or crafts. I print it out, bind it, and send it to the required address.

I wait impatiently for some response, and eventually am delivered a small receipt that indicates that this contribution has indeed been handed on – though I recognise at once that it has already reached the end of the line, having clearly not travelled far. I'm deeply perturbed since the public has been *asked* for suggestions. So back to the printer I go, and by the next day several copies are on the Governor's desk. From there the list moves, travelling from department to department, and months later complete strangers are still remarking that they've stumbled across it in someone else's office and loved some of the ideas. It seems, then, a natural move for me to join the Tourism Association which is now advertising its AGM – an organisation of whose existence I was previously ignorant.

Chris and I both attend, he as interested in the tempered improvement of St Helena as I am, though with his long absences, it would be fruitless for him to join the association himself. However, I will happily pay an annual subscription and become a member. I've lately pulled back from all charities except the time-demanding RSPCA, but a tourism chat now and then can be fitted in.

As the committee seats itself, it quickly becomes apparent why I've never heard of this group before. There's no verve anywhere, and the brief discussion that brushes questions on tourism displays a terrifyingly parochial attitude, topped by an indignant complaint from a hotelier that *"tourists are demanding"*. Chris's eyes widen in shock. *Of course* they are demanding. They're paying big money – even at these hotels!

The sitting Chairman, who does not anticipate being replaced at this AGM, views the few strange faces on the floor and inquires who might be interested in joining the association as ordinary members. One or two put up their hands – livewires I respect for their forward-thinking – and so my hand goes up too. "Then," announces the Chairman to the room, "we must ask all other non-members to leave the meeting." *Leave the meeting?* This is a public AGM, advertised in the press! Chris is utterly nonplussed. While I'm permitted to observe the Election of Committee Members, must my husband wait for me in the pitch dark without a bench or chair to sit on? He looks over at JJ who is already muttering a colourful lingo of disdain, and though JJ has contributed enthusiastically to our now-dubbed *22 Pages* he never again will darken the doors of the Tourism Association, I can tell. He and Chris exit the hall together, with other discharged guests, leaving the rest of us shaking our heads.

And so, like the sun after rain, comes light. Astonishingly, there will be a reshuffling of committee members tonight after all, and the energetic, worldly-wise Joe Terry of SHELCO is voted in as a new Chairman while the old Chairman vacates his chair in shock. Even the new vice Chairman is tourist-friendly, the new secretary bouncy, and everyone else is rolling up their sleeves in anticipation of action. Now the expelled guests are hauled back in from the deep shadows of the TEC car park – all except JJ who has legitimately gone home in a huff – and business proceeds in an efficient manner. As I pay my £1 membership, I lay a copy of the *22 Pages* before the new Chairman: "Seen this before, Joe? It's a compilation of tourism suggestions from right across the island."

He peers at it, shaking his head, and slides it into his briefcase.

The next day he phones. "Some of those suggestions are easy enough to implement right away. I love the movable trees-in-tubs for beautification of the Wharf, and the local music suggestions. We can get going on the music right away." It will be good working with him.

So a short time later when the RMS coincides with the visit of a cruise ship, there is – quite magically – a group of casual old-style musicians playing for sheer enjoyment just outside the Canister building. The veranda railings at the Consulate Hotel are lined with delighted visitors who love the trio of sax, guitar and fiddle, while other tourists are proffering coins to the players. However there is no hat or tin to put them in, and consternation reigns briefly because remuneration was never part of the equation. But the government's nearby Tourist Office eventually supplies a receptacle, and it's decided that perhaps the collection could go to charity. The civilian Tourism Association, when next it meets, is ebullient. Tourists were ecstatic, the musicians hauled in substantial revenue, and the exercise was a huge success. Now a scaled-down Ladies' Orchestra is vying to play the next time that a cruise ship calls, which will be soon in this autumnal quarter of the year.

The next ship is large, with a significant passenger complement, and Tourism Association members – by now brandishing personal copies of the *22 Pages* – are in gear under its new leadership. The sale of cool drinks and water at the top of the Ladder is the focus of the moment, and because a sellers' licence is needed, Tamsin, who already has one, volunteers to supply the refreshments. It has long been a horror of my own that those, so often elderly, visitors who feel a lemming-like compulsion to conquer the daunting 699 steps of Jacob's Ladder are met with absolutely no facilities for refreshment at the top of an exhausting climb. No teashop, no kiosk selling Cokes, not even a miserable drinking fountain. But as a starter we are organising Tamsin's ice keg of drinks this time around.

The day dawns brightly. The ship comes in. Christopher and I are occupied in the country for most of that morning, but when we return to town through Ladder Hill I see no Tamsin. There are a number of tourists still milling about at the head of the Ladder, some looking faint and wan which is not unexpected in this heat, but not one is clutching a can of liquid. "What happened to the drinks?" I ask Joe when I bump into him near the Canister where the Ladies' Orchestra is nowhere to be seen either.

"Tamsin decided that as there were only 1 600 passengers on the cruise-liner, it wasn't worth her while to spend a morning selling drinks at the top of the Ladder after all." We both sigh the exasperated expatriate sigh of the oft-thwarted before he continues: "And in case you haven't heard, the Ladies' Orchestra were happily strumming away outside the Canister to the great enjoyment of our tourists, until the police strolled up, told them they had no licence to perform there, and sent them home." And then we laugh, Joe and I, both old hands at frustration.

We are beyond surprise, sadly. As we head for home Chris and I recall another instance a few years back when a bus loaded with seriously geriatric tourists intent only upon the famous philatelic collections of St Helena, paused to offload them at the Post Office door one Sunday when the office had especially opened for them. The first, on sticks, had barely alighted and was just turning to assist a doddery friend, when a policeman admonished the bus for stopping. "You can't park here," the driver was informed. "You must unload your passengers at the Wharf and they can walk up." The man on sticks hauled himself back on board, and at unanimous request the entire busload was delivered back to the Steps where they boarded a ferry and immediately returned to their ship. All we can do, really, is bang our heads against a wall.

In anticipation of the important Commonwealth Games to be held in Melbourne, Australia, the Queen's Baton has arrived in St Helena – and it's a truly momentous day. Making its circuitous way around the world, seeking out the scattered remains of the British Commonwealth, it has not forgotten little us, and thanks to a fortuitously well-worked RMS schedule, it has even timed its arrival to coincide with the upcoming St Helena's Day. This visit has been minutely planned by the local Queen's Baton organisers. Chris and Stuart and I are positioned near the head of the Ladder to view this unusual object when it ascends towards us, while below us in the Parade Virginia is overseeing young schoolchildren who are enjoying an incidental break from studies. We're advised there will be flag-waving and dancing girls down there.

It alights from the ferry, makes its way along a comparatively deserted Wharf because crowds are clustered in the Grand Parade this morning, and as it enters Jamestown through the Arch, its bearer raises it aloft. There are cheers and whistles, miniature flags go berserk, cheerleaders do their thing with exuberance while the blasé teenage students of the island's Secondary School, feigning total disinterest, lounge languidly against the ascending railings of the Ladder where they have been posted as another reception line.

Then our turn comes to behold this majestic symbol. One unfortunate Australian has volunteered to run up the Ladder, sight unseen, and he starts off with energy. But soon he decides that discretion is the better part of valour, and running up this vertiginous stairway for the first time with handholds barred by draped scholars and a large cylinder conveyed above your head, is not wise. He hands the Holy Grail to a Saint to run instead. It is a long, very shiny chrome object of somewhat phallic design, and sports winking coloured lights down its front. At the head of the Ladder it is reverently handed to assorted helpers in designated Queen's Baton-receiving T-shirts to stroke, and even some of the bored students extend a hand to it. I myself am accidentally caught in a knot of baton-gazers from whom it is difficult to extricate myself, and before I can step away from this mesmerising object, it's shoved towards me. "Would you like to *touch* it?" I am asked. I extend a dutifully deferential hand. The chrome is cool and smooth to the touch, like most other chrome. I resist prodding any of the winking lights. When I wiggle my way back to Chris and Stuart, I exaggerate the honour: "I touched it! I *touched* the Queen's Baton, touched by the *Queen* herself!"

Stuart sees at once that I am teasing, and guffaws. "So did I. But I heard they brought three different batons with them in case some of the little lights go out – and I don't suppose the Queen touched any of them!"

We wait while the T-shirted brigade piles into the open green charabanc which has laboured from Jamestown to meet them, and watch the Baton raised aloft again like Liberty's torch as the old bus winds back down the Ladder Hill Road to fulfil the prescribed duties. "I really think the Queen's Baton should have dressed up smarter than just a T-shirt," remarks a woman nearby. "After all he's a very important person." She's not alone in this misguided opinion, I soon discover; but at least he's been properly welcomed.

When we next see the baton it is doing a lap of honour around the playing field at Prince Andrew School on St Helena's Day, where the Bishop is blessing the festivities.

"That baton has done the rounds of every old-age facility on the island," he tells us after the ceremony. "But half the poor old things didn't have a clue what it was all about – they've never heard of the Commonwealth Games! But one old duck did acknowledge its massive celebrity – she touched it, promptly burst into tears, and told the Aussies she had never dreamed that she would live to see anything so important in her lifetime. I wonder if the Governor – the Queen's actual envoy here – heard that."

22.

Wigs and Wine

May to June 2005

It is almost exactly a year since I last sat in this courthouse beside Marie, the judge's wife, attending Giles's prosecution. Now we are back here together, Christopher with us too, hearing a wishy-washy psychiatric assessment of one of the Two Boys, delivered via video link. This psychiatrist, one of two offering assessments in the coming days, is British and apparently attached to a London hospital. And we learn that at some time in the past few months he visited St Helena on such a fleeting visit that his presence passed virtually unnoticed by anyone. I suppose the police knew he had come, but not even Stuart remembered him knocking on the prison door. Boy Two – the younger one, seventeen at the time of the murder – is the accused in question, as his fluctuating moods cause concern to those around him, especially since incarceration eleven months ago. Psychiatrist Brit eventually divulges that he spent, during his consulting visit, a total of four hours with the accused.

We have an impressive array of lawyers before us: on the elevated Bench, the Lord Chief Justice in scarlet and black and well-worn wig, and below him two imported British barristers, an imported solicitor, and our own Scottish Public Solicitor, all also gowned and wigged. All four are clued up, alert, paying attention, asking sharply pertinent questions while Psychiatrist Brit, filmed in close-up on a large screen to one side of the court, quails under their interrogation. We can see him longing for this to end.

At some point there's a mighty fluster about a document he needs to see, but he is 4 000 miles away; so, simultaneously, the four modern lawyers flip open their laptops and prepare to email him.

But here's a stumbling block. Psychiatrist Brit is not in his own office while he faces this daunting video link camera. He is, in fact, three London blocks from his own computer and reaching it will demand an adjournment of some length before he returns to us.

"What about fax?" inquires the septuagenarian judge.

"*Fax?*" The lawyers exchange shocked glances. This hearing has, in an instant, metamorphosed from learned legalism to palaeography. They're too stunned to respond.

The Judge accosts his own camera. "Is there a fax machine near you?" he asks the man in London.

A young woman, previously unobserved on screen, leaps to her feet and scoots about the room while the psychiatrist entirely abandons us for a moment or two. Perhaps both have gone to seek the tools of archaeology.

Finally he returns. "Yes, we have a fax machine in the room next door." Our four younger lawyers slump in their seats and close their laptops with definitive snaps.

The Judge smiles a little smirk of victory. "Then, in the interests of speed, we shall send a fax." Chris is nearly hysterical with laughter. He will send no email, and will initiate no call – or God forbid, a text message! – on a mobile phone unless under the direst duress, and firmly believes that the world's finest achievement since the invention of the wheel was the introduction of the facsimile machine. I grant him that in this case it's certainly faster than email.

Psychiatrist Brit's assessment seems thin to us, almost vague sometimes, and a measure of uncertainty lurks beneath his findings. He is put through the mill and his voice grows fainter as the hearing progresses. He does not in the least impress Chris or me with his arguments, or imbue us with confidence in his findings, yet he insists that Boy Two is "psychiatrically unfit" to stand trial for murder.

The next day we hear an assessment by a South African psychiatrist whose professional experience focuses largely on criminals and such legal cases as this. He is considerably older and more life-battered than Psychiatrist Brit, and his points are succinct and positive. We all noted when he visited St Helena, because during the full week he spent on the island he was frequently observed entering and exiting HM Prison. Life-battered he might appear, but he knew what he was looking for, found it, and now assumes that the lawyers share his own confidence in his abilities – but for one fatal mistake on which the legal team pounces. He has submitted a formal written assessment of Boy Two which is presently laid out before all the lawyers, in which the young accused is assessed to be cunning, game-playing, and extremely bright given the tools for academia (the psychiatrist himself has taught him to use a laptop to download guitar sheet-music, which he grasped with speed). And he is adamant that the youth is quite fit to stand trial. He has interviewed family members as well, and if a boy, barely eighteen, of his circumstances claims confusion at legal proceedings, it is understandable, he says. However, the psychiatrist has thrown away the original notes he used for his report and the lawyers mince him to shreds for this, though as no detail has been omitted from the official report, we wonder why on earth he should keep the scribbled jottings from which he compiled it? This is a trick of legalese to shake him, but he's a professional and remains unshaken. He simply looks irritated.

We do not discuss the case with Marie when court adjourns, though her expression indicates that we are probably all three thinking alike. And when she and the Judge come to dinner this same night, all eight of us – our guests carefully chosen not to trespass upon any case connection, and Stuart prudently on duty at the prison – exercise huge restraint in avoiding any mention of the day in court. The Judge will present his own findings in a brief sitting tomorrow, deciding whether Boy Two stands trial or not; yet as far as Christopher and I are concerned, the presentation was cut and dried. It makes for a relaxed evening with a good meal, much laughter, liqueurs after dinner that carry us into the early hours before guests disperse. "See you in court," we call after Marie and the Judge as they recede down the path. We're already gripped by this case.

The Saturday morning sitting is indeed brief, but Marie and Chris and I are there again. All the lawyers are hastily adjusting wigs, shuffling papers, opening laptops, when three thumps of the gavel announce the Lord Chief Justice. He does not indulge in lengthy preamble today, and soon we are out in May's midmorning sunshine again, under the purple jacaranda trees, old courthouse cannon beside us, peaceful doves *croo-crooing* from above. There's not much to say, really. The Judge has made his decisions, and so a case against Boy One can proceed. Boy Two, the younger, subject of the week's debates, has been found *unfit* to stand trial. "I really didn't know how he was going to rule," says Marie, as shocked as we are, "but I rather assumed…"

"So did we."

Chris and I attend all the court hearings. It is interesting stuff, but the more the case progresses, the more sobering the murder's background becomes. Boy One, the elder, has pleaded not guilty to the charge of murder but guilty of manslaughter and is forthwith removed from the court, handcuffed for the short crossing of the Grand Parade back to prison until the Judge points out that such restraint is hardly necessary in St Helena. Boy Two, 'unfit to stand trial', is allowed to stay for his own hearing. We keep an intrigued eye on his unflinching body language as he sits in the dock while young witnesses are brought in, one after another. There were many that fateful Saturday night nearly twelve months ago, some joining Ryan and his cousins in the rough skirmish that started at the Consulate Hotel bar, others joining in the extended fray a little higher up the town. And by the time Ryan and the Two Boys had moved down to the Arch to amuse themselves by hurling calumnies at innocent crew members returning to the visiting American supply ship, all three boys were pretty drunk.

It was at the Honeymoon Chair, however, that things turned really ugly. A fight ensued, Ryan taking the brunt of some seemingly motiveless onslaught by his two cousins. He was already bleeding heavily when he toppled over the railing into the waterless moat to crash through the rusty tin roof of the former shooting range below. But, as it transpired to our horror, Boy Two then took the trouble to run down the moat's steps to his cousin's injured body and finish him off by bludgeoning with a nearby chair.

Day after day we sit behind Ryan's mother in the courtroom, watching her shoulders tremble as she weeps through descriptions of her son's last moments. She is warmly supported by Father Chris of her parish at St Matthew's, both friend and counsellor to her, sometimes by Ryan's natural father, sometimes by her life partner, but nothing alleviates the grief she is suffering. Across the aisle sit the other family members, parents of both accused, faithful supporters of their errant sons but as far out of their element here as goldfish in a shark tank. They neither weep nor register any flicker of emotion throughout, but they do not miss a session.

By the end of several days depression is weighing on us. Through hearing evidence in this case it has become distressingly plain that, whatever the Judge may finally rule for this murder, it's not only the Two Boys who are in severe trouble. Several young witnesses have been in the dock themselves before for one misdemeanour or another. But boredom has emerged as the real killer here. Come weekend nights, these teenage youths – some barely thirteen – set out from home with the sole purpose of getting drunk and picking a fight. And while domestic violence has long been a well-concealed secret on the island, the blatancy of this new teenage aggression seems to have developed in a shockingly short time. It shakes me that just three years back Virginia felt safe walking the mile home from Donny's disco, through Jamestown on her own, at two in the morning – never depriving my anxious-mother instincts of sleep in those days – yet now even Richard, at eighteen, feels nervous alone in town at night. Especially after 11pm when brutality gets going. Drunkenness is established by then, and cannabis is illegally puffed behind the walls of the derelict Duke of Edinburgh playground in Market Street. Later, when further alcohol has been imbibed, rivalry over a woman enters the equation, and suddenly there is a recipe for friction. These youths, we discover with alarm, are no strangers to broken bottle attacks, knife threats, and broken bones. Insolence has come to the fore, crass language, rude gestures, vandalism, and a noticeable element of racism among those less bright who perpetrate violence. The brighter teenagers of this island, it must be said, have mostly packed their new British passports and left.

Christopher and I stay to the end of the case when Boy One, charged with manslaughter, is sentenced to four years' imprisonment at Her Majesty's pleasure, in St Helena. He's a lucky guy. Conjecture has long held the possibility that one or both of them might be introduced to a British penitentiary, perhaps for life, which would show them another side of the world altogether. But the sentencing of Boy Two is delayed, and now legal ramifications cite that the Governor, as Commander-in-Chief of St Helena, holds some sway in deciding the outcome of this particular case. So it is he who'll announce the sentence later. Rumour has it that four years is what Boy Two, also, will serve – for murder.

*

It is not only beer that is frothing at Donny's this Friday. The three visiting lawyers are seated at our table when Chris and I join it, and all are in a ferment of indignation. From Stedson's ears, great clouds of steam are metaphorically billowing. Before them, on the table, lies a copy of this week's *St Helena Herald*. It's the Editorial that has sent blood pressure soaring.

"Picture this," it says: *"Two pretty scared Saint boys who are confronted with an environment purposely designed to instil awe and even fear – red-robed judge with sash and wig, black-robed barristers also with similar ridiculous wigs..."* Ah, poor little murderers, how beastly of everyone to make them uncomfortable.

As the article goes on, our eyes widen in disbelief. It rants about witness boxes putting the accused in the spotlight, about the legal system's roots in Medieval England, about gavel-knocks on the door... *"But what's worse,"* it continues, *"is that all those with the power to decide the boys' fate are expats... all of them effectively unconnected with St Helena in all but the most peremptory way."* An almost accusatory tone is then directed at the Lord Chief Justice, the two visiting barristers and the visiting solicitor, the incumbent Attorney General, and the incumbent Public Solicitor who is already in extension of his three-year contract on the island.

Fire flashes from the Prosecutions' eyes. "And who would have handled this case if we were not here?"

I look at Stedson for confirmation, but he's speechless. "I know of only one fully qualified St Helenian-born lawyer," I offer, "and she has a high-powered job in England where they pay her a proper salary."

It is hard to fathom what complex emotions Stedson is experiencing over this article for which, as a member of the Media Board, he is feeling certain responsibility. But my personal reactions – surpassing, that is, my amazement at such a crassly stupid editorial – are of overwhelming chagrin that these professionals are publicly disparaged in this way. Liberalism is fine; questioning, a prerequisite; criticism, part-and-parcel of a good editor's job. But sensitivity is essential. And with a lack of the latter for some time past, this article is the straw that has finally broken the camel's back. "Who *is* this editor?" asks one of them, stabbing the article with a finger.

Stedson finds his voice at last, a mere quaver of his normal bellow. "He's an expat himself! Not only can St Helena not supply a legal team qualified to present a murder case in court, but we can't raise a Saint newspaper editor!"

Stedson's wrath endures, fanned by the ire of the insulted lawyers. And by the time Chris and I are trussed up in finery at Plantation House a week later, celebrating yet another Queen's Birthday, the editor has resigned from the newspaper and Stedson from the Media Board.

"Who's the new editor?" I ask.

Stedson flashes his blinding grin. "Another expat, of course. I just hope the new one has some sense."

Though a handful of modern island houses now stand just below the grounds, and Mr William Balcombe's fine house and garden have given way to the Cable & Wireless headquarters nearby, little else has changed the view since Napoleon Bonaparte stood on this lawn at the Briars Pavilion and gazed wistfully out to sea. As always, the great walls of James Valley soared up on either side, to his right the untarred Side Path of his time laboured up into the country, and on the left the high dramatic cliff-form of the Heart Shape Waterfall was tucked into its own quiet curve of the landscape. Perhaps some part of the old fortifications at High Knoll peered over the cliff upon the *"little Corsican tyrant"* as he drew in the sweet scents of white roses, geraniums and orange trees that grew among the fuchsias, myrtle, pomegranates and vines of his surrounding garden, but the omnipresent fort as we know it today was completed only in 1874, some sixty years after Napoleon stood here.

The year was 1815, the month mid-September, when an English ship, *Icarus,* swept into James Bay with news, not only of Napoleon's escape from the Mediterranean island of Elba in March that year, but also the Duke of Wellington's glorious victory over him at the Battle of Waterloo in mid-June – tidings promptly celebrated by a royal salute on the island and a festival held for the local garrison, *"with extra wine allowance for every soldier".* Even the release of all prisoners, both civil and military, was joyously promulgated – quaintly excluding that of one single soul awaiting trial for burglary – and fun was had by all. It is no wonder that the jubilant little Island of St Helena could hardly credit then that within a month the leader of that opposing army himself – not a captive of battle, as erroneously believed, but in fact a victim of certain dishonoured deals between England and himself – would arrive to take up residence on their island; a hostage restrainedly described in a letter to St Helena from His Majesty's Government as *"a man whose conduct has proved so fatal to the happiness of the world"*.

And so, in due course the fallen Emperor arrived, brought on HMS *Northumberland*, an ancient ship recently destined for the scrapyard but hastily refurbished and very ill-equipped for such a long voyage, affording maximum discomfort to the loyal French Household that accompanied him and offering Napoleon only a tiny, cramped cabin. The prisoner travelled under the watchful eye of Rear Admiral Sir George Cockburn who carried orders to temporarily replace the incumbent Governor, Colonel Mark Wilkes, until a new Governor was appointed. Wilkes was a gentle aesthete with a classical education and a passion for replacing the forests of Longwood so carelessly hacked down by 150 years of English settlement. But gentle men were redundant now. And after six months of Admiral Cockburn, the pedantic Sir Hudson Lowe – doomed to an acrimonious relationship with the French Household – would eventually take up the reins of guardianship of this most valuable prisoner.

What Napoleon thought when he first saw St Helena is always an early point of conjecture as new visitors now steam in on the RMS. And perhaps the journals of a certain Lieutenant James Prior, then a 23-year-old Ship's Surgeon who had passed this way just two years before him, sum up the dispirited impressions of Napoleon and his accompanying Household as HMS *Northumberland* nosed into James Bay during that eventful October: *"It is impossible to approach and see this singular island, for the first time, without wondering how the deuce it got there. A vast mass of rock, rising abruptly from nearly the centre of the great Atlantic ocean, jagged and irregular, cut and slashed as it were into pieces by the great hatchet of nature – too large to be passed without examination, and too small, and unfruitful, and badly situated, to be of much use..."*

Prior also gives us a picture of Jamestown at the time,

patronisingly describing his first view of the town as *"not unpleasing"*. *"It is formed by one principal street, of some length..."* he tells us, *"tolerably broad, paved, clean, and resembling an English village, though more neat and compact. The houses are small and white-washed; they consist principally of shops and lodging-houses, the former retailing the wares of India and Europe at an advanced price, the latter giving a temporary home to the passenger in the India fleets. It also contains a church, a tavern, barracks, and (what would be better in any other situation) a burying ground. Several batteries and posts surround it on all sides."*

And so this, too, is what Napoleon saw when he finally opened his eyes to daylight in Jamestown from a room at the house of Mr Porteous, to which he had been guided the previous evening. The late disembarkation was his own choice, while for two days he had lurked on board to shun the great crowds gathered to gawk along the shoreline. And even when, after sunset on the second day, he finally made the short journey from the old landing steps and alongside the ramparts to the house that stood just opposite St James' Church, the crowds were still pressing enough to be held at bay by soldiers with fixed bayonets. The landing that Napoleon used is still intact, sitting apart from our present day Steps, yet not defined with any historic plaque that tells us so.

Napoleon did not care for Jamestown, its perceived stuffiness, or its staring crowds, and his first day ashore was not yet over before he resolved to remove himself from the capital as swiftly as possible. A house, investigated the previous day by Admiral Cockburn and Napoleon's accompanying Grand Marshall Count Bertrand as a likely residence for his captivity, lay five miles distant at Longwood – the somewhat ramshackle summer residence of the island's Lieutenant Governor Colonel and Mrs Skelton. And so Napoleon took to a horse and the cool mountain air, and gladly left the town behind. However, though the threesome took breakfast with the Skeltons at Longwood, the house was far from habitable, and Napoleon was glumly forced to retrace his steps towards Jamestown.

But luck was on his side. Descending the steep curves of Side Path as he once again approached the town, he glanced down into a snug hollow and spied The Briars - a small house fully occupied at the time by Mr and Mrs William Balcombe (an agent of the EEIC) and their five children. It caught his fancy, and so, after diverting to investigate, and spilling charm over the bemused owners, it was agreed that – at least while Longwood House was under renovation – the notorious ogre of Europe would take up temporary residence in the tiny summerhouse that stood in the grounds of The Briars, some thirty yards from the main house. Within hours Napoleon had sent for his collapsible iron campaign bed, and he never again set foot in Jamestown.

The pretty pavilion consisted of just one room in which Napoleon made himself comfortable, though Colonel Bingham, Commanding Officer of the garrison, considerately extended this space by having his men set up a marquee on the lawn outside it. The Balcombes donated a small round table, for eating and writing at, an armchair and other chairs, and he lived here in the *"friendliest of atmospheres"* for nearly two months while Longwood House was being renovated, spending the mornings dictating his memoirs to the faithful Count Las Cases who, with his young son, had moved into the cramped attic above. After dinner he strolled in the garden. Or, sometimes, if they had no other guests, Napoleon would pass an evening with the Balcombe family – whom he described as *"excellent people"* – playing whist, singing songs in French and English (even though he preferred Italian opera above other music), or discussing novels. And over these months a diverting friendship that grew between him and the Balcombes' vivacious French-speaking 13-year-old daughter, Betsy, filled the emptier hours. Though much has been written to decry this unusually close association between the 46-year-old General and a young girl, there is no historical evidence whatsoever of romance between the two. The fact is, Napoleon was fond of children and so, separated from his own – a son now wrested back into the maternal bosom of Napoleon's wife, the former Princess Marie-Louise of Austria – he understandably made much of Betsy's company.

Testament to his attachment to his family, soon hung on the walls of the Pavilion – miniature portraits of the erstwhile Empress and his adored young son, the King of Rome – which had always hung in his campaign tents. From his cargo of possessions on the ship, Napoleon also sent for a favourite silver-fitted dressing-case which resided atop a chest of drawers, and, dating from his magnificent Tuileries days, the highly decorated gold and silver Athenian tripod washstand made for him by his Paris goldsmith, Martin-Guillaume Biennais who, incidentally, had also styled the gold laurel wreath with which Napoleon had famously crowned himself Emperor of the French in 1804. Also, Marchand his faithful valet, had so detested their first congealed evening meal brought to the Briars from the town, that he had soon sent for the official chef, Pierron, together with a cottage stove and appropriate linen and silver for the Emperor; and with improved dining accomplished, Marchand, and Ali the second valet, then settled down for the night as bodyguards to Napoleon, wrapped in cloaks and sleeping on old mattresses from the *Northumberland* outside his door. (Born Louis Etienne Saint-Denis, Ali was in fact a well-educated young Frenchman whom the Emperor, for apparently whimsical reasons back in 1811, colourfully transformed into his personal Mameluke – a slave-soldier of an ancient and powerful scimitar-wielding Muslim military caste – dressed him in Oriental wear, and had him rebaptised. But Ali was later, perhaps more suitably, appointed librarian and copyist to the French Household in St Helena, of the scores of letters and memoires that eventually flowed from Longwood.)

Though the Balcombes' house was long ago demolished, some of the trees around the small patch of lawn where we stand gazing at Napoleon's view are the originals, JJ tells us as we wait for the imported lawyers to join us. And, as an illuminating tour guide for the French Properties, he is identifying them for Chris and me when we hear a joyful shout: "We're here at last! We got lost!" And Edgar the Defence appears from an unexpected direction, trailed by Mike and Tony. It was Chris's idea to join this group, reminding me that we have not been on a guided tour of Longwood House – as is the habit when local sights are close to home – since a gardener casually showed us around the museum seventeen years ago. So now is the hour, with Chris's holiday wearing down, JJ giving the talk, and this tiny group of fellow-tourists as company.

With the small Pavilion quickly disposed of, we drive in convoy up Side Path and past Alarm Forest to the Tomb, parking at the side of the shady road that rims the Devil's Punchbowl, making our way down a precipitous grass path into Sane Valley. This burial spot was personally chosen by Napoleon when illness persuaded him that he would never return to France. Still overlaid with tall trees and birdsong, a plain slab marks the empty grave, uninscribed because his petulant English captors refused to add *Emperor* to his name. So there it lies today, undeclared but protected by staunch iron railings that replaced a bored sentry who guarded the spot throughout the nineteen years of Bonaparte's peaceful interment after his death on 5 May 1821, until his remains were finally fetched away to Les Invalides in Paris in 1840.

The French frigate *Le Belle Poulle* was the ship commissioned to bring the warrior home, carrying with it HRH the Prince de Joinville and several members of Napoleon's Longwood household that initially had comprised an illustrious band of Marshall and Countess Bertrand, Count and Countess Montholon, General Gourgaud, Count Las Cases and his son, and eight servants. To avoid prying eyes, the exhumation took place at midnight on 14 to 15 October, in a sturdy downpour, commemorating that long-ago anniversary of Napoleon's arrival in 1815. And at last the coffin was set upon a hearse fashioned from a former Governor's carriage and sombrely drawn by four horses to Jamestown – a long and impressive procession headed by a detachment of St Helena Militia, the French contingent of dignitaries and their ship's officers, the island's Governor (now General Middlemore), and his officials. Bringing up the rear of the cortege, came a company of the Royal Artillery, all wending their way at such a snail's pace down the mountain to Jamestown that it was four o'clock in the afternoon before the town's outskirts were reached. From this point the route was lined all the way to the Landing Steps by soldiers bearing reversed arms, and at the steps a short handover ceremony was held between General Middlemore and the Prince de Joinville before the imperial coffin was lowered into a boat from *La Belle Poulle*. Then, accompanied by a volley of salutes fired from all the French and British ships in the roads, the dead Emperor was carried into the custody of his countrymen. Three days later, the French started on their journey home.

It is an island on its own, the spot that marks the tomb, a quiet and secluded place, indisputably rural. More emotive, by far, than the marble edifice of Les Invalides in Paris where Napoleon's body now rests in extravagant splendour. For the sylvan little dell that he selected, even as a temporary place, shows a gentler, perhaps more human side of the great megalomaniac Emperor whom we more commonly see in our mind's eye astride a great white horse in battle, or raising an imperial crown to his own head. And one cannot help but wonder at his ignominious end. How are the mighty fallen.

Longwood House was hardly a palace either, though the house that now represents the residence of Napoleon's captivity is so elegant a world-class museum that JJ's description of Napoleon's household at dinner almost defies imagination. There they sat, the gathered throng of Emperor, ladies and gentlemen – nightly attired in up-to-the-neck full evening dress and tight bodices – crammed together around a medium-sized table in a medium-sized room. There were gaps in the floorboards where rising damp caused mould on the wallpaper, while rats played in the corridors just outside. It was a room where fires were kept burning in the grate day and night in the hope of combating the dreadful dampness, which only caused insufferable humidity in the room. "Dinner," says JJ, who describes with imaginative flair the fine Sevres china, the crystal glasses, and the precious silver brought from France, "was a ten-minute affair. The poor people could not stand the surroundings, the smell, the smoke, or the heat. They gobbled their food and were out of there as soon as possible." Next door is Napoleon's bedchamber where he would lounge in bed and read, sit in a chair and read, or lie in the deep iron bath in an adjoining room, and read. What else was there for him to do?

By the time he grew ill, he had already dictated his memoirs, using the grand billiard table to lay out maps of reference rather than play billiards, and after his enjoyable picnic breakfast with Colonel Doveton at Mount Pleasant in 1820, he never took another meal outside Longwood. The house was ringed by watchful soldiers round the clock, recording his every move, and their presence inhibited any sense of freedom he might even have gained from the gardens which he himself designed with sunken paths and gazebos where he might hide from view a little. And by then, anyway, he was ill with what intelligent research defines as cancer of the stomach, a condition that killed not only his own father but also a sister and a brother, since suggestions of arsenic poisoning by the English have never gained foundation. At Longwood House there is just one portrait that does not show the normally podgy cheeks and pouting lips with which the world is so familiar. This is not a picture painted to gratify a glorious Emperor; but it is, oddly, the portrait we like best of him – rather as one feels empathy with his solitary burial spot in Sane Valley – for it shows the lines of illness and tired eyes of a weary man, and brings a touch of reality to a truly extraordinary legend.

The lawyers are just as entranced by the tour as Chris and I, and so it falls to me to photograph them for posterity against a backdrop of Napoleon's house before we leave. And it is while they pose in the late afternoon sun, before the famous green lattice porch of Longwood's front entrance, that JJ wrings magic. "It's such a beautiful evening," he announces, unexpectedly reappearing around a corner with an irresistible basketful of glasses and wine bottles, "that if you're not in a rush, we should have a drink in the garden." And so it is that as the sun sets in glorious technicolor upon a tiny British island in mid-Atlantic – the evening bathed in brilliant pink and orange that brings to an end an entirely marvellous afternoon – a congenial group of friends and acquaintances arrange ourselves along the rim of Napoleon Bonaparte's tricorn-shaped fishpond and happily demolish two bottles of deep red wine.

23.

Flying without Wings

January to June 2006

Christmas 2005 has passed, with the family together as usual, our sixth at the Villa. After eighteen months of residence with us, Stuart is becoming accustomed to pinning the top star on the veranda's Christmas tree while Virginia and I fuss around with other details of tree-dressing. Christopher, with a fortifying glass of wine beside him, helpfully loops hooks into ornaments for hanging, and hands them on to us while traditional snowy songs from old Christmas CDs are challenged by an exuberant but repetitive *Jingle Bells* from the deafening electric keyboard at New Bridge. Only Richard, having written the last of his final school exams just days before he flew to Namibia to board the RMS at Walvis Bay – a call that conveniently shortens what has already become for us Michel's forecast "long bus ride" – is not yet part of Christmas. He is still in post-school shock, his skinny length extended in a wicker chair, arms hanging limply at his sides as he mentally tweaks plans for a gap year backpacking trip around Europe in the coming year. Though we've spent hours planning his itinerary together, I'm already suffering pangs of separation anxiety. For if anything goes wrong over there, I can't reach him. I can't even reach his mobile phone from here.

However, he can reach me, I soon discover once both my menfolk have returned to Cape Town and Richard has duly been forwarded to the wild blue yonder. He sends a few wildly abbreviated emails as he crosses from London through Holland to the rest of Europe, which tell me where he is. And then I receive a call *from* his mobile: "Mom, I've just arrived by train at Hamburg station and I don't like the look of this city. Where shall I go now?" Here, as far from the Outside World as one can be, I frantically conjure up a mental map of Germany as seconds of airtime tick by. "Berlin?"

"That's next week."

"Lübeck?"

"Okay, 'bye."

I can't construct a full sentence on Lübeck, but the next email informs me it was a good suggestion. He spent Easter there and visited the biggest church-organ in the world. Some weeks and many short emails later I receive another call: "I've just arrived in Basel by train, but I forgot my camera in Munich. I'm bleak. Just to tell you I'm going back for it." *Oh? Okay.* Six hours later he phones again, St Helena's heart-jumping international call double-ring echoing through the house. I snatch it up.

The voice is infinitely more ebullient now: "I got my camera – they had it at the hostel. Just to let you know. 'Bye." The boy's alright on his own and he's seen every stick and stone of Europe, from the sublime to the ridiculous, intelligently. "I told you not to worry," says my friend Mabel who understands, like all Saints, about distance from family. "He's fine on his own. Cape Town's not really closer if he doesn't need you."

As months advance through this fresh year of 2006 we, in St Helena, are adapting to new changes. At Villa Le Breton chaos reigns, with pneumatic drills juddering the house as tracts of our hideous back yard are uprooted and trundled away on wheelbarrows. I am now paying the price, of course, for the brilliant notion, conceived so easily last year, to extend and improve this wonderful old domain with a large *en suite* bathroom for our bedroom and a small private sitting room alongside. The space below will metamorphose into a generous utility room with a wall of store cupboards, and give us also a much needed downstairs loo. But the birthing of preparations for this task was not an easy one, naturally. And delays from our draughtsman, and from Legal & Lands, while I counted hours to boarding the ship to Cape Town, took their toll on my placid nature. It was necessary – vital, in fact – to gain approval for our plans before I left the island in order to shop, in that great metropolis, for all the building materials (barring cement blocks) that I would need for the entire operation. And without approval we would not proceed.

But approval came through as I headed for the Wharf, and when I returned to St Helena in October, I brought with me everything from Italian tiles to six-inch nails. After these mounting years of residence, I am now fully familiar with St Helena's retail shortcomings, so nothing was left to chance.

Enclosed on three sides by thick walls, the noise in the yard is deafening, and Iris – sister-in-law of faithful Zander and just returned from a few years in England – fights a losing battle with dust as she settles into Annette's three-year-vacant place. Mimi has cleared off in a huff to the neighbours' more peaceful garden at Blundens, and sad though we are, I'm half-relieved that Harry's quiet death in December released him of this traumatic intrusion for a cat of such venerable age. Succumbing to a series of light strokes, he now lies comfortably beneath the guava tree behind the ornamental pedestal at the bottom of the garden, with banana leaves lining his bed and a frangipani bloom between his paws.

The whole house feels like a warehouse. Richard's requisitioned bedroom stores planks of African rosewood, and light fittings, doors, handles, paints, varnishes and grouting, ornaments for the new bathroom, mirrors, framed pictures, screws and bolts. It should be housing four large Georgian sash windows as well, but Cape Town supplied Victorian ones in error, which have already sailed back there with Chris, at great palaver. A cracked lavatory cistern was another discovery we made upon unveiling the many cartons of bathroom furniture stacked on the upper veranda, and that too has been returned across the seas. It all spells added expense and delays while our carefully chosen wares make their way through the rigmaroles of import all over again – especially as the RMS is undertaking a voyage to distant Tristan da Cunha this February, followed by a voyage to England, leaving us stranded for much longer than usual. If the replacement windows aren't on the next voyage, it could be nearly mid-year before I receive them.

The hardstanding under the jacaranda tree is stacked with cartons of terracotta tiles for the utility room and Italian marble for the bathroom, protected from rain by flapping tarpaulins. It took six of us to pile them there, hauled from Larry 'Nails's container at the Wharf into his truck with stevedore assistance, but by our own fair hands from the truck parked outside the gate at Villa Le Breton. Stuart and Larry worked manfully, and the rest of us helped as best we could, whinging a little, with Virginia and I comparing calloused fingers afterwards. All of it might have been easier if the Duke Boys' truck was not in the repair shop at the time – the only private truck on the island fitted with a crane that could have hoisted the loads over the wall and straight to the hardstanding.

Our new team of builders, reputedly blessed with knowhow and efficiency, does not display the light-heartedness of my familiar former merry trio of Pat, Gibby and Growler. There are no jokes or banter, no laughter during working hours, and I miss the jollity. But the job is going well. Our ancient sewage pipes are now exposed and we see how they run at an upwards slant towards Cambrian House, so now are not surprised by past years of troubles in that department. I leave them to level things out, and take refuge on the veranda, watching fire engines droning up Side Path all day with tanks of water for Longwood which has run out of it again. The entire expanse of Longwood is serviced by two meagre tanks, it appears, and I'm puzzled that another couple have never been added to supplement them. "The trouble is, the government doesn't play chess," says Bish when he pops in for coffee and watches the coming and going on the hillside with equal fascination. "No one thinks ahead in this place. Everyone's content with two small tanks when they're full, but no one plans for a drought. Yet there's enough winter rain at Longwood to see everyone through summer." It crosses my mind that everyone has lately begun voicing grievances more openly. That is one of the more subtle changes to which we are adapting.

St Helena is advancing into a new era of free press that offers alternative reading to the government-sponsored *St Helena Herald*, and it's a brave new world we face these days. Headed by the same Mike Olsson who set up SaintFM radio not quite a year ago, the quarto-sized *St Helena Independent* has burst into print media with blaring headlines, outspoken editorials, and questions asked that are thrusting and vital, and the government squirms beneath the onslaught. Suddenly political taboos are brought to shining focus. And, most interestingly of all, letters to the *Independent* begin to reflect the voices of islanders in a litany of uncertainties that reveal for the first time what the population is really thinking. The government hates it. DfID deplores it. The *St Helena Independent* – like its big sister SaintFM Radio – is available for instant download on internet all over the world, and our secrets are out.

There's continuing confusion about the Airport, of course; for in the ten months since Governor Clancy's go-ahead announcement at Plantation House last Commonwealth Day, March 2005, nothing has materialised except a rather overzealous publication, last December, of a government brochure entitled *St Helena Strategy*. For all to savour, a jaunty timeline predicts that Airport construction work will start between 2005 and 2007, meaning that air services will be ready to commence in 2010. This will apparently bring St Helenians flooding home from much more lucrative employment in the United Kingdom, Ascension, and the Falklands, to return the resident population to above 5 000 for the *"first time in twenty years"*. (Could they mean: For the first time in *four* years, perhaps?) By then we also will be welcoming daily air movements at the Airport, *plus* monthly cruise ship traffic… *Monthly? Does this infer that fleets of cruise liners will suddenly prefer the wild South Atlantic Ocean in the midst of winter to returning to Europe for the northern summer as they have done for decades?* The jauntiest item, however, is the information that from 2020 St Helena can expect 20 000 tourists per annum to visit this island, at which point all UK government budgetary aid will cease. Good for DfID. Not so good for St Helena which, by the very nature of this island and her people, cannot possibly be financially independent by then.

By this first quarter of 2006, SHELCO, so buoyed by new enthusiasms just a year ago, has once again been elbowed out of the picture, and we can only guess that perhaps the motives are greed on DfID's part, since this fine UK government department is now in charge of planning. Yet they have done little but talk about environmental impact studies, more feasibility studies, arrangements for management policy, developmental work, and construction procurement plans; talk that means nothing at all to the average St Helenian now entering the seventh year of waiting for a single sod to be turned at Prosperous Bay Plain. The only tangible thing the island has gained from this takeover is another DfID Air Access Project Manager, and it is he, in faraway London, who leaps to life in the face of some caustic printed comments about inactivity. Into print he falls: *"Please have confidence in all those…who are working hard to deliver the airport, and don't believe everything you hear on the rumour mill."* Nicknamed Guitar for good reason, this expert's overplayed enthusiasms for St Helena's future prosperity under an Airport are a tad relentless, and pleasant though he is, some sigh at yet another onslaught of his Utopian ideals at each of his frequent visits. So frequent, in fact, that he permanently stores his recreational guitar on the RMS so that he is not forced to lug it about the world with him, and plays it long and often on his voyages. Wondering how many guitars he owned, I was, in fact, once moved to inquire, "Do you gather your wife and three children around you each evening when you open the front door, and give them concerts like you do on the ship and the island?" He looked amazed at such a notion. "No, I never play my guitar at all except on the ship and the island."

The *Independent* swoops on this latest press release concerning our golden future: *"Methinks he dost protest too much!"* it screams in an editorial, asking as we all do: *"Are we really sure we are looking forward…to a bright and prosperous future; or on the contrary to a slow, irreparable collapse of our infrastructure, accompanied by a continual exodus of the most skilled and valued people on the island… Is St Helena crumbling, or is it on the edge of a dramatic period of economic expansion? Is it Paradise Island, or a box of chocolates with no chocolates inside?"*

Indeed there seem to be minimal chocolates inside these days, and none with luscious fillings. But those who carry St Helena in their blood or in their hearts still keep tight hold of its truly beautiful box, looking back with nostalgia on the chocolates once enjoyed. And as the island inexorably deteriorates, Saints begin to wonder if the British government has some ulterior motive for this airport since the surviving population is no longer young enough to man it and all that it entails.

Within the first four months of 2006, Guitar is back on the island, this time accompanied by a full contingent of other DfID experts. Suddenly there is much afoot. Graphic drawings and plans are displayed outside the Tourist Office at the Canister, meetings are held across the island, and I join a well-attended talk at the Consulate

Hotel one Tuesday night. With SHELCO's short-but-steep airport-machinery access plans now jettisoned for good, half the meeting deals with DfID's projected and massively expensive 13km "Haul Road" to be built from the stony beach at Rupert's Bay, up the steep valley behind, across Deadwood Plain and the settlement at Longwood, and over the desolate wastes of Prosperous Bay Plain to the site of the Airport – just to transport machinery and materials for constructing a runway. A small dock for ships will also be constructed at Rupert's, the next bay to Jamestown, and it seems natural that the RMS could tie up there. "Oh, no," says DfID with some surprise at such a preposterous idea from the floor. "It won't be deep enough for the draught of the RMS, and besides, we won't need the RMS once the Airport's here." Guitar doesn't live here, you see. He does no shopping, for a start, and someone else feeds him.

But it's the second half of the meeting that gets to me. I am stunned by what I witness in that hall. Afterwards I go home and write all my agitation and disbelief into a letter to the *St Helena Independent*. The next morning I am no less angry, so I send the letter. When it is published it takes up a full A4 page of the newspaper. It starts: *"On Tuesday night when public discussion regarding HIV/AIDS arose at the Access Meeting at the Consulate, I could not take the mike because I was lost for words – struck absolutely speechless by the naïveté of those who so eagerly leapt to their feet around me. St Helena, what are you thinking? What extraordinary complacency leads you to believe that HIV – the scourge of the entire globe – has miraculously bypassed this chosen island?...Aids has been an identifiable sexually-transmitted disease for over twenty years – during which time the island has certainly not remained celibate..."*

Well, that's an understatement if ever there was one. Many St Helenian girls – pretty, vivacious, and generously warm-blooded – are world-renowned for their eager favours, on ships, in the seedy side of ports, with anybody's husband, ready and waiting even as yachts drop anchor in the bay, while certain RMS crewmen happily make free with prostitutes in Cape Town. Yet the public line is: *"We have no HIV on the island."*

At this meeting I hear much about singling out African workers who *might* be contracted for heavy work on the airport, and nearly the entire vociferous meeting rises to its feet to object. Africans will bring HIV, we hear. They must be screened for HIV before they get here, or the whole population might succumb to this dreaded scourge through breathing their air – or so is the ignorant implication. But at no point is a suggestion made that women might simply resist sleeping with these workers (even though Africans are almost universally despised by Saints) to avoid contracting the disease – or, God forbid, use a condom. No suggestion of local screening is ever made. No yachtsmen are screened, no visitors from strange countries, no white or Coloured South African visitors – but here the whole island is decreeing that all South African blacks *must* automatically be tested before setting foot on this hallowed ground. I find the screamed discrimination ugly, and the sheer ignorance about AIDS nauseating. Before long, even cries of Africans "raping and pillaging" are offered in the hysteria, and I let fly in the letter, voicing my anger at both issues: the attitude of mistaken belief that this island is the centre of the universe, warning that the nation had better learn to accommodate foreigners if indeed we do, actually, get the promised Airport; and at the island's unforgivable ignorance regarding this illness at this late stage, and its presumptuous belief in natural immunity from it. It is not as though the threat has been ignored by the medical fraternity; five years ago the *St Helena Herald* ran a double-page spread on AIDS in which one of the island's doctors wryly commented: *"Condoms are not showing any signs of being increasingly popular whilst sex remains very popular."* And as long ago as the late '80s, the then Senior Medical Officer was writing warning articles in the newspaper about the horrors of free sex and AIDS. *"Based on the spectacularly uninformed reaction from the floor at the Access Meeting,"* my continuing letter suggests, *"real money should be spent on a massive and dedicated sex-protection education campaign that includes the free and ready-availability of thousands of condoms throughout the island."*

Within hours of Friday's publication I receive eleven phone calls commending me on my "courage" to write what needed to be said and agreeing with my sentiments, and I am vastly relieved. It could so easily, in this climate of increasing racial hatred, have gone the other way. But the ignorance is indisputable. An expatriate who once worked with AIDS victims told me she was asked by a worried Saint: "What do

HIV sufferers actually *look* like?"

"Just like you and me," she replied, explaining patiently that until full-blown AIDS develops, there are no physical signs at all.

Others ask: "What if HIV sufferers come into our restaurants?" There's only one answer, really; they're probably there already, even if we dare not speak about it. But there is one good spinoff from that meeting. Within a year, we will welcome a South African AIDS counsellor on a three-year contract, with condoms soon clearly displayed for the taking at many shops.

Since the Rupert's Haul Road showed up on a drawing, the Airport has crept inexorably closer. Of course, it still exhibits the old dance we have long grown used to – one step forward, three back. And while in March the *Independent* reiterates that *"We are two months away from issuing tender documents for airport construction,"* by May we are being informed that there's been a "delay". Rumour says September, but DfID reminds us that in July *"three visiting consortia"* will arrive on the island. Of course, by the time July comes, the three consortia have pulled out of the project altogether – because DfID expects them to foot all the bills for risks!

However the project wins marks for sheer tenacity. At a private sector seminar hosted by the Chamber of Commerce, the Governor comments on an *Investment Policy for St Helena* draft document developed from various reports offered by outside experts and recently released by the Castle. *"You need investment, and you need to be looking to tourism as the main economic driver for that investment,"* explains the Governor. Perks are offered to new businesses starting up within six months of the Airport opening; which leads to a question about proposed tourist development of some of the more attractive buildings in Jamestown, presently utilised by the government. The Governor warms to his subject: *"Jamestown needs to develop a carnival atmosphere,"* he replies disarmingly. *"We could do things like closing the road on Sundays so that restaurants could put out their tables and chairs on the street."* He's clearly studied those *22 Pages* quite closely, but alas, a year after they appeared there are still barely any restaurants. And St Helena, in any case, never would open on a day of rest, not for a tourist.

Joe Terry of SHELCO – again inexplicably flying the island without wings but doggedly pursuing the proposed environment-friendly hotel on SHELCO's behalf – puts up his hand. *"What guarantees would be in place for businesses wanting to invest here?"*

"None!" replies the Governor. *"There can be no guarantees. All we can do is offer incentives, rather than guarantees."*

Joe knows that at first hand. Perhaps he just asked the question out of irony. For into one of our periodic surges of Airport-projection-and-tourism-upgrade-fever a few months back, came one of the happiest occurrences St Helena has enjoyed in years. An advertisement of Intent published in the local press, as the law demands. In it Joe's wife, Daisy – a multitalented product of the Philippines – expressed her plans to open an Oriental restaurant in Jamestown. The site was already chosen, all furniture and equipment already on provisional standby with suppliers abroad, and she was ready to start as soon as the technicalities of a licence had been breached. For weeks no one talked of anything else, for the restaurant promised a popular mix of Asian dishes, and in this culinary desert which we inhabit we can't wait for a real restaurant to open.

It was Bish who brought the news when it broke, heading down our garden path at a veritable sprint. "This place will never survive on its own! The fools have turned it down!"

I'd just emerged from long communication with a book about ancient olive trees in Europe and was on some placid foreign plain altogether, not sure what had been turned down this time. But as the cogs of my mind hazily readjusted to the vagaries of St Helena, I assumed that it had something to do with the Immigration Control Board which shows a distinct fetish for turning down anything that might benefit the island – a recent victim being a Namibian company that wished to set up game fishing for tourism in St Helena, bringing its own boats. Another expatriate application, this one for setting up a small hotel in the long-empty Porteous House at the bottom of Main Street, was denied on the grounds that the St Helenian owners of the Consulate Hotel "would not welcome the competition".

"Who's turned down what now?"

"Those Mother Grundies at the ICB have *turned down* the Oriental restaurant!"

"WHY?"

"Because, evidently, 'we don't need any more restaurants', and 'anyway Saints can cook eastern food themselves.' I've never heard such rubbish in my life!" I saw I might need to dispense a whisky and soda to soothe him – and perhaps one for me too – but for the moment I was too shocked to move. St Helena, we all know, is a funny place, and I was supposed to laugh – *ha-ha-ha-ha!* But I really wanted to burst into tears of frustration. Weren't we promised the Airport so that tourism would render us financially viable? There was too much to ponder in one go, most of it taking energy just to move into the same mental galaxy as the Immigration Control Board… *Oh-oh-oh-oh!*

Bish sank into a chair. "Racism here is something terrible!"

I knew at once what he meant. And it is not only pale Saint against dark Saint in their own island, but also Saint against foreigners. What chance did Daisy stand as an expat *and* a Filipina?

But after Chris had returned to Cape Town in January, he delivered some welcome news on this perplexing subject. "The Governor and I were chatting on the ship," he told me, "and he whispered that he had carefully considered the impassioned letter you wrote him about the restaurant fiasco. He's going to overturn the ICB's decision on the Oriental restaurant. He has the power to do that. Because when the island gets an airport, St Helena *has* to start moving into the 20th Century." Chris laughed. "He knows, like everyone else, that island tourism is still light years from the 21st Century!" Later, with the Governor's decision made public, the battle gained momentum. Five members of the Immigration Control Board resigned forthwith, and even though a new Board was set up a month later, letters continued to flow to the press on the subject. So much so that by mid-March even the feisty *St Helena Independent* was pleading for a stop to *"hatred for individuals or people of certain origin"*, but it did not halt the vitriol.

The old ICB, sadly, did not hold the patent on hatred. We have for some time been visited by American Supply ships – those that carry vast armament stores and mobile hospitals in anticipation of World War Three starting at some country nearby – which drop anchor in James Bay for several weeks at a time while their crews enjoy a little R&R among the friendly inhabitants of St Helena. And one such American sailor, witnessing a drunken brawl between two Saints in Jamestown, made a benevolent attempt to separate them. For his trouble, he was beaten to the ground and kicked so badly in the head, and his eye so badly damaged, that he was promptly rushed back to his ship and flown to New York. Yet, notes the *Independent* some long time later, no official mention was ever made locally about the incident, and since then there has been a noted absence of American Supply ships in James Bay.

And then Chris phones from Cape Town. "I have just read the strangest article," he tells me. "It's in the *Financial Mail*, and it's written by a passenger on a little Russian ship returning from a cruise to Antarctica."

I name such a ship that calls each year.

"That's the one. Apparently one of their crew went ashore at St Helena, got set upon by Saints, and was horribly injured. But they didn't take him to Jamestown hospital – they took him back to his ship. The ship set sail for Ascension, and the man died on the way. That's manslaughter – but you've never mentioned it."

"Because I've never heard anything about it!" Wondering how I'd missed such a dire event in the news or at the Coffee Shop, I rush to piles of back copies of both *The Herald* and *The Independent*, but not a line refers to this calamity. We never do hear a single word on the island to hint of it, yet there are the facts, in clear black and white in the revered South African *Financial Mail*. I ask one of our local legal fraternity about it, and he dons a discomfited expression: "I might have heard something…" And then he walks away. I don't like cover-ups. Ugly and deeply unsettling, they surely emanate from some government source for the *St Helena Independent* would not have let this go willingly. Cover-ups issue also from letters that whine petulantly, *"Media should only write nice things that make St Helena look good,"* to which the *St Helena Independent* retorts: *"We don't believe you can promote anything without being truthful."* The sad truth is, of course, that if things were really as good as we wish, there would be nothing to cover up.

24.

The More Things Change...

May to July 2006

South African doctor's wife, Elsa, has not drawn breath since she climbed into my car in Maldivia Road. She sits in the back with Stuart's youngest sister, Toni, and talks. And she talks and talks and talks. It is all cheerful chatter, amusing, ebullient, bestowing on our sortie the exuberance of a school outing – which it is, in a way, since every schoolchild on the island is headed in the same direction. History is being made today and Elsa, Stuart, Toni and I, for all our worldliness, are as excited as everyone else. We've brought a picnic, and as usual are armed with everything from sunhats to zip-up rain jackets piled in the back of the car. And cameras, of course. Today we're going to see an aeroplane.

Though this event was planned for July a year ago, in the way of St Helena time it is happening ten months late. But finally the whole island is gathering to watch an overflight of the proposed Airport site at Prosperous Bay Plain by a South African Hercules C130 which took off from Walvis Bay at dawn this morning, exercised to test wind and visibility issues and to assess the lie of our proposed runway. Only one runway now, since SHELCO's sensible dual-runway plan has been tossed out of the window. Hercules aircraft are not the planes planned for St Helena's illustrious new life, of course, but in the present scheme of things, are among the few that can carry enough fuel for a return journey to Namibia.

We are a cheery party arriving at the small buildings called Bradley's Garage which stand solitarily in the semi-desert wastes of Prosperous Bay Plain. Hundreds of cars and buses are parked all around it and, gathered on the ridge before the terrain drops down to the Airport site, almost all the able population of the island is staring skywards. Among dozens of teachers I recognise, Virginia is supervising her class of eight-year-olds from Harford Middle School, and beyond her I soon spot the white hair of the Governor shining like a beacon in the black-haired crowd, the suits of half the Legislative Council, and hundreds of familiar faces among the throng. We zip up our rain jackets against the chill breeze, wear sun hats against the damp, and wish we had brought gloves while we take up position with eyes glued to the south east. Morning fog swirls – as always around this site – with light rain falling and the Peaks behind us invisible through low cloud swathing the central island. So our gaze yields little to entertain us while we wait, except an occasional view of the old signal house that tops a peak on the far side of the airport. Here a dastardly deed was committed in 1904, when two brothers shot a watchman there one night in a murder so foul it is today remembered in the New Museum. However, though the story is well-published in most histories of the island, the museum has somehow 'forgotten' the surname of the perpetrators in order to spare family connections – one of the most common names on the island.

The land around us is rough and uneven, given to little rifts, bumpy hillocks, and occasional spreads of wild *mesembryanthemums* greening the yellow-brown view. Now and then wirebirds skitter across the lenses of binoculars, highlighting concern for the continuing survival of this island's only existing endemic bird whose habitat will soon be an airstrip. But we're confidently assured by airport planners that these shy little birds will be perturbed by neither building operations nor the terrifying roar of modern pterodactyls swooping over them from time to time. Beyond Signal Point the lands drops away in those daunting cliffs observed from the arriving RMS, and according to plans presented to us, any aircraft landing or taking off from this place will be faced not only by fog, but in their absence, crosswinds. Today burning tyres, with vacillating columns of thick black smoke spewing into the pristine air, have been laid along the runway route to outline the projected airfield for the coming Hercules. All that's missing is the actual plane.

It was due here at ten, but ten o'clock passes and our eyes are already watering from staring into the white glare of the morning fog.

The children are noisome and growing restless, and Virginia rolls her eyes when I glance at her. Elsa has wandered off to engage others with her ebullience, and Stuart and Toni are chatting. Toni, a single mother around thirty, is a quiet girl, rarely speaking without necessity; but Elsa's infectious loquaciousness has drawn giggles in the car and a bounce in her manner unfamiliar to me. Wearing disarming pigtails under a soft cloth hat, she looks little older than a schoolgirl herself today, and is clearly enjoying this unusual expedition.

A man from Air Safety Support International is supposedly on board the incoming Hercules, to look at the topographical layout – a heartening arrangement – and also two aviation consultants from the consultancy firm that wrings massive sums from DfID for the pleasure of chatting about our Airport. This should be quite a fun junket for the consultants, I imagine as we continue to wait for something to happen, for their coffers have already been generously enriched by DfID, with little to show for it but an incessant string of visiting experts. Their several millions, we feel, might have found far more practical use in St Helena itself, where roads deteriorate with every rain; where water is scarce in one area, brown in another, periodically contaminated in a third; where electricity is diesel-driven by aged ferry engines that frequently break down, supplying power that is expensive while the new second-hand wind turbines seldom turn. Education is also short on budget, as are medical and social-service care. And tourism, for all the talk of a glowing future down that road, cannot fund anything at all.

Someone shouts. Good grief, we can hear a plane! Forty-five minutes late, but it approaches somewhere through the misty dazzle. And then it bursts into view and we cheer. The schoolchildren, who have never seen a large aircraft before but know about space shuttles from television, give a requisite squeal of interest before resuming the games they started some time ago. The rest of us watch with the fascination of an imminent alien landing. The Hercules doesn't land, of course, because there is yet no runway, but it flies up and down, back and forth according to the black route offered by the belching tyres, and makes simulated landings and take-offs. It's really exciting – an event so unique here that I am rushing about with my camera, capturing every swoop and soar over the airport, searching frantically when it disappears into the slowly rising fog, and pointing again when it reappears. Once, it dives to little more than fifty feet above the ground, and though I cannot ascertain what the wirebirds are feeling, I suddenly realise that total panic reigns among the feral donkeys on the far side of the plain. They are running in terrified circles, unsure where to go, and even across the great distance between us and above the fading roar of the engine, we can hear their frightened screams. Why did no one herd them away?

The Hercules entertains us for a good hour, then makes a final sweep around the whole island, and the *Independent* later laments that if the RMS, staggering towards us from Namibia with a broken clutch, was not running thirty-three hours late, it might have made a marvellous photo-opportunity to snap both together at James Bay. Also in that report, the local St Helena Access Project Manager remarks that the trials had been very successful *"but also had taken their toll on the persons involved, due to the tensions and excitement of the day"* – leading cynics promptly to suggest that perhaps no more stressful aircraft should ever be brought to this beautiful haven again. However, perhaps the greatest irony lies in the fact that nearly twenty years ago, an identical pre-airport trial-flight – also by a Hercules C130 – was conducted over a similar stretch of this island. For all I know, it might have been the very same aircraft.

"At least a C130 was a good choice of plane for a test-drive," comments Bish over a family supper a while later. "It could be the plane of choice for alternative airport plans."

"Hardly," I scoff, recalling those Boeings in the Q5 posters. "No fare-paying passenger will travel in a Hercules!"

Bish bestows a smug smile upon the table. "What if, despite all the tourism talk, the British government has a hidden agenda, as rumour suggests?" He looks at Stuart. "DfID's Prison Reform Co-ordinator has been here recently, hasn't he?"

Stuart nods. "He brought plans for a High Security prison to be built in St Helena – way out in the country." A dawning light then passes over his face. "The site overlooks the *Airport*!"

"Why do you think we want a High Security prison in St Helena?"

A few names spontaneously leap to my mind: Charles Taylor, Saddam Hussein, Osama bin Ladan... This would not be the first time

St Helena was used for political prisoners. All eyes meet around the table as we ponder the implications of this news, and we're all thinking the same thing. Does not our very remoteness provide the solution to incarceration for today's terrorist? I can almost hear our new nickname: *St Guantanamo!*

"I've actually seen the signed blueprints, though hardly anybody knows about the existence of these plans. What do you think of that?"

"I think," I start slowly, "that nothing will enrage the island more than a cover-up. I think, if that's what the British government really wants to do here, they should have told us years ago and we could be moulding our lives around facts, rather than the fiction of a thriving tourist industry. I think, actually, that a prison like that might be St Helena's saving grace."

Virginia's aghast eyes are like saucers. "You want us to be a *prison* island?"

"We've been one for most of our history. An historian once also pointed out that, through the ages, the only times St Helena has ever been financially secure was when the military were stationed here – and that would probably happen again. I'm inclined to think that prison island status would be the better option, because I don't see how we will ever survive through tourism."

"Perhaps they want tourism *and* political prisoners?" suggests Stuart.

"Well, if DfID's experts are to be believed, one told me that a viable tourist industry needs 900 000 visitors a year! As it is, we can't hope to cope with the projected 20 000 we can evidently expect by 2020!"

Bish does quick sums in his head. "Nearly a million visitors means around 2 500 people a day! With overlap, it could mean 17 000 or 18 000 visitors here on any one day, milling around Jamestown, searching for somewhere to eat, a beach to lie on, and a little resort shopping. With no RMS to bring food."

Stuart asks, "Who comes up with these crazy ideas?"

Bish gives a wry chuckle. "Some chap at a desk in London who thinks we're in the real world. Like that visiting British MP who expected to find us in the Caribbean!"

"Maybe," comments Virginia thoughtfully, "we'd be better off as a prison island after all."

Bish resumes eating. "So we're back to the Hercules, aren't we?"

Not since Q5, over four years ago, has the island been in such cheerful mood. Outside the hospital, where participants are gathering, there's a scene of festive flamboyance and so many costumes, textures and vivid colours are intermingling that simply standing there is like swirling through a psychedelic whirlpool. Music blares from a lorry bedecked with palm fronds, bunting, balloons, streamers, bright paper, shining spangles; and the musicians who entertain us from the back of it are squeezed into the limited space the decoration has left. The Carnival hasn't yet started, but body-painted men, men in outlandish costume, girls in grass skirts or frothing with ostrich feathers, and broad-beamed women enveloped in wobbling balloons, are already dancing. The atmosphere is electric, vibrant, filled with shouted banter across the crowd as more and more people fill the square, and with laughter which has been in such short supply around here for too long. The lorry's keyboard, sax, and drums echo against the surrounding houses of Hospital Square, and then beat back at us from the cliffs on either side. This is St Helena's first Carnival procession, a fundraising drive devised and organised by Malcolm, a lively Assistant Purser on the RMS, who is home on leave to start up the brand new *"Cancer Support and Awareness Group"* – a society aiming to assist families suffering under the multiple stresses of that disease.

It's come too late for Margaret, Stuart's mother, who valiantly struggled under its onslaught until just a month ago when she died in Jamestown Hospital with four of her six children around her bed. She was a charming woman to whom I warmed immediately on the few occasions we had a chance to meet, and since it was her hope to join this very procession in a wheel-chair today, I would have been honoured to push her in it. I find her absence here poignant, but Stuart's sister Toni, and even Virginia – neither girls naturally given to public exhibition – have dressed up to join the fun in her behalf, for Margaret was a splendid mother.

The Carnival is one long party. After it starts from the hospital square, it snakes its way down Market Street, jangling money boxes, singing and shouting in sheer enjoyment, throbbing with recorded South American music when the band rests. The mood is infectious. Those who have not joined the dance itself are lining the route all the way to the congested bend at the Market, and everyone is smiling. People reach out to drop money into boxes, and once the dancers spread into the broader reaches of Main Street, spectators join in too, jigging and clowning happily among the splendid costumes that still are swirling and leaping. It takes two hours to cover the one-mile distance from top to toe of Jamestown, and by the time the Grand Parade is reached it is almost growing dusk. This is when the real party gets going, of course, but about that time I am making my way home to the sanctuary of my lovely half-chaotic house to enjoy a glass of wine in splendid stillness now that the builders have left for the day.

Six days a week the builders start at 8am, and I rush to be brushed and cleaned and downstairs before their tentacles probe the upper floor like the waving arms of an octopus. My bedroom has been commandeered and all its furniture, covered in old sheets, is huddled bemusedly in the middle of it, drawers, boxes, lamps and stools piled on the high four-poster bed, because a hole could be bashed through an outside wall there at any time, I am warned. As I work at my computer on the landing, planks of wood, lavatory cisterns, and drums of paint lurch past me in procession. If I sneak to the loo in the old baize-green bathroom, a face almost certainly will appear at the window, as they're working right outside it – so those excursions are curtailed to lunchtimes or, if I time things well, to a moment when they briefly confer on the ground floor. But sewage pipes are level at last, and the yard is covered with a smooth flat floor devoid of its old raised manhole covers and awkward gutters.

One new exterior wall, two bricks thick, encloses a room on the lower level, together with the solid walls of the kitchen, main house and boundary walls. But - I am assured by Boss Builder as his work ascends – two-brick thickness is *"defin'ly"* not viable for the upper storey, because *"this is the way things are done in St Helena"*. I am anguished by this revelation because my new Georgian sash windows (replaced in Cape Town) will now sit flush in their walls in a highly non-aesthetic arrangement. But Boss Builder is an expert in local construction and I soon learn that I cannot – and absolutely *may* not – argue with him on any score. Things are done differently here, I must accept. So, secretly mourning the sturdy brick cavity walls of South Africa that are more familiar to me, I hold my tongue while I watch the rising rows of ugly cement breeze-blocks that are the only local option, and when my blood pressure rises, I take myself into the garden. Hypertension is always an issue, I think, when builders take over your domain.

But tonight, euphoric from the fun of the Carnival, and with the house to myself for an hour or so, my little world is at peace. Two exquisite fairy terns are chatting in the jacaranda, making the funny tissue-paper-on-a-comb sound that is their conversation. Mynah birds have already set off for the roosting trees downtown, leaving relative quiet around me. Peaceful doves forage for supper before retiring while Mimi watches with beady eyes from the veranda, and the smaller birds – the chatty Java sparrows, tweeting canaries, vociferous waxbills – are crisscrossing the garden purposefully, homeward bound. Tessa and I wander to the lower terraces and once beside my heart-warming Shrubbery, I turn round to look inland, past the high white edifice of my gracious house, beyond the lush mango orchard at Cambrian House peeping from behind it, up the narrow curving valley to its very head where a cluster of the rounded volcanic-shaped hillocks of the Briars fill the gap around the Heart-Shape Waterfall before the Ridges start. Beyond those is a skyline of trees, and all is green up there, contrasting with the brown of these dramatic coastal cliffs that guard the town. How can one not absolutely adore this place, even as hope fades for its faltering future? Before I head back up to the house to pour a sunset glass of wine, I bend to wipe dust from the engraved pink marble slab at my feet, which we laid in the garden ourselves, and read the sentiments of my decades-long romance with this little place: *God gives all men all earth to love, but since man's heart is small, ordains for each one spot shall prove belovéd over all.* It is seven years since I came to sign the papers for this house, nearly six since the Season of Desolation, five since I started spending more time on this island than at my primary home. Have my sentiments changed? In the time that I've lived here, I have learned things about the island I never dreamed before. I have been stabbed in the back a few times, discovered streaks of personality I do not care for in a population world-famous for its charm, seen an overnight exodus of the island's brightest youth and a viable future go with it, and witnessed a smothering onslaught of politics quite beyond the island's control. But we, none of us in our family, came here expecting paradise, and our expensive and momentous move was akin to a marriage in some ways. For better or worse, in sickness and in health. And yes, strange but true, this is still a spot belovéd over all.

As the last of the applause fades in the packed Consulate Ballroom, the crowd heads for the door. The Ladies' Orchestra has tonight offered up *Supper and Soothing Sounds*, providing a melodic concert accompanied by Spaghetti Bolognese and Apple Crumble as a tempting menu, and an enjoyable evening. But it is late, after eleven-thirty, and I'm ready for bed. As the crowd disperses, Bish and I fall into step down the long length of the hotel's courtyard bar together, through the narrow neck of entrance passage to the front door, and out to the veranda steps.

"Where are you parked?" he asks as he stoops to pet a tiny stray kitten appearing at our feet on the pavement.

"At the bottom of the street, near Castle Gardens."

"So am I. I'll walk with you." Two steps later he turns. "This kitten's following us."

We leave the brightly-lit precincts of the Consulate, pass Solomon's darkened offices, pass Miss Helen George's neat blue house, and the kitten is still with us, skipping merrily between our feet, a most enchanting tiny thing, all colourful blotches and large round eyes. She is also – I discover as I investigate more closely in the street-light – alive with fleas and worms. She flops against my ankles affectionately and purrs. She's thin and barely more than six weeks old. "Calico cats, tortoiseshells like this, are my favourites," I idly remark into the night.

We walk on, past the Corkers with the old charabanc parked behind, and the newly-built Armstrong's house that has resuscitated a previous ruin. Past the still-empty Porteous House that could have been a guest house, and the large iron gates into Castle Gardens where Ann's Place is. My car is close by. "This kitten's still with us," I remark. She is rubbing up against my tyres, in fact.

"I suggest," says the Lord Bishop, senior cleric of St Helena and Ascension Islands, "that if she climbs into your car, you should take her home. She's too young to be allowed to wander the streets alone at midnight."

I completely agree, but I look around furtively nonetheless. "Would she need some help, do you think?" I whisper.

"Probably. She's very tiny and your car is high." He turns away to gaze up at the clock-tower of St James' Church in holy contemplation for a moment or two.

"Look, she's in my car after all!" I exclaim in surprise, and Bish steps up to look.

"Isn't that lucky! And she seems quite happy. She wants a good home. Off you go now."

Stuart, newly back from his shift, is in the kitchen when I walk in with this new acquisition, and either his exclamation of surprise or some sixth sense of occasion brings a sleepy-eyed Virginia all the way from the Cottage to investigate. "I knew something was going on," she observes matter-of-factly, immediately relieving me of the purring kitten and nestling it into her neck as though flee-infested midnight arrivals are a frequent occurrence. "She'll sleep in the cottage with us, and Stewey will bring some food and water. I'm going back to bed."

The union between Tessa and the kitten is unusually close. Just as Mimi welcomed Tessa's arrival with an admonishing "I'll suffer you only if you acknowledge that I am Boss Cat," so Tessa has become Louise's nursemaid. She plays with Louise, protects Louise, rough-and-tumbles with Louise, sending her flying in amiable games. She screeches angrily and bares her teeth when Louise sharpens claws on upholstery, and teaches Louise to investigate arrivals at the gate. Louise, now believing she's a dog, learns everything well, except how to bark.

When Stuart and I take her to A&NRD for worm pills and a check-over while Virginia's at work, the animal carers coo over her prettiness. "Same colours *ezzac'* as your dog!" they exclaim.

"Well, yes," I explain with a poker face. "Louise, being so small, was made of off-cuts from Tessa's coat, you see." They smile thinly, without humour, and tactfully refrain from commenting on my gross stupidity.

I've done my bit for the RSPCA so far this year, and gross stupidity wasn't involved in much of it. With the plight of our 150 retired donkeys suddenly plunged into the limelight by an expat with free time to investigate their conditions, the urgent need for a Donkey Sanctuary has emerged. Donkeys were, for generations, the island's workhorses, the carriers, the means for travelling to market, a family member that everyone nurtured. But in these days of excessive car imports (currently sixty to one hundred arriving twice a year when the RMS has visited England), the old donkey is forgotten. Seriously neglected in many cases, and shown cruelty in others. The expat we call Penny 'Donkey' – a fit and forceful individual – treats their chafed ankles, suppurating sores, softened hooves, and the rope-burns on their necks. She has even removed certain animals from their owners in an effort to save their lives, and feeds them herself. But now the island itself must take responsibility for them.

When the local RSPCA St Helena changed its name, for complicated reasons, to the St Helena SPCA, it was pointed out that our remit was not to *care* for animals but, as the title suggests, to *prevent cruelty*. So once we had set up a sanctuary, care of the donkeys would be out of our hands. Setting it up was, however, a project not unlike the Airport – first the consultations, then the reports. Michel, our Chairman, looks at me, and I know that look. "Alright," I sigh, "I'll do it."

The research takes me weeks and weeks. I am thorough to the last crossed *t*, though previously I knew little more about donkeys than to exclaim "Ah, sweet!" as I passed one on the road. They are lovable beasts, we all can see that, but I soon learn that they enjoy being in groups and should never be separated from a best friend, love peppermints and being scratched behind the ear, can live till fifty, but need this housing, that food, this medicine, so much water, hard floors, this tack... By the end of my research I have produced a tome of finely detailed information regarding every possible aspect of donkey comfort known to man, plus a little history (donkeys have worked since the Pharoahs first used them 6 000 years ago, and the first mention of them in St Helena is 1709 when there were nineteen on the island.). My document is so formidable, in fact, that I absolutely know that no one will read it except perhaps a builder who could use these specifications for a donkey shelter. So I start an additional, edited version, radically cropped for popular consumption, bringing the most salient facts forth in a Q&A style for the ordinary public.

By the time all is finished, I'm exhausted. Since I joined this society soon after the Heritage fiasco, Michel and I – combining my thrusting Anglo-Saxon business-letter style of writing with the garlands and lilies of his Gallic diplomacy – have waged a frustratingly arduous four-year campaign to extract from the Castle, a *public* vet's report which was mystifyingly barred to the RSPCA. In the end we won, were able to read the fictitious calumnies printed in it about the society's perceived enmity with the animal-carers of the A&NRD and smooth the ruffled feathers, eventually leading to satisfying teamwork between the two groups. But in the meantime, the Christmas Tree at Spar has continued to employ just Chris, JJ and me, without any local assistance, for a hectic week at the busiest time of each year. There have been charity fundraisers, falling to JJ and me, including a successful Table Decoration Lunch as a requested follow-on from the previous Fashion Lunch. The Diet pet food sagas, that concerned JJ and me, are now thankfully running smoothly from Larry's shop, the Rose & Crown, and there are noticeably more healthy pets on the island. In addition JJ and I have spent months of Friday afternoons issuing radio tips to SaintFM listeners on how to care for their pets. Working with JJ is fun – he's energizing and enthusiastic, and we're a good team. But we're both growing tired now of doing everything alone. We've done this for years.

Michel is delighted with both donkey files when I finally deliver them, thanking me over and over again, and I am touched by such a show of gratitude in a land where thanks are scarce. But I've given up too much of my free time for too long, and I'm aching to take my life back. I want to paint and write and listen to music, read in the hammock under the mango trees without feeling guilty, cook imaginative meals again, sit still in the garden and watch the birds, linger over a chat at the Coffee Shop… I'm missing my life.

I attend meetings on the proposed Donkey Sanctuary until Michel sees it into the capable hands of expatriate volunteers who will negotiate land with the government, start it up, introduce fundraising *Adopt-a-Donkey* programmes, *Riding for the Disabled*, and seek support from abroad... *And what will happen when these expats leave, I wonder secretly?* What happens to every project here, of course. A death, be it fast or slow. But we've done as much as we can.

"I'm taking a sabbatical from the SPCA," I inform Michel when all is at last secure. "I need a rest." Michel takes a long deep breath, but he nods understandingly.

And then comes the shock announcement. "So am I," says JJ. "Someone else can do fundraising for a while." The look that now crosses Michel's face is one of mild panic. It's accolade enough for the time JJ and I have given.

Chris has barely unpacked from his mid-year arrival before we dress him up and take him out to dinner. The destination's proper and attractive designation is, in fact, the *Orange Tree Oriental Restaurant*, or so the pretty sign tells us, but here it will forever be familiarly dubbed 'The Chinese' and left at that. The sign is posted at the entrance to a short arcade through the ground floor of tall Association Hall which will soon, we believe, offer both an enlarged DVD-hire outlet and a daily sandwich shop in the two attractive spaces that once were the derelict bar of an old hotel. On the floor above them, the miracle of health foods are available from Y&T in an expensive emporium of vitamin pills, whole-wheat crisp-breads, pesto, olive oil, and other welcome intimations of 21st Century good health. While further up, ascending the building's gracious wooden staircase, are the offices of the flourishing SaintFM Radio – *Heartbeat of St Helena* – and the *St Helena Independent* newspaper.

Once through the arcade, we cross Smith's Yard, an old cobbled courtyard where lights blaze welcomingly from the new restaurant up some steps in the far corner, and Daisy greets us with kisses and her characteristic smile. Enrobed in a crimson satin *cheongsam* she immediately sets a tone of elegance as she shows us to our table, unfurls linen table napkins across our knees, and offers a wine list and a menu. For a glorious moment we're too stunned to speak. *This is like-it-or-lump-it St Helena?* Muted jazz is playing in the background, candles are lit, long voile curtains drift elegantly in the breeze through large windows, while the menu offers so many inviting dishes that it takes time to debate them – to decide how we will share this marvellous oriental feast among the four of us. *Was this delight really smothered by the Immigration Control Board?* Chris gives me a conspiratorial grin. "Thank goodness the Governor overturned that decision." Thank goodness.

Daisy's brother, Gilbert, is cooking in the kitchen – a tall smiling Filipino garbed in chef's jacket while his wife, Meryl, also in *cheongsam*, helps Daisy wait tables. There is such an air of grace about them all, a friendliness and ease with which they attend to the wellbeing of their guests, that we feast and linger and feast some more to delay waking from this dream. I glance across the table at Stuart enthusiastically tackling sticky ribs, the honeyed marinade spreading around his mouth and over his fingers, and Virginia wielding chopsticks around chicken with cashew nuts, and I can't help smiling. "Your troubles are over," I grin. "I know exactly where you will celebrate your next Valentine's Night!"

"Only if she opens that night!" Stuart mumbles through the ribs.

"Daisy is from the Outside World. She'll open on Valentine's Night, you'll see."

Both of them look ecstatic.

25.

Sticks and Stones...

August 2006

Stuart meets me at a sprint as I return home from coffee with JJ, eyes wide with anxiety. "I tried to phone you but you'd already left. Virginia's in hospital again. I took her down a few minutes ago."

"Again?" I have no need to ask why. The attacks that started four years ago have lately increased to a point of regularity. Heart-wrenching, stomach-churning, mind-numbing for us who witness them. Excruciating agony for her to suffer. Starting with tell-tale rings like panda eyes against her fair skin, she quickly sinks to a marked heaviness of spirit. Arms instinctively protect her stomach, and soon she is complaining about sternum and back pains and breathlessness. Stuart and I meet eyes across her, familiar with the next stage. She will swallow a pill prescribed for migraine of the stomach which, the internet informs us is a rare but valid illness, but within minutes she will throw it up. Costing the equivalent of £6 each in the wider world, the hospital orders only five at a time and has given her three. She uses them sparingly but they're of little benefit if she can't keep them down. The writhing starts soon afterwards, the groaning, and by the time she sinks to the floor because the cosseting of soft cushions aggravates the pain, she's crying out "Don't touch me! Don't touch me!" Stuart and I are helpless to hold her hand, stroke her arm, to comfort in any way.

We all resist – as long as possible – resorting to the hospital, since no one there is wiser than we are about her predicament. In the earliest stages she was x-rayed, scanned for gallstones, had ECGs to test her heart, blood tests by the score, stomach scopes, and so far nine different doctors have assessed her since the pains started so long ago, with no positive conclusions except the suggested stomach migraine. We know the drill now. Often at night when these attacks most usually occur, we deliver Virginia to the hospital's reception desk where she's told to wait on one of the cheap plastic chairs in the passage until someone comes. One of us sits with her, testifying to the great discomfort of those seats, while she eventually chooses the floor as a better writhing surface. If it's really late, no doctor-on-call actually appears but will deliver by phone the required permission to administer pethidine – a powerful pain-killing injection often used on women in labour – which will put her to sleep but treats absolutely no cause. It also runs a risk of addiction which frightens us, since she's received this at nearly every attack for the past four years. If the daytime floor is busy, the friendly nurses – who know her well – step across her prone form in the corridor with a sympathetic: "Ahh, lovey, you back here again?" as they bustle to and fro. But once, for two hours she was stepped over, back and forth, by a British locum doctor who completed all his morning rounds before he agreed to examine her, then prescribed a light antacid – as usual.

Growing thin, she looks wan and exhausted as the attacks become more frequent. She tries her best to keep working, but attacks are now starting at school and I have already made a few five-mile dashes to Harford Middle School at Longwood to fetch her home. She's terrified of eating anything that could trigger an attack, yet the careful lists of foods we have kept over the years show no common denominator. We're stumped for clues, and sleepless with worry. The only recourse now is to undergo specialist tests in Cape Town, I feel, and if we were not already due – all three of us – to depart next month for a long-planned three-month holiday there, we would definitely book that voyage now.

After this latest overnight visit, she returns home, but just days later the next attack starts. Considering her state, there's no option but to drive her back to the hospital, and this time she is shown into the rooms of a visiting surgeon I have not met before. Dr Desai is a good-looking man with fire in his soul. He clearly does not care for interfering mothers who sit in on consultations. His eyes flash at me angrily, but I don't care; Virginia is so far beyond speech she cannot possibly describe her pain. He prods and pokes at her stomach but senses nothing untoward. Eventually he faces me with clear antipathy at wasting his time, and suggests I take my malingering daughter home. "I will fetch her some pills," he offers grudgingly. "It's nothing but a little stomach infection." He is already at the door, opening it wide, hand firmly shoving my shoulder through as he speeds me off in departure, frantic to be rid of this pestilent matron.

"A little stomach infection?" I stop in my tracks, appalled. I am a cobra now, spitting venom. "She's had a little stomach infection for *four years?*"

He takes a step backwards, a fleeting glance of wariness passing through the flames of his antagonism. "Four years?" he echoes more meekly.

"FOUR YEARS!"

He clears his throat. "I'd like to run further tests on her. We'll keep her for a few hours."

I am shaking with anxiety by the time I reach home, head throbbing, and cheeks – I notice in a mirror – as crimson as two overripe strawberries. I will soon be in a hospital bed beside Virginia if I don't calm down, I know. But Boss Builder does not have any calming effect. He brings me the exquisite little Italian hand basin intended for the new downstairs guest lavatory, bought at vast expense in Cape Town, and shows me the crack that occurred when one of his boys dropped it. The basin is aeons removed from any of Jamestown's bathroom offerings, so I won't even try to look for a replacement here. I shrug. "I'll think about it tomorrow," I say in my Scarlett O'Hara voice, and retire in a prone position on the sofa to sip soothing honeybush tea. I lie there all day, playing at relaxing, while hammers are securing a complete new roof along the length of our enlarged house, but the strawberries are still with me when I'm called to fetch Virginia home.

She's waiting in the passage, slumped in one of the plastic chairs, visibly dopey, when I arrive. Nurses pass, as well as a doctor friend who hijacks me into her office to measure my roof-venting blood pressure and issue some pills. Yet no one knows what Virginia's tests have revealed though I ask everyone I see. Even Virginia doesn't know. This doesn't bode well. When Dr Desai opportunely emerges from theatre, there's no escape for him. He instantly recognises the harridan in his path and advances bravely. "We have done a scan," he informs me in the pronounced accents of his subcontinent. "And we have found – well, there are – We-have-found-gallstones."

"Gallstones!" But she was scanned for these four years ago.

"*Multiple* gallstones – that's what we have found. We will operate tomorrow week, on Thursday."

I take Virginia home, as much aware as she is that Thursday week is eight days and probably several attacks away, but Thursday is the hospital's operating day and no one will be moved from that timetable. The Thursday that will dawn tomorrow is already over-booked, I'm told. She is limp and worn out and I don't see that she can possibly teach in this condition, but at least she is washed with the relief of at last *knowing*. I ring the school to say that she will not be at work for the rest of the week.

On Friday, as I enjoy fried grouper and chips with Stedson and Joyce and Bish at Donny's, under the velvet canopy of a late July evening, I'm called to the phone. "Just to let you know she's back in hospital," says Stuart.

"How bad is she?"

"Not good, but she's already knocked out by the drugs. I've just left her. There's no point in you visiting tonight."

But I visit tomorrow, as early as I can. I walk down from home, just a few yards really, taking the back way shortcut through a rickety paint-peeling gate, along a weed-grown path past St John's Villa Community Clinic and through an outdoor passage crowded with rusted stoves and pre-Neolithic equipment. Then I haul in the deep breath that must see me round the corner to the hospital entrance beyond the men's ward where an open drain below their windows exudes a nauseating stench of urine. Only as I enter the reception foyer do I dare let it out.

I find Virginia accommodated at the far end of the long women's ward, near a window, and to reach her I walk past numerous crones in various sad stages of demise. A large screen shields her from prying eyes; but she's far beyond caring, I realise by the time I lean over to kiss her. This girl is seriously ill. Her face is gaunt, eyes rolled back, jaw slack with weakness. She barely recognises me and all that escapes her is a soft sigh as I reach for her hand. She's clearly sedated, but there is more to her apathy than that, I can see. I sit with her for two hours before her pains start again. I know this when she hauls herself out of bed and more or less drops to the floor on its far side, wedged into the narrow space between the screen and a small table, her way of dealing with things. She is keening now, in high-pitched bursts of pain, and I call a nurse who shakes her head sadly as she checks the card. "We took her off pethidine and gave her a new drug, but she can't have no more for another two hours." Virginia is right under the bed now and neither of us can reach her. "Are any doctors in today?" I ask. There should be four to choose from.

The nurse shakes her head again. "Today Sat'day. Maybe someone will come in but prob'ly not."

I don't know what to do. I vacillate wildly between accepting that I may simply be an over-reacting hysterical mother and so should be working on calming down, and wanting to raise hell somewhere around here. I walk up and down the corridor to escape her keening. Eventually I stand on the wide veranda watching cardinals flit in the flowerless jacaranda just beyond me, the traffic coming and going in Market Street directly ahead, and the sea beyond it. I haul calming breaths despite the proximity of the reeking drains and wish with all my heart that Chris were here to hold my hand.

As I turn back inside Dr Desai himself crosses my path. The very person I want. He is meeker today, a lot less antagonistic now that he has spotted those multiple gallstones, but he is still not mother-friendly. Besides we are evidently suffering some language problems today and he takes me for a fool. "I know you are supposed to operate on my daughter next week but – " I begin.

"Yes, yes, next Thursday."

"I wonder if you could bring it forward. She is in terrible pain."

"I have her written down for Thursday."

"I know, but she's – "

"Can you not understand?" he snaps. "I have her name in the book. Operate Thursday for gallstone."

"She'll be dead by then. It's five days away."

"Yes, yes, five days is Thursday. Come with me, I show you the book."

He hauls me into a small office and flicks over the pages of a massive diary, stabbing his finger at the 10.30am slot. "See, there is your daughter. Victoria. We operate many patients for gallstone next Thursday."

I lean over and flick the pages back to today, equally emphatic at stabbing the whole gloriously empty page. "She will not survive till Thursday. Please can you operate sooner?"

He shakes his head in utter exasperation. "I think you must go to your home. On Thursday we will remove your daughter's gallstones and she will be well. Do not worry."

I am not a worrier without reasonable cause, but the encroaching death of my daughter is good enough reason to keep me right here. By the time I return to her cubicle, she has been tucked back into bed by a nurse but has broken out in a massive rash. It would be splendid to behold if her condition were not so desperate. These are red-ringed saucers of various size and shape, but a uniformity of buttercup yellow within their circles lends her physique, from top to toe, a somewhat surreal artistry. I wonder whether it's time to call for Stuart, but between night shifts at the prison and Virginia's attacks, he hasn't slept for days and is himself almost at a point of collapse. I hang on, watching her breathing grow uneven and effortful. When a sister looks in I beseech her: "She needs the operation urgently. Couldn't you please ring one of the doctors and suggest it for me?"

"It's the weekend," she says. "They don't operate except on Thursdays."

"She won't last like this till Thursday." She nods in silent agreement and my hopes rise. "Dr Desai thinks I'm just a hysterical mother – I can't get through to him."

"I also think she need the operation now," says the Saint sister, "but it not my place to suggest it to the doctors. Sorry, ma'am."

And so the hours pass. At some point Virginia is mysteriously hauled away under Dr Desai's command, to undergo another gastroscopy – her fourth in as many months, I think, and when she is wheeled back in, he grudgingly reassures me there is nothing wrong with her stomach. *But we knew that,* I want to shriek, *you found stones in her gallbladder three days ago!* In calmer moments I am grateful that he is being thorough, yet I doubt she wanted the added discomfort of a camera pushed down her throat just at this time.

For the rest of the day, she is sedated until the drug wears off, then she drops to the floor again and keens. I can't tell if she knows at all what's going on. Mostly her beautiful blue irises are somewhere under her forehead, leaving yellowed whites in their place. The nurses look in only rarely, no other doctor appears at all. My heart is breaking, and when Stuart arrives to relieve me I go home and cry. *Am I really just a hysterical mother after all?* I'm confused, and so exhausted by my own high blood pressure that I can't think clearly… As her mother *I know* she's near the end of her rope, but the visiting Dr Desai is a highly-recommended surgeon who will not listen to me. *Could I go above his head and phone the Senior Medical Officer, Elsa's husband, and tell him of my worries?* But mothers are always deemed hysterical, aren't they? If I fail to convince him, there's no hope for Virginia…

We all ride out the night somehow, and when Christopher makes his eight o'clock Sunday morning call to me, I open the floodgates. He once had multiple gallstones too, and though I am familiar with his agonies those many years ago, only he can truly empathise with her suffering. He is utterly horrified. "The pain is unbearable!" he exclaims. "Leave it to me – I'll phone the SMO."

Within half an hour I hear the SMO's deep voice at the other end of our telephone. "Just to let you know, we're operating on Virginia at ten this morning. We just need time to bring in theatre staff from around the island."

I phone Chris back. "What on earth did you say to him?"

"I explained that I have suffered that pain myself and it's excruciating, and I said from the way you described her I don't think she'll live till Thursday. But what did it, I think, was phoning him at home, from Cape Town, at eight on a Sunday morning! I also said I'd pay extra to operate today!" It's a man's world, definitely.

The phial that sits beside Virginia's ward bed when she returns from surgery and Stuart and I are allowed to see her, contains thirty-four little black stones. She doesn't want to look at them, but she does examine the three neat dressings on her stomach. "Is this all? I thought there'd be a huge gash."

"Keyhole surgery," we tell her gladly. "Dr Desai brought the equipment with him." I want to find Dr Desai now, throw my arms about him, and plant kisses on his cheeks. But he strenuously avoids me.

We're already in the earliest days of August when Virginia's operation takes place, and now just three weeks remain before she, Stuart, and I leave for our Cape Town holiday. But there is another problem. Virginia does not hold a valid passport – and it wasn't for want of trying. At the time that her expiring South African passport needed renewing in Cape Town, the South African Home Affairs Office happened to be demonstrating the highest level of inefficiency ever adopted by a state department in the history of the universe. Armed with absolutely everything he could require for the procuring of a new one for She who lives nowhere near a Consulate – multiple photographs, current passport, identity document, downloaded application form filled in and signed by her own hand, a full set of fingerprints extracted and witnessed by the St Helena Police, a thick dossier of documents in fact, by the time it was stacked – Chris, as far back as January, had duly taken up position in an early morning passport queue that never budged. This soon became the manner of his daily employment, taking with him his *Cape Times* and a swatch of financial magazines to read while he waited to be seen. But when he finally reached a desk he was curtly informed that Virginia *must* appear in person, no argument. He explained why this was not possible.

"Then she must fly home."

He explained again. The woman shrugged petulantly, shuffled papers and shouted: "Next!"

Weeks passed as he met one brick wall after another, getting nowhere while I, in St Helena, considered other options. There was a chance, I had discovered by studying the shipping schedule, of sending Virginia home via Walvis Bay, flying her down to Home Affairs in Cape Town during the Easter school holidays, meaning that no teaching time would be lost – a short turnaround voyage that would solve all her problems. But by April, we eventually realised, there would not be *more* than six months left on her passport, so the Namibian Immigration would not allow her into their country, even to pass through it. Cancel that idea.

Anxiety mounted month after month as our August holiday steadily approached and still Virginia's passport application was getting nowhere. Again and again Chris was informed that no exceptions could be made and she must "appear in person", that her photographs must be verified, that the submitted fingerprints were too smudged to use... Then, at last, in May, he struck gold. By this time he was so familiar a figure at Home Affairs that he'd found his way into a back office, and after a succession of irksome delays there, was eventually ushered through to a Mrs Ali in yet another room where he explained the problem all over again. But even Mrs Ali, like the others before her, had no clue where St Helena was, and didn't share concern about his daughter's passport problem. The logistics of living in a place so remote are, by and large, beyond the wildest imaginings of average mortals.

Then his eye fell on that day's *Cape Times* on her desk, folded open at page three where, waiting for the doors to open this morning he had read, in his own copy, an article commenting on the outrageous racial discrimination demonstrated at an HIV/AIDS meeting in the far-off Island of St Helena a few weeks back. Mrs Ali, it transpired, had read it too. "My wife," announced Christopher conversationally, "attended that meeting herself and was so angry about the racism displayed there that she wrote a furious letter to the local island newspaper about it!"

Mrs Ali straightened in her chair. "Really? Your *wife*?" she uttered in an entirely new tone of voice. She cleared her throat, "Well. Now, how can we help you, Mr Cooper?" Within half an hour Virginia's faxed fingerprints had been verified and accepted in far distant Pretoria, and Mrs Ali took possession of the other data. "The passport will be ready by mid-June."

By mid-June Chris was already back in St Helena for his half-year visit – without the passport. But when he once again darkened the doors of Home Affairs in Cape Town (only to discover that Mrs Ali no longer worked there), he was *promised* it would be with him by a given date in late July – the RMS's last voyage north to the island before we three departed south on it. This, too, was a vain hope, because Christopher only received the document two days *after* the northbound ship had left Cape Town, and now was the proud possessor not only of Virginia's *new* passport, but also her expired one, as well as her vital South African identity card – with absolutely no way of getting them to her.

But we are old hands at being prepared, Chris and I; and while he warned the Cape Town shipping agents of her predicament, and the ship's Bureau staff, he also explained everything minutely to the ship's senior master, our old friend Martin Smith. On St Helena, Governor Clancy issued Virginia with a Letter of Safe Passage, outlining her passport problem and verifying her identity, which would allow her to board the RMS without the requisite document. And this, in turn, alerted the Governor's Staff Officer (moonlighting as British Consul), the St Helena Emigration department, and the St Helena Police, of the facts of her unusual circumstances. No stone was left unturned.

By the third week in August, Virginia is slowly recovering from her ordeals. The school has given her sick leave, and Stuart does her packing while she recoups her strength. We kiss Tessa, Mimi and Louise goodbye, urging them not to harass the elegant canine, Timba who, with his friendly expatriate owners, will look after the house in our absence; and at last embark on our well-deserved holiday.

On board the RMS, the Bureau staff, familiar with our family and aware of the problem, present no obstacle when Virginia reminds them that she has no papers to show except the Governor's Letter of Safe Passage. "We understand," they reiterate, "that Chris will give the Cape Town shipping reps your new passport to bring on board as soon as we dock in Cape Town on Saturday morning. We'll let you know immediately it's here, and then you can go through SA Immigration as usual when the officials come aboard later. No problem."

No problem. What a wonderful phrase! Given the opportunity to relax at long last, I unpack at leisure, seek out the ship's doctor for an anti-seasick injection before the voyage starts, and hang over the railings as usual watching our dear island disintegrate into the clouds until we can see it no more. Then I settle into the familiar rituals of our long bus ride home for the next five nights.

The vagaries of a high sea swell are not kind to my exhausted disposition, and for three nights I manage to stagger to the dining room only for sociable dinner exchanges with the pleasant company at the Captain's table, but the rest of the time I keep to my cabin, reading and dozing, striving to combat queasiness despite the injection. Virginia and Stuart, both excellent sailors, look in to chat from time to time, but mostly they are enjoying the cruise with a good deal more verve. By the third morning, feeling heartier, I venture forth from my cabin armed with an exciting book, aiming to select a chair in the airier light of the Main Lounge. But I have barely seated myself in my favoured position halfway down the long room, when a small shudder announces the death of one of the ship's engines. As a regular sailor on the RMS I'm not unfamiliar with the muted tones and slightly laboured progress of sailing on only one engine, but the troubles lately have grown so frequent that on the island, "delays due to bad weather" – as officially announced by Solomon's Shipping Office and relayed to the radio stations – are universally greeted by: "Engine trouble again!" This breakdown feels just a bit different, however.

The lounge is fairly empty, a few people at the far end, and one stranger reading under the clock opposite me, while the majority of passengers are probably playing sports on the sundeck. I have no idea where my children are but... My book is not yet opened when the Captain's voice blares over the tannoy: "Ladies and Gentlemen, it is necessary for us to stop both the ship's engines for a few minutes, which might cause a little swaying."

Thanks for the warning. Within a moment the other engine falls silent and the ship involuntarily swings her bows with the current, lurching slightly as she does so. But in the next instant she is broadsided by a wave that sends her heeling so violently to starboard that the horizon shoots into the air. My whole person is on the move, at high speed and against my own volition, and before my life has a chance to flash before my eyes, a clear image of the movie *Poseidon* leaps to mind. There are screams. A very long moment later the horizon is still above us somewhere, while the view through the windows is almost entirely water, and this feels horribly like the end. I turn my head to discover the man-under-the-clock is still opposite me, but no longer backed by the timepiece, since the square of carpet we inhabit usually covers the dance floor and, being unfixed, has travelled as far as it can go down the length of the Lounge, skimming us along with it.

It is an aeon before the ship decides to haul herself upright again, heels to port, to starboard, to port, and then slowly, uncertainly, steadies herself. But by then I am seriously frightened. I cannot recall that I have ever been so scared in my life. But soon after one engine has been restarted and the room put to rights, an elderly lawyer table companion comes staggering into the Lounge, clearly terrified. Almost incoherent with fear and knowing that I commute quite regularly on this ship, he is now looking to me for reaction. We still have two days to go on this voyage, and our present position is hundreds of miles from help of any kind – beyond the reach of any plane or helicopter and well clear of frequented shipping lanes. Ours is a lonely, lonely sea but I dare not announce this. I visualise either a lawsuit or a heart attack emanating from this man, and since it has evidently fallen to me to forestall both I give him a bright, broad smile: "That woke us all up!" I jest. "Are you alright?"

"Fortunately I was sitting down in my cabin – but I really thought we were going to turn turtle…!"

Be assured, so did I. I give a forced but jolly little laugh. "Oh, no!" I lie baldly. "This sort of thing occasionally happens if there's a large swell, but the engineers and the Captain have everything under control." More times than I care to count I have woken to the wild slamming of drawers and cupboard doors rocketing back and forth as we lose engines, but this was the worst I have experienced. This ship, built fifty feet short of its designed length in a late '80s British cost-cutting venture – a fact that accounts for more of a corkscrew motion and a slower speed than she would otherwise possess – looks, to the layman, exceedingly top-heavy. But however much I am assured that she carries an exceptionally deep draught to compensate, these rolling experiences are not convincing.

"I honestly thought this was the end!" the old man exclaims. "So I'm wonderfully relieved to see you looking so calm. How many voyages have you made on this ship, did you say?"

"Between twenty and thirty, I think."

He sits down and prepares to resume his life. "Whew! This woman here," he announces to the next passengers to appear in the Lounge, "says this often happens but the crew have it all under control. And she should know – she's a regular passenger and has been sailing back and forth for *years!*"

Years ago, my friend, we did not have regular breakdowns. But while the island's masters dream only of an Airport, safety at sea appears not to be an issue. I finally open my book just as the Hotel Officer comes to check on us: "Well," he announces jovially, to cheer us all up, "the soup is at one end of the galley and the pot's at the other. And little Naomi fell off her chair in the Bureau." Everyone chuckles, but it is a distinctly nervous sound.

By evening everyone's more or less regained their equilibrium, but when I join my designated table companions for dinner, the lawyer is clearly still shaken by the morning's terror. With the Captain on my right (not the senior Martin Smith this time but an alternative captain, a Saint I've known for years), the lawyer is on my left, and I offer distractions in general chatter. The Captain, presumably already informed, is all ears when I recount the hilarious details and dramas of renewing Virginia's passport. He laughs along with the reviving lawyer, but makes no comment at all about these unusual circumstances – until I catch up with his reactions twenty-four hours later.

"Let me buy you a drink," says the Hotel Officer after dinner the following night, and sees me into a quiet corner on our own. "This business of Virginia's passport – you realise you're breaking the law by bringing her on board without one?"

I'm a bit startled by this. "We've tried our damnedest not to."

"The Captain is *furious* about the whole thing. He had me on the carpet this morning and really chewed me out, and then I had to chew out the Bureau staff too. He should have been told."

I tell him tersely that the ship's *senior* captain knew all about this long ago, as does His Excellency the Governor, both St Helena's and Cape Town's shipping agents, the RMS Bureau Staff, St Helena Emigration, St Helena Police, the British Consul in St Helena, and the South African Home Affairs offices in both Cape Town and Pretoria.

"The Captain wouldn't have let her board if he'd known."

"Virginia is carrying a Letter of Safe Passage from the Governor who is Commander-in-Chief of St Helena. This ship is also under his jurisdiction."

"Not while the Captain is on board. The Captain has the final say."

This absolute lie is his shot in the dark, aiming at my ignorance of such technicalities. But it misses the mark. I maintain a dignified calm despite the two familiar skin-searing strawberries that have swiftly risen back into my cheeks. "If you knew the background to this story you would realise that we have moved heaven and earth to get her passport to the island in time, but it missed the ship by two days. Virginia is a South African Citizen and with an ID number to show to Immigration on arrival, they cannot refuse her entry to a South African port. Besides, her new passport will be handed in by the ship's reps as soon as we dock."

He still doesn't smile. "As you know, since yesterday's engine breakdown we've been running late. Instead of docking at Cape Town in the early morning tomorrow, we're only arriving at the pilot light at ten o'clock at night. There'll be no rep to hand in the passport at that hour, but Immigration in Cape Town work twenty-four hours a day, and when they see that Virginia is on the manifest but has no passport to show them, they will fine us, *the ship*, £5 000. This is how much trouble you have caused."

I don't sleep after the tirade has ended and I'm permitted to return to my cabin. I have seldom been so angry in my life. I toss and turn in my bunk all night bringing down imprecations upon a Captain too cowardly to approach me himself, and on a whippersnapper who uses such tones to a full-fare paying passenger who has spent a small fortune in passages over many years on a very expensive ship. And I am also panicky in case the passport is not brought in time and there's a scene with the Immigration officers after all; but a £5 000 fine for the ship is the least of my concerns. I resolve not to worry Virginia or Stuart with a whisper of this added complication until we stand at last on *terra firma*.

It is deepest winter darkness when the RMS finally sidles up to Cape Town's dock, and the business of tying up to the bollards is executed by shadowy figures below us. Virginia and Stuart and I have been hanging over the railings for hours, watching the lights of this most beautiful of cities grow clearer as we approach. I regret, for Stuart's sake that he has not been treated to a daylight arrival, for this is one of the world's great experiences, though he is happy to be awed by its endless sea of tight-packed glittering lights stretching into infinity. He is also making much of the strange and pungent city smell which is new to him, exaggerated by the dampness of Cape winter air even though it is not raining while we stand here.

But while the two of them exclaim and giggle together about their surroundings, I am practically falling overboard in my efforts to spot a shipping representative. Two cars are parked down there, although it is now the dead of a cold night, but no one alights from either because the service gangplank has not yet been lowered. My heart is thumping, hands shaking so much I keep them in my jacket pocket lest Virginia see how nervous I am. A white van arrives, and my heart sinks. It has the undeniable stamp of government on it. Immigration, two men, braving the chill, get out and wander up and down the dock. My eyes are pinned on the other two cars. And at the moment that I hear the clang of metal touching the ground, one car door flies open and an utterly unfamiliar figure leaps out to mount the small gangway. The Immigration chaps are right behind him.

The suspense is almost too much to bear. I leave the railings and dart downstairs to the Bureau, pretending to look in the windows of the shop and at the notice boards. Almost no passengers are around, but a knot of men are chatting in the Bureau square, none of whom I recognise except the Captain and the Hotel Officer. I have no wish for either of them to see my anxiety, so I retire to shadows – until, eventually, one of the younger Bureau staff subtly catches my eye. His merest nod is all I need. The passport has made it. The husband of one of the woman shipping reps, I learn later, has especially come out at midnight on this dark, cold Saturday to see it safely on board. *Thank you, rep and rep's husband! I can sleep tonight.* But I still won't mention anything of this ugliness to Virginia until we have stepped on to home soil tomorrow morning.

26.

Extended Perils

April 2007

At Villa Le Breton we have passed a seventh Christmas on the island, quickly falling back into step with St Helena life since our November return, with Richard in tow, home from Europe's adventures. All had gone well at the house during our three-month absence, and our housesitting friends evidently enjoyed a Jamestown change from the dampness of Piccolo Hill where they are stationed, just as their dog Timba enjoyed the company of Tessa and Louise. Only Mimi, ever the drama queen, took exception to the new long-legged dog in her domain, and petulantly took up residence in a mango tree for the duration – specifically in an abandoned mynah bird nest in which she was still demurely composed when Zander pointed out her hideaway on our return. She's come down now, and resumed a more regular feline life.

While Virginia happily returns to Harford Middle School where the children are younger and more polite than the wild youth of Prince Andrew Secondary School – lately much in the news for vandalism, graffiti, cannabis-dealing, and most notably the hospitalisation of the Deputy Head Teacher when a boy bashed him on the head with a plank – Stuart, finally released from prison duties, has resumed his expert plumbing. Richard, hopefully inclining towards a sojourn of leisure, was – under vociferous protest – harnessed into driving lessons with patient driving instructor Hensil Peters. Negotiating St Helena's hills and switchbacks is a far cry from driving the freeways of the Outside World, of course; but we reasoned that if he mastered these he could drive almost anywhere. And Hensil saw him through the course with such aplomb that the first time Richard ever drove alone, he took our car through a pea soup fog to a vague address on the hairpins of Sandy Bay, found the house, was welcomed by the girl he sought, and served a dish of mackerel curry by her grandmother. "Wow!" says Stuart, agog. "Mackerel curry! You know what an *impression* you made on the old lady?"

The building work, continuing long past its due date, finally comes to its end in late January, completing nearly a year of noise, dust, and intrusion. And Boss Builder and I, on a final tour of inspection, wander this enlarged home with delight. In the new terracotta-tiled utility room which houses extra fridges, freezers, washing machine, and a wall of cupboards filled with overflow china and glass, the horrible metal kitchen window that once overlooked our hideous old yard now sports custom-made American shutters that marry the kitchen to its new addition. To one side is an elegant new guest loo, painted the same rich baize-green as the old upstairs bathroom but humoured by two large white framed posters of collective nouns which invariably detain visitors there for longer than necessary. With the expensive Italian replacement hand basin also in situ, I revel in the simple convenience of having such a facility downstairs without the old trek we used to make. But upstairs – ah, here's the thing! The hole eventually beaten through our two-foot-thick bedroom wall now introduces a spacious travertine-tiled bathroom with a huge shower, African rosewood cupboards and modern fittings, a place of such luxury in this old house that we barely know ourselves – and no longer do we need to negotiate midnight stairs.

Beside the bathroom, a door opens to a cosy three-windowed room that gazes on one side across rampant purple bougainvillea and up the stubbled slopes of the dramatically high mountain above us, and on the other over the tranquil mango orchards of lovely Cambrian House to the hillocks of the Briars. It's a calm room, exuding invitations to burrow into its cosy sofa with a book, to listen to music, to paint at the artists' corner I have set up there, or simply to relax – earning its nickname: the Chill Room. There's only one thing that disappoints in this peaceful sanctuary, and that's the lack of any sill or indentation around the three lovely Georgian sash windows, given the described necessity of one-brick-thick-upstairs-walls-in-the-St-Helena-way. But when I reiterate this regret to the expert Boss Builder, now champing to snatch our final payment from me, wash his hands of Villa Le Breton, and move on with greater wealth, he says tetchily: "But I *could* have built it two-brick-thick. The downstairs wall was quite strong enough to take the weight. *You* said – " I leave the room quickly before I seize him by the throat.

Our island years have marched at ever-quickening pace, months tumbling through them like over-exuberant children, leaping and flailing, often falling flat, eventually hauling themselves up again to dust down and proceed on their ungainly course. But the path lately travelled seems bumpier than ever, littered with obstacles slowing the way of real progress while the island psyche is invaded once more by lethargy.

At the tail end of last year had come some Airport news, intended perhaps as a magnanimous 2006 Christmas Bonus, though no one threw parties to celebrate. Not here, anyway. Delivered as an announcement from DfID, we heard that *of six compliant responses* to their quest for Expressions of Interest in providing scheduled flights to St Helena, *three* companies had finally been shortlisted. None was intelligently expected to be in the British Airways mould of world renown, of course (though that might have been the general island supposition); but it turned out – and these were the best options – that all three were tiny British charter companies. So tiny, in fact, that one was still in the process of being set up, but they offered, respectively, a Boeing 737-800 with 189 seats, and a Boeing 737-700ER (extended range) with 126 seats.

The third option, though based in England, planned to use charter aircraft flying from South Africa which would offer a non-stop four-hour flight from Cape Town in preference to a refuelling junket all the way from London. However, as charter companies do not generally imbue confidence in comfort or safety standards, this Christmas bonus was received with barely a shrug by the indifferent populace for whom these distant decisions are made. Then we heard that that one of the happy *compliant responses* actually owned no aircraft with range enough to fly over an ocean, and the small planes they did own were currently employed in gun-running into African countries.

Clearly we, on the island, are not unique in our cynicism. For following hot on the heels of this announcement, was published in the *St Helena Independent* a lengthy *"View on Air Service Statement"* by aviation industry correspondent Duncan Mayhew, who is engagingly familiar with matters St Helenian. He writes: *"So long as DfID do not lose their appetite for subsidising both the Island of St Helena, and access to it, nor expect any significant acceleration in the long haul to financial self-sufficiency which they have set out to achieve, the island should look forward to a satisfactory air service coming into being. The only real casualty will be the credibility of those Government spokesmen and their consultants who consistently asserted over the past five years that air services commissioned or originated by the public sector would (or could) be subsidy-free. They will not, and nobody with a serious grasp of public finance ever really believed otherwise."* Bravo, Mr Mayhew. We also believe that this airport is going to prove a weightier millstone around DfID's necks than they have ever known before. And Mr Mayhew does not even mention, as Chris comments, the added – and ongoing – costs of properly qualified air traffic controllers, the overseas training of aircraft maintenance technicians, the apparatus with which to service planes properly, the employment of runway maintenance crews, reliable meteorologists for our windy and foggy airport location, permanent fire and rescue crews with adequate equipment (including standby fire engines close to the airport), sea rescue crews with adequate boats on standby... Nor does Mr Mayhew ask this vexing question: Should 'our' airline ever be granted St Helenian livery as so fondly suggested in government-sponsored brochures over the past five years, on exactly *whose* tarmac will our plane sit gathering dust, rust and declining efficiency in the rests between the proffered once-a-week flights? None of these extra expenses has been publicised by DfID, so presumably all those responsibilities have been shoved over as part and parcel of the DBO (Design, Build and Operate) arrangement expected to be signed by prospective airport building contractors; when some are found. The buck will thus be neatly passed. But how many reliable construction companies out there are completely *au fait* with airport management?

April rain is bucketing down. This used to be a month of calm air and manageable warmth, as far as I remember, but the world's climate changes are capricious. And as I lie in bed, I hear it clanging on our new green corrugated iron roof that shields an older inner roof and a thick new layer of insulation, and still it keeps me awake. It's been raining off and on for days, but this is a real downpour, terrible in its force, thundering against every surface, driven by wind that is hurling it down the valley. I enjoy its fulsomeness as I lie cosseted by pillows, listening – until I hear another sound. The new sound is that unmistakable, heart-sinking, gut-wrenching *drip-drip-drip* of a leak. I know immediately where it's coming from and am out of bed in a trice, into the new extension, clicking on the light of the pretty Chill Room. *A leak?* In horror I observe water pouring not only through the two ceiling down-lighters but all along the joins of the ceiling board itself. We are practically awash! I yank up the new white floor rug, fling myself into the linen cupboard, bringing out towels to soak up pools already strung across the shiny new iroko floors, and see that, by the grace of God the water has not touched the floor-to-ceiling bookshelves yet. The books somehow are protected, but the rest is not a pleasing sight. Fetching bowls from the kitchen, I set them up strategically, cast a protective rug over our pale sofa, and shutting out the horror behind a crisply closed door, retire once more to bed. But the rain continues mercilessly.

I am barely downstairs in the morning when Stuart points out the swamp in the new utility room where water has poured down its wall through the seam of the new skylight which, we suddenly notice, has never been sealed to the wall at all. Further in, water is streaking swiftly through electric fixtures for the iron and washing machine, as well as into the broom cupboard where our electric vacuum cleaner is already sodden. The bottles, papers, plastic bags also kept there are drenched. This is not good. "He'll have to come back and fix things," Stuart observes. "But – "

I realise what the 'but' means, and simply don't know what to do about it. So when the world gets to work, I ring Jane the new Public Solicitor. "The trouble is," I explain, "Boss Builder's little company has been dissolved since he finished my extension. Two of his former employees have left the island, and he's taken a government job which has nothing to do with building."

"Have you paid him?"

"We paid the final instalment in January, but it wasn't raining then."

"It's still his responsibility. The law says he must fix everything at his own expense. If it entails hiring new men to do it in his spare time, it's not your problem."

I'm about to put down the phone, when she hails me again. "And take my advice on this too: make a list of everything that's wrong, decide a reasonable date when the repairs must be finished, and have either me or a lay advocate present when you meet with him, or it could get ugly. There's no charge for a lay advocate."

I am not looking forward to any of this. I call Boss Builder, set up a meeting for five o'clock this evening, and then call John Newman – former Chief of Police, former Speaker of the House, former Chairman of the RSPCA, former head of just about everything, and current lay advocate. I outline my predicament. "I'll be there," he says, arriving punctually and inspecting the problems himself. But when Boss Builder finds Mr Newman ensconced on my veranda, his expression is panicked. I dispense my list in triplicate, trying to soothe the ruffled feathers as best I can, explaining why I spoke to the public solicitor at all and why a lay advocate is present. I lose count of the cigarettes he is smoking (despite an island-wide shortage), in the agitation that raises his voice several frightened pitches. "I'm not intending to sue you," I explain. "But I am obviously disappointed that the job was not properly finished, and now I *have* to ensure that the leaks are fixed as quickly as possible at no added expense to myself. Mr Newman will witness your signature of agreement."

We all investigate the leaks again, Boss Builder's sharp face gaunt with worry. "But I have no men anymore," he squeaks.

"Find some," growls Mr Newman, and Boss Builder suddenly perks up with inspiration: "Stuart can help me!"

I am not so inspired by this notion. "Stuart will not help you – it's not his problem."

When they leave I'm like a wrung-out rag. I *hate* altercations, and I'm exhausted from no sleep, and since it's gone six o'clock I contemplate a calming whisky for medicinal purposes. Virginia, completing class planning in the dining room, packs up her books as I extract a glass from the sideboard, and she heads for the Cottage. But too soon she's back. "Mum, the electricity's out in the Cottage – and there's water pouring down the wall!"

My shoulders slump like a rag doll. The detailed list of leaks, signed and witnessed in triplicate, has gone away with Boss Builder and the lay advocate – and it makes no mention of a glitzy-hotel water feature knocking out lights, stove, and fridge in the cottage, clearly emanating from the new, improperly sealed cottage roof. I laugh when I view the scene, and Virginia looks at me warily: "What's funny about this?"

"I don't know."

"You'd better pour that whisky. You've had a very bad day."

With darkness comes chill and we move indoors. I've forgotten to dig supper from the freezer, so we make submarines with a baguette that needs eating while Stuart fries conger eel for himself and, all exhausted, we carry our repast to the television. But at the instant of first bite, a loud bang resounds from somewhere unknown, causing a frown of puzzlement all round. "It's the Chill Room door, I think," Stuart suggests. "A window there is opened a crack, and with this wind…" Probably. We'll look later. We're on bite two when Bish walks in, plonks himself down to complain about the climate, and calls for coffee once we are finished eating. Then, with supper finally accomplished, Stuart and Virginia excuse themselves while I head towards the kitchen and the coffee maker. With the island out of cigarettes again (even though Boss Builder clearly has a secret and generous supply), Stuart is rationing his father to five a day, and it's time to deliver tomorrow's quota to Ladder Hill where he lives. But the two have gone no further than the gate before they both come tumbling back again. "You'd better come and see!" they splutter. "A rock has hit your car – and there's a huge dent in the bonnet!"

So that bang was *not* the Chill Room door.

When we raise the bonnet, we find the engine quite intact – *thank you, dear strong workhorse!* – and the car is mercifully driveable. But St Helena law compels us to inform the police that a rock from the mountainside has damaged our property, so Virginia makes the call while I tiredly consider the day I have enjoyed. The culprit is lying in the drive, in fact, at rest halfway between the car and a gatepost, neatly sheared on one side where the force of hitting the raised road above our drive has split it. So it bounced on the road, bounced again on my car and –

"I nearly fell over that rock when I came in," Bish announces suddenly, "and I wondered why on earth you'd left a stone right there! See how it's hit the gatepost so hard the plaster's fallen off on the *far side*?" The gateposts are massively thick, and large plaster shards of plaster are lying inside the property. We realise simultaneously that if he had arrived just a few seconds earlier and been hit by the rock, he would now be dead.

"Someone's obviously watching over you," I observe as he clutches his pectoral cross like a lifeline. I rather hope he doesn't have sole rights to guardianship.

When the police arrive in a roaring Land Rover, they bring with them teams of Rock Guards and Health & Safety crews in luminous vests, who morosely set about the business of strafing the ink-black hillside with sweeping torchlight, clearly preferring to be snug at home on such a night. Among them is Boss Builder too, but we do not chat. Ordered to remove our cars to places of safety in Upper Market Street (recent scene of all the China Lane rockfalls), we manoeuvre our three cars and Bish's through the present traffic of Land Rovers at our drive's awkward reverse turn and park them there, supposedly out of harm's way. Then we trudge back home to stand chatting to the police who remain seated snugly in their van. Maldivia Road and its mountain swarm with disembodied vests fanned in all directions on the slippery, prickly slopes; and when eventually they coagulate into a group once more, we are informed that as the rest of the mountain looks reasonably safe (as far as can be ascertained in the pitch dark), it should be alright for us to sleep at home tonight. They will be back in daylight to scan the mountain properly. The simultaneous roar of large government vehicles starting up trembles the surroundings, and when they have all departed Bish utters in a parched voice: "Cancel the coffee – I think we now need strong whisky!" While he is clearly shaken by his near-death experience, I am fairly sure that I, by now, could down a bottle of Scotch singlehandedly.

The cigarette mission is cancelled too, and Virginia and Stuart join us on the veranda to exclaim about size and momentum and lucky escapes. Rockfalls of any size are chastening events, descending without warning, without assured direction. Sometimes it's the forceful rolling of just one large stone that hits with the velocity of a cannonball if it descends from high enough; sometimes a shower of rocks bouncing, splitting and wildly dancing as they cascade. Sometimes it's the most dreaded of all, the avalanche. But all are unavoidable, and only luck plays a part here. As we sip our soothing spirits the nerves gradually calm, yet even so Bish and Stuart remain the more visibly rattled among us. Stuart's upbringing on the heights of Ladder Hill, and Bish's home in the high country have precluded them from the ever-present danger of living between two tall cliffs; and though Stuart has spent three years in the valley with us already, his eyes are ever roaming the hillsides for threats. Tonight, though, nothing can be seen beyond the bounds of the veranda, and we must simply accept the Rock Guards' assurances that this was a single stray rock loosened by the recent rains.

I refill the glasses and we have just settled into less frenetic conversation when, through the calm night air – broken only by an insistent pounding of the electric keyboard at New Bridge – we hear a sudden rushing sound. It's loud enough to halt chatter as we meet perplexed eyes, wondering why someone might be viciously shaking banana palms on the other side of our hedge at ten o'clock at night, it seems so close. And then the rush diversifies into that marrow-freezing rattle –

Stuart is on his feet in a second. "Rocks rolling!"

We're all on our feet now, but we hardly know where to turn. We can see nothing, and sound in this narrow valley neck reverberates from cliff to cliff. It could be coming from anywhere… "Quick! Under the lintel!" I grab Virginia with one hand, Tessa's collar with the other, give Bish a directional shove towards our big front door. Stuart has scooped up Louise and holds her in his arms, but we don't know where Mimi is –

Somewhere out in the night the avalanche continues, crackling and crashing like kindling in a starting fire, under-laid by a roar that is terrifying in its growing velocity, until at last it subsides and separates once more into just the rattles and cracks of the last descending stones, bequeathing the scent of damp vegetation and hot rocks to the heavy air. The four of us and our two animals are clinging together in the broad front doorway, protected by two-foot thick walls and 200-year-old lintel, simply hoping for the best. When all is calm once more, Virginia reaches for the phone. "It's Virginia again," she tells the police. "There's been another rockfall in Upper Jamestown – this one's huge…! Where? We have no idea! All I can say is, it's somewhere near Villa Le Breton."

Bish selects a chair in the sitting room over the hazards of outdoor living in these dangerous regions. "Where's that whisky?" Amazingly there's still some left, and I dispense it once again. When the roar of the police van again shivers the mountainside, more chatting takes place out in the drive and we can almost make out the weary expressions of the Rock Guards with Health & Safety again their wake. More torches are shone, again the luminous vests fan out in the dark, but no destruction is discovered anywhere up our road. When they leave to search the other side of the valley, Bish hitches a ride to his car in Market Street. "I don't know how you can live down here," he tosses over his shoulder as he scrambles into the police van. "I'm much safer up the hill."

"Closer to God," hisses the policewoman, laughing. "And he don't even invite y'all to sleep on his floor up there in safety!" In a louder voice she admonishes: "You better at least pray for these poor people, Bishop, after you runnin' away like this!"

At midnight the phone rings. We've spent the last two hours watching beams of torchlight crisscross the eastern flank of Upper Jamestown, hearing shouted communications as the vests comb that area, wondering – since the avalanche clearly occurred on that side – if cottages are buried under debris. Our hearts have pounded with anxiety ever since it happened, and we pick up the phone with dread. But the news is good, Virginia informs us when she has spoken to them. The rockfall emanated from the Side Path pass, hugely high above us, where a whole section of mountain under the road gave in, crashed down the slopes and landed on the edge of the Run where there are, thankfully, no cottages. The result: no damage to private property and no injuries to anyone, since the someone watching over the Bishop so carefully has also watched over our whole neighbourhood. Now we can sleep in peace…

Well, almost. Since the Cottage is a swamp without lights, Stuart lays cushions on the sitting room floor while Virginia opts for the sofa. I wonder how safe I am upstairs where rocks might crash through the roof above me from either side of the valley, and for just a moment I contemplate the dining room floor as an option. But cockroaches tickling me awake are a more frightening hazard, so I take myself up to my own bed, and – without the taxing drip of fresh leaks in the Chill Room next door – I sleep the sleep of the utterly exhausted.

When the sun rises on a new day, things look better. Repairs to Side Path will close the road for six weeks, we hear; but at home, Boss Builder is already preparing to seal our leaks – even the cottage roof – without Stuart's help. Best of all, because our insurance includes an optional policy entitled Extended Perils, Solomon & Company will pay for a new bonnet for my car. And it will only be a three-month wait for that.

Christopher arrives at mid-year bringing exciting tidings of an impending tour to St Helena led by a well-known Cape Town tour leader to far-flung places. I'm interested in meeting him since we share mutual friends in Cape Town who have enjoyed amazing Antarctic and Arctic adventures with him, so I see this as a golden opportunity to become acquainted. "I was given this information by the RMS's shipping office in Cape Town," Chris tells me. "Hans is bringing a music tour to St Helena in November. Their voyage is booked."

We allow some time to pass before we assail the Tourist Office, giving them room to gather dates and details that might help us know how to meet him. But the girl at the desk looks blankly at us. "Hans? I never heard that name, ma'am. But there are a music tour coming in November, and they playin' for us. Classical music."

"Classical music? The visitors will be *playing*?"

"I think so. You better ask Stacey, ma'am."

Stacey gives a puzzled frown. "I don't think they playin' classical music. I heard they was playin' jazz."

"Jazz! Where, when, how many?"

She is startled by my interrogation. "Perhaps you should speak with Pamela, ma'am. She know more about it."

Pamela laughs. "The visitors aren't playing at all. As far as I know, there's a group coming here just to listen to local music."

For a moment I sway dangerously at the concept of a dozen strangers making this adventurous expedition to hear Country-&-Western music on a keyboard, but regain my cracked voice to ask: "What about Hans? Is he leading this tour?"

"Never heard of him. Some radio personality from South Africa is leading it."

When I get home I phone Joe Terry, still Chairman of the Tourism Association. "What have *you* heard about this music tour?"

"Nothing! It's all news to me."

"So you have no idea how the island might be entertaining all these music buffs with our local music?"

Joe makes one or two unrepeatable exclamations and then offers to come back to me. "Some investigation shows that just one concert has been arranged for them," he tells me over the phone. "And no one feels there's any need for more than that. The Ladies' Orchestra are the chosen ones."

I clear my throat. I'm still a paid-up member of the Tourism Association which presumably offers me the right to make suggestions. "Perhaps we should haul out the buskers again, get them a licence to play outside the Canister? And when these visitors come through Customs perhaps we could belt out local CDs instead of American pop on the radio." I name some of the rash of new CDs recently issued by local singer-songwriters.

"Bring this up at the next meeting," says Joe, "and we'll see what we can do."

When the next meeting comes around I am ill in bed, and Joe offers to make the suggestions on my behalf. But he is ominously silent afterwards. "What happened?" I ask when I next see him.

He shrugs wearily. "I offered all your suggestions and we talked a bit about this tour, but the previous Chairman stated that 'it isn't the business of the Tourism Association to involve ourselves with this sort of thing', and so they chucked out any further talk of it. As it stands, this music tour is travelling nearly two thousand miles just to hear the Ladies' Orchestra in one concert. But it's out of our hands."

"Then what is the business of the Tourism Association?" Chris asks.

I am helpless to answer that – until I find an advertisement, by accident, in an old edition of the *St Helena News* (predating even the *Herald*):

ESTABLISHING A TOURISM ASSOCIATION FOR ST HELENA

The TA will be a discussion based group to start with, that will bring together people from both the public and private sectors who are interested in tourism development on the island. Once the TA is established and fully functioning, it could also be involved in assisting with the organisation of tourism activities and events for visitors and locals and for helping to expand our visitor programme.

So where did Joe and I go wrong?

The Most Beautiful Dog in the World has her picture in the *St Helena Independent*. Below it is the caption: *Tessa Struts her Stuff*, and Stuart is garrulous with pride when he phones us in Cape Town (I am on my annual visit home) to describe her advent into Society. The occasion is a series of canine obedience lessons lately introduced by the new owner of Buzz and Millie, the Drug Dogs – a former dog handler from the British police, recently settled on the island. I hear marvellous things about Tessa. "Out of all the dogs in our class, she is far and away the smartest!" Stuart enthuses. "You don't need to show her anything twice!" If Stuart and Virginia are the proud parents of our beloved Island Special, I am just as swelled with grandmotherly affection at the other end of the line.

"Will the classes still be going when I get back to the island?" I inquire.

"We're on number three of six now, but you'll be here just in time to catch the final demonstration. You've *got* to see this – she's the star of the show!"

Within weeks I'm back in the bosom of Villa Le Breton, and by the next afternoon Stuart and Virginia are driving me and our marvellous hound to the Final Demonstration. "You'll see straight away why we're so proud! Tessa is not only the Most Beautiful Dog in the World but also the Smartest!"

Yeah, right.

An hour later we are on our way home again, but now silence reigns in the car while Stuart grips the steering wheel with intense control of his utter humiliation. Virginia has turned to the window and studies the rain in abject shame. This dog beside me in the rear seat, happily smiling and panting and nudging my arm for gestures of huge affection, has disobeyed every single order issued this evening. She has not only disproved every word of praise gushed from Stuart's proud lips over the past six weeks, but has utterly chagrined us all. Even the masterful trainer, Paul Laban, is left stunned by Tessa's total disregard for everything he has taught her, and all but the actual perpetrator of this embarrassment are now returning home with tails between their legs.

"I can't believe this," Stuart growls as we arrive home. "Yesterday when we practiced, she was perfect! Tessa, come! Sit!" Tessa follows him to the lawn and sits like an angel. "Heel!" Tessa heels. "Fetch!" Tessa takes off at a sprint and fetches the ball he throws. "Stay!" I watch from the veranda as he goes through the whole gamut of commands, and the dog's obedience is quite above suspicion. On return to the house he glowers at me. "It must be you," he says. "Until today she's never put a foot wrong. She was showing off this afternoon because *you* were there!"

"Perhaps she was showing off because you'd told her she was such a star," I mutter defensively, yet the bottom line is, Tessa has disgraced us all in this final hour of glory. Nevertheless, I have seen her obey the requisite instructions and she has now proved herself the Smart Dog that she definitely is, if a contrary one. After we have licked our raw wounds we forgive her.

So, I decide, now that she is clearly a trained and disciplined companion – despite her showing-off exercise – I can take her about in the car a bit more often than before. And late the next afternoon I drive her to the Wharf when the RMS is readying herself for departure to Ascension.

This is a mistake, I soon discover, because though I am intending only to run over to wish a quick farewell to a departing friend and then immediately return home, Tessa evidently likes the looks of the gathering crowd and slithers through my opened door like quicksilver. "Tessa!"

I yell, and am completely ignored. "Tessa!" She is greased-lightning itself, streaking the length of the long seafront, wildly weaving between knotted bystanders and manoeuvring cars, now disappearing into the thick of arriving traffic, now reappearing to happily greet perplexed strangers and friends alike, tossing her head coquettishly in response to my crescendoing calls. "TESSA! COME HERE!"

She has a sense of humour, this dog, and uses it now to good effect as she returns down the Wharf at speed, rolling her eyes and lolling her tongue at me as she shaves past. I am screaming her name, and having ascertained that no lead nor rope nor belt of any kind lies within the shambles of my car, am now galumphing gracelessly after her, several paces behind, as she crosses the moat and passes beneath the Town Arch. Here we have a serious situation. Traffic is not paying attention to unleashed dogs dicing with death as it sweeps down Main Street and across the Parade, converging at the narrow Arch to jostle for parking places on the already crowded seafront. I am desperately lunging for her collar, screeching shrilly at the top of my voice, making inelegant feints at thin air as she streaks ahead, dicing with death myself in my efforts to slow down the approaching cars, when there is a loud and ominous screech of tyres ahead –

A car passes me and exposes my dog at a halt, momentarily caught by surprise by the sudden proximity of a huge 4x4 towering over her. And, thank heavens, she's still on all four feet! "TESSA! STAY!" I reach her just as she regains her equilibrium and heads off for another foray of freedom. But I've caught her at last, by the tail. With one hand I rip off my cardigan and thread it through the collar from which she knows how to evacuate herself in moments of rebellion, and now she finds that the extra stuffing has tightened the pretty leather necklace she wears. Defeated, she relaxes into obedient and compliant stance and reluctantly agrees to heed my commands, so that I can now raise my head and thank the hovering and watchful 4x4 driver for not squashing to a pulp the Most Beautiful Dog in the World. And when I do, I see to my unparalleled humiliation that the driver is none other than Paul Laban himself, the dog trainer, with both Buzz and Millie Drug Dogs yelping with laughter in the back of his vehicle.

For the first time ever, the post for our next Governor has been advertised in the overseas press – meaning that the new Commander-in-Chief will not necessarily have been drawn from FCO circles as in the past, but may apply for the job as for any commercial position. This, of course, prompts applicants from the sublime to the ridiculous, many of whom are known to the island; and the Bishop, our continuous fount of knowledge, offers some of their names to us with rollicking amusement as he learns them. "Things don't necessarily improve for us here," he says, "but this new method's good for a laugh."

In the long run, the man finally selected to lead us at least has Overseas Territories' experience and, though vaulting out of retirement, comes to us with a spell in another island state in his back pocket. He was never a Governor there, but with the end of our likable Michael Clancy's three-year term, the new man is pleased to take up gubernatorial reins in St Helena, and it is assumed that he might be familiar with the workings of far-flung governance.

Quite coincidentally several senior office posts on the island have fallen vacant at the same time, and while we await the arrival of the new Governor in the early weeks of November, he is preceded by a brand-new Chief Secretary by just a fortnight. A tall good-looking man with a pleasant-looking wife, they step ashore casting before them an aura of self-assurance and capability, and the newspapers are quick to introduce them to the public. But this is a relationship doomed at the outset, for the *St Helena Independent*, quite inexplicably, takes violent exception to the new Chief Secretary's conservative Panama hat and double-breasted blazer.

Intrigued by this couple, I turn on the radio to hear the new man's introductory address, and am at once heartened not only by his reassuringly educated English accent, but also by the authoritative manner of his delivery. This is a man used to taking control, accustomed to organising, and dedicated to getting things done, just as his history testifies. We are lucky indeed to have captured him. And if his public manner appears slightly testy by some accounts, it may, I think, be excused by the unfairly bad press he is receiving.

Within hours, somewhat bizarrely for such a new arrival, he is sworn in as Acting Governor in the absence of a substantive Governor present within territorial waters, and for this short but solemn ceremony he adopts a line of respect for this position, assuming immense dignity by tastefully donning morning dress. It is a stroke of genius, I decide, having entirely forgotten about this very English substitute when protest at the demise of our Governor's uniform raged three or four years back. But this, according to the proletariat paranoia that has lately overtaken reasonable thinking, is just another trademark of the upper middle classes who are to be despised under all circumstances, regardless of the work they do, and vitriol quickly spreads, turning to a mild mass hysteria in which this unlucky couple is criticised at every turn.

But the order achieved by this new official is a revelation, and Stedson, as a Councillor in close collaboration with the new Chief Secretary, is impressed. "At last we have someone really *good* for the island!" he exclaims. "This man knows what he's doing, knows what needs to be done, and gets on with it. He's the best thing that's happened here for years!"

I am keen to meet his wife and show friendship in this hostile world in which she suddenly dwells, but 'flu holds me back from inviting her to coffee. And by the time I'm better, the incoming Governor has arrived and everyone's swept up again in official functions. It is another Remembrance Sunday when the new Governor arrives, and a rather rushed programme has been devised for his Inauguration. The RMS, also carrying the Bishop on return from holiday, has been urged to make all speed with her important cargo to allow for a dawn disembarkation, a 9.30am gathering of the troops in the Parade for the Inauguration, and then the eleven o'clock procession to the Cenotaph for the Bishop to conduct the service and the new Governor to lay the wreath for the Territories. I take up position early on the Parade, accompanied by Wendy, Stuart's older sister visiting from London, both of us intrigued to see whom we have been sent this time. And before long the Governor's car glides down Main Street and disgorges the new incumbents. Like our erstwhile Governor Clancy, the man mounting the podium is tall and white-haired, but the resemblance ends there, though he seems pleasant enough as he quips about the Sheriff's pretty purple hat replicating the flowering jacaranda that leans over the assembled dignitaries. His speech is lively and promising, diction clear, delivery animated. But what has jolted me to real attention is his all-embracing greeting: "My Lord Bishop, Honourable Speaker, Honourable Members of the Executive and Legislative Councils, Honorary French Consul, Madam Sheriff, Distinguished Guests, Saints of all ages, Incomers, Expats, and Welcome Visitors…"

I look at Wendy. "Did he say *expats*?" She nods. Expatriates! Someone, at last, at *last*, acknowledges that we also exist here, that we – tiny number of inward-investing settlers that we are – are not after all the scum of the earth, or no more than a mere interference on this island. Someone has *welcomed* us today! I think I might like this man.

Two weeks later I find myself seated at dinner beside the new Governor. It is the first time I've met him and our proximity presents an ideal opportunity to speak up. "I've been wanting to thank you so much," I say as he pours wine for me, "for including us expatriates in the welcome at your inauguration speech. It was a small thing but it meant a great deal to us – "

He plonks down the wine bottle abruptly and almost draws away. "I wasn't meaning people like you," he snaps. "I meant the Brits on contract."

Oh… *Oh?!* I might have hoped that somewhere in that lengthy preamble there could have been a tiny space for us settlers who spend lots of money on the island and take no salary away…

I am not a little taken aback by this unexpected rudeness, but in order to sidestep a potential international incident in these social surroundings, I quickly turn my attention instead to his wife who sits opposite me. English football is, somewhat surprisingly, her chosen topic and she is quick to announce her devotion to West Ham, which is fine by me since I know absolutely nothing about that club. However I do fairly enthusiastically follow the beautiful game from time to time, thanks to Richard's fervent persuasions, and, relieved to have discovered that our conversation did not involve maths or synchronised swimming, I bravely throw in my ha'penny's worth. "I'm a Chelsea fan myself," I offer congenially, based solely on having attended one game against Fulham at Stamford Bridge once upon a time.

She hauls a surprising dose of air through her nostrils before her face withers. "Yes," she opines, "*yoouu – would* be." And with that I am flung back on the slag heap where, apparently, snobbish expatriates belong. There's some truth, after all, in that old adage *Bad go, worse come,* I realise. And, excluding the likeable Michael Clancy whom we miss, it seems to me that worse is definitely here.

Yet another Festive Season is soon upon us, and Christopher and Richard, travelling separately this year, duly arrive with the December soft fruits and the season of merriment. We see in the New Year with Gay and her new husband at a jolly party at Blue Hill. Not much political talk passes our lips on this occasion, but over dinner the new Governor (let's call him Guy Rude) promises us fervently that by April of this incoming 2008 we will know, absolutely definitely, who will build the Airport – the South African company or the Italians who have lately expressed interest and visited the island. Yes, well… Chris and I have been around here rather longer than this new man, and a knowing look passes between us. *Absolutely definitely?*

Richard returns to Cape Town in January, followed, on our February wedding anniversary, by Chris and me. But by then all hell has broken loose in the Castle. Rumours abound, of course, but the story that most forcibly reaches us is one of yet another of the cover-ups that, lately, appear to be *de rigueur* in the local government, on our ship, and at DfID. This version tells of an Executive Councillor detained for drunk driving, but at Legal & Lands a decision is made not to prosecute the man because "it would not look good for the government". When the upstanding new Chief Secretary makes this discovery he is outraged. "There is not one law for the ordinary people and another for executives," he rants. "Prosecution *must* take place!" Utterly fazed by such extreme integrity, the senior Legal & Lands official runs hotfoot to the Governor who promptly agrees that prosecution of the councillor is out of the question. And this minor tear causes the final split between the Chief Secretary and Governor Rude, a simple excuse for their vibrant personality clashes; perhaps, also, for the very blatant class differences that evidently rankle our upstart Commander-in-Chief. The Governor, the story goes, lifts the phone and speaks to London. "I can't work with this man!" he announces, and within days the new Chief Secretary is relieved of his post. Stedson is appalled: "If I've said it once, I've said it a hundred times, this Chief Secretary is the most efficient government appointment we have had here in years – he's got things done! *And* he is a gentleman!" Perhaps that heritage is the poor man's greatest sin.

27.

Voyages from Hell

February to July 2008

Things are dire on the RMS. Last September, visiting England on one of her twice-yearly jaunts, the ship was surprised by a random safety check. The davits for the lifeboats were stuck, SaintFM promptly informed us, so lifeboats could not be lowered into the water. There were also *"other safety issues"* that didn't comply with regulations, the radio station added, notwithstanding all the stringent EU rules that St Helena is compelled to obey. And since recent fuel-saving regulations decree that the ship must now crawl at eleven knots (rather than fourteen knots), it seems to have broken down on every voyage. Officially, however, we are informed that the RMS has again – and again and again – been delayed by *"bad weather"*. (The past 18 months have presumably seen persistent and merciless vicissitudes of climate.)

The ship left England immediately after the safety check, with davits still stuck and the other mysterious faults unresolved, and sailed 4 000 miles to the island, then a further 1 700 to Cape Town, without any disaster fall-back. We were horrified. Nothing more was said on the news, but delays continued. Richard, on his way north to the island in November, ahead of Chris, had been caught up in one at Cape Town docks where, having boarded the vessel at the required time, then lay captive for more than thirty-three hours while hectic banging emanated from the bowels of the ship. It might have been assumed that this delay presented a good opportunity to fix the faulty davits, but according to an officer on board there was "too much else to do"; so lifeboats clearly were not a priority. In the early dawn hours of eventual departure, Richard soon awoke to the slamming of cupboard doors and drawers in his cabin – tell-tale evidence that both engines were down; and a glance through the porthole confirmed they had travelled no further than Table Bay's breakwater. "As you know, when the ship was built in Britain eighteen years ago," an officer conspiratorially explained to JJ who was also on board, "the British government not only compromised comfort on board by building the ship fifty feet shorter than she was intended – which causes its strange corkscrew motion – but she was given ferry engines. What you may not know is that those engines were on their way to the scrapyard when they were rescued and fitted into the RMS." Indeed, that last detail, many people do not know.

By the time Chris followed Richard north in mid-December, the ship was rushing to make up lost time, and his voyage, run at full throttle contrary to fuel-saving tactics, was the smoothest he has ever experienced. "The engines sang," he enthuses, "and we simply cut through the water." But we are still concerned about the odd silence that has fallen across the faulty davits, the whitewashed engine breakdowns, and the things we are clearly not being told. What else is faulty?

Chris is moved to voice his concerns. While still on the island, he writes a letter to the new Governor. *"As a frequent passenger on the RMS* St Helena, *preparing to embark on my 32nd voyage on this vessel..."* he begins, then lashes out in his controlled and gentlemanly manner at the issues of safety, ship's water and health, air conditioning and health, bunkering surcharges, unreasonable schedules, and finally the lack of openness and transparency regarding truthful information from the ship itself. He ends: *"Though the ship somehow manages to retain its delightful and uniquely charming character, I cannot help but remark that if disturbing breakdowns, safety fears, delays, discoloured water and airborne viruses are benchmarks for the high fares demanded, there is little hope for St Helena's tourism by air which will prove to be many degrees more demanding – and not a little off-putting to those who value their life in the air!"* Maintenance is the unspoken watchword here, for we are sensitive to the fact that we have lately lost the island's only Sea Rescue Boat to lack of it, and no other island boats are suited to the purpose. *"I wholly trust...that the RMS may soon revert to engendering the happy and relaxed atmosphere enjoyed on board in former years. And not least, as we relentlessly march towards tourism, to once again acting the fine ambassador she once was for the entire Island of St Helena."*

It is to be hoped that something of this might be taken on board, forgive the pun, or at least passed on to the relevant bodies governing the ship – but no one knows quite who is responsible for the RMS. Onus for the ship's recent vagaries is passed like a hot coal from hand-to-hand, from the St Helena government to the shipping line that manages the ship, to the obscure London office that owns the ship, back to the St Helena government that claims the ship, back to the shipping line, ping-pong, ping-pong... "It's DfID," we are eventually informed by someone who claims he *really* knows. "The shipping line would have put in proper engines years ago if the British government had only agreed to it. But DfID is so obsessed with the airport it has worn blinkers for the past nine years, and can see nothing else." *When the RMS turns twenty,* we were warned years ago, *she will be retired because by then the Airport will be up and running.* Of course nine years on there is still no airport, and the ship is eighteen years old already. Is she destined for the scrapyard in two years' time?

No, is the answer, *she will stay in service until the Airport comes.* And if she had been retired at twenty, would she have gone to the scrapyard then? *No. She would have been sold and refurbished and put into service somewhere else.*

We clutch at the word *refurbished* like a drowning man's straw. So, as there's no sign of any airport here for at least another four years, some say seven or eight, why can't she be refurbished for us?

Well, she can't, because DfID is simply not interested in our ship any more. When the Airport arrives, we learn, *some sort of cargo ship* will be contracted to bring our goods, but it is likely to accommodate no more than two passengers – *if* we are lucky. Never mind the fact that it is exceptionally hard to find a ship with a cargo derrick these days, and we are helpless without one. *"I'm really sick,"* writes a senior St Helenian official, *"of us islanders always being treated as second-class citizens. It's happened for centuries and it doesn't get better. London never listens to anything we say – and we do have real concerns. We* must *have a passenger ship even if we have an airport."*

In a mood of faint apprehension Chris and I board the RMS together in mid-February of 2008, freeing up Virginia and Stuart to celebrate Valentine's Night â deux at 'The Chinese', and then to run the house until my projected return in June. There is an exciting period ahead, with a trip to Vietnam for Richard and me soon after arriving back in Cape Town, and four weeks in Italy with Chris a short time later, and I'm geared for a busy four months off-island. We settle into our cabin and a few minutes before we're due to sail I walk down the long A-Deck corridor to seek out the doctor for my essential anti-seasick injection – but I can't reach his surgery for a barricade of sorts set up just before it. Then I spot four uniformed St Helena policemen seated just beyond, in what is fancifully known as the Hospital. One of them is our friendly Deputy Police Chief himself, and I raise querying eyebrows at him. He smiles enigmatically; but the doctor, when I locate him, tells me the facts. "We are accommodating a prisoner in the hospital – one of the stowaways that arrived on the island at Christmas. The police will hand him over to authorities at Walvis Bay, who will presumably put him on a plane back to the Congo." Presumably. Who can say what will actually happen to this boy back in Africa?

It was something of a shock, we imagine, for a farmer at rural Blue Hill, out in the fields one afternoon shortly before Christmas, to be suddenly confronted by two black-skinned African boys asking for food in a foreign language. He called the police, of course, who immediately detained them as illegal immigrants. But how did they get there? The story was slow in extraction, for obvious reasons of cloudy communication, but it transpired that these youths – aged twenty-one and twenty-two – were loading cargo on to a ship in the port of Mutadi, Democratic Republic of Congo, when the notion came to them to flee their turbulent homeland by stowing away in the hold of the vessel they were lading. They took supplies of food and water into hiding with them, sensibly enough, but after three days of sitting in harbour and a further three days at sea, the supplies ran out. And so they gave themselves up.

Common practice on many ships, we were told some years ago, is to throw stowaways overboard to drown, thereby saving a huge amount of red tape, paperwork and unwarranted expense. But their more humane ship, evidently registered in Vietnam, did not do that. Instead, the next day, once inside St Helenian territorial waters and about five miles off the island, they cast off the boys in an unmarked life raft kitted out with lifejackets, paddles, and four packets of water, and pointed out the daunting western cliffs they were passing. That the Congolese boys arrived alive was little short of a miracle, however, for the seas at that point are less than accommodating. But though the long-gone ship was admired for its kindness, the problem of their stowaways was now ours. During the weeks that followed, ceaseless negotiations took place in efforts to return them to the DRC – an act that many considered almost as cruel as drowning them – and a few suggestions were made that these able young men, in return for a safe haven, might be harnessed into some healthy manual labour on the island for a period of five years before their status is reviewed. But this was evidently not a consideration because, officially, *"it would open the door to thousands of other refugees from Africa."* "Perhaps out of fears of rape and pillage or infecting HIV into the air we breathe," someone cynically suggested, remembering that long-ago vociferous AIDS meeting at the Consulate Hotel.

"How," Chris asks, "are they likely to stowaway in their hundreds on the off-chance that a kind Vietnamese ship will give them life rafts and water to get here? Or will they set off from West Africa in open boats and battle head-on trade winds and currents in order to reach an island no one has heard of? Really, isn't it easier to keep on heading for the Canaries as they've been doing for years, which are closer?"

It is not as though this island is besieged by stowaways. The last one was nearly eight years ago. But as he happened to choose the same March voyage that brought us and our household to settle into Villa Le Breton for the first time, we have been able to dine out on his story for some years. This was a bright boy, going places, one who carefully watched the ship in Cape Town, noted crew movements, noted the fact that the ship said *London* on its stern, acquired for himself a pitch-black track-suit to match his skin, some apples and vitamin-C sweets, and boarded the RMS by one of the ropes binding it to the shore. The random stowaway search conducted on board before setting sail did not turn up anything untoward, and so the ship confidently upped anchors and set sail for St Helena. But a day or two later, a steward venturing into the dining room one afternoon when all was quiet, was taken aback to glimpse a stranger ducking behind a table. And so a story emerged.

Having foiled the stowaway search by hiding in the ship's dark funnel in his black track-suit, with eyes and mouth tightly closed, he'd grown hungry after consuming his apples and sweets, and eventually decided to raid the dining room. Now forced to explain himself, but speaking only French-of-sorts, an officer's wife was summoned to translate, though the lines between her schoolgirl threads and his pidgin-lingo were quickly blurred. She did her best, however, and soon informed us that the boy was a 16-year-old Hutu from Burundi, caught up in the all-too-familiar tragedies of Central Africa when, the previous month, February just past, he had witnessed the murder of his parents, brothers, sisters, uncles and aunts. Alone in his escape, he then, over the next three or four weeks, covered thousands of miles to South Africa, hitched a ride on a lorry to Cape Town, and happily spotted the ship with *London* on its stern.

There was instant sympathy on our ship, and exclamations at the resilience and resourcefulness of one so young with the wounds of his grief so raw. A hat went round the passengers in a trice, garnering several hundreds of pounds for his benefit. Cupboards were raided and new sets of clothes presented. Lavish trays of food were delivered to the ship's hospital where he was detained for the remainder of the voyage, at which he picked with criticism and demands. But our kind-hearted Captain Smith did not throw him overboard.

Once on the island, the long reeling-in of red-tape was begun, and in the meantime the boy was comfortably housed with a minder at Piccolo Hill, taken shopping, given every indulgence he could command. And as a measure of consolation, the French Consul visited him long enough to deduce that it was not last February after all, that he had suffered his terrible bereavements and started the epic journey south, but in fact some several years previously – after which our eloquent Michel was fired by the Burundian "for not speaking proper French". What was never quite determined, though, was just how many *actual* blood relatives were lost in his tragedy, thanks to the African habit of bestowing respectful 'connections' on all seniors in a village. When we saw him around town, we soon noted that he now favoured smart black trousers for day wear and plain crisp shirts in brilliant red, lime green or fluorescent yellow, Nike trainers and a smart watch. At Ann's Place, where Governor Hill frequently enjoyed lunch with colleagues from the Castle, the boy, arriving to enjoy his own meal, took consummate care to shake the hand of every dignitary at the high table, greet them in English and offer a little bow. And in the end he got exactly what he wanted – a free voyage on the RMS to England where the British government was pleased to offer him British citizenship within a very few months, and a place at a Midlands university.

The Congolese boys, we fear, might not fare so well. For reasons involving a suicide attempt in prison, it was decided to repatriate first one and then the other – perhaps to forestall another such attempt on the RMS; or to see if the first one survives his return to Africa, as with the DRC's track record it is difficult to imagine their welcoming arms receiving home two able-bodied youths who have fled that country's anarchy in the first place. When we finally dock at Walvis Bay, Namibia, after a long and eventful voyage, we watch the stowaway disembark ahead of us. At the bottom of the gangplank stands a Namibian policeman and a man in civvies, who both escort the boy to a small truck parked nearby. They talk animatedly as they go and, somewhat reassuringly, there is a spring in the step of the captive. I hope he survives his homecoming.

There's something different about the anti-seasickness injection the doctor gives me when, because of the stowaway blockade, he appears in person in our cabin to minister this vital antidote. It just doesn't feel familiar. Too short, too fluid, without the momentary warmth through the veins I'm accustomed to at the start of each voyage. I don't challenge the doctor, but I comment to Chris: "This doctor's convinced that seasickness is all in the mind; I'm sure that injection was a placebo."

Chris is reassuring. "Give it a chance. The sea's smooth and the forecast looks alright. Besides you already have wristbands on." I cannot describe what a shocking sailor I am, but Chris is right. Thursday, our first night, and the second day are fine. I survive the first dinner happily; go down to breakfast, lunch, even dinner again despite the slight roll we are demonstrating by Friday evening – and then the sea changes. Everything changes. Through Friday night I am up and down to the bathroom, sick as a dog, and in the age-old tradition of seaborne sufferers, I soon recognise the growing wish to die. At 5am on Saturday a ship's engine goes down. We recognise the sensation instantly. But at least we are safe with one engine, and still moving. The good engine is stalwartly puttering along through a rolling swell and all I can think of is getting up speed to pass quickly through this extreme vexation.

The pared-down sound from the engine room extends through the breakfast hour which I forego by remaining on my bunk, and as the hours drag by, the voyage becomes inexorably longer and fraught with more discomfort. We are crawling now, while the sea enjoys capricious games with the ship. Only at 2.30 in the afternoon, after nearly ten hours of trouble, does the faulty engine revive, but I have long ago stopped smiling. By the time the Chief Purser calls a meeting in the Main Lounge at 5pm, I'm stone-faced. Already weary of being cooped up in the cabin by nausea, I haul myself upstairs alongside Chris to find out what's afoot.

"I've called this meeting for all passengers intending to disembark at Walvis Bay," begins the officer. "According to my list of 104 passengers on board, fifty-three of you are booked for onward flights to Johannesburg or Cape Town from there. But because of our long engine-breakdown and the heavy swell, the ship will now be late, arriving at Walvis Bay at midday on Monday instead of early morning, and you'll miss your lunchtime flights."

A groan circles the Lounge. Daisy Terry's chef brother, Gilbert, travelling with his wife and their newborn baby, looks horrified. His midday flight to Johannesburg was a connection to Dubai, to connect again to the Philippines, and his plans are now seriously out of kilter. Ours are only irksome by comparison. "For those who would prefer to stay on board for an extra three days to Cape Town," the Purser continues, "the next leg will be at the company's expense. But those preferring to disembark at Walvis Bay should hand in your names now, and we'll reschedule your flights and book your overnight accommodation. Regrettably, because of this swell, we won't be able to make up the lost time."

Chris looks at me. "You've only got two weeks to get your

Vietnam visa which takes ten days – we can't afford the time to stay on board." In truth, I want nothing more right now than distance between me and this unbearable rolling. I leave Chris to organise details, and race back to our cabin and its bathroom.

By Saturday night Chris, the good sailor, has also succumbed and Eileen, our stewardess, brings soup and rolls to the cabin. "A lot of people are down," she says. "But thank goodness the A-Deck loos are working again – they were blocked all last night." As was our B-Deck loo earlier today, for which we summoned a plumber. But by 7pm it had seized up again and did not flush for the next twelve hours. The seas are worse now, and through the course of Saturday night, as I regularly plunge from bunk to bathroom, we hear the engine fail three times more, screaming in protest as the engineers fight to restore it.

There is nothing left in my stomach to expel by the early hours of Sunday morning when I bend over the lavatory retching my heart out, and it is the dire trauma of this action that rips, audibly and in an all-too-familiar fashion, that poor old fragile and worn-out ligament in my back that has torn three times before. The pain is horrendous. I clutch the grab-handles around the tiny bathroom for support, lean against the door which fortuitously opens outwards, and somehow propel myself to my bunk. I am faint with agony, the world spinning into a vicious black vortex, and Chris rouses himself in queasy surprise to observe the opening of another inevitable chapter of walking sticks and painkillers. But all I can think of is Vietnam. We have so long wanted to go there, Richard and I, and this holiday has been researched and planned and booked for nearly a year. But suddenly I can't stand or walk unaided. I can't even turn on the mattress, prop myself up, or – as I soon discover – get out of bed to reach the bathroom. Chris administers what painkillers he can find in my travelling pouch, but they're not nearly strong enough to cope. Then he takes fifteen minutes of hauling and cajoling merely to ease me to a sitting position where he might gently hoist both my legs over the little wooden ridge of the bunk and on to the floor, and from there into an upright chair from which it is easier to gain the bathroom. It's the most agonising and challenging manoeuvre I have ever made, and I am in unspeakable pain.

When the doctor arrives, his face is all contrition. But I am too far out of things to vent accusations about placebos (for which our bill shows the going rate for the proper medication). He is now attention personified, instantly jabbing me with a healthy flow of real seasick antidote, fetching the strongest painkillers he can find short of morphine, disappearing again to gather aluminium crutches, walking sticks, and a very sturdy Zimmer frame. The last draws a weak laugh from me, in respect of my perceived youthfulness, but he is in deadly earnest. "Use whatever you want," he exhorts me. "Take it with you when you disembark tomorrow, and return it to the ship in Cape Town." He fusses about my safety in the straight-backed chair from which I hold court in the shabbiest nightdress I possess, and calls on us frequently.

By Monday the extra breakdowns have caused further delays, long past the promised lunchtime, and we do not dock in Namibia until nearly seven in the evening. But by now the ship's management (or owner, or subsidiser, or governing body) has resolved to exclude breakdowns from reasons for the delay. It's the old bad-weather story, and Chris, who has learned much from local island cynicism, says: "If they claim breakdowns, they'll have to pay for our hotel accommodation. Bad weather is an act of God, so now *we* pay." It's true, of course, but pain-management is my lot at present. I can't much care about the rest.

I select an aluminium walking stick and my husband's comforting arm, and with these two aids, step-by-painful-step, disembark from the voyage from hell, today bestowing no fond backward glance on the familiar little ship over my shoulder. Tourists around us, about sixty on this voyage, are ranting, and I wish that the powers, whoever they are, were here to witness this embarrassment. The shipping office women have flown from Cape Town to handle the mess of rescheduled flights and emergency accommodations, and Chris and I – perhaps by virtue of our frequent voyaging – have been assigned to a delightful B&B on Walvis Bay's lagoon front. But what I want is home, my own familiar bed, stable ground, and Paul my friend who fixes backs. First, though, we have to live out the rigours of a night in a strange accommodation, and then the two-hour flight to Cape Town tomorrow at midday.

It is at the airport that we meet up again with several co-travellers and one of them is the Chief Engineer from the RMS. Waiting in the check-in queue I ask him conversationally: "As a matter of interest, which engine was it that broke down this time? The old troublesome port engine or the starboard one?"

His eyes instantly douse their friendly twinkle. "Breakdowns? We had no breakdowns!" Ah. So we're back to the familiar whitewash.

Paul sees me nearly every day for two weeks – at a price, of course – but finally I stand unaided in his room and ask the burning question: "Do you think I'm mad to go to Vietnam like this?"

He refuses to meet my eyes. "No," he says. "Go. But please be *very careful.*"

So Richard and I board a flight to Singapore, connect to Hanoi, and love Vietnam to bits. Offering minor hindrances to his youthful energy, my back carries me around somehow and I am *very* careful – at least for the first four days until we reach the stunning World Heritage Site beauty of Halong Bay where I am so enchanted by the splendid junks and their backdrop of fascinating limestone islands that I cease to watch my footing. My headlong crash across a jagged pavement is full-length and utterly graceless, entertaining to scores of onlookers who gaze in open-mouthed amazement at my collapse until a devastatingly handsome Frenchman materialises at my side. Once he has hauled me up, dusted me down and disappointedly discovered my years, he melts back into the crowd and I resume a rather ungainly limp to our luxury junk. My fragile back has held, miraculously, but my right knee is now seriously sore. It soon swells like a football, turns black to my ankle, paints my toes navy-blue and once more calls forth the trauma painkillers the doctor issued me on the ship. But, refusing to consult an Asian doctor's acupuncture needles, I stoically keep going and, a whole month later, the knee (having visited my own doctor at home, by then, who suggests a cracked kneecap and pulled tendons behind it) subsequently carries me through Venice and all of Umbria with Chris, before the swelling begins to subside.

By the time I return to Cape Town from Italy at the end of May, I am exhausted by pain and effort. Now the thought of sailing back alone to the island in June on a suffering ship that is only due for dry dock in July, fills me with palpable horror. And so we postpone the booking until late July (after dry dock) and I settle in to rest at home, renewing acquaintance with Cape Town friends I usually see only on rushed shopping sprees, and snuggling down for the Cape winter. Dry dock will see to the recalcitrant engines, we assume, and maybe at last the lifeboat davits will be fixed. After everything's mended I'll be happier on the RMS.

From St Helena, Virginia passes on all the news by costly overseas phone calls. "There's huge excitement here!" she exclaims. "The French have brought in a helicopter! We keep rushing into the garden when it passes overhead! Mimi runs inside."

"How big?" I ask, immediately concerned about rockfalls in our valley.

"Tiny, just a two-seater. They use it to raise the netting at the Wharf. Their work's going well. They'll be finished by August."

"This project represents a fine example of private initiative versus government waffling," cited Bish when the first announcements of intent were made. "It just takes one sensible woman to apply for EU funding while Legco still bickers over who should fix the public showers at the Wharf – and she gets it." €15.47 million was what she gained for St Helena and its Dependencies eighteen months back, which allocated a full €10 million to St Helena specifically for Wharf improvement. This meant cliff stabilization in the area, a new crane, wharf widening, a *real* Customs terminal, and safer landing facilities for cruise ship passengers. And by last Christmas a team of French engineers had already arrived to start work on wiring up the threatening cliffs of Munden's.

It wasn't, however, very long before the local government grew petulant about the project; perhaps because it wasn't really theirs. And as we sat at the Coffee Shop one day, watching the men at work with their little spider crane that crawled over the mountainside as it pulled and threaded wires, we clutched our sides with laughter at the latest swish of gubernatorial petticoats. Someone of substantial authority, it transpired, had taken umbrage at not being officially informed about the presence of this small crane on the island, and feeling disregarded, had promptly demanded that the spider crane be licensed as a road vehicle because it possessed four wheels. That the crane would never have business on any place besides Munden's cliffs, seemed to have no bearing at all on the matter. But work nonetheless ceased for a full day while the poor little machine was loaded on to a truck and then hauled slowly up the Ladder Hill Pass, through steep Half Tree Hollow to

White Gate's vehicle testing centre where none of the employees knew anything about cranes. They declared it fit for licensing anyway, and then it was slowly trundled back to work. "The idiocy of this operation defies comprehension," Bill Bolton exclaims. "Especially as the Chief Licensing Officer himself knew nothing about this fiasco!"

By June, Chris and I in Cape Town, are once again clutching sides with laughter. We have found on the internet an article lately published in London's *Observer*, written by a clued-up journalist who recently visited St Helena. For once, unlike the vast majority of compulsively-written stories of this fetching island, she gets her facts right, and in the course of her research conducts some amusing interviews. The first is with Governor Rude, in which she inquires why he feels the Airport would be good for St Helena. The answer reduces us to shrieks of mirth. He feels, so claims the writer, that an Airport would be good for rich South Africans to send their children to boarding school in St Helena, and also as a high security escape for South Africans *"when Zuma comes to power"*! Can we be reading this correctly? This man, as far as we know, has visited South Africa *once*, for a couple of days perhaps, before embarking on the RMS voyage that first brought him to St Helena. He clearly does not know that rich South Africans would not *contemplate* a boarding school in distant St Helena for their beloved progeny, but would prefer to offer them excellent education at South Africa's own top-notch private schools – where even quite a few *British* children, for a fraction of the cost of an English public school, fly to South Africa for a fine education in academies where basic good manners, for one thing, are still a prerequisite, and where teachers are not bashed on the head with planks. And why on earth, we ask, should ultra-expensive St Helena provide such an attractive safe haven *"when Zuma comes to power"*? There are far cheaper places in the world to run to, should the need arise.

The question put to the *St Helena Independent* is no less disturbing. The Airport, the interviewee claims, will be good for making St Helena a safe haven for finance, *"like the Caymans"*. Chris blanches when he reads this. *"The Caymans!* Oh my God, drugs and money laundering!" is all he can gasp. We're getting good value out of this article, but the cake is taken by the Tourist Office who then states unequivocally that the Airport will be good for... *"the likes of Madonna and Nicole Kidman"* who want a paparazzi-free environment!

No comment. We're laughing too much. This Airport is the farce of the century.

We stop laughing when Virginia phones in early July with news of the ship. "Have you *heard*?" I hardly dare to listen. "The RMS was half an hour out of Ascension, on its way south to St Helena, when it hit a whale or a submerged container, and now one of the stabilisers is damaged."

"So it turned back to Ascension?"

"No, it carried on and will arrive here tomorrow. But divers have to go down and inspect it, so it's running late again."

Bits of kaleidoscope are tumbling about in my head. "A whale *or* a container? If it was a whale, surely there'd be blood? Half an hour out of Ascension people would have seen what it was!"

"Well, that's the ship's story."

When the RMS reaches St Helena it is thoroughly examined by the Dive Team, and the accepted conclusion – one of many options, of course – suggests that the ship hit nothing. Metal-fatigue reputedly accounted for the fact that one of the stabilisers, just too weary to carry on, collapsed with a great clanking noise and so was hanging rather limply from its support, threatening at any moment to fall off completely and open a leak into the hull. (That's the story that was intended to reassure prospective passengers.) Another version, rather more hotly denied, suggests that it was hanging weakly because the last time it docked in Cape Town someone carelessly forgot to pull in those stabilisers before the ship connected with the quay. In any event, we are aghast that she never turned back to Ascension immediately, so that passengers weren't put at risk; and now St Helena's divers are left with the task of patching things up. The potential hole is what worries them, and they decide to pin the broken stabiliser back against the side of the ship on the outside, while securing the interior mechanism with cement. The trouble is, there's another shortage of cement on the island, and so it is the French who eventually come to the rescue with two and a half tons of their own supplies. "Now they're waiting for it to dry. It will take a few days," reports Virginia later.

"Will the stabiliser get properly repaired in dry dock in Cape Town?"

"Not yet," laughs Virginia. "An expert from Rolls-Royce will fly to Cape Town and look at it, but they'll have to custom-build a new one which will take some time. They're talking about December, six months' time."

"This is madness," Chris interrupts. "You can't travel without stabilisers. Not with your back still so delicate."

I have to say, the very idea of retching over a loo again makes my fragile ligament shiver. "Presumably she's cancelled all her southbound passengers while she limps back to Cape Town with a potential hole ready to open up?" I continue to Virginia on the phone.

"They thought about taking only a skeleton crew with them, but Lloyd's gave the go-ahead for a full complement of passengers. They're moving very slowly, and they'll hug the coast of Namibia all the way down."

Laughter is seldom far removed from things St Helenian. Chris and I can't help ourselves, and we roll about with humour once more. The desolate coast of Namibia comprises one of the most dangerous coastlines in the world – the notorious 900-mile-long Skeleton Coast, killer of more than a thousand ships that we know of. And now our poor little disabled RMS is hugging it – as the safer option. God bless her, and all who sail in her.

28.

Voices from the Graves

August 2008

"The news is not good," says Stedson on the phone. After a hard-won battle to get his beloved Joyce medevacked from the island, he has finally accompanied her to Cape Town for advanced medical consultations. For six months or more she has suffered agonies in her hip, and despite protests, the island hospital insists her problem is no more than a pinched nerve. "It's really bad," says Stedson, and I immediately think *cancer*, "in fact it's the very worst." I pick up the changed timbre of his voice. Then we know.

The last time we see Joyce everything about her is grey, and the bright roses we have brought flare like fire against the ashes of her former self. The cancer, which was never only in her hip, it transpires, has spread all over her body in this past month and we do not expect her to recognise us. Yet her innate desire to make others comfortable commands Stedson to bring up a chair for Chris while I hold her soft, beautiful, manicured hand. Two of her sisters have flown from England to see her and among their last gifts to her are nails elegantly shaped and prettily painted in pink. "Get Chris and Lindsay some tea," murmurs Joyce, and though she's in a private ward and facilities are there, we decline. It is clear that Stedson can't tear himself from her side.

She dies in the night three days later and I hear the weight of his pain in the early morning call to us, the news casting a pall of terrible sadness over Chris and me too. Joyce was our friend, our dear friend, and this new order takes some assimilating. Stedson spends the day with us before he boards the ship home with Joyce in a casket, and his eyes are pools of weariness and grief. "But I am also angry," he says. "The island hospital kept insisting there was nothing seriously wrong with her, and I only got her here through intervention from high places. Yet there was a man on our ship, rushed on board after a 'suspected' heart attack, who partied the whole way, had a massive shopping spree in Walvis Bay, and was pronounced perfectly healthy by the doctors in Cape Town – and he happens to be a cousin of a woman making medevac decisions. There's something very wrong in that."

We agree. There's evidently quite a lot around the hospital that seems to be wrong lately. Back-biting, finger-pointing, carelessness, misdiagnosis, and far too many costly accidents. A good shuffle around – or out – of some staff would be no bad thing, we have heard. And Virginia's four years of undiagnosed gallstones are convincing enough from our own point of view.

Three months later Stedson is back in Cape Town. "Now *I* have cancer," he tells us in a flat voice. "And they say it's aggressive. Can you believe this on top of everything else?" If Chris and I are panicked at the thought of also losing Stedson so soon after losing Joyce, we can only imagine how Stedson feels. But extensive Cape Town medical tests show that his cancer is not aggressive at all, is a slow-growing type, and in fact is so mild that it can be treated with oral medication. "How dare they tell you it's aggressive before they have proof positive! It's unethical!" Chris explodes. But a small thought niggles that maybe Stedson's wrath at the hospital upon returning with Joyce in a coffin had rubbed up some backs the wrong way. Could this have been retaliation of the cruellest kind?

Time out is what Stedson needs now, and we invite him to spend a long weekend with us. "Just put your feet up and do whatever you like for a few days," Chris says. "And before you leave on the ship we'll also get you up to our house in the mountains to show you some clear night skies."

For Chris and me this journey into the country will be an educational tour, we know, for Stedson's prodigious knowledge of astronomy and geology appears infinite to philistines like us. But it's also a way of bringing Joyce among us again. This jaunt was meant to happen three years ago on their return through Cape Town from a holiday in Arizona – a sortie much anticipated by both – and Joyce had exclaimed: "I know Stedson will look at the stars, but I simply love wild countryside!" So, at the last minute, when the trip was cancelled due to severe floods and washouts of all access roads to the area, their disappointment was profound.

Now, with the four-hour drive to this wild-country area behind us, and having learned more about the ancient geology surrounding our mountain house than we've ever known before, having watched the sun set in African splendour across the valleys and seen the craggy massifs around us burn copper in the evening light, we are relaxed on our wide wooden deck under the night sky. The coals of a barbecue are dying nearby and bottles of Cape wine are at hand. Above us the Magellanic Clouds are clearer than Stedson has ever seen them, and while Chris and I count shooting stars and satellites, he points out constellations with names we have never heard before. "Joyce would absolutely love it here," he exclaims suddenly, and though I know he's right it hardly needs to be said. Personally, I feel as though Joyce is right with us anyway, sitting at this little table, delicately twirling a glass of white wine with those beautiful smooth fingers of hers, and also counting shooting stars.

A strangeness pervades St Helena's Rupert's Valley. It is the only place on earth where I have actually heard the *deafening silence* to which poets refer, and was so moved that I myself wrote a poem about it, a long time ago. I had walked from Jamestown, up the climbing gradient of Side Path in the gentle light of early evening, and then, in my pedestrian explorations which were new to me so long ago, took the proffered left turn that straddled the long mountain divide between James Valley and Rupert's. The descent from there was smooth but steep and I had made it halfway down before I realised that shadows were warningly deep in this area, and that night was fast drawing in. So I stopped for a few minutes to gaze into the deep place below which, through much of its history, has acted as more of a utilitarian valley than one of bucolic delight.

In its depths a town was once conceived by a past Governor who had dreams for the place, but it never grew much further than a dwelling named Hay Town House which still stands today, and a few cottages. The Boer prisoners built a useful yellow-brick desalinisation plant at the sea's edge at the turn of the 20th Century, which stood for years as a monument to their practicality before it was condemned to redundancy, and this was later followed by a power station, a bulk-fuel farm, and a couple of fish factories. Today a tiny landing stage built against the high cliffs, and the valley's stony beach offer a rough recreation area for islanders who swim and hold barbecue parties in one of the island's few areas where the sea can be easily accessed, and Stuart and Virginia frequently fish here for red snapper, mackerel, conger eel, old wives, bull's eyes and the sundry other marine delights that adorn our plates from time to time.

I still remember the shrouding atmosphere of that valley as I stood alone on the deserted pass that evening. The telling shadows reaching across the deep dark scrubby valley and climbing the walls of its eastern flank. The absolute and indescribable stillness of the air, and its weightiness. The complete absence of any rustle of grass or insect wing or sigh of breeze. No faraway voice calling below, no distant engine sound, no ocean's surge, no cricket or bee or fly to break the smothering oppression. Just total, total silence, as un-giving as punch bags squeezed against my ears, until the roar of it utterly confused my brain. I remember shivering and quickly turning for home, walking up the slope with brisk, urgent steps until I reached the high saddle and once more could look down on the familiar toy-town of Jamestown, living and breathing in its happier place.

Now I understand what I experienced that evening, for something deep, deep inside me must have stirred my subconscious. I knew nothing then of Rupert's Valley's real history, its sadness and the terribleness of that sadness. But the reality of it comes to light when Virginia informs me by phone to Cape Town that a team of four archaeologists has been on the island for the past few months, exploring the route that the new Haul Road will take. The Haul Road forms a significant portion of the Air Access Project, beginning in the bay itself with a projected jetty big enough to land large machinery brought for the Airport (but not big enough for the RMS to tie up at). From there a brand new 13km road is to be constructed to convey this machinery, cutting through the valley itself, displacing the fuel farm and the power station on the way, and then wending its laborious way uphill until it reaches the plateau of Deadwood and eventually crosses close to the settlement of Longwood, to deliver the goods to Prosperous Bay Plain on the very far side of the island. But someone connected with this massive project, with rare and commendable foresight, has suggested that an historical survey of the valley be carried out *before* actual roadwork begins. And so the four archaeologists are presently on the island, sifting sand around the area where human bones were once unearthed during one of the valley's previous building projects many years ago; and their finds are becoming more chilling by the day.

It was the passing of the Slave Trade Act in 1807 that set the ball rolling for the suppression of the slave trade in the Atlantic. And by the following year Britain's Royal Navy had already set up, at great expense, the West Africa Squadron which patrolled the vulnerable coast of that continent, eventually creating Great Britain's first colony in Africa, Sierra Leone, where freed slaves might live in safety under British rule. However, such humanity did not come so speedily to St Helena which, in the scheme of things, lay not far-off West African waters; and it was only some ten years later, around 1818, that the question of slavery actually arose within the island's Council, to any effect. A few days later, Governor Hudson Lowe convened a public meeting of inhabitants, explaining that public opinion across the seas was fast becoming favourable to the abolition of slavery, and then went on to advise his listeners that the Court of Directors (of the English East India Company which had run the island since 1659) viewed *"with regret"* the fact that St Helena was the only spot under their government where slavery still existed in any shape or form. Suggesting that the island follow the lead of Ceylon where all children born of slaves after a certain date should be deemed free, he handed over the debate to the slave owners themselves, who took a mere ten minutes to decide that the Governor's suggestion be adopted and that the cut-off date would be 25 December that year. All children born of slave women from then onwards were pronounced free.

This did not mean that St Helena was suddenly relieved of all slaves of course, for at the initiation of Hudson Lowe's abolition exercise in 1818, there were as many as 1 540 slaves on the island. In a quirky little Record for 1824 responding to proposed tax on *Free*

Blacks, the succeeding Governor Walker sanctimoniously pointed out that Legislation could not recognise any distinction of colour, and that in the matter of hundreds of individuals it would not be an easy matter to determine whether they ought to be classed as blacks or whites (such was the mixed hue of the growing new St Helenian population). The Law recognised only three classes, he explained: The Military, who were governed by the Articles of War; Slaves, by a special Code; and the rest of the inhabitants who did not fall within these two descriptions. However, just three weeks later, the Governor's own *Minute on the Progress of the Population* listed, out of a total population of 4 700 inhabitants, 1 066 *"Free Blacks"*.

Another long wait. Fourteen years following Hudson Lowe's initiating suggestions ensued before Abolition of Slavery was formally recognised in St Helena in 1832, the East India Company themselves purchasing the freedom of the 614 slaves held by planters at that time, for the sum of £28 062.17s. *"At one time,"* writes Stedson, himself a slave descendant, in a newspaper article published a few years back, *"the slaves outnumbered the whites, so why did they not revolt? In 1694 an impending uprising was rumoured. As a result every male slave on the island was rounded up, but it was decided to put only three of them to death, the others to 'receive great punishment'. One was hanged in chains on the top of Ladder Hill and left there to starve to death. The other two were hanged and then disembowelled whilst still alive, after which they were dismembered and their quarters and heads stuck up at the crossroads as a warning to all slaves. Cruel and inhuman punishments were meted out on slaves at the least provocation. In 1687 a slave was burnt to death and a proclamation was issued that all slaves were to be present at the execution and that every one of them should bring a piece of wood for the fire."* Abolition, in that case, came none too soon.

By two centuries later, great political and financial changes were occurring on the island. From London, just a year after abolition in St Helena, came the surprise announcement that from 22 April 1834, the island would no longer be governed by the privately-owned English East India Company but now would become a Crown Colony – meaning, in practical terms, that the substantial sums of money lavished on the island by the EEIC throughout its generous tenure would fall, virtually overnight, to around a mere quarter of that sum, as offered by St Helena's new government masters in London. Added to that, just a few years later the first distant warning death-knells began sounding for the lucrative shipping trade that St Helena had so long enjoyed, when the P&O Line opted to commence a regular service to Egypt, meeting the EEIC ships on the isthmus at the Red Sea and thereby counting down dramatically the number of their ships rounding the Cape or calling at St Helena in future. When the Suez Canal finally opened in 1869, of course, things were to grow far, far worse for this ailing island.

However, for the moment there was still much to attend to on St Helena while the busy West Africa Squadron was hard-pressed in their labours as they busily pursued slavers thither and yon across the Atlantic. Inevitably, the slavers had initially responded by swapping their merchant ships for faster vessels, with a marked preference for speedy American clippers that for years were able to outrun the naval ships. But, eventually, enough clippers were captured by the squadron to allow pursuit of the slavers at comparable speed. One such famous captured clipper, somewhat sickly renamed HMS *Black Joke*, even found fame for successfully seizing eleven slavers in just one year. By 1820 the United States Navy had come to the aid of the West Africa Squadron with the USS *Cyane,* and over the years gradually built up enough force – capturing twenty-four slavers themselves – to warrant the merging of their unit with the Royal Navy, in 1842, into the combined Africa Squadron. In the fifty-two years between 1808 and 1860, however, the West Africa Squadron is credited with capturing 1 600 slave ships, and freeing their cargo of around 150 000 Africans who were aboard those ships.

And so it was that St Helena eventually came into play. Whether Sierra Leone was now too crowded to cope with these vast numbers, or perhaps St Helena's proximity to the action was simply more convenient, the Records do not make quite clear. But by early 1840 substantial numbers of these unhappy cargoes were being landed at Rupert's Bay, the slave ships sold and broken up, and the slaves fed, clothed and nursed at the Liberated African Depot, especially built for this purpose in this valley. In an ideal world, perhaps those miserable Africans who survived and eventually grew to strength might have been returned to joyous family reunions in their lands of origin, but even the goodwill of the Royal Navy did not extend that far, for many poor souls who regained their health were then reputedly shipped off, anyway, to the West Indies where there was evidently much demand for their labours.

By 1850, just ten years after the Liberated African Depot was established, a total of 15 076 Liberated Africans had already passed through this forlorn place. And Bishop Robert Gray, visiting the island from the Cape around that time, states: *"If anything were needed to fill the soul with burning indignation against that master-work of Satan, the Slave-trade, it would be a visit to this institution."* On the occasion of his visit there were not less than 600 *"poor souls"* there, he tells us, of which more than half were in hospital suffering from *"dreadful"* ophthalmia, severe rheumatism and dysentery, with a reported twenty-one deaths in a week.

However, a far more grisly account of events, painting a truly frightful picture, comes from John Charles Melliss, a colonial surveyor and engineer who published, in 1875, his own account of boarding one of the slave ships that had been brought into Rupert's Bay: *"A visit to a full-freighted slave ship arriving in St Helena is not easily to be forgotten; a scene so intensified in all that is horrible almost defies description. The vessel, scarcely a hundred tons burthen at most, contains perhaps little short of a thousand souls, which have been closely packed, for many weeks together in the hottest and most polluted of atmospheres. I went on board one of these ships as she cast anchor off Rupert's Valley in 1861, and the whole deck, as I picked my way from end to end, in order to avoid treading on them, was thickly strewn with the dead, dying, and starved bodies of what seemed to me to be a species of ape which I had never seen before. One's sensations of horror were certainly lessened by the impossibility of realizing that the miserable, helpless objects being picked up from the deck and handed over the ship's side, one by one, living, dying, and dead alike, were really human beings. Their arms and legs were worn down to about the size of a walking-stick. Many died as they passed from the ship to the boat, and, indeed, the work of unloading had to be proceeded with so quickly that there was no time to separate the dead from the living."*

After Melliss's shocking experience of 1861, the Liberated Africans continued to be off-loaded at Rupert's Bay for a further thirteen years until, in December 1874, the Records simply announce: *Liberated African Depot in Rupert's Valley closed.* No fanfare, no explanation, little beyond a cursory mention that two years earlier, 260 slaves had been returned to Lagos and Sierra Leone, presumably as part of a winding-down process, and we are not told how many were still in St Helena in 1874, or how many of those opted to remain on this foreign island to marry local girls and start a whole new branch of St Helena's diverse family tree. Nonetheless, it is with this simple announcement that we thankfully reach the end of one of the sadder histories of St Helena.

Somewhat bizarrely, from the slaves' profound misery had actually sprung some alleviation for the rest of an island heavily weighed down by the burden of distress brought on by the transference of St Helena from the EEIC to the Crown in 1834, coming in the form of employment at the Liberated African Depot and revenue from the naval ships that brought in the slavers. But then, with dwindling employment at Rupert's together with the departure of the anti-slaving squadron, St Helena sank into such a depression that by 1872 the St Helena Mutual Emigration Society was already set up to aid those bent on greener pastures in the Cape Colony and in Natal.

Now, nearly a century and a half later, Virginia, across the airwaves, says: "The four archaeologists already here are discovering so many slave burials in Rupert's they've sent for six more archaeologists to help them. There're far more bodies there than anybody imagined. They're even finding some graves cut into the hillside!"

I am utterly appalled to think that at this most historic time I am a full 1 700 miles from the action. Not that my feeble back would allow me to actually sift sand with them, of course, but at least I could watch. "What sort of numbers are we talking about?"

"A lot, really a lot. They're only concentrating on the area that the Haul Road will go through at this stage; but they say the area they're busy with is only one to three percent of the total area, and they've already lifted a hundred bodies. There are probably 250 just in that small section. They know that burials start fairly low in the valley, but they're digging quite far up the valley near the Fuel Farm, and there're also large burial areas near the old Leper Quarantine Station."

"But that's high up the mountain!"

"Mum, they estimate that there may be between 8 000 and 10 000 slave burials in the whole valley. They're saying that this is now a major excavation site, and one of the largest slave grave sites in the world. It will really put St Helena on the map for historians."

"Are these single graves?"

"Most of the graves seem to be a standard 6ft by 2ft, according to their interview, but they're discovering two or three bodies in each. They even found one with four, and they think they'll find more like that. Some of the bodies are laid out, but these four have just been thrown in. All the bodies are buried straight into the ground, of course, but they have also found one tiny coffin belonging to a stillborn baby wrapped in a shroud of cloth with tiny little brass pins. It's the only body they've found in the whole valley in a coffin, so far. The others are all naked except for a few necklaces or beads buried with them. The archaeologists say that anything valuable they wore when they were captured would have been sold before they were put on the slave ships, so there's not enough jewellery to give clues to ethnic identity."

This is so much to assimilate. Eight to ten thousand bodies in Rupert's Valley! "What's happening to the bones they're lifting?" I ask, fearing the worst of an island that does not halfway appreciate the value of its extraordinary history.

"Each skeleton is being separately boxed, and a sample from each will be sent away to analyse their origins. But we already have an osteologist here, who's measuring the bones, looking for age and sex and disease, that sort of thing. Some bodies have tribal notches cut into the front two upper teeth, and that might help with identification. The archaeologists are also pushing for a proper reburial eventually, when something more is known about them, and they feel strongly that the bodies should all remain in Rupert's, perhaps somewhere near little St Michael's Church up the valley, whether Christian or not."

"They've got my vote on that."

A short time later, the archaeologists hold an Open Day which Virginia and Stuart attend, wandering around the site, talking to the specialists, taking photographs of the diggings marked out across this unexpected corner of the valley. By now 327 bodies have already been disinterred, as well as several heads and other 'remnants' evidently separated from their bodies. There's even been talk of one grave containing seven bodies, though little is publicly advertised about that.

Eventually a few of Virginia's photographs make their way through the temperamental antics of our Cape Town computer to show Chris and me the current scene in this arid valley. There are pegs and brown patches of earth climbing the slopes where the land has been disturbed near the Bulk Fuel Farm. There are archaeologists pointing out jumbled bones and fragments of human remains to those few hundred people interested enough to come and look. There are close-ups of holes in the ground that have revealed their stories. And then – and then suddenly my stomach tightens. I am gazing at a perfectly intact skeleton in close-up, quietly at rest and undisturbed. And somehow, in one swift second, the archaeological excitement of this project has given way to profound sadness, a sudden understanding of the unendurable misery this person suffered before he found peace in the good earth of St Helena. Did he die on the slave ship of smallpox or measles or another of those other diseases that spread so rapidly in confined quarters? Did he die even as they tried to pass him to shore, brought to safety at this foreign island by the Africa Squadron? Perhaps he (or she) died from the effects of amoebic dysentery, or malnutrition, at the Depot itself? Perhaps we'll never realise the true horror of his story, but at last I know why I felt that oppressive weight on me as I stood on the descending pass to Rupert's in the evening shadows so many years ago, and heard that deafening silence. The noise was the voices of all these dead.

29.

Rocks and Rolls

February to June 2009

After a full year away, I am at last on the Landing Steps again. My delicate back, taking fright at a rocking voyage undertaken alone, had postponed again and again my return to the island, until Virginia and Stuart celebrated Christmas with us in Cape Town at the end of that year, 2008. Returning to St Helena in February 2009, I sailed with them, surviving the voyage north without further mishaps, and now am looking about at the changes wrought in my absence. There are no signs of spider cranes or bright-vested Frenchmen on the cliff face any more, for their project was completed last August, and the tall cliffs of Munden's are now softly shrouded in a mist of netting. It's surprisingly inoffensive, and there is a definite sense of greater security in these lower reaches of the Wharf as we wrench ourselves out of the ferry lifejackets and head for a gleaming new white bus on offer today for our ride to Customs. Someone, of course, is quick to inform us that the netting selected above is of such a cheap variety that it is banned in France, and will wear out in five years' time. But we just shrug. It's St Helena's way, like the second-hand wind turbines that have lain unused at Deadwood Plain for the past eighteen months, like the cheap tar that melts, like the ferry-engines that supply our power… It's good to be back in this frustrating but familiar world.

The familiarity doesn't last long, however. At the far end of the Wharf, Donny's has had a major revamp, indisposing his old container kitchen to broaden the deck and start building a *real* kitchen where the bar used to stand. The bar container has, I see, been moved to the forefront of the deck now and totally obliterates the sunset. "I trust that's very temporary," I laughingly hint to Donny as I recall our years of Friday drinks with Stedson, Joyce and Bish, watching out for the green flash at sunset and competing for first views of Venus from our regular table at the railings.

"Of course." But *temporary* on the island usually has some other reality. Like the village of temporary pre-fab housing for expats built at Piccolo Hill in the 1960s and still in regular use today.

There is now an incomplete second storey at Donny's too, and I gaze up at its gaping window apertures. "Fine dining soon?"

"Everything's come to a stop," he shrugs. "I don't need to tell you why." Of course not. Inevitably the stop is linked to the Airport. Donny's shoulders are slumped and his exuberant personality seems to be on leave.

But at the Coffee Shop, expatriate Bill and Jill are just as cheery as usual, busily feeding the crowds who have poured down to the Wharf to meet the ship. And after the requisite hugs of greeting, Bill says: "I think you'll notice some changes. A whole new crowd of expats are here now: new Chief Sec, new Financial Sec, two Economists, a new Public Solicitor, and a whole army of people we don't recognise at all. Experts, I think. They just keep coming and coming!"

I soon see what he means. Three strangers in business suits strut towards the Coffee Shop as we speak, and sit down with two others. They hadn't travelled with us, so they must have been here a few weeks already. Like Bill, I'm already starting to feel overwhelmed by this influx. Up Main Street, traffic is parked on the pavements as usual – nothing new there – but immense packing-crates are stacked on the verandas of the Consulate Hotel which was sold to a South African businesswoman while I was away. There's much activity inside, I see, which at least bodes well for its desperately-needed restoration.

So why, today, do I feel so oddly dislocated? Is it because so much has happened in my absence? Already I am sensing that all is not well with this vulnerable place. In the street there are not the wide smiles that used to warm the welcome, and even waved greeting seems less energetic. The *Observer's* journalist, visiting last year, referred to this island's "*melancholy state*", and I feel now that she could not have chosen a more apt phrase.

"Is High Knoll still standing?" I ask, slightly facetiously, thinking of that presently out-of-sight symbol of strength and might straddling its hill and overseeing its sea-girt domain. Just a year ago, our great solid fortress was declared out of bounds to the public because, like too many other historic buildings, it began falling down. Through latter years we've witnessed chunks of the fort breaking off, leaving gaps like baby teeth on the skyline; but in February last year, a substantial portion on the western flank gave in without warning and tumbled, in a resolute mass of old stone and rubble, down the side of its little throne. So as not to endanger any local builders, no repairs would be made, announced the island government; or at least not until professional restorers arrive. But will anyone come in time to save it?

"It's still there, but crumbling fast," advises Stuart, negotiating the traffic after retrieving our waiting car from the Wharf.

Though no shot has ever been fired from High Knoll, its bearing is one of stoic protection for its people. Succeeding an earlier fort built in 1790 – a high, square structure with two outer towers and stone ramparts – this greater stronghold seems to have been built during England's so-called *fortification mania*, a period reigning from the early 1860s to the 1870s. As far as can be ascertained, the new fort was begun in 1874 – the task of building it falling to Royal Engineers who kept units in St Helena at the time, promising some sort of protection to the people should the island ever come under attack. In point of fact, beyond housing some recalcitrant Boers there between 1899 and 1902, and later some quarantined animals, it has never ever been used as a fort, and lately has best served my family for enjoying a bottle of chilled wine at sunset or letting Tessa run free there on a Sunday afternoon. But it is, nonetheless, a kind of symbolic matron to the island.

Our homeward progress up Market Street demands a stop outside the brownstone Baptist Church, and Stuart waves an arm out of the window at a scene of devastation. Behind the church, on the mountainside, there is still the tell-tale swathe of a major rockfall cutting a path from the very crest of the mountain, nearly a thousand feet above, careening through the Ladder Hill Road, and finishing behind the tightly packed buildings below. It occurred at around ten o'clock on a weekday morning a few months back, the sound of it audible high up the valley where Stuart was working at the time, and terrorising the children out for morning break in the Pilling School playground directly across the road. But miracles were high on the agenda that day, for as the avalanche started, a car with passengers, making its way down the Ladder Hill Road, unexpectedly copped a large rock on its bonnet, seriously shocking them but not injuring anyone inside. Gathering momentum as they rolled, 300 tons of rock then cascaded across the pass, taking out a chunk of the retaining wall, and down the steep mountainside they roared. Once in Jamestown, they completely demolished the nursery schoolroom beside the Baptist Chapel, destroyed an entire carpentry workshop behind the building next door, and slammed into the back of the church itself and the unoccupied bathroom of its Manse. It hardly seems credible that all the small children and their teacher, who could have been gathered in the schoolroom at the time, happened to be across the road in the Pilling playground, while all the carpenters had just popped out to a nearby shop to buy midmorning snacks. The Baptist pastor and his young family, together with a visiting family, were in the Manse at the time, and though the pastor himself was barred by a huge rock from descending the stairs until rescued, not one of the eight inhabitants was injured.

The rest of the town knew of the disaster the minute the lights went out all over Lower Jamestown, and shattered water mains spewed like geysers in Market Street. The schoolroom has nothing left of it but broken stone walls, I see, so now provides off-road parking for the pastor's car.

The Governor – never the soul of tact – quickly attempted to soothe a nerve-ruffled nation: *"The rocks of Jamestown are all volcanic in origin. There are two major types – the massive basalt rock which forms the large blocks that tend to stick out from the hillside, and the looser, more gravelly-looking deposits known as breccia…* The Fairhurst Report *indicates that there are few days when some kind of small movement of rocks does not take place. This movement does not pose a danger; it is when the large basalt blocks become displaced that a serious problem is posed."* Are we soothed, we wonder; those of us who live under the shadow of massive basalt blocks? Back in the 1970s, Jamestown was actually assessed unfit for habitation by dint of this very threat, and yet the reassuring truth is that, in the past 100 years, only two people have been killed by rockfall in Jamestown.

"And we told you about last year's floods," Virginia adds, as we move on up the hill. "Those also happened while you were away." Serious floods are not common enough in St Helena to rustle many pages of the history books – a bit like thunderstorms that earn infrequent mentions – though the valleys of the island are susceptible to mud in wet weather. As a Jamestowner, my imagination's arrested by the flood of 1871 that poured down the slopes of Ladder Hill and Munden's, causing rockfalls and considerable damage to the houses at the base of each, and extensively damaging Side Path. But far more horrific was a house in Friar's Valley, simply swept into the sea by deluge and huge rolling boulders in 1873, drowning a father and six of his seven children, with only the mother and one daughter saved. This same flood wrought such havoc in Jamestown, a few valleys away, that the brute force of the Run, blocked by rocks and roaring down the valley, carried with it huge iron troughs (roughly a cubic metre in size), poultry, donkeys – and a woman who was most fortuitously saved by her voluminous Victorian skirts! The similar flood of 1878 – destroying several buildings and drowning two people – is the one best remembered by a plaque on the wall of the Town Arch, showing the height of the waters that passed that way.

It had rained from the moment Christopher and I left the island a full year ago, Virginia and Stuart complained – for months and months and months. By April the ground was saturated, especially in the countryside, and couldn't cope with accumulated water. Storm-water drains blocked up in Jamestown, overflowing through streets that were already lined with mud, loose stone and grit, and at one stage all exits from town were closed to traffic, due to inevitable small rockfalls round and about. At night, unable to sleep under the hammering rain on the tin roof of the Cottage, Virginia and Stuart eventually moved upstairs where the double roof of the main house affords some insulation from the noise. But Stuart still lay awake nervously listening for the distinctive rattle of rocks on the mountainsides alongside, while Virginia noted the thundering of the Run as it passed through New Bridge, taking rocks, bridges, logs, all kinds of vegetation, and an unfortunate pig with it. Of major impact on Villa Le Breton, was the fact that the roaring cascade also carried away the vital water pipes that feed our garden with untreated water from the Run. And when the rains finally thinned out and the rest of world returned to normal, our beautiful half acre slowly and inexorably began to die.

With the long-instituted Zander just at this time departing our service for other occupations across the island, the responsibility of saving the garden summarily fell to Virginia and Stuart, both working long hard days in other fields. The struggle was arduous, according to their exhausted descriptions. The lawns were brown and brittle, the banana palms dead, the precious frangipanis in my hard-earned Shrubbery emaciated and ill. A whole corner of crowded trees in the far reaches of the garden – my precious African thorn tree and a young jacaranda among them – was threadbare, and as Virginia imparted this woe over the telephone at the time, my heart had sunk at the thought of yet another struggle to salvage our garden's remnants as I did eight and a half years ago through the Season of Desolation. But, with a gift of private water through a hose generously slung over the wall from Cambrian House, things slowly began to burgeon again. And so, as we round the familiar bends at St John's Church to enter *tungi*-flanked Maldivia Road, grating to a crunching stop on the rough gravel of our drive, I hardly dare guess what we will see. Virginia, ahead of me, gives a little gasp as she flings open the wide black gate. "Look!"

Dare I? I open one eye, remembering my past Gobi only too clearly, and steeling myself. And I see… *Green.* Everything is green! Smooth, mowed emerald lawns, trees, bushes, thick and luxuriant; all shades of vivid, healthy verdancy. Along the path, border plants are flowering, scarlet and pink hibiscus among them, tall golden cannas towering over the rough little birdbath whose ugly base has always previously been depressingly prominent. Sky-blue plumbago shows on the hedges, heavy-scented white frangipanis flower near the front door – and even the Shrubbery's seven frangipanis are bedecked with palest pink. I turn to Virginia and Stuart. "You both did this?" By the time they left for Cape Town in December, the pipes – carried off in April – were finally restored.

"We started it. But it was nothing like this when we left! Alan's done this."

Alan is a Saint in every sense of the word. He is also Stuart's energetic older brother who, some months back, took a long appraising look at this ailing garden and then gathered it under his wing. He shrugs off my cooing and grovelling thanks when he follows us from the Wharf, yanked along by a grinning and joyous Tessa on a lead. "I just gave it water, nothing else," he says. There are cabbages and tomatoes, fennel, parsley, *pak choi,* thyme and basil, and tell-tale signs of conscientious digging over and probable fertilising in the vegetable patch. There is the making of a tiny bunch of bananas on a resuscitated palm, and there are three slowly ripening granadillas on a fence vine that has barely shown any sign of life before. Mangos are weighing down the branches of our ten or eleven trees. "That smallest tree has the sweetest fruit," Alan advises, proud of his achievements but still shrugging off praise. "All the garden wanted was water. Look, here come Mimi and Louise to say hallo."

It's really, *really,* good to be back.

Among many well-travelled English tourists escaping a northern winter, a handful of Saints, and an inevitable tranche of experts aboard the RMS on our February return voyage to the island, was a small British parliamentary deputation on a fifty-seven-hour familiarisation visit to St Helena. Two MPs from the House of Commons – who kept themselves aloof from the common herd of co-passengers – and one member of the House of Lords who was a good deal more democratic. Introduced to the lord over drinks one evening, I was promptly quizzed about my island impressions as a resident and, not surprisingly, also about my thoughts on the Airport, eliciting from me my usual forthright views. But only later did he mention that no Airport discussions were expected to take place during their very brief stay, as the Airport issue had been *scrubbed* from their agenda. I smiled to myself, foreseeing the extreme unlikelihood that these men would pass through St Helena without being verbally accosted about the way the island has been handled by the British government through these many years of promises, now broken.

Virginia and Stuart, arriving in Cape Town for Christmas, had brought the huge news with them. After a year of heightened Airport expectations after an Italian construction company had finally won DfID's unusual DBO tender, with a deadline set for the final signing of the Airport contract on 12 December 2008, a statement from

London on 8 December, changed everything. With just four days to go, after *ten years* of negotiations, the British government Treasury, it transpired, had perused *"the papers at Downing Street"* and decided that St Helena's Airport Project should be put on *"pause"*. No signing would take place with the Italians after all, and the whole question of an airport for St Helena was to be reconsidered.

"Cancelled!" shrieked the island angrily. "That's what they really mean!"

We, in Cape Town, did not question its halt. With the world buckling under the weight of 2008's sudden financial duress, with established Banks in dire straits, with thirty-six airlines gone to the wall in the past twelve months, with the British prime minister fighting for political survival in a country turned against him out of sheer panic for personal survival, it would have been a lunatic move to promise a £300 million airport to an unknown island just at this time. Chris and I, with financial papers at our disposal in the Outside World, TV business channels from America to Asia at the ready, and God-given intelligence, had realised back in September that our Airport would be shelved. But protest from the outraged island was so shrill that, indeed, the parliamentary deputation *was* accosted despite scrubbing the Airport from the agenda. "Money has been invested to raise standards because the Airport was coming!" shouted islanders. "And now we've lost that money!"

Perhaps it's possible that the invested money might still raise standards, we observe ruefully, though St Helena would not necessarily think that way. We are also a little aghast that St Helena, as a nation, actually swallowed all DfID's hysterical hype about wealth through air-tourism. Did anyone really believe that Jamestown would flourish with those quick-turnaround comfort-loving tourists living twenty minutes' drive away? No, our fly-in tourists – probably not much interested in nature or history, collapsing battlements, hiking, or exploring Georgian towns – would spend their days being pummelled in SHELCO's spa (they at least are still clutching their hotel plans) while chilly mists swirl around Broad Bottom, and then they would fly home. They might visit Jamestown once, just to look at it – or twice if there is game fishing from smart white motor-yachts at the seaside, though we cannot forget that the Immigration Control Board has once already turned down such a business offered from Namibia. There's little else to entice them in the capital, so DfID's message of future riches somehow always smacked of little more than a crafty ploy to hand self-finance over to a small population that has no clue how to manage it, and then say: "Well, sorry chaps, we gave you the Airport you wanted and you didn't make a go of it. It's out of our hands now."

The abysmal history of this latest Airport issue is a sorry tale. Over the first months of this year, heated debates have flurried through Britain's House of Commons, the House of Lords, all through Westminster, it seems, and occasionally through the British press. Never before has the name of St Helena Island been so frequently uttered in its Mother Country. Interesting impressions have emerged from these flurries. In the House of Lords, there is an anguished protest about the delays to which the island has been subjected by DfID over the long haul. In the Commons, voices carry across the House in similar protest.

Our visiting parliamentarians, after their lightning-flash call, having soon discovered that the Airport issue could not simply be *scrubbed* from the agenda, are drawn into the House debates too. Lately a lady Member of Parliament in London – a former Foreign Office Minister, as it happens – has also taken up the gauntlet and is granted half an hour to relate the story of St Helena's Airport. Clearly trying to defend St Helena's right to air access, she does not omit mention of our current shortage of potatoes, as though this deprivation would not occur with an airport on the island. Her naïveté in this respect is unsettling, considering the myriad more urgent supplies that should be flown in if a plane could possibly board them. But she makes a good case against DfID's apparent ineptitude. She is vociferously supported by the Member for Swindon who somehow feels responsibility for all those in her constituency with family on the island (not forgetting that she might well be counting their election votes at the same time). Then the unfortunate Minister for DfID (the Department for International Development, after all) is called to his feet to reply, and it is this trembling attempt at departmental-vindication that will be longest remembered for his distressing ignorance of matters St Helenian and the infamous slip-of-the-tongue that referred to St Helena as "an occupied territory"! Well, did the *St Helena Independent* go to town on that, granting the poor man front-page headlines. But shock and outrage at this gaffe were not restricted to local condemnation. Even a long article by a recognised UK journalist quickly took to referring to him as 'Mr Occupied Territory'.

However, DfID did not stand alone under public censure. *"It is conservatively estimated that [the Consultancy Firm] have been paid something in excess of £20 million in fees by DfID on St Helena's behalf, over the past six years,"* announces one informed contribution to the *St Helena Independent, "and the net product has been nothing of value whatsoever."* Certainly, under their auspices, the price of the Airport rose by leaps and bounds, within three years hitting the £145 million mark, and the year after that, jumping to nearly £250 million. Amazing this, for not so long beforehand – only about six years earlier, in fact – the figure still hovered around the original £26 million. And it was, apparently, this same consultancy firm that offered DfID the extraordinary notion that tendering airport contractors would be happy to agree to a fixed-price contract for DBO (Designing, Building and Operating) our Airport – which, of course, saw all three self-respecting and sophisticated South African construction companies walk right out of DfID's office three years ago, *"privately disclosing that the contractual expectations advanced by [these] 'Management Consultants' on DfID's behalf were totally unworkable, unreasonable, naïve and entirely outside of industry norms for the type and scale of job involved."*

The shock of this unsurprising desertion of the three companies so stunned DfID and their consultants at the time, that they were apparently not able to get their act together again for another eighteen months, after which time only one of those three South African companies bothered to re-bid. They and the Italian company were the final bidders two years ago (after a large Chinese consortium and an Irish one had both withdrawn just days before embarking on a familiarisation tour of St Helena), and were invited to submit their tenders by the end of November of that year, 2007, which they duly did. The final choice was to be announced the following April, as faithfully promised by Governor Rude at Gay's New Year's Midnight Feast just over a year ago.

Well, of course, the announcement never came, though a raft

of gushing excuses followed from DfID's Air Access Project Team, ever-intent on promising St Helena the earth. *"The inordinate delay in DfID's performance during [last year, 2008] remains unexplained except as inefficiency; it is known that both sets of bidders [Italians and South Africans]were equally bemused by the interminable silences which emanated from their prospective employers,"* the article comments. *"Meanwhile the public were spoon-fed homely comments from the DfID Air Access Project Office in April to the effect that the contractors' submissions were 'over a foot thick' and 'take a lot of reading, which we are doing as fast as we can'."*

Six months passed after the tenders were received. Then in June, the two bidding contractors, South African and Italian, were invited to meetings in London to discuss their submissions. But yet another silence followed from the Air Access Project Team. September 2008 slid by, bringing no Access news other than the Haul Road archaeology dig, undoubtedly one of DfID's more enlightened projects. But rumour afloat by early October suggested that the two contractors were now growing restless and wearied by dealing with DfID, and though we shall never know what actually transpired between them, lo! suddenly in mid-October there was an announcement. The Italians had won the contract, setting free the South Africans to pursue more energised fish.

Losing no time in their eagerness to get started on the project, the Italians promptly sent a small group of logistical executives to St Helena to tie up ends with the island government, coinciding with the projected signing of the contract in London by Her Majesty's government on 12 December 2008. Imagine then, their horror when the entire project was brought to that cowardly *pause* just four days before the final signatures were expected to be scrawled. Later in the month, at a pleasant lagoon-straddling restaurant in Walvis Bay, as they all passed through Namibia from an RMS voyage, Virginia and Stuart had enjoyed conversation with the three Italian executives. "In Italy we have big containers already packed with equipment waiting to be shipped to St Helena within four months!" they exclaimed. "We were all ready to go! We have been ready and waiting for months!"

In some ways I am relieved that I was not in St Helena at the time of the *pause*, for the anger of the Saints can only be imagined. But was it anger that no Airport was forthcoming after all, or greater anger at the way the island has been fobbed off with fantastical promises for so many years?

The UK-based air-transport journalist, Duncan Mayhew, bursts into print again in the *St Helena Independent* soon after our return to the island, and his article makes fascinating reading. By dint of his particular familiarity with the island, he now offers detailed options for our future. Clearly he has a Pisa-like leaning towards air transport, going out of his way to slate the very notion of a new ship instead, and goes so far as to opine: *"Passenger shipping as a means of purposely getting somewhere was simply the victim of technological generational change, like the monochrome TV set and the brick-sized mobile phone. Although much folklore and hocus-pocus has been allowed to develop over the years about the possible costs and risks of flying to St Helena, most of it is demonstrable to aviation economists as complete bunkum, a good deal of which could fairly readily be traced back to people with a vested interest in preserving the anachronism of St Helena being served by a ship..."*

I am slightly peeved. The whole of St Helena, my good man, is an anachronism and is likely to stay that way until the seas dry up and reveal the golden beaches that were here nine million years ago, when this island was twice the size it is today. The flying world of these times demands instant gratification: sun, sand, sea, and shopping. But the truth is that we, perched here in the middle of earth's loneliest ocean, can offer almost none of those commodities, which is why St Helena attracts a special breed of intelligent traveller, mainly those mature in mind, those who shun the crowded beaches of Ibiza and Majorca, and those who know where they're headed and why. These people do not mind *thrashing along* on a comfortable ship, making friends as they go – friends they will keep through the passage of time, actually – and feeling, by the time they have made the expedition to this unique dot on the map that they have been truly rewarded. Of course, the argument about time still rages on, and planes would not involve ten to twelve days of two-way travelling between London and St Helena, via Cape Town. But people who want to get to St Helena, make the time. They have done so for centuries and are still doing it quite happily. So let us not relegate the ship option to a scrapyard just yet.

Mr Mayhew's article cuts deeply into DfID's tender flesh. And he also gives no quarter to the consultancy firm whose well-remunerated advice over the years is now being thoroughly trashed. Dwelling for a moment on DfID's repeated bleating that they have no wish to subsidise a ship for St Helena, and an airline would spare them this fee, he tartly reminds them of their ignominious attempts three years ago to glean any interest at all in procuring an Air Service Provider. Not from any *bona fide* airline, anyway. "*Thus...it became clear...that DfID themselves would stand to be extremely grateful indeed for any interested air operator kind enough, rich enough and insightful enough to purchase and operate an aircraft which could technically manage the extreme demands of the Air Navigation Regulations in relation to serving such a remote destination as St Helena. The only, and highly probable, alternative...is that in order to achieve any air services at all from St Helena's new airport, post-2013, it would be necessary for DfID themselves to become the owners – or more likely, lessees, of a suitable variant-type aircraft, and thereafter contract an aviation operator to fly it for them. Thus DfID would, exactly as with the RMS, become monopoly operators themselves, and with an aircraft specific to the characteristics of St Helena's airport.*"

After some continuing history of the bungling that has served us in the name of progress through the past several years, and the consequent jettisoning of Plan A (our International Airport), Mr Mayhew offers some detailed and practical alternative suggestions, putting forward various ideas for shorter runways and different planes which would save everybody a lot of money. So at last we have some positive suggestions for a move forward, some practical tips to work on to wrench the island out of yet another trough of despair, and at least three informed and much more economical alternatives for DfID to ponder if they are truly interested in our 'urgent' need for Air Access.

But isn't something missing from that article...?

Oh, of course! Nowhere at all in it (or in other articles, for that matter) is mention made of our dire need to obtain cargo – and the writer has fallen into the same snare that DfID and various consultancy firms have floundered around in for a decade. For, let's face it, only when you live here do you appreciate the vital importance of watching a ship dropping anchor in our bay and proceeding to transfer containers of necessaries from its decks to our lighters. Why else have we been served by cargo-passenger ships since time immemorial? Why else do we repeatedly ask of DfID with now hoarse-voiced cries: "What arrangements are you making for our cargo?" It would be not quite truthful to quote a response along the lines of "Oh, we'll eventually sort out something for you if we can find a ship somewhere with its own derrick," but that's certainly the impression we are given. If our old friend, the indefatigable Guitar, actually comes to live here under his hastily reconstructed job-title of Infrastructure Project Manager for DfID, he will at last experience, at first hand, the ongoing necessity of a regular ship in our lives, and the urgency of having that detail secured before we remotely begin to dream of entertaining 20 000 tourists. But by then it might be too late to get what we need and what many have requested for years: a bigger, more efficient *dedicated* ship that can carry more passengers in more comfort than our present RMS, travel faster, sail more smoothly, and carry more cargo if necessary. Being dedicated specifically to St Helena, it might even travel routes that suit the island, rather than routes with schedules devised by an economist at a desk in London (who occasionally, to the rollicking amusement of an entire island, publishes the information that the RMS will depart at 14.03hrs or arrive at 07.47hrs, thereby advertising his very limited knowledge of a world beyond the London Underground!)

Lately, however, it has been announced, as a sop to island anger probably, that £35 million could buy us a new ship. What sort of ship they do not describe. A second-hand Korean rust-bucket with cabin space for two? Please, let's not forget that our own beloved RMS – after substantial money was saved in the building of it in 1989 by cutting out fifty feet of its middle section, omitting to fit twin rudders or fore and aft thrusters, and opting to install scrapyard ferry-engines, fuel units, superchargers, blowers and air-conditioning units of such inferior quality into our brand-new vessel that they have ceaselessly given trouble – cost £30 million twenty years ago! While this somewhat demeaning display of fobbing off is acted out yet again, it cannot but bring tears to our eyes to note that the present annual budget for mere Members of Parliament in London purports to exceed *twenty years'* projected worth of our RMS's miserable little £17 million annual subsidy. And yet, who knows: with an efficient ship and proper marketing of this gorgeous island, we might eventually not need a subsidy at all.

However much we love the island when the RMS is not here – revelling in St Helena's particular quietude then, her familial drawing together, the time we are granted to get on with private matters and to complain about shortages incurred by her absence from the island – there is no emotion quite so heart-warming, quite so reassuring, quite so joyous as the sight of her resting in our bay. She's a mother, a favourite aunt, a dear friend, a beloved nanny, a lifeline, all rolled into one; indisputably part and parcel of this island's existence. If only our decision-makers could recognise her significance in the great scheme of our lonely little lives.

30.

Carved in Stone

June 2009

Already the year is halfway through, midwinter in these inverted climes, and the garden is illuminated by lush winter hibiscus once more, doubles and singles, bursting like can-can girls in brilliant frills from emerald curtains along the garden path and the borders of our property, and in soaring crimson clusters beside the house. The four corners of the garden dazzle with bougainvillea, in lilac, orange and deep salmon. At the gate our mauve variety billows over the wall like February Rollers on the Wharf, splashing its abundance throughout that corner, stretching inquisitive arms into a nearby tree to grab surprised branches and haul itself ever upwards, spreading its brilliance even more generously.

Down in The Shrubbery yellow blazes from Brazilian tacoma bushes (*yellow-pops* here), while the blue plumbago hedge, demarcating the vegetable garden, matches scraps of cerulean winter sky that show between bobbled oceanic clouds in this less humidity-draped season. No summer offers such abundance of colour in our garden as this time of year, and a glow of nostalgia recalls my amazement at such vividness as I walked for the very first time down this garden path, in this month, exactly a decade ago.

The years since then have barrelled by, hurtling along like mere months since the incoming Governor Duncan Hill and I sipped gin on the RMS while he promised an Airport "up and running within five years". But already five years have overshot that deadline. And all we have to show for it is the *pause*.

Yet we still discuss the Airport all the time, this subject that affects every one of us in this small place, even if we have nothing directly to do with it. "DfID *had* to reopen consultations with us," Bish announces one day, stroking Louise affectionately as she relaxes on his lap, "because if they don't, that department will face a judicial review of the way they've handled St Helena over the past ten years." This, of course, explains why a soft-voiced Irishwoman, purporting to be an *independent* assessor (even though the internet clearly advertises that she once was employed by DfID herself), has lately made the daring leap from *Gannet Three* to Landing Steps. We hold nothing against her or her remit, of course, as she has ostensibly come to hear the island's feelings voiced. But the local floorshow held on her behalf is side-clutching. The Chamber of Commerce, silent to the point of muteness when it needs to be heard, now rears from deep slumber with a mighty roar. "*Option A!*" it screams as its Chairman distributes piles of printed A stickers at every retail outlet, for shoppers to paste on their cars. In five minutes the stickers are everywhere, slapped on office doors, on shop windows, on vehicles driving about their private business. *Build our airport now!* is the demanding stance of *Option A*, and by noon on Day 1 their canvassers have set up tables on street corners and are yanking unsuspecting shoppers over to sign a letter of support.

Option B supporters – those who see the necessity for a new dedicated ship to bring our necessaries – have their breath beaten from them. But it takes just one brave man to drive to town with a large *B* on his car, and the ball starts rolling. "After a month we have *one thousand* votes in favour of *Option A*," whoops the Chamber of Commerce. And a quieter voice announces calmly that in under three weeks, an *Option B* letter has garnered over six hundred signatures, with no coercion at all or pre-printed *Bs*. All were obtained from supporters who actively sought out the three venues where they might add their voice. *Option C*, yet another pacifier offered by DfID in these beleaguered times, gets no votes at all, as this final choice invites support for a five-year postponement before airport consultations start all over again. Everyone ignores this one.

This mid-year, in a sudden turning back of the clock, three comfortingly familiar faces have reappeared on the island. Doctor André, returned after a long absence, for a three month locum bellows "'*MORNING!*'" in rich-voiced Afrikaner resonance as he passes on his way to the hospital while we enjoy breakfast coffee on the veranda, his arm waving cheerily, head just visible over our tree-lined stone wall. His return provides a delicious sense of *déjà vu*. But it's the Hipgraves – Royce, our Chief of Police in the early days of Governor Hill, and his bubbly wife Denise – who keep us rollicking with reminiscence. "Were you at St James' Church," asks Royce, back for a six-month stopgap following the sudden retirement of our local Police Chief, "when little old Dot fell headfirst into the tuba and sent the collection plate flying across the choir? Do you remember when somebody's teenager gave Father Chris a glass of neat gin as a joke, and he danced his way through Evensong? I'll bet you've never forgotten that quiz night on the RMS when Gloria caused chaos over dinner…?"

Who could forget that? Who could forget Gloria? In this mood of reminiscence I suddenly recognise how much I now miss her tempestuous presence on the island. I miss the colour and excitement of her character which – though of sometimes dubious entertainment value – exceeded by light years her comparatively prosaic successors. I miss her benign and well-intentioned husband who made a few mistakes as Governor but harboured, I think, a genuine love for the island, and a far deeper interest in its wellbeing than those that followed. I miss those many expat friends who fulfilled their government contracts and left over the years, and I miss those many Saints who have sailed north in the great post-Q5 exodus. It's a quieter island these days, and older; but the remaining young (and perhaps the naïve) still anticipate a future life built upon tourist riches when the Airport finally arrives – even though a clear picture of such a future resolutely evades our personal imaginings.

"Would you and Chris ever sell this house?" Denise asks suddenly, and the shock of her question startles me. I hide its quick surge of emotion with a giggle: "Well, we evidently did. Last year."

"This sounds like the start of a typical island tale," Royce comments drily, waiting.

And so I recount what good friends Brendan and Lee-Ann had told us after they had housesat Villa Le Breton while Virginia and Stuart celebrated Christmas 2008 with Christopher and me in Cape Town. Brendan was putting out the rubbish one morning when a neighbour passed by. "Hey," the neighbour commented, "I didn't know the Coopers advertised this house for sale! The people sayin' Chris and

Lindsay have left the island and gone back to Cape Town for good, and have sold the house. And Virginia and Stuart will rent the place from you when they're back here."

"From *me*?" queried Brendan, somewhat nonplussed.

"Well, ain't it your wife's daddy that bought the place for you for a Town House, and is lettin' you live there until the young people come back and pay you rent?" Brendan evidently smiled noncommittally. "Hey," he called as the neighbour moved on, "did you hear how much Lee-Ann's daddy paid for this place?"

"'Hundred fifty t'ousand," the neighbour said knowledgeably, and disappeared.

I recall how the laughter, when Brendan told this story, trembled the summer-blooming night-cactus flowers on the hillside across the road, their yellow petals glowing luminously against dark rocks and their scent wafting over to us in the heaviness of that February night. I remember our jollity disturbing the families of brown geckos catching moths on the veranda ceiling above us and one of them protesting with a yapped-out *chup-chup-chup-chup*, a sound as synonymous with this house as the comb-grating conversation between our roosting fairy terns in the jacaranda. Even the zeppelin-sized summer cockroaches buzzing past our conversation couldn't detract that evening from the certainty that Chris and I will never sell this gorgeous house, not as long as we are allowed to live here, not as long as we are physically able to drive the hairpins, or negotiate the potholes of Jamestown on foot, not as long as there's still something to laugh about in St Helena. "No," I answer Denise's question. "We'll never sell. It's completely part of us all."

So today Tessa and Louise gambol along with me as I wander down to our blooming Shrubbery, and I wipe the dust from the pink marble slab that lies nearby. Today it is ten full years since I signed for this house – arriving on that well-remembered voyage with Duncan Hill's fervent plans for this island – and, like his dreams, the marble slab's enamelled words have been weathered in their time and now are faint. But I move aside a tumbling miniature orchid with its flimsy red flowers that have blocked some dirt, and the last words of my Kipling verse jump at me:

> *...One place shall prove*
> *Belovèd over all.*

One place. This is not the centre of the universe, as many locals erroneously believe. Regrettably, it is not even a place of importance among Britain's Overseas Territories or, more worryingly, among those who manage our affairs and would, understandably, prefer to be freed of responsibility for an island which, as young James Prior remarked so intelligently two centuries ago, is *"too small, and unfruitful, and badly situated, to be of much use"*. This is no more than a truly remote island in the middle of nowhere, with an absorbing history and stunning natural beauty. But it is this very remoteness that endows it with such singular charm, and tragically, that charm is now under threat.

Epilogue

April 2014

The years have eclipsed again, and 2014 started sadly with the shocking death of Tessa, knocking us all for six. It was her nightly habit, after quaffing supper on the veranda, to charge the mynahs who promptly swooped in for their share, and fling herself down the front steps after them. This was old practice, notwithstanding her gammy leg, and on this early-January evening she landed just too hard on the brick path below. There was then nothing to be done for her crushed hip, already disintegrating with years, we were assured by the resident vet (Michel's outstanding work with the St Helena SPCA had eventually worn the government down and won us a compassionate permanent vet). So, based on his capable and professional judgement, a difficult decision was made. Tessa slipped away quietly, just three weeks short of her ninth birthday – living perhaps four or five years longer than her shaky start had augured – remembering a happy, love-filled life as the dog her first owners nicknamed Lucky because she came to live with us, and the one we called the Most Beautiful Dog in the World.

One of Stuart's brothers fielded all of that, looking after the house and our other dog and new cat (successors to Mimi, and to little Louise who had mysteriously vanished one day without trace), while Virginia and Stuart, now happily married, were visiting Cape Town, again staying with Christopher and me. Their wedding, back in 2012, did not, thank goodness, entail a 'team' rolling back the hard-won lawns of Villa Le Breton or repotting all our vegetables in favour of a backup dance floor, because they chose to celebrate their marriage in Cape Town where everything they needed for a memorable day was readily available. JJ made the dress, but the design was Virginia's own.

It was an eventful January, with the later arrival of their first child, born in South Africa because medical facilities are at such questionable lows in St Helena that Virginia was medevacked out two months before the birth. "Things have got worse since you left," Stuart was informed by phoning friends and family. "Seven doctors here now, hardly working... not enough equipment... forty medevacs sent to the Cape in January and February... someone got fully prepped for surgery last week, before doctors realised they didn't have proper instruments to operate..." I think again of the IATA recommendation I once heard about, that an Intensive Care Unit (not currently existing in St Helena at all) should be easily accessible from an international airport, and wonder if the island's masters know this.

Basil Read, the name now on everybody's lips, is the South African contractor that finally won the new £300 million contract on offer, after the Italians had justifiably pulled out following the 2008 fiasco, and building the Airport finally began in January 2012. They have their own paramedic unit, of course – not trusting to the vagaries of Jamestown's General Hospital. They have built their own village at Prosperous Bay Plain for those overflow staff who cannot find enough accommodation among island houses. They have their own work canteen on site and import much of their food in their own ship, the NP *Glory 4*, which docks at the temporary quay in Rupert's Bay, that they built – the first ship in St Helena's history to offload cargo directly on to shore. They have brought in massive earthmovers, carved the steep and twisting 14km (8.6 mile) Haul Road from Rupert's Bay on one side of the island to Prosperous Bay Plain on the other, and have so far provided jobs with healthy salaries for 340 Saints who wish to work for them, some of whom they have even sent to South Africa for training. They have long been labouring around the clock, and are progressing well with filling in a plunging 100m deep valley with 8 million cubic metres of blasted rock and concrete to level out the 2 000m runway, and work is already underway on the terminal building.

The first flight is anticipated in early 2016 – provided an airline has been procured by then, of course. Its presence at that august event is not definite, because no one seems to be able to decide where this flight should originate. England? Europe? Will it be allowed to refuel at the American base at Ascension which has, for decades, strenuously locked the door on any suggestion that our civilian flight might call there? Which South African destination – Johannesburg or Cape Town? One flight a week? Two a week? The conjecturing is worse than it was fourteen years ago when SHELCO produced a clear prospectus that covered every detail. But no one has yet explained why any self-respecting airline should *want* to go off the beaten track to St Helena for relatively few passengers. We smile at what is, perhaps, the most pertinent suggestion ever made (in jest, we hope) regarding this questionable project: its fantastical naming as Wirebird International Airport – after the island's very own (semi-flightless) bird.

Dragging their feet, waiting for answers, are sophisticated hoteliers loath to invest money before flights are assured. The Mantis Collection, famous for upmarket boutique hotels and unusual eco-escapes around the world, is keen to convert the historic colonnade, Georgian buildings, and depressingly disfigured parade ground of crumbling Ladder Hill fort at the lofty head of Jacob's Ladder, into a 5-star hotel. The eco-famous Oberoi Luxury Hotels have pranced about in the wings for years. And SHELCO, who has partnered Oberoi for even longer, has clung tenaciously to their plans for a green 5-star hotel in the rolling vales of Broad Bottom. But until very lately all have resisted investing real money in St Helena in case the steadily progressing airport turns into a military base instead (as, inevitably, has been questioned yet again). Once flamboyantly cited as the would-be *"greenest hotel in the world"*, Oberoi's best intentions for St Helena have since lost their whimsy – and now almost their entire interest as well. But the latest news informs us that, bravely, SHELCO has finally decided to start a hotel project anyway (without the association of Oberoi at this early stage), so that at least there will be some beds available to visitors when the first flight arrives. After all, practically nothing else has happened to shape up local accommodations for those so-called *demanding* tourists.

It is said that mobile phones will operate on the island from Christmas 2014, and their masts are already being erected; and ATMs may be introduced by the Bank of St Helena (established in 2004 and inevitably nicknamed BOSH). All this is reassuring indeed, for while Basil Read forges ahead, keeping on track with their contract and taking on, also, the construction of a permanent dock at Rupert's, the building of SHELCO's hotel, and some professional resurfacing of main roads, little else has progressed in St Helena. Infrastructure is as slow in improving as it ever was, and along with all the old frustrations of expensive electricity, questionable water supplies and erratic internet services, our Saint friends exclaim in exasperation about the island's general decay.

Stuart sighs. "It also seems that the old courtesy is going now – fewer friendly waves in the street, fewer cheery greetings. And don't imagine that two cars can ever again stop in Market Street and chat like they used to, while others patiently waited. Those lovely old good manners are disappearing." Something uglier has come in their place. I first sensed it five years ago, after Joyce had died and, while Bish was on overseas leave, I sat alone with a grieving Stedson, stalwartly keeping up Friday night tradition at Donny's. It is racism, and it came – not from those Saints grown used to seeing our integrated family around the island – but rather shockingly from the new rafts of white British expatriates sent over on contract. Stedson, as a prominent Saint with a compelling personality, sometimes briefly secured their attention. But I, sitting with him, was purposefully ignored, their rudeness blatant and their clear disapproval of me sickening, as they tightly kept to their own. "You're a white woman," explains Stuart candidly, "sitting alone with the darkest man on the island – and they can't handle it. The new people, they're all White Ants." He's got me smiling at the old island nickname for expats who tenaciously cling together.

Beyond Daisy's hard-working 'Chinese', there are no world-standard restaurants yet, and grocery shortages still occur with monotonous regularity. And yet there is, alarmingly, no certainty yet of any cargo ship contracted to feed either the islanders or their numerous tourists after the RMS finally retires, or before the Airport opens in early 2016. Indeed, in current news, London appears to have only just awoken to this conundrum, though it has been a question consistently asked of them by savvy islanders since that long-ago referendum in 2002. Some several years back, querying this problem with the most senior DfID official at the time, Virginia was casually told not to worry because "*tons* of cargo ships will call", and I remember her shocked expression at his bald mendacity. Tons of cargo ships? St Helena, as he should have acknowledged, is not on the sea route to anywhere – so why should ships come out of their way for us? Besides, with the distressing dearth of fresh fish in St Helena's territorial waters over the past few years (possibly fished out by pirate trawlers that consistently hover just over the horizon, and against which St Helena has no resources), the island cannot offer any export to fill those emptied containers that have delivered our goods, for which reason a dedicated ship is absolutely essential to this island.

There is always the possibility of sending away the island's rubbish in them, of course; but as the cost of that freight would be untenable if left to the devices of the mysterious people who currently run the RMS, un-recycled garbage is inexorably mounting instead, already sullying the view of one of St Helena's least-known but most fascinating tourist sights, the multi-coloured sands at Bottom Woods.

As for those "*tons* of cargo ships" eager to serve the island: each one will require either a draft shallow enough to tie up at the new permanent jetty being built in little Rupert's Bay, or, more realistically, they will need on-board derricks to handle over-side cargo, which are seldom fitted to ships anymore. Those are just the supply concerns; we dare not even ask about a sailing option for medevacs who cannot fly.

We should be joyful in this brave new world of progress, but even some islanders once stringently pro the thought of flying, are realising that the changes wrought by air access to their unique lifestyle are irreversible. "We are bringing St Helena closer to the Outside World, leaving behind a very special legacy for the people of this island far away in the South Atlantic Ocean," announces Basil Read with the fondest of intentions, for the company has integrated well in St Helena and also has contributed more charitably to community events than was ever in their remit. But the fact remains, St Helena will soon no longer be remote, no longer unique, no longer the place of interest and fascination that it has been for centuries; and certainly, without beaches and fair weather, not a popular tourist attraction. Many of us, envisioning what probably lies ahead, still doggedly believe that good marketing, with a faster, more affordable ship would be key to St Helena's best tourism aspirations, and that air access won't be the answer. But we dearly hope to be proved wrong; very wrong.

Illness eventually returned me to my primary home a few years back, for necessary proximity to proper medical care. So now Christopher and I pay only visits to our beautiful house which Virginia and Stuart have made their permanent home. They are deeply happy there, and their child will grow up in a charmingly historic house with a bird-filled garden; he will swing in the twisted old mango trees, and learn to grow healthy vegetables with his father. His mother will supplement his education with books and music, and he will be kept, as far as humanly possible, from taking drugs and picking youthful fights on Saturday nights, from boredom.

I do not love the island less for seeing it from a clear distance now, but I am inordinately sad for it. And I think back with acute nostalgia to those years I lived there, watching the Airport antics; witnessing the ever-changing tides of cheerful contracted expatriates arriving and departing; gossiping with Saints and expats alike about our frequent frustrations. And the easy laughter that held us all together still rings in our memories. This was then a very special place, an island whose whole personality and extraordinary uniqueness were shaped by its great distance from the Outside World. I write this in remembrance of that remoteness.

SALIENT CONVERSIONS

St Helena size: 10 x 7 miles = 16 x 11km
47 sq. miles = 121 sq. km

Distance from Africa: approx 1 000 miles = 1 600 km

Distance from Ascension Island: approx. 700 miles = 1 126 km

Distance from UK: approx. 4 000 miles = 6 500 km

Distance from Brazil: 1 300 miles = 2 092 km

Height of Diana's Peak: 2 700 ft = 822m

Gumwood treeline (ancient) 400-600m = 1 300-1 900 ft

Villa Le Breton from Wharf: approx. 1 mile = 1.6km

Runway length: 2 000m in length = 6 561 ft, with a landing distance of 1 550m = 5 085 ft

AIRPORT NITTY-GRITTY

By April 2014 Basil Read had imported into St Helena:

Their own ship, the NP Glory 4, to bring 30 000 tons of cargo to the island, which included:

> *8 million litres of diesel fuel*
> *300 tons of explosives*
> *6 200 tons of cement and pulverised fuel ash*
> *500 tons of sand from Namibia*
> *120 items of construction equipment*
> *900 containers*
> *1 200 tons of reinforcing steel*
> *5 000 tons of miscellaneous cargo*

There is yet more to come, including all apparatus necessary for air traffic control, runway lights, electricity connections, and the building of a 1.5 million litre fuel farm for air fuel. The company, according to the DBO contract, will manage air access for ten years once an airline is installed, and thereafter the Island of St Helena will take over all responsibility for maintaining and running air access and tourism – and (supposedly) be financially independent.

LGC April 2014

FURTHER READING

Birds of St Helena – Beau W Rowlands – pub. British Ornithologists' Union 1998

The Endemic Flora of St Helena – Q C B Cronk, Nelson 2000

Fernão Lopes: a South Atlantic Robinson Crusoe – Beau W Rowlands – pub. George Mann Publications 2007

Fish & Fisheries of St Helena Island – A Edwards, Newcastle Univ 1990

A Guide to the Birds of St Helena and Ascension Island – Neil McCulloch 2004

A Guide to the Geology of Ascension Island and St Helena – B Weaver 2002

The History of Plantation House, St Helena 1673-1967 – Margaret, Lady Field – pub. The Patten Press, Cornwall 1997

Infernal Traffic: Excavation of a Liberated African Graveyard in Rupert's Valley, St Helena. A Pearson, B Jeffs, A Witkin & H MacQuarrie 2011. Council for British Archaeology Research Report 169

One Man's Island – St Helena – Ian Baker. Wilton 65 2004

St Helena – Robin Castell, 150+ photos of buildings + part reprint of Melliss 1875 text - pub. Wensley Brown 1979

St Helena 1502-1938 – Philip Gosse – first published Cassell & Co 1938 – new edition Anthony Nelson, UK, 1990

St Helena 500: a chronological history of the island – Robin Gill and Percy Teale – pub. Teale & Gill, Cape Town 1999

St Helena: the Chinese Connection – Barbara B George – pub. Barbara B George 2002

St Helena: the Historic Island – EL Jackson 1903

Further lists of new and second-hand books on the South Atlantic islands are available from **Miles Apart** (Ian Mathieson), Barwood House, Grants Lane, Ramsbottom, Lancs, BL0 9DB, UK Tel: 01706-826467, email: imathieson2000@yahoo.co.uk

Made in the USA
Middletown, DE
10 August 2022